The Agricultural
Scientific Enterprise

About the Book and Editors

The State Agricultural Experiment Stations have played a fundamental role in the development of science and agriculture in the United States. From their inception in 1887, the experiment stations have attempted to wed basic research with practical application and have helped institutionalize a utilitarian approach to agricultural science. Agricultural research and the new technology it helped to generate were major factors in the transformation of U.S. agriculture into a high technology, mechanized, science-based industry. Moreover, the experiment stations, as the first large-scale, publicly supported scientific research institutions in the United States, have also long been models for scientific institutions both here and abroad.

Compiled for the 1987 centennial of the State Agricultural Experiment Stations, this volume critically examines past performance, current issues, and future directions for public agricultural research in the United States. Each of the authors, drawn from disciplines as diverse as philosophy and agronomy, focuses on a central concern for the scientific enterprise. Issues include priority setting, maintaining and promoting disciplinary and inter-disciplinary effectiveness, supporting higher education for agriculture, and efficacious dissemination of research findings. By setting these issues in their historical and philosophical context, the volume suggests new approaches for meeting the continuing challenge to achieve equity, efficiency, sustain-ability, flexibility, conservation, and consistency with other objectives of U.S. society.

Lawrence Busch and **William B. Lacy** are professors of sociology at the University of Kentucky. They are the authors of *Science, Agriculture, and the Politics of Research* (Westview, 1983) and the editors of *Food Security in the United States* (Westview, 1984).

Published in cooperation with
The Experiment Station Committee
on Organization and Policy and
The Cooperative State Research Service, USDA,
in commemoration of the 100th anniversary
of the Hatch Act, 1887-1987,
establishing State Agricultural Experiment Stations

The Agricultural Scientific Enterprise

A System in Transition

**edited by Lawrence Busch
and William B. Lacy**

Westview Press / Boulder and London

Westview Special Studies in Agriculture Science and Policy

This Westview softcover edition was manufactured on our own premises using equipment and methods that allow us to keep even specialized books in stock. It is printed on acid-free paper and bound in softcovers that carry the highest rating of the National Association of State Textbook Administrators, in consultation with the Association of American Publishers and the Book Manufacturers' Institute.

Published in 1986 in the United States of America by Westview Press, Inc.; Frederick A. Praeger, Publisher; 5500 Central Avenue, Boulder, Colorado 80301

Library of Congress Cataloging-in-Publication Data
The Agricultural scientific enterprise.
  (Westview special studies in agriculture science
and policy)
  Bibliography: p.
  Includes index.
  1. Agriculture—Research—United States.
2. Agricultural experimental stations—United States.
I. Busch, Lawrence. II. Lacy, William B., 1942- .
III. Series.
S541.A485 1986   630'.72073   86-15801
ISBN 0-8133-7241-0

Composition for this book was created by conversion of the editors' computer tapes or word-processor disks.
This book was produced without formal editing by the publisher.

Printed and bound in the United States of America

∞ The paper used in this publication meets the requirements of the American National Standard
   for Permanence of Paper for Printed Library Materials Z39.48-1984.

6   5   4   3   2   1

Contents

Part Three
Disciplinary and Interdisciplinary Research

Part Four
Commodity Studies

Part Five
The Experiment Stations and Science Education

Part Six
Dissemination and Impact of
Experiment Station Science

Part Seven
Future Directions

Part Eight
Conclusion

Foreword

From the beginning of American agricultural development, science and technology have been major forces in improving production efficiency. Until the 1940s, the principal changes were in shifts in power sources—from human to horse to mechanical.

The post–World War II period brought the first full phase of scientific agriculture. The key factors were the development of hybrid crop strains, widespread use of pesticides and herbicides, improved nutritional and medical practices in animal husbandry, and the increased use of energy and fertilizers. As a result of these new methods, each farmer now feeds and clothes seventy-nine people here and abroad—up from only seventeen at the turn of the century.

Today, the United States is the recognized world leader in agricultural production. The agricultural system, including related input and marketing components, generates about 20 percent of the nation's gross national product and employs 23 percent of the U.S. labor force. Because of the diversity and efficiency of this system, American consumers spend only about 16 percent of their disposable income for food, only 12 percent on groceries, and 4 percent on eating outside of the home.

American agricultural products are highly competitive in world markets. Their sales represent 18 percent of our total exports and contribute substantially to the balance of payments. As an industry, American agriculture has had a high rate of growth in productivity—a rate more than three times as high as that of the nonfarm business sector of the economy since World War II.

In the 1970s, U.S. farm prosperity seemed assured. But today, not everything is as healthy in the farm sector as expected, nor is the outlook as bright as it once was for expanding markets. In February 1985, both *Time* and *Newsweek* magazines carried cover stories featuring the changing fortune of farmers. The plight of farmers is front page news across the country, and Secretary Block is a prime participant in national radio and television broadcasts.

A significant increase in the value of the dollar in comparison to other world currencies, as well as expanded world production, tends to place some U.S. farm exports at a competitive disadvantage. These market changes and their subsequent impact on commodity prices have been major factors in lowering farm land values in the United States. The credit crisis now facing the nation's farm belt can be traced in large part to these developments and to high interest rates relative to inflation.

What can be done to turn this situation around? The administration and several others suggest that U.S. agriculture must become more market oriented and rely less on federal support programs. The President's proposal for the 1985 Farm Bill was based on such a focus. Although the resulting Food Security Act of 1985 differs from that proposal, it still emphasizes a return to a market-oriented agriculture economy. However, rather than commenting further on the matter, I will direct my comments to the roles of science and education in addressing these and other farm issues.

Need for New Technologies

For the next decade and on into the next century, the economic viability and international competitive position of U.S. agriculture will depend heavily on gains in productivity. This means reducing production costs and providing higher quality goods and services, including more value-added products for the export market. The combination of traditional research methods and the new biotechnologies offers tremendous potential for improving the competitive position of U.S. agriculture.

New and improved animal technologies point to faster growth rates, less feed per unit produced, increased disease resistance, and more offspring per animal. Animal diets can consist of more forages and crop by-products, supplemented with minerals, vitamins, amino acids, and other nutrients.

By using biotechnology techniques and conventional plant breeding, crops will have increased resistance to disease, insects, and nematodes. New, more resistant varieties of food and feed grains, fruits, and vegetables will be affected less by variations in temperature, water availability, and competition from weeds. Similar scenarios are possible for fiber and tree crops.

Through biotechnology, scientists have the capability of providing the blueprint for future generations of agriculturally important species—plants, animals, and micro-organisms. Researchers can intensify their efforts to maximize the usefulness of agricultural products.

Among the many forces that are creating a need for changes in approaches to agriculture and thus the development of new technologies, the following come easily to mind:

1. Changing food consumption patterns;
2. Increasing concerns about the continued availability of soil and water resource bases;
3. Changing demands of domestic and foreign customers for forest and range products;
4. Increasing public concern over the effects of scientific, economic, and technological developments on human health and quality of life.

These points should be elaborated. There are indications that the public has a growing appreciation for the relationship of dietary regimens, good health, and physical fitness. In addition, scientific and etiological data suggest a possible relationship between the onset of some chronic disease conditions such as hypertension, diabetes, and cancer and what and how much we eat. These developments suggest that we should increase our emphasis on the study of nutrition *per se* and on how the meeting of nutritional needs should relate to production and processing of food and food products.

Second, there are increasing concerns about continued availability of soil and water bases. Improved resource-saving technologies need to be incorporated into current production practices. We need to know what resource use patterns are consistent with sustained agricultural uses over time.

Third, 71 percent of our total land area is in forest and range resources. These resources provide wood, wildlife, water, forage, and energy, plus jobs and an array of recreational opportunities. As with crops and domestic farm animals, improved forest and range technologies can increase yields, better protect the resource, reduce input costs, and enhance the quality of the products—all to meet changing demands of domestic and foreign customers.

And fourth, public debate has recently increased over the relationship between scientific, economic, and technological developments on the one hand and human health and quality of life on the other. There is vigorous debate over the enforcement and adequacy of our laws and regulations. Such activity gives rise to these types of questions:

1. How do we evaluate low-level carcinogenic risks from multiple sources?
2. How do we effectively monitor unwanted contaminants in our food supply?
3. How do we evaluate the safety of genetically engineered microbes that may be used in food processing or production?

This last item is a particularly good example of the transitional nature of the agricultural scientific enterprise. The need to assure the citizens of America that biotechnology is not fraught with a significant potential for developing and turning loose some new, unknown, and devastating monster has attracted a great deal of attention. On December 31, 1984, a proposed set of regulations was published in the *Federal Register*. A central aspect of the regulations was to design a secure, yet nonoverbearing, set of standards that would assure (1) that proposed research experiments were reviewed by the highest qualified scientists in our nation, and (2) that it was not only scientists who were engaged in this review process, but the public as well. These proposed regulations suggest the establishment of a recombinant DNA advisory committee (RAC) for each major agency, very much as NIH has now. Thus, the NSF, the NIH, the DOD, the EPA, as well as the U.S. Department of Agriculture, would each have a RAC. Representation from each of the RACs would be placed on an overall coordinating board to assure that standards are consistent among the RACs.

National Biological Impact Assessment Program

There is a related idea that was first presented by the Biotechnology Committee of the Division of Agriculture at the National Association of State Universities and Land Grant Colleges meeting in Denver, Colorado, in the fall of 1984. It is called the National Biological Impact Assessment Program (NBIAP). If implemented, it would serve three functions:

1. Provide a ready inventory of the highest qualified scientists to call upon to review either proposals or protocols within proposals upon the request of any of the five RACs. Perhaps scientist Smith at Cornell or scientist Jones at Arizona is among the very best in the world with respect to micro-organism X and its interaction with pathologic condition Y. This would provide a consistent quality of counsel and advice across all the RACs.

2. Provide information about existing and potential test sites that could be examined for their applicability and appropriateness for a given set of experiments. The heart of this inventory would be the state agricultural experiment stations and their branch stations, as well as the biological stations at non–land grant institutions, including Harvard, the University of Oklahoma, and others. These are test sites at which the biota have been well documented. Experiment stations, for example, know the crop rotation systems, know a great deal about the soils, the water situation, the micro-organisms within that soil, air pollutants, weeds, insects, and bird pestilence that are a part of the history of that site. Armed with these data, perhaps the ideal site for a given set of experiments can be selected. If additional data need to be obtained before the experiments begin, they could be identified and efforts could be designed to fill the gap. If there is need for covering the area with screening material to keep birds from flying in, or if a windbreak is needed to keep the situation from being exacerbated by wind drift, all of this can be accomplished. In any case, it provides a test site system that builds upon the enormous amount of base knowledge that is already available.

3. Finally, NBIAP can be a major contributor to the enormous task toward which all of us interested in the biological sciences must strive, specifically, the development of a catalogue or an inventory of the biota, not only within the United States, but around the world. In this third aspect, one can see how the many science agencies funded by the federal government can join forces with those funded by state and private industry to develop a most extensive and impressive intelligence system with respect to planet Earth and her biology. NBIAP is not so pretentious as to assume the overall role of such a program, but at least it can contribute markedly to this nationwide and worldwide inventory system.

Sustaining Increased Productivity

As agriculture becomes more dependent on sophisticated technologies to produce and process food and fiber products, it will take increasing effort to sustain the effectiveness of those technologies. This is an area with several names—maintenance research, productivity-sustaining research, protective research, and defense of gains research, among others. The concept of maintenance research applies to many aspects of agriculture—from plant breeding to work on soil and water resources, pest control, and livestock production.

Just like buildings and equipment, technology depreciates in usefulness and must be updated. Research investigations and the people who perform them are inexorably linked. We can't have one without the other. There is a growing need in such fields as nuclear biology and systems analysis for highly trained scientists who also understand the unique needs of agriculture.

We needn't look far to find evidence of industry's recognition of the benefits of working with universities in research, in development, and on the application of new technologies. This is a part of the great American story. There are far too many new alliances and partnerships between universities, federal agencies, and private industry to mention here. They are well known. This issue was the focus of a forum at the Academy early this year. Instead, two final topics should be addressed.

Concerning Surpluses

Because this nation enjoys an abundant supply of agricultural products, we occasionally hear opinions expressed that research causes surplus or is ahead of its time. Or with a plentiful supply of food and fiber products, someone will ask, "Why spend money on research?" The premise on which such statements are made is not valid.

As mentioned earlier, a major premise of agricultural research is to sustain and improve productivity growth. Improved productivity of off-farm inputs, labor, and natural resources is the key to a profitable and competitive agriculture. It is absolutely vital to a healthy industry.

Surpluses are basically a marketing problem that research attacks by improving product quality and reducing product cost—the most important factors in expanding market shares. Research continually provides options for current management and production practices.

Periods of surplus or scarcity are not the times for knee jerk overreaction in terms of changing research policy. Indeed, it is precisely these issues that define the overall objective of agricultural research. It is always difficult to come in exactly "on target" with respect to the production of a given commodity or commodities. If one has to err on one side or the other, then let it be the surplus side. But in times of surplus, we have an obligation to find new uses for the surplus or new uses for the land freed up by reducing the production of a given commodity. Let us remember that increased productivity is not synonymous with increased production.

The International Community

The United States has a long and enviable record of sharing its resources and knowledge with other countries in a continuing effort to contribute toward economic stability, reduce poverty, solve world food programs, and promote peace.

While international programs in the agricultural sciences make up a very complex system, U.S. agriculture has the basic ingredients to assure itself of a leadership role. These ingredients include:

- A strong and viable U.S. agricultural science system
- A solid and proven university-USDA relationship
- An effective partnership with the private sector
- A dynamic scientist development program through funded research
- A model information delivery system serving every country
- Experience in a wide range of international cooperative activities

There are many reasons why cooperation with the international scientific community pays real dividends. Exchanging knowledge and training programs provides a foundation for *trading* partnerships and allows the U.S. to keep abreast of new developments in other countries.

There are other issues facing scientific agriculture, but those we have outlined are enough to illustrate that we are in the midst of exciting times.

The agricultural sciences are going through a transition period. The changes have implications for education in agriculture at the baccalaureate and graduate levels. There is a new sense of interdependence among the sciences, especially in biology as it relates to agriculture. There is considerable excitement over the potential for innovation and development of new products that will find widespread application in agriculture.

For these reasons, the interaction of universities, federal research laboratories, and industry is being explored in an effort to find productive and mutually beneficial bases for endeavors and to foster greater cooperation. Interaction of the clientele with the publicly supported research and education programs in the United States has been one of our strengths.

With the introduction of new and sophisticated scientific developments and innovations, we anticipate that these relationships will grow and become a more important element of what we know as the "federal/state, public/private sector" partnership that makes up the U.S. research and education, food, and fiber system.

Orville G. Bentley
John Patrick Jordan

Preface

Centennial celebrations are occasions to stop, pause, reflect, and rethink, to compare the needs of yesteryear with the needs of today, and to consider the appropriateness of goals and objectives to a future undreamed of one hundred years earlier.

Passage of the Hatch Act in 1887 established the State Agricultural Experiment Stations. This Act was a compromise between the interests of basic research and application, the state and federal governments, urban and rural America, advocates of production and conservation, banks and farmers, and science and tradition. Under the terms of·the Act, federal funds were provided to each state to establish an experiment station in affiliation with its land grant college.

During the past century, agricultural science and the state agricultural experiment stations have played fundamental roles in the development of science and agriculture in this country. Agricultural research and the new technology it helped to generate were major factors in the transformation of U.S. agriculture into a high technology, mechanized, science-based industry. This new agricultural system has become the most productive in the world, and the food and agricultural sector as a whole, the largest of all U.S. industries. Today, the experiment stations are important components of the U.S. food system and key forces in determining future U.S. food sustainability and security (Lacy and Busch, 1984).

From their inception in 1887, the experiment stations attempted to wed basic research with practical application. Prior to this time, science in the Western world was primarily the domain of intellectually curious, isolated individuals. With the establishment of the United States Department of Agriculture (USDA), the land grant colleges, and the experiment stations, the U.S. Congress institutionalized a utilitarian concept of agricultural science. Knowledge was to be pursued for its usefulness in improving the material conditions and general welfare of the population.

The pursuit of agricultural science in the experiment stations had other important consequences for the development of science and agriculture. The joint funding of experiment stations provided one of the earliest examples of a state-federal organizational partnership. The increasingly specialized, commodity-specific nature of scientific inquiry encouraged the development of a commodity orientation among clients. Moreover, the linkage with teaching and later with extension became a model for national research systems.

Despite widespread support for the experiment stations, at their inception there was extensive disagreement over even the most fundamental points. The terms of the Hatch Act itself were vague and would only be clarified by the passage of time. Many questions arose including: What type of research should be conducted by the stations? Could research conducted in the laboratory be transferred directly to the field? Were field trials in Maine valid for Mississippi? Should stations test commercial products for farmers? Should they accept gifts and grants from commercial organizations? How should they establish their research priorities? How should they transmit their knowledge to farmers? And, how could they insure continuing relevance to the farm and rural population? Consequently, the role of each experiment station was defined through continual negotiations and compromise (Busch, 1980, 1982; Busch and Lacy, 1983).

With the passage of amendments to the Hatch Act and other Congressional acts, the scope of the stations was widened further. Research in home economics, marketing, forestry, and rural life became part of the already broad mission of the stations. At each step, this mission and the research decisions and processes implementing it were renegotiated.

With their diverse clientele, decentralized organization, and internal diversity, the experiment stations often have been forced to redefine their role in order to insure their continued existence. The complex negotiations and conflicts within the stations have frequently mirrored the conflicting demands of actual and potential clientele. Arbitrating amongst these diverse groups while maintaining continuity in the research program has required both political skill and a little luck. Occasionally, scientists caught in the conflicts and debates paid heavy personal and professional costs (Hardin, 1955; Lacy and Busch, 1982).

Today, on the occasion of their centennial, the stations again face conflicts and decisions regarding their role. In the 1970s, U.S. agriculture entered what many people regarded as an era of limits and critical choices, requiring significant adjustments in the use of resources and in the very nature, structure, and capacity of agricultural research itself. Corporate interest in the products of biological agricultural research, as well as burgeoning corporate support for research, has raised new questions regarding the appropriate types of collaboration and roles for public and private research. Moreover, a group of approaches, usually labeled the "new biotechnologies," has promised to open avenues for agricultural research which have profound consequences for the structure of U.S. and even world agriculture (Hansen et al., 1986). At the same time, the research community has been confronted with increasing consumer interests and concerns about the products of the food system.

In the political arena, new demands for accountability have been articulated (e.g., GAO, 1981; Rockefeller Foundation, 1982). Moreover, overproduction and the depressed farm economy of the 1980s have raised questions regarding the desirability of increased productivity. Finally, the public has begun to raise broad questions about the success of the nation's food and agricultural research system in achieving fundamental goals, including equity, efficiency, sustainability, flexibility, conservation, and consistency with other objectives of U.S. society.

The seemingly settled structure, organization, and mission of the experiment stations are once again the subject of debate and renegotiation. It is within this context that our volume traces the historical and philosophical foundations of public agricultural research; research management and priority setting processes; selected issues in the development of disciplinary, interdisciplinary, and commodity research; contributions in education and training; dissemination of research findings; and future directions for the agricultural research system.

Part One focuses on the unique historical and philosophical context for experiment station research. Marcus delineates the difficulties faced in establishing the stations as viable scientific institutions. Chapters by Schweikhardt and Bonnen, and Burkhardt present contrasting views of the values incorporated into agricultural experiment station research at its inception. Dundon reviews how conflicts amongst these values have affected specific scientists, while Randall shows how these value conflicts have shaped and limited policy research within the system.

Since its inception, a key problem for experiment station research has been priority-setting. This is the focus of Part Two. Lipman-Blumen documents the enormous range of interests incorporated into all agricultural research priority-setting. Christensen and Robinson, and Zuiches examine priority-setting from the viewpoints of the federal funding agency (Cooperative State Research Service) and the state agricultural experiment station manager, respectively. Holt reviews ways that computers have changed and will continue to change the priority-setting and management process by making more and better information available to administrators.

Experiment station research has been conducted along disciplinary, interdisciplinary, and commodity lines. Part Three focuses on disciplinary and interdisciplinary research. Evenson demonstrates how experiment stations have tended to avoid both product development and fundamental research, in which economic implications are of little consequence, focusing instead on what he calls 'pretechnology science.' Swanson and McIntyre provide vivid examples of the problems and successes of interdisciplinary endeavors in the areas of soil conservation and pest management, respectively.

In addition to disciplinary and interdisciplinary research, a portion of experiment station research is organized along commodity lines. The three papers on major U.S. cereals included in Part Four trace this approach. Flora and Flora review the different ways in which regional economic and political needs impinge upon rice research and production. Fitzgerald traces the shifting line between public and private research in the development of hybrid corn. Finally, using Kansas as a case in point, Flora demonstrates how wheat research has responded and contributed to the changing structure of American agriculture.

Experiment station research has always been intimately linked to education. Virtually all Ph.D. scientists graduating from the U.S. land-grant universities have received training in conjunction with experiment station projects. In Part Five Huffman reviews the production of scientists for domestic agricultural research, while Swanson examines the impact of experiment stations on foreign agricultural research.

While agricultural extension services have long disseminated specific results of experiment station research, the cumulative effect of these results has been to transform both domestic and international agriculture. The two chapters of Part Six examine this issue. Gajbhiye and Hadwiger review the key role played by the experiment stations and their scientists in the establishment of the international agricultural research centers. White reports how this research has transformed American agriculture and in the process transformed itself.

Finally, in Part Seven, we look to the future and explore three major issues that confront the system. Madden addresses the capacity of the system to respond imaginatively to the chorus of critics that have emerged in the last decade. Feller examines the potential effects of a weakened Extension Service on research. Then, using Cornell University as a case study, Buttel *et al.* evaluate whether new ties between experiment stations and agribusiness can resolve fiscal problems without undermining the value commitments that insure continued public support of the system.

In the Conclusion, Wittwer links the many political, social, economic, philosophical, and technical issues and provides a tentative agenda for the experiment stations' second century.

No published volume represents merely the work of the authors. All are social products, the result of interaction amongst authors, editors, typists, copyeditors, and others. Moreover, an interdisciplinary work demands not only multiple contributions but integration, organization, selection, and rewriting, such that style, grammar, vocabulary, and citations follow a uniform pattern. It requires a group effort.

This edited work represents selected papers presented at a symposium held in March, 1985, in Lexington, Kentucky. That symposium and this volume are one of a series of symposia and books commissioned by an Experiment Station Committee on Organization and Policy (ESCOP) subcommittee for the centennial of the Hatch Act. This subcommittee, chaired first by Nolan VanDemark and more recently by James Zuiches, was instrumental in stimulating moral, financial, and technical support for the project. James Halpin, director-at-large for the Southern Region, was particularly helpful in handling details. Dr. John Patrick Jordan, administrator of the Cooperative State Research Service, supported the project and supplied the financial resources necessary to bring it to fruition. In addition, the Kentucky Agricultural Experiment Station provided the necessary staff support and space to insure the success of the project.

Our conference coordinator, Carol Calenberg, played a major role in organizing the original symposium held in March, 1985. She arranged meeting space, found audiovisual equipment, resolved travel difficulties, organized meals, and much more. After the symposium, Ms. Calenberg coordinated correspondence with the authors, typed each of the papers in a form compatible with the publisher's typesetting equipment, and otherwise assisted in organizing the manuscript.

Ann Stockham proofread the manuscript, helped to ensure stylistic consistency and eliminate duplication, and, with help from Ms. Calenberg, prepared the index. In addition, graduate student Jayant Deo assisted with various facets of the project. All of these individuals have contributed to making this volume a success.

Lawrence Busch
William B. Lacy

References

Busch, L. "Structure and Negotiation in the Agricultural Sciences." *Rural Sociology* 45:26–48, 1980.

——— . "History, Negotiation, and Structure in Agricultural Research." *Urban Life* 11(3):368–84, October 1982.

Busch, L., and Lacy, W. B. *Science, Agriculture, and the Politics of Research.* Boulder, Colorado: Westview Press, 1983.

General Accounting Office. *Long-Range Planning Can Improve the Efficiency of Agricultural Research and Development* (CED-81-141). Washington, D.C.: General Accounting Office, July 1981.

Hansen, M.; Busch, L.; Burkhardt, J.; Lacy, W. B.; and Lacy, L. R. "Plant Breeding and Biotechnology." *BioScience* 36(1):29–39, 1986.

Hardin, C. *Freedom in Agricultural Education.* Chicago, Illinois: University of Chicago Press, 1955.

Lacy, W. B., and Busch, L. "Institutional and Professional Context for Rural Sociology: Constraints and Opportunities." Pp. 404–13 in D. A. Dillman and D. J. Hobbs (eds.), *Rural Society in the U.S.: Issues for the 1980s.* Boulder, Colorado: Westview Press, 1982.

——— . "The Role of Agricultural Research for U.S. Food Security." Pp. 289–320 in L. Busch and W. B. Lacy (eds.), *Food Security in the United States.* Boulder, Colorado: Westview Press, 1984.

Rockefeller Foundation. *Science for Agriculture.* New York: Rockefeller Foundation, 1982.

PART ONE

Historical and Philosophical Context

its state connection. The former evoked images of the German stations, which scientists took as a tacit recognition that they were central to agriculture and which farmers understood as a formal acknowledgment that scientists in some capacity could aid agriculture. The latter indicated that the station's staff was responsible to the public; it suggested that the constituency who had pushed for the station's creation—farmers—possessed the authority to circumscribe station labors and adjudicate its effectiveness.

The Connecticut station continued to function in a similar manner until the mid-1880s when it started to conduct scientific research. By then, however, the Connecticut station had ceased to act as a leader in the experiment station crusade. Its place had been taken by the New York station, which was formed in 1882. That station's creation marked the institutionalization of the compromise between advocates of scientific research and proponents of practical applications. It was the New York station that proved a model for later state efforts. Indeed, the New York station was the embodiment of the intellectual compromise upon which the Hatch Act would be predicated.

None of this is meant to deprecate the important role of the Connecticut station. Getting a legislature to finance America's first station was no small matter. In addition to Connecticut's initiatives, over twenty-five station proposals had been offered in eleven states between 1870 and 1875. Although most enthusiasts claimed to pattern their plans after German stations, all had been different (Marcus, 1985:65-72). But perhaps it was only just that Connecticut formed the nation's first station. Yale's Samuel W. Johnson certainly had campaigned the longest. Author of the highly regarded *How Crops Grow* (Johnson, 1868) and *How Crops Feed* (Johnson, 1870), he had not missed an opportunity since the late 1850s to champion the station cause (Rossiter, 1975:127-160). Generally speaking before audiences of farmers, Johnson stressed in every instance that agricultural science, particularly agricultural chemistry, was the determinant of agricultural practice; he repeatedly maintained that a station's true objective was to impress upon farmers the primacy and utility of science in agriculture. Reducing agricultural processes to agricultural chemistry, he envisioned stations as chemical laboratories operated by men trained in laboratory methods. There they would engage in scientific inquiries; they would determine the laws upon which agriculture rested (Connecticut, 1874:52-71, 76-80, 92-93).

Ironically, it was not Johnson's vision that Connecticut put into practice but that of Wilbur O. Atwater, Johnson's former student. Recently appointed at Wesleyan, Atwater proved far more practical than his mentor. He realized that farmers would not yield primacy in agriculture to agricultural scientists. As important, he recognized that they saw no benefit in scientific investigations. As a consequence, he proposed a station that would avoid these difficulties by trading on its staff's technical—not investigative—skills. The issue he seized upon was fertilizer frauds. Aware that farmers expressed concern about purchasing adulterated fertilizers, Atwater's proposed station would be manned only by chemists and charged with regulating the

Connecticut fertilizer industry; the station would analyze commercial fertilizers and determine their percentages of phosphoric acid, nitrogen, and potassium. Other activities would be secondary and attempted as time and money allowed (Connecticut, 1875:247-276). And that provided the framework of the Connecticut law (Connecticut, 1876:191-192).

The Connecticut station did little besides analyze artificial manure during its first years. The situation persisted even when in 1877 the legislature relocated the station at Yale and placed it under Johnson's direction (Johnson, 1879). In retrospect, Atwater's approach to the station question had worked too well. It was not an institution that conducted research but rather a large state chemistry shop. The station differed from other state chemistry operations, which several states formed in the late 1860s and early 1870s to regulate the commercial fertilizer industry (Marcus, 1985:42-46) only in size; it employed more chemists. The station's pursuit of that mission was essential to retain legislative approval and continued funding. That meant that the station stood as an institution dependent upon its scientists' technical abilities, not their investigative ones. Both Johnson and Atwater complained about the station's limited scope but found the fertilizer work so overwhelming as to preclude new duties. And for most Connecticut residents, who regularly applauded station efforts, those duties were sufficient.

They also seemed sufficient to citizens of several other states. Within a year of its inception, the Connecticut agency received inquires from at least seven states about the enterprise (Connecticut, 1877:97-99). These missives led to the creation of two other permanent entities designated as stations. North Carolina formed its station in 1877 (Battle, 1912:136-139), and New Jersey followed three years later (New Jersey, 1880:8-9, 248-249; Sidar, 1976:193-194). Both employed men who had earned their spurs at the Connecticut station, and both were merely state chemistry facilities; they attempted to do virtually no science.

The only state-supported stations during this period were closely patterned after Connecticut's pioneering effort. Other proposals were offered, but they failed to become law. Most were presented by agricultural college professors or their advocates (Marcus, 1985:81-86). Almost all involved agricultural schools in some integral way. But joining colleges to the station cause proved politically inept; farmers tended to treat agricultural schools with suspicion, dissatisfaction, or disgust. Repeatedly, farmers accused agricultural colleges of doing nothing for American agriculture and, as a result, expressed more interest in reforming these institutions than in increasing their funds or expanding their responsibilities (Nevins, 1962:52-68; Nordin, 1974:62-63; Scott, 1972:53-56).

Cornell and the New York Station

Colleges often did more than outline plans. They also lobbied legislatures but to no avail. At least one college went further, however. Without state sanction or funding, Cornell University declared in 1879 that it would open a station (Colman, 1962:205; Lazenby, 1880). Sentiment for an agricultural experiment station had been particularly intense in New York—there was no state fertilizer law—and Cornell apparently decided to get a jump on the field. In that way, when the legislature finally acted, Cornell would seem the natural site for the state station.

The station that Cornell set up most closely approximated Johnson's vision of an experiment station. Manned predominantly by chemists, the Cornell venture would seek to discover the underlying laws of agricultural science. Its faculty would then preach those laws to farmers, who would practice what was preached. Not surprisingly, few farmers looked upon Cornell's scheme with favor. They saw no indication that the college, its scientists, or scientific investigations had, would, or could help agriculture. And to prevent Cornell from preempting the station question, they called on the legislature to establish a board of control, composed of representatives of state farm organizations, to decide it. The board would be empowered to establish the station's location, define its objectives, and employ its staff; it would be the guiding force. And farmers persuaded the legislature to follow their plan. In late 1880, it appropriated the then princely sum of twenty thousand dollars a year to create a state station in line with the farmers' proposal (Curtis, 1880).

From the start, state agricultural organizations sought to influence the board. They suggested several different station formulations. The lack of consensus among farmers about what the station should attempt, where it should be situated, and who ought to serve there posed difficulties for the board (Anon., 1881a; Crandall, 1881; Harris, 1880). It remained until 1882 for the station control board to work its way through the morass. E. Lewis Sturtevant was instrumental in that endeavor, and the board rewarded Sturtevant by appointing him station director (Swan, 1882:1-3).

A South Framingham, Massachusetts, farmer, who was trained as a physician, Sturtevant had gained the respect of both farmers and agricultural scientists. His standing with farmers came first. In 1876, he converted a major part of his Waushakum farm into a model or demonstration farm. Opening it to the agricultural public on certain days, Sturtevant used his farmstead to show others the benefits of farm management techniques (Philbrick, 1877; Sturtevant, 1878). He systematized farm operations, adopted double entry bookkeeping, and ran various variety tests (Sturtevant, 1877). He also edited the agricultural newspaper, the *Scientific Farmer*, and was an active participant in the Massachusetts State Board of Agriculture (Sturtevant, 1876).

Those activities established Sturtevant's credentials as a farmer. His scientific respectability came from his research and his role in the professionalization of agricultural science. Sturtevant pursued several investigations into soil physics, using the first lysimeter in America, and studied the chemistry and physiology of milk secretions. He also examined Ayshire cattle and attempted to develop a "thoroughbred" corn. This last endeavor was particularly noteworthy. Along with Byron Halsted and William J. Beal,

Sturtevant was one of the few Americans in the 1870s explicitly exploring the principles of plant hybridization (Plumb, 1899). But his scientific research was insignificant in comparison to his professional efforts. Sturtevant was the driving force behind the formation of the Society for the Promotion of Agricultural Science. Established through his initiative in 1879, the society's members constituted a veritable who's who of American agricultural science. The organization strove to "come to be regarded as an authority in the field of agriculture, as does the National Academy of Science in its special domain"; it sought to set agricultural science's agenda and to become America's agricultural science tribunal (Marcus, 1985:92–97).

Sturtevant's enviable position among farmers and agricultural scientists provided him insights into the ambitions of both. He was able to combine them to chart a course for the New York station, which was different than earlier stations. It was based on a different relationship between agricultural scientists and farmers. He began his analysis by acknowledging that stations often must undertake some "political duties," such as fertilizer control, but argued that those tasks did not constitute "the true agricultural experiment station," which was "in a sense industrial in its conception and existence." To Sturtevant, stations needed to determine "what the farmer wants to know" and "why he wants to know it." Put more directly, farmers desired a catalogue of rules, the sum of which was successful farming, to make as large a profit as possible. Sturtevant then focused on the factor of profit as something that divided station endeavors. It resulted in two types of enterprises, agricultural investigation and agricultural experimentation. The former sought knowledge as its outcome and included the processes of discovery and verification. The latter took this knowledge to determine practical, profitable farming methods. In effect, it was the processes of application and verification (Sturtevant, 1882a:39–42).

Sturtevant's emphasis on verification was crucial. He felt it the essence of the scientific method and, as a consequence, asserted that only those trained in that method—scientists—could function at stations. But he also used verification in another sense, as dictating the form of station research activities. Verification required the division of agricultural science work into its minutest constituent parts. Only those elemental processes could be verified; each step commanded an expert researcher in that area of inquiry to verify by weighing, counting, and measuring. In other words, Sturtevant defined a station as a kind of research institute in which agricultural scientists with varied specialties participated in different aspects of a single investigation (Sturtevant, 1881:237–242).

The elegance of Sturtevant's vision gained him the New York post and contained facets appealing to both farmers and agricultural scientists. While it satisfied scientists by mandating that only they could engage in experimental work and that the work must be pursued according to the highest tenets of science, the acknowledgment that stations existed only to advance agricultural practice pleased farmers. Scientists would achieve public recognition for their investigative skills, not their technical expertise, and farmers would gain the fruits of station labors as well as retain an implicit say in its destiny. The use of the concept of profit served to strengthen this bond. The division of experimentation into agricultural investigation and experiment not only explicitly linked science and practice but also provided a rationale for that union. As the earlier stations had, Sturtevant's proposal offered something for both agricultural scientists and farmers. Unlike those predecessor institutions, however, it was conceived in such a way as to allow scientists to engage extensively in research.

Sturtevant did not hesitate to translate his plan into action. During his first year as director, he had a laboratory, library, barn, chicken coop, plant house, silo, and feeding stalls built for station use. He also employed a horticulturist, veterinarian, and chemist and their several assistants. He would add five more specialists in the next few years. Sturtevant demonstrated a similar initiative in his selection of station tasks. In 1882, the staff worked in tandem on the following agricultural investigations: corn-growing techniques, potato yield increase, effects of soil temperature and depth on growth, the relationship between dairy feeds and milk production, and methods to exterminate quack grass. It also pursued agricultural experiments. Variety tests predominated. It tested during the year eighteen varieties of grasses, ten varieties of oats, fourteen of sorghum, and four of barley (Anon., 1881a, 1885; Sturtevant, 1882b).

Sturtevant proved as adept at publicizing station operations. He rarely missed an opportunity to discuss his institution before state agricultural societies in the north. Reports on station activities appeared frequently in the three agricultural newspapers with national pretensions, *American Agriculturist*, *Rural New-Yorker*, and *Cultivator and Country Gentleman*. Prominent farmers visiting the Empire State often were given tours of station facilities. Scientific publications and organizations also got the word. The journal, *Science*, regularly featured the New York station, and Sturtevant no doubt communicated its accomplishments to the Society for the Promotion of Agricultural Science. Because of his judicious use of these various forums and the perceptiveness of his vision, Sturtevant received numerous letters from legislators requesting further information about the station enterprise. Some came from as far distant as Alabama (Marcus, 1985:102-106).

Significance of the New York Station

The New York station, then, became known nationwide. Its establishment according to Sturtevant's principles marked a milestone in the history of American experiment stations. In the five years following his appointment, the Connecticut and New Jersey stations changed their approach and added at least some of the features that Sturtevant first instituted. They even tried to abandon fertilizer control work (Jenkins, 1886:129-130; Neale, 1886:272). By 1887, they more nearly resembled in emphasis, staff, and plan of action the New York station than Atwater's original agency. The significance of the New York approach extended well beyond established stations. During the same period that Connecticut and New Jersey redirected their endeavors, Ohio, Massachusetts, Wisconsin, and Maine erected stations. Each new midwestern or northeastern station showed remarkable similarities to New York. None was just a laboratory, and all devoted a considerable share of their resources to agricultural science problems aside from fertilizer analysis. They not only had broad research agendas and mixed research facilities, but they also were equipped with more diverse staffs. Finally, they combined in most cases the labors of several investigators on any single set of scientific issues (Goessmann, 1883:1-3; Henry, 1884:6-16; Lazenby, 1882:5-123; Smith, 1980:8-13).

Southern Experiment Stations

Curiously, few aspects of the New York station model were adopted in the south. That seemed the result of a conscious decision. Although southerners hailed the work of northern stations for the north, they suggested that those labors were inapplicable to southern farming. Indeed, they complained that the south's agricultural problems stemmed directly from imitating the north; following rules derived for farming in the north had misled southern agriculturists. As a consequence, southerners focused on the application of scientific principles, not the principles themselves. Arguing that southern agriculture had fallen so far behind the rest of the nation's agriculture that it demanded remedial action, they called on their legislatures to create stations that would translate established farm science into peculiarly southern practice. In particular, southerners wanted station personnel to test methods of cultivation, varieties of seeds, and types of breeds for their suitability to the various southern soils and climes. They also desired regulation of the commercial fertilizer trade (Anon., 1881b; Henderson, 1880:370-372; L. O., 1886:86-88; Page, 1886).

That was the rationale for southern stations. It led in the mid-1880s to the opening of stations in Kentucky, Tennessee, Alabama, and South Carolina (Dabney, 1888:4-5, 19-20; McBryde, 1888:56-60; Scovell, 1888:5-6; True, 1937:101-102). These four stations held one important attribute in common. As with the North Carolina station, none of their mandates depended upon their staff's research skills. Rather, it was their technical, methodological, or practical expertise that landed them their commission. Sturtevant's breakdown of agricultural experimentation into agricultural investigation and experiment possessed no meaning for these southern stations; they were not established to function like the scientific institutes of the north. Southerners demanded a distinctly southern practice, based on science, perhaps, but science applied to the uniquely southern situation. As a result, southern experiment stations were to create a southern agriculture distinct from that of the north.

Conclusion

Although southern stations pursued a different mission, it was the northern station experience that was incorporated in the compromise that produced the Hatch Agricultural Experiment Station Act. That compromise preserved the terms of the tacit agreement between farmers and agricultural scientists first enacted at the New York station. In fact, the act's initial section contained two sets of phrases that stood as explicit references to that compromise. The pairing of "investigation and experiment" as well as "principles and applications" reflected its sentiments. So, too, did the act's second section, which outlined station duties. It included as appropriate station activities original research and practical inquiries, such as variety tests (U.S. Congress, 1887). The basis of that compromise stemmed from Sturtevant's political acumen and the example of the New York station. His explanation of station activities struck a responsive chord among farmers and scientists, while his station's endeavors demonstrated that it was possible not to offend either of two competing, often antagonistic, constituencies. Farmers received a station that provided practical advice, and scientists had a place in which to employ their investigative skills.

References

Anonymous. "Farmer's Talk. Central New York Farmers' Club." New-York Farmer and Dairyman 1:145, 1881a.

———. "Experimental Farms and Stations—Their Necessity in the South." Southern Planter and Farmer 42:401, 1881b.

———. "State Experiment Station." Cultivator and Country Gentleman. 50:962, 1885.

Battle, K. P. History of the University of North Carolina. Two volumes. Chapel Hill: University of North Carolina Press, 1912.

Colman, G. P. "Pioneering in Agricultural Education: Cornell University, 1867–1890." Agricultural History 36:200, 1962.

Connecticut Board of Agriculture. Report of the Secretary of the Connecticut Board of Agriculture, 1874.

———. Report of the Secretary of the Connecticut Board of Agriculture, 1875.

———. Report of the Secretary of the Connecticut Board of Agriculture, 1876.

———. Report of the Secretary of the Connecticut Board of Agriculture, 1877.

Crandall, P. B. "N.Y. Experiment Station." New-York Farmer and Dairyman 1:162, 1881.

Curtis, T. D. "An Experiment Station." New-York Farmer and Dairyman 1:72, 1880.

Dabney, C. W. "Report of the Director." Report of the Agricultural Experiment Station of the University of Tennessee. Knoxville: University of Tennessee, 1888.

Goessmann, C. A. Massachusetts State Agricultural Experiment Station, Bulletin No. 1, July, 1883.

Harris, J. "Among the Farmers—No. 55." American Agriculturalist 39:306, 1880.

Henderson, J. T. "Annual Report of the Commissioner of Agriculture of the State of Georgia." Publications of the Georgia State Department of Agriculture for the Year 1880, 1880.

Henry, W. A. "Report of the Officers of the Station." *Report of the Wisconsin Agricultural Experiment Station for 1884,* 1884.

Jenkins, E. H. "[The Connecticut Station]." *Report of the Secretary of the Connecticut Board of Agriculture,* 1886.

Johnson, S. W. *How Crops Grow: A Treatise on the Chemical Composition, Structure, and Life of the Plant.* New York: Orange Judd and Company, 1868.

———. *How Crops Feed: A Treatise on the Atmosphere and the Soil as Related to the Nutrition of Agricultural Plants.* New York: Orange Judd and Company, 1870.

———. "Report of Agricultural Experiment Station." In *Report of the Secretary of the Connecticut Board of Agriculture,* 1879.

Lazenby, W. R. "Cornell Experiment Station." *Cultivator and Country Gentleman* 45:105, 1880.

———. *First Annual Report of the Ohio Agricultural Experiment Station,* 1882.

L. O. "Experimental Farms." *Southern Planter* 47:86, 1886.

Marcus, A. I. *Agricultural Science and the Quest for Legitimacy: Farmers, Agricultural Colleges, and Experiment Stations.* Ames, Iowa: Iowa State University Press, 1985.

McBryde, J. M. "Report of the Director of Experimental Stations." *Report of the Board of Agriculture and Commissioner of Agriculture of South Carolina,* 1888.

Neale, A. T. "Our Experiment Station, Its Past, Present and Prospective Work." *Annual Report of the New Jersey Board of Agriculture,* 1886.

Nevins, A. *The State Universities and Democracy.* Urbana: University of Illinois Press, 1962.

New Jersey State Board of Agriculture. *Seventh Annual Report of the New Jersey State Board of Agriculture, 1879–80,* 1880.

Nordin, D. S. *Rich Harvest. A History of the Grange.* Jackson: Mississippi State University Press, 1974.

Page, J. R. "A Plea in Favor of Experimental Farms." *Southern Planter* 47:1, 1886.

Philbrick, W. D. "Waushakum Farm." *Cultivator and Country Gentleman* 42:489, 1877.

Plumb, C. S. "A Biographical Sketch." *Annual Report of the Missouri Botanical Garden* 10:71, 1899.

Rossiter, M. W. *The Emergence of Agricultural Science. Justus Liebig and the Americans, 1840–1880.* New Haven: Yale University Press, 1975.

Scott, R. V. *The Reluctant Farmer. The Rise of Agricultural Extension to 1914.* Urbana: University of Illinois Press, 1972.

Scovell, M. A. "Report of the Director." *Report of the Kentucky Agricultural Experiment Station,* 1888.

Sidar, J. W. *George Hammell Cook. A Life in Agriculture and Geology.* New Brunswick: Rutgers University Press, 1976.

Smith, D. C. *A History of the Maine Agricultural Experiment Station, 1885–1978.* Orono: Life Sciences and Agricultural Experiment Station, 1980.

Sturtevant, E. L. "Onward." *Scientific Farmer* 1:108, 1876.

———. "Waushakum Farm Notes." *Scientific Farmer* 2:2, 15–16, 30, 72, 86–87, 100, 114, 128, 142, 155, 1877.

———. "Second Annual Field Meeting." *Scientific Farmer* 3:97, 1878.

———. "Experiment Stations." *Transactions of the New York State Agricultural Society,* 1881.

———. "Agricultural Experiments: What the Farmer Wants to Know, and Why He Wants to Know It." *Report of the Secretary of the Connecticut Board of Agriculture,* 1882a.

———. "Report of the Director." *First Annual Report of the Board of Control of the New York State Agricultural Experiment Station for the Year 1882*, 1882b.

Swan, R. J. "Report of the Board of Control of the New York Experiment Station." *First Annual Report of the Board of Control of the New York State Experiment Station for the Year 1882*, 1882.

True, A. C. *A History of Agricultural Experimentation and Research in the United States, 1607–1925*. Washington, D.C.: Government Printing Office, 1937.

U.S. Congress. "An Act to Establish Agricultural Experiment Stations in Connection with the Colleges Established in the Several States under the Provisions of an Act Approved July Second, Eighteen Hundred and Sixty-two, and of the Acts Supplementary Thereto." *U.S. Statutes* 24:440, 1887.

2

Policy Conflicts in Agricultural Research: Historical Perspective and Today's Challenges

David B. Schweikhardt and James T. Bonnen

Introduction

Agricultural research policy was once concerned primarily with the allocation of resources, but now it involves a growing list of new issues and conflicting interest groups. As a focal point of agricultural research activity, the agricultural experiment stations find themselves the center of a rising level of policy conflict. After several years of debate, most defenders and critics of the experiment station system understand each other's positions on these issues. Too often, however, these policy conflicts are seen simply as factual misunderstandings or political disputes between institutions with competing interests. In fact, some of the most intractable differences arise out of vastly different value beliefs.

All decisions involve the use of normative (values) and positive (factual) knowledge. Value knowledge—about the goodness and badness of situations, conditions, and things (Johnson, 1984)—is a form of information necessary in making decisions. By providing an assessment of existing and potential conditions of society, values, when combined with positive knowledge, allow political decision makers to determine the existence of a problem and its more desirable solution. While positive matters and jurisdictional questions are in dispute, the rising level of conflict today over agricultural research policy can, in part, be seen to result from conflicting value perceptions about the consequences of different policy options. These conflicts are more difficult to deal with and tend to be poorly understood by those (especially scientists) whose positivist philosophy places values outside the realm of objective knowledge (except in the sense of knowledge about who values what). This chapter is based on a systematic analysis of the role of values in the formation and behavior of critical institutions in the development of U.S. agriculture (Schweikhardt, 1983).

The present structure of the experiment station system arose, like all institutions, out of an earlier problem context that resulted in a political decision based on positive knowledge, value beliefs, and the exercise of power. The institutional characteristics responsible for the performance of the experiment stations are evaluated in this discussion as a product of choices and compromises made during the writing of the Hatch Act of 1887. The role of values in a number of present-day policy problems is then examined.

The Role of Values in Agricultural Research: A Historical Perspective

The state agricultural experiment stations are unique in that they combine (1) public financing of research not supported by private interests, (2) an emphasis on applied research, (3) interaction between the research of the stations and the education and extension activities of the land grant system, and (4) a geographically and administratively decentralized system capable of addressing the research needs of farmers facing many different ecological conditions.

The rationale for such a system is apparent to the careful modern observer. The decentralized structure and applied nature of the system are credited with a significant portion of the growth in U.S. agricultural productivity (Evenson et al., 1979). However, this is an *ex post* assessment. The nineteenth century builders of these institutions had no coherent, *ex ante* criteria for selecting the most effective system. Instead, the decentralized system of applied agricultural research was far more the product of values held by scientists, farmers, and politicians. Value preferences were expressed about the conduct of science, the type of research to be performed, and the appropriate relationship between the federal government and the states. These values influenced the Congress and, ultimately, the success of the stations at improving agricultural productivity.

Values Affecting the Hatch Act

This section provides a historical and descriptive summary of the value perceptions that influenced decision makers in writing the Hatch Act. The historical materials on the Act are surveyed, and contending groups and values are identified. Similar values are aggregated, and a sampling of quotes is provided here to demonstrate the expression of these values by decision makers.

Because values are a large, complex category, the effort here is limited to those values expressed clearly in the prescriptions of groups that were in public contention over the form of the Hatch Act. In some cases, these values could be described as ideologies or fundamental philosophic value positions held in strong, if not absolute, form (e.g., the strict constructionist view of the Constitution). Others are value positions to which groups adhere either out of self interest or in the belief that agricultural research can only be successful as a social institution if the espoused values (e.g., scientific or utilitarian values) are accepted.

The Values of Science. There are certain values, held primarily by scientists, that define a good environment in which to perform research. According to the scientific view, it is good for researchers to be free to follow any lead in the pursuit of truth in order to make their maximum contribution to society; pursuit of other goals that distract scientists from their mission of acquiring knowledge is bad. At the 1887 meeting of the Association of American Agricultural Colleges and Experiment Stations, scientists Samuel Johnson, Wilbur Atwater, and George Cook reminded their colleagues that individuality and freedom were the "first conditions" of successful research (Association, 1888:30). One year later, U.S. Commissioner of Agriculture Norman Colman supported this view, warning that political manipulation of the stations would lead to "deterioration in the workers and the work" (White, 1963:249).

Scientific freedom remained an essential value for scientists and administrators during the formative years of the experiment stations. Addressing the Association in 1909, President A. B. Storms of Iowa State warned that a "dry rot" in efficiency and morale was certain to result from political interference in the operations of the stations (Association, 1910:56). Director W. H. Jordan of New York agreed, adding that the scientist must remain "mostly within the atmosphere of inquiry," unhampered by duties "foreign to his general trend of effort" (Association, 1909:115). Two years later, Jordan reiterated this value, claiming an investigator need not "smell of the soil" to be an effective researcher (Association, 1911:159). Director J. L. Hills of Vermont echoed Jordan, likening the researcher to a marathon runner who must not be distracted by administration, teaching, or extension and the station director to a "Cerberus who guards the inmates of his domain against the insistent demands of those who would withdraw them from their tasks for work in the outer world" (Association, 1911:164).

Utilitarian Values. Many nineteenth century men of practical affairs strongly believed that it was good for science to improve the lives of those who worked in the vocations of life. Historians have often called this "vocationalism"; to the utilitarian, increased productivity and welfare of workers are the sole sources of utility that derive from a scientific discovery. As a result, applied research is viewed as having a higher priority than basic research. This does not imply that a conflict of scientific and utilitarian values is inevitable. Indeed, agricultural scientists were quite vocal in expressing utilitarian values in the nineteenth century.

The objective of research, according to a utilitarian, is to improve the material well-being of the working class and, in the case of the experiment stations, farmers in particular. Farmers, of course, expressed this value; as one farmer complained at the 1882 meeting of the Wisconsin Agricultural Society, "We do not want science floating in the skies; we want to bring it down and hitch it to our plows" (Carstensen, 1960:18).

Early agricultural scientists shared this attitude. The objective of inquiry, according to Pennsylvania State College President George Atherton, was "to cheapen the means of subsistence and thus to give man more leisure" (Association, 1888:33). Director Isaac Roberts of Cornell was more blunt: "So long as teachers study science for science's sake the farmer will swear at the bugs for the bugs' sake" (Association, 1898:70). His successor, W. H. Jordan, maintained this utilitarian tradition, claiming the stations should have "nothing to do with knowledge that cannot be brought into the service of humanity" (Jordan, 1908:134).

The Values of Strict Constructionism. Strict constructionists insist that the Constitution is to be interpreted literally and, therefore, any rights not explicitly reserved for the federal government are to be exercised only by the states. This interpretation of the Constitution views the use of federal power not explicitly authorized in the Constitution as leading to (1) the expansion of federal influence in all areas, and (2) an undesirable concentration of power in the central government.

During Senate debate, Senator John Ingalls of Kansas spoke against the Hatch bill on strict constructionist grounds. The bill, he contended, was nothing more than the product of "a certain select class of self-constituted reformers," set on the "continual interposition of the National government in state and local affairs." A continuation of such efforts would result "in absolutely destroying the independence and freedom of individual conduct and subverting the theory on which the Government is based" (U.S. Congress, 1887:723–724). As the next section demonstrates, the values of strict constructionism were critical in the establishment of an administratively decentralized research system.

The Writing of the Hatch Act: A Policy Prescription

By the time the Hatch bill was introduced in Congress in 1886, the major issue to be resolved was the degree of control the federal government would have over the stations. The Hatch bill, supported by the land grant colleges, only allowed the U.S. Commissioner of Agriculture to establish standards of value for use in fertilizer analysis by the stations. The USDA supported this proposal but added that a central office in the USDA should be established to collect and publish research results.

Introduced in the Senate by James George of Mississippi, debate on the Hatch bill began in July, 1886. The provisions of the bill included:

1. The objective of the bill was to "aid the USDA in acquiring and diffusing . . . practical information on subjects connected with agriculture";
2. The experiment stations were to be departments of the land grant colleges;
3. The stations were to be under the control of the trustees of the colleges and a director appointed by the trustees;
4. The U.S. Commissioner of Agriculture would determine a "standard of valuation . . . upon which the analysis of fertilizers . . . shall be based";

5. Each state would receive $15,000 annually to support such stations (U.S. Congress, Appendix, 1887:120–121).

Senator Preston Plumb of Kansas offered the first amendment, an attempt to eliminate the Commissioner's power to set standards of valuation for fertilizer. Plumb's objection was that such a provision would give the Commissioner "the power to determine the commercial value of all the fertilizers in the markets of the United States." Rhode Island's Jonathon Chace responded that the section was harmless, simply wanting to establish "not a standard of value in money, but to establish a standard of . . . chemical quality" (U.S. Congress, 1887:722). Joseph Hawley of Connecticut rejected this argument, claiming the federal government had no constitutional authority to establish standards for any articles: "Why not establish a standard hoe, . . . pill, or . . . anything else? We have a right to make these articles exactly as we please in spite of your law and in spite of your Commissioner of Agriculture" (U.S. Congress, 1887:723). Finally, even after proponents such as Chace expressed concern about "clothing the Commissioner of Agriculture with too much power over this matter," the amendment was accepted, and all references to fertilizer values were removed (U.S. Congress, 1887:721–28). This amendment marked the first victory for the strict constructionists; they had eliminated federal control over fertilizer standards and, in the process, had eliminated one form of USDA control over the stations.

George Edmunds of Vermont next offered an amendment requiring that 15 percent of the funds be used as the U.S. Commissioner of Agriculture directed. His stated purpose was to achieve "uniformity of methods and results." The Massachusetts Grange also supported the amendment as a means of assuring that college administrators could not divert all of the money to teaching or other uses. This amendment ran into opposition from strict constructionists. Senator John Ingalls of Kansas led the opposition, claiming that no "bed of Procrustes" should be erected to fit the stations to the Commissioner's desires and that local institutions providing a "collision and contest between opposing views" would ensure "the greatest good for the greatest number." Again, the strict constructionist view dominated, the amendment was defeated, and federal control of the stations was avoided (U.S. Congress, 1887:721–24).

The last amendment offered by the strict constructionists also limited the role of the federal government by striking out all references to the USDA in the bill's first section, leaving its purpose to be the acquisition and diffusion of knowledge but not necessarily to aid the USDA in doing so. Again, the colleges' control over the stations was strengthened, not because college-controlled stations were thought to be more efficient at improving agricultural science but because the strict constructionists in the Senate wanted stringent constraints on federal control of these state institutions.

In the House of Representatives, William Hatch of Missouri guided the Senate version to passage by a 152 to 12 vote with no amendments and minimal floor debate (three pages in the *Congressional Record*). President Grover Cleveland signed the bill on March 2, 1887. In its final form, the Hatch Act provided that the experiment stations would be established under the direction of the land grant colleges. If independent stations or colleges existed or were established in the future, the state legislature would designate which institution would receive the Hatch funds. The USDA had no formal control over the stations; it could only provide forms for recording experiment results.

The Experiment Station System Viewed as a Product of Value Compromise

The Hatch Act produced an agricultural research system with an applied orientation that is both geographically and administratively decentralized. This unique arrangement was the result of a compromise of conflicting views regarding the proper conduct of science and the appropriate relations between the states and the federal government. Scientists, stressing the value of scientific freedom, were seeking to control the selection, conduct, and publication of research. Farmers and many college scientists, however, placed one constraint on scientific freedom: truth was to be sought, not for its own sake but for the utility it could provide farmers. Within this applied or utilitarian boundary, scientists were to control the research process. With this compromise, scientists were able to secure the support of progressive farmers (and, therefore, legislators) yet still maintain their intellectual autonomy. It was, admittedly, a boundary that required continual restatement and defense in subsequent decades, but the legislative intent was clear.

The role of strict constructionist values is also worth noting. By establishing the principle that the experiment stations were state institutions, the strict constructionists had the effect of placing control of research in the hands of local administrators and scientists. As a result, the scientific freedom enjoyed by experiment station scientists is due, in large part, to the strict constructionist view of the proper relations between the federal and state governments.

One must recognize the serendipity in the compromises made and the decentralized institutional form chosen. Evenson and associates' (1979) quantitative analysis has shown that a significant portion of the improvement in U.S. agricultural productivity is allocated with the decentralization of research from the state station to the substation level. The economic logic of diminishing returns implies that the national to state segment of decentralization, if one were able to measure it, would generate an even greater impact on productivity. Today, it seems obvious that the large land base and diverse nature of U.S. agriculture require a physically decentralized system. However, it was the values of political decision makers—in particular, the values of science and strict constructionism—that produced a decentralized decision-making system allowing scientists to respond to the research demands of farmers in thousands of specific ecospheres across the U.S.

Furthermore, the results of Evenson *et al.* (1979) also indicate a significant complementarity between disciplinary (i.e., basic) research and various types of applied research. This, of course, is understood by those who see research to improve agriculture as a process that requires investments in a number of research activities: disciplinary science, the development of technologies via applied research, the adaptation of applied results to the myriad of specific ecological niches in agriculture, and, eventually, the maintenance of biological productivity gains against the inevitable biological and physical attacks that develop in any ecosystem. All of these research activities are necessary. The productivity derived from an investment in any one type of research is lower without an investment in the others.

The success of the agricultural research system in its first century was made possible because the experiment stations, in conjunction with the USDA, exploited the complementarity of disciplinary and various types of applied research and were responsive to the problems of agriculture. This is a more complex and significant task than it may appear. It involved, of course, the funding of research institutions and projects reaching across the full research and development spectrum. Just as importantly, it involved a system of interlinkage of functions and communications that attempted to keep applied scientists aware of the problems of agriculture and abreast of the developments in disciplinary research while, at the same time, disciplinary researchers were generally informed of the advances in basic science needed in applied research. It also involved sufficient administrative linkage and cooperation to facilitate setting national priorities. If the system is to make similar contributions in its second century, this element of integration and coordination must be sustained and improved. Finally, when considering the allocation of resources between disciplinary and applied agricultural research, it is worth noting that the success of the system is also based on its ability to address both long-term productivity growth and short-term crises in agricultural production. Thus, the appropriate ratio of disciplinary to applied research spending will vary over time and across commodities. This is a flexibility that ought to be maintained as the system enters its second century. One can only conclude that, in establishing a decentralized, integrated, and flexible system, values were selected that enhanced the system's capacity to improve agricultural productivity.

Policy Conflicts in Agricultural Research:
Today's Challenges

The original goals and values of the experiment station system remained unchallenged, at least from the outside, for over half the twentieth century. The last quarter century, however, has seen a rising level of conflict as critics from inside and outside the scientific community have begun to question these traditional goals and values. Some criticism has come from scientists who believe the contribution of research to societal welfare arises almost exclusively from disciplinary research—and that public budgets for applied research would be better used for disciplinary science. Other criticism comes from applied scientists who believe the contribution of research to societal welfare arises almost entirely out of applied research. Both are chauvinistic views that are factually wrong. In addition, there are various advocacy groups in society today that believe the benefits of agricultural industrialization do not or cannot outweigh the costs. The challenge for the agricultural research system in its second century is to respond to legitimate criticism with appropriate policies, to educate policymakers on the contributions and nature of the system, and, when necessary, to defend the system against unwarranted charges.

On-Going Conflicts Between Disciplinary and Applied Science

The tension between the developers of disciplinary and applied knowledge has never, of course, been completely absent. Nevertheless, until recently this has been a tension that existed mostly within the system; as such, it was resolved within the boundaries established by the goals of the system. As a consequence, decision makers sought to exploit the complementarity between disciplinary and applied research.

In the past decade, a more decisive tension has arisen. This higher level of conflict has resulted from chauvinistic views that exist within the agricultural and the larger scientific community (Johnson, 1984). On the one hand, those with the view that only disciplinary science and complete scientific freedom can provide the ultimate source of economic growth greatly underestimate the role of applied science in relaxing the constraints of nature. Conversely, those with an applied science chauvinism underestimate the role of disciplinary science in providing a foundation for advances in applied work.

What is new and unfortunate about this higher level of tension is that it has developed between the system and the "outside" scientific community rather than within the system (Marshall, 1979; Mayer and Mayer, 1974; Wade, 1973). Primarily, it has pitted the land grant colleges against the non-land grant colleges and the disciplinary scientists that dominate the National Academy of Sciences and the National Science Foundation, often over such matters as competitive grants versus institutional funding.

Chauvinists on both sides, limited by their values of disciplinary and applied science, have an excessively narrow view of the research process and the sources of productivity growth in agriculture. Some of this chauvinism, no doubt, is simply a form of political cannibalism; as budget growth stagnated, the political leaders of research were forced to examine their brethren more closely and, in a defensive reaction, sought to acquire or defend available funds in a more aggressive manner than usual. If our objective is an intelligent, effective policy, however, we must seek instead to exploit the complementarity of disciplinary and applied research by providing support for projects across the entire agricultural research and development spectrum. The difficult task lies in discovering and maintaining the appropriate balance of investments in these diverse research activities. The agricultural research system has managed to do this reasonably well. Fragmentation, or loss of effective linkage of all parts of the system, would lead to a considerable loss in the potential productivity that can be derived from any given investment in agricultural R&D.

Conflicts Between Science and Its Critics

Concurrent with the rising tension among scientists has been a growing conflict primarily between scientists and a bevy of critics outside the scientific community. These critics have lodged a variety of complaints, focusing mainly on the alleged insensitivity of the agricultural research establishment to the side effects of technological change and the lack of accountability in the research process.

Conflicts Over the Side Effects of Industrialized Agriculture. The list of allegations lodged against industrial agriculture is well known: the growth of farm size and capital requirements have limited entry into farming and made farming financially unstable; chemical pesticides, herbicides, fertilizers, and animal medicines threaten farm workers, consumers, and the environment; soil erosion destroys the productivity of the land; the declining number of farms diminishes the quality of life in rural areas; mechanization displaces willing workers; the gains of industrialization are inequitably distributed; the rights of animals are violated in modern production systems (Berry, 1977; Hightower, 1973; Mason and Singer, 1980). The groups that have placed these issues on the public policy agenda bring an entirely new set of values to research policy, values that often conflict with the values of science. Just as the experiment stations cannot be credited with all the gains in agricultural productivity in the past century, neither can they bear full blame for these side effects. Nevertheless, as an institution explicitly charged with the duty of developing new technology, the experiment stations are an obvious target for all these accusations and have a leadership role in contending with these criticisms.

Agricultural research is in an uncomfortable position; it cannot take credit for transforming agriculture or for the high rates of return often claimed of it without also taking some responsibility for the side effects of industrialization. The challenge for research managers will be to accommodate some of these values, possibly through research itself, as is being done with integrated pest management in an attempt to avoid the environmental impacts of chemical pesticides.

Conflicts Over the Research Process. A separate but similar issue is the management of the research process. The entire research community is under increasing scrutiny, with outside groups calling for greater accountability for researchers. The rights of animals in the research process, the regulation of genetic research, and the *ex ante* assessment of research are all issues now facing the research system (Bellew, 1984; Biemiller, 1984; Mackay-Smith, 1983).

Again, these issues bring new values to the political arena, and, once again, these values conflict with the values embedded in the Hatch Act that provided local, self-regulating control of scientific research. In this age of greater public sector accountability, however, the research system has little choice but to face these issues. The challenge, as with the side effects of industrialization, will be to address legitimate concern without impairing the benefits that the experiment stations can rightly claim they provide.

The Changing Social Context of Research Policy

The confidence in science held by the public that endured during the first half of this century has declined substantially in the second half. With this change has come a growing doubt that science always serves in society's best interest and, with that doubt, a growing interest in research policy. Furthermore, the political process has evolved in the direction of a broader participatory democracy. This is affecting agricultural policy. Since agricultural research policy is inevitably made within the larger agricultural policy arena, the political climate of agriculture cannot be ignored.

The Erosion of Confidence in Science. The decline of America's confidence in the inevitability of progress, that tomorrow will always be better than today, can be attributed to a number of causes. Whatever other causes may exist, the public's declining confidence in science has been a contributing factor. Whether measured by public opinion sampling or anecdotal evidence, the public has exhibited a loss of confidence in science for at least two decades (Etzioni and Nunn, 1974). A number of root causes can be identified. The public no longer sees science as a neutral force contributing only to the progress of society. Apprehension exists that technology is inevitable; that is, anything that can be done in the laboratory will eventually be imposed on society. Science is sometimes perceived as creating new and larger problems than it solves. Also, when scientists disagree publicly about the potential impacts of science, the public is left with the impression that, unlike the idealized scientist who is objective and honest, some scientists must not only be wrong, but also biased or dishonest (Etzioni and Nunn, 1974; Graham, 1978).

Scientists are not blameless in this loss of confidence. Too often, scientists have disclaimed all responsibility for the impact of scientific discoveries or failed to appreciate and explain both the potential and the limitations of science. This is perhaps understandable; political debate is not the scientist's forte. In a democracy, however, public funding can only be sustained if the public maintains its confidence in the funded institution. Not every scientist must be involved in public dialogue, but a larger number must, as must research managers and political leaders with an understanding of agricultural research.

More fundamental for research policy, however, is that changes in the public's values have led to a redefinition of what we as a society consider to be progress. The notion that progress could be measured as a strictly positive function of output is now challenged by the view that increases in output must be measured against the potential social or environmental externalities arising from technological change. Underlying this challenge, of course, are the values of the critics of research, values that conflict with those embedded in the experiment station system since its inception.

Changes in the Political Climate of Agriculture. Not only has a new and potentially conflicting set of values been injected into the agricultural research policy debate, but the issues raised must be resolved in a political environment that is increasingly uninformed about or unable to resolve agricultural policy issues. Until World War II, while the problems were numerous, the policy agenda in agricultural policy was short and the decision-making process was relatively uncluttered. Research and education occupied a premier position on the farm policy agenda. The decision process was controlled by Congressional committees, USDA personnel, land grant leaders, and general farm organizations. The leadership of these groups collectively understood the subtleties of politics as well as the needs of agriculture. They generally listened to the scientific leadership in agriculture on the policy agenda of science. Thus, they were able to provide a consistent, cohesive policy for the development of agriculture.

In the post-War period, this cohesion has broken down. As agriculture became specialized and industrialized, the economic and political interests of agriculture fragmented. The general farm organizations lost influence to commodity interest groups, each with its specific, often conflicting, demands. Under the impact of progressively greater specialization, even the economic interests of commodity groups have fragmented. The rise of the modern farm input and output sectors introduced a new set of agribusiness interest groups into the process. More recently, as the share of farm production exported has risen, a greater number of federal agencies and officials became interested in the political and economic impacts of food policy. The rising share of the USDA budget spent on food stamps, price supports, and other programs with well-organized clientele has pushed research and education further down the policy agenda and further down the list of budget priorities (Bonnen, 1980). The scientific needs of agriculture have been ignored and the priorities often distorted in budget and policy decisions. The passage of each new farm bill is now a major political struggle; only the coalition of farm interests with urban consumer, labor, and welfare interests, trading support for their respective programs, can achieve results. The task of legitimizing agricultural R&D is becoming more difficult since research is seen to be guilty of political association with increasingly unpopular farm programs; as a result, the future of research funding is more uncertain.

Policy Conflicts to Be Resolved

As the experiment station system begins its second century, a number of conflicts must be resolved. Just as the values chosen during the writing of the Hatch Act helped establish the original capacity and limits of the system, the values chosen in making critical policy decisions over the next few years will establish and limit the future effectiveness of the system.

The disciplinary and applied chauvinists create a conflict between disciplinary and applied science. The former view the basic disciplines as the ultimate or sole source of economic growth and place a high value on the unrestrained scientific freedom of "basic scientists" to establish the research agenda. The applied chauvinists, guided by the high value attached to the practical results of science, seek to constrain the research agenda; agricultural scientists are to be free within the boundaries of an applied research agenda. The Hatch Act resolved this conflict in favor of practical results, and the existing system reflects this bias. As agriculture has become a science-based industry, however, its dependence on disciplinary research has become greater. Thus, calls for increased attention to disciplinary science do have some validity. However, disciplinary research without an applied science follow through will have limited practical utility.

To resolve this conflict in favor of either extreme position will reduce the system's ability to exploit the complementarity of disciplinary and applied research. Furthermore, any resolution, of this conflict that includes an increase in agricultural research spending in basic disciplines at non-land grant universities should emphasize activities with expected relevance to the needs of applied researchers. It should also invest in a network linking these researchers with applied scientists in the land grant system. The failure of scientists in basic disciplines to understand the problems of agriculture and the potential uses of their results will leave the research process incomplete, resulting in delays in research and utilization of knowledge and consequent losses of potential productivity.

Another conflict is at hand between scientists and the critics of agricultural industrialization. While the issues involved vary from environmental quality, to health and safety, to the displacement of workers, to the welfare of animals, advocates concerned with these issues often share a common perspective. In each case, they place a higher value on eliminating the side effects of research than on scientific freedom or increased agricultural productivity.

The most extreme critics of agricultural industrialization wish to impose a zero-risk tolerance on the system. To them, any change in technology or institutions, regardless of its benefits, is undesirable if its development or implementation is accompanied by any environmental, social, or economic risks. If this view prevails, much research cannot be pursued, benefits will be forfeited, and major costs will be imposed on farmers and consumers—on the slightest chance that some external cost may be created. The leadership in the agricultural research community must explain the necessity of some risk taking in science. Furthermore, they must maintain their trustworthiness by recognizing that risks do exist and, where necessary, withdrawing from lines of work where risks demonstrably outweigh benefits. There is a range of tradeoffs where risks must be balanced and prudent decisions made in the interest of society.

This may seem hostile to the research process. It is not. Science has always had a pragmatic tradition, following one path toward an objective then, when that route proved infeasible, following another. In the past, these decisions were based on the criteria of technical feasibility or agricultural productivity, primarily because the existing system placed high value on increased agricultural efficiency. If the stations are to avoid the costs of excessive research regulation, they must recognize that new criteria, based on new values, must be applied to the pragmatic tradition of the research process.

If the leadership of the agricultural research community insists on defending absolute scientific freedom to the exclusion of all other values, it is very likely destined for political defeat. The loss of agriculture's political power base, combined with the legitimate concerns of reasonable critics, will force greater accountability on the system. To oppose such changes could play into the hands of more extreme critics, possibly resulting in limits to research funding and more restrictive control of research.

While the experiment stations will be responsible for addressing a number of the issues raised by critics, a number of the side effects of industrialization would be better addressed by policies other than research policy. The financial frailty of capital intensive agriculture, for instance, would be better addressed by appropriate monetary and fiscal policies than by changes in research policy. Similarly, the displacement of workers will require education and employment policies beyond the control of the experiment stations. To repeat an earlier comment, the experiment stations are not due all the credit or blame for the industrialization of agriculture. They cannot and should not be expected to address all the side effects of industrialization.

If the agricultural research system is allowed to fall into disrepair, a unique American contribution to science and food production will have been lost. A hostile relationship will likely develop between the land grant and non-land grant universities, and the system will likely lose a growing number of scientists to private industry. If the critics of research are successful in placing extreme limits on the scope of public research, private sector researchers could pick up these lines of research, often without the scrutiny applied to public research. As a result, there could be less of the accountability sought by research critics. In addition, many costly lines of inquiry with highly uncertain payoffs will not be pursued or will be long delayed in intellectual development.

A century ago, the challenge for leaders of the agricultural research movement was to forge a system out of a set of conflicting goals and diverse values. The product of their efforts was a system that brought together the disparate elements of science in the service of agriculture. Today, the leadership of the agricultural research system faces a similar task of mediating the differences between conflicting values. Different values and a different distribution of power exist. If the leadership fails to acknowledge its responsibility, it faces the possibility of political defeat or exclusion from important policy decisions. In its second century, the challenge for the system is to find an accommodation with the legitimate concerns of a new set of political participants while maintaining the integrity and contributions of the system to a stronger agricultural sector—an agriculture supportive of the long-run goals and welfare of the society.

References

Association of American Agricultural Colleges and Experiment Stations. *Report of the Committee on Station Work.* Washington, D.C.: Government Printing Office, 1888.

———. *Proceedings of the Annual Convention of the Association of American Agricultural Colleges and Experiment Stations.* Washington, D.C.: United States Department of Agriculture, Office of Experiment Stations Bulletin, 1898-1911.

Bellew, Patricia A. "Agricultural Research, Once Little Noticed, Grows Controversial." *The Wall Street Journal.* November 21:1, 1984.

Berry, Wendell. *The Unsettling of America.* New York: Avon Books, 1977.

Biemiller, Lawrence. "Social and Political Dilemmas Hit Agricultural Research." *The Chronicle of Higher Education.* July 5:1, 1984.

Bonnen, James T. "Observations on the Changing Nature of National Agricultural Policy Decision Processes." Pp. 309-27 in Trudy Huskamp Peterson (ed.), *Farmers, Bureaucrats, and Middlemen: Historical Perspectives on American Agriculture.* Washington, D.C.: Harvard University Press, 1980.

Carstensen, Vernon. "The Genesis of an Agricultural Experiment Station." *Agricultural History* 34:13-20, 1960.

Etzioni, Amitai, and Nunn, Clyde. "The Public Appreciation of Science in Contemporary America." *Daedalus* 103(3):191-205, 1974.

Evenson, Robert E.; Waggoner, Paul E.; and Ruttan, Vernon W. "Economic Benefits from Research: An Example from Agriculture." *Science* 205:1101-07, 1979.

Graham, Loren. "Concerns about Science and Attempts to Regulate Inquiry." *Daedalus* 107(2):1-21, 1978.

Hightower, Jim. *Hard Tomatoes, Hard Times.* Cambridge, Massachusetts: Schenksman, 1973.

Johnson, Glenn L. "Academia Needs a New Covenant for Serving Agriculture." Mississippi State: Mississippi Agricultural Experiment Station, Mississippi State University, 1984.

Jordan, Whitman H. "The Authority of Science." Pp. 128-45 in Thomas C. Blaisdell (ed.), *The Semi-Centennial Celebration of Michigan Agricultural College.* Chicago: University of Chicago Press, 1908.

Mackay-Smith, Anne. "Animal-Rights Fight Against Pet Projects Worries Researchers." *The Wall Street Journal.* November 30:1, 1983.

Marshall, Eliot. "Agricultural Network Fights Unwelcome Gift." *Science* 205:1108-09, 1979.

Mason, Jim, and Singer, Peter. *Animal Factories.* New York: Crown Publishers, 1980.

Mayer, Andre, and Mayer, Jean. "Agriculture, the Island Empire." *Daedalus* 103(3):83-95, 1974.

Schweikhardt, David B. "The Role of Nonmonetary Values in Induced Institutional Innovation: The Case of the State Agricultural Experiment Stations." Unpublished M.S. thesis, Michigan State University, 1983.

U.S. Congress. *Congressional Record*. Forty-ninth Congress, Second Session, 1887.
Wade, Nicholas. "Agriculture: NAS Panel Charges Inept Management, Poor Research."
    Science 179:45–47, 1973.
White, Leonard. *The Republican Era, 1869–1901: A Study in Administrative History.*
    New York: MacMillan, 1963.

3

The Value Measure in
Public Agricultural Research

Jeffrey Burkhardt

Introduction

The research agenda for public agricultural research is currently the subject of considerable debate. Changes in the structure of American agriculture have brought with them the need for public sector scientists and administrators to reconsider the mission of public research. Indeed, the question of the proper mission for public research is a pressing one, since with the upcoming centennial of the Hatch Act in 1987, there are increasingly calls from both inside and outside the agricultural research establishment for a "new commitment" to the *public* purpose in public sector research. What *this* means is, however, far from clear.

What is clear is that the current debate is over values. In this regard, political and philosophical analysis of the value dimensions of public agricultural research is not only theoretically, but also practically, important. Funding, programs, and people are affected by the outcome of the debates.

My aim in this chapter is to present an analysis of the value dimensions of agricultural research with an eye toward providing a model and a criterion that can resolve conflicts over the proper direction for public research. My initial argument is that the decision criterion currently in use in prioritizing research agendas is a species of the philosophical doctrine of utilitarianism— service to the greater good of the greatest number. In the first section of the chapter I show how this criterion is used to resolve conflicts over the direction of science. In the second section of the chapter, I argue that the current interpretation of the utilitarian principle tends to ignore or minimize the importance of certain values or interests, specifically "new agenda" considerations. Finally, I wish to maintain that without a change in that criterion, we cannot legitimately claim to have achieved the public purpose in a public research agenda. What I propose is that a criterion of "human needs" should be taken as definitive of the good in "greatest good for the greatest number." This, I believe, is consistent with the best reading of the history of the public mission for public research.

The Meaning of "Values"
in Agricultural Research

In the philosophical literature on the subject, values are variously characterized as attitudes, beliefs about good things, preferred states of affairs, motivating ideals, and so forth (see, e.g., Rescher, 1969). The vagueness and ambiguity of the term "value" in ordinary language suggest that each or all of the characterizations may be appropriate, depending upon the context or theory in which it is offered. In the present context, I suggest that values be understood not so much as attitudes, commitments, or beliefs about good or ideal states of affairs, but instead as ideologies—interests parading as ideals. This view on "values" is more revealing of the dynamics of agricultural research agenda setting than are the other characterizations of values. This is because most of the values defining the value context of agricultural research are broad and institutionally oriented ones, easily capable of a wide variety of radically different interpretations, which reflect economic and political interests. That is, individuals and groups of individuals stand to gain or lose in real terms by having a particular view of values definitive of agricultural research acted upon. Thus, while most of the values already there in agricultural research institutions in accord with the official reading of the Hatch Act and subsequent "mission" legislation appear to be commonly held, they are not. Commonly held values are in fact held with very different understandings of what subscription to that value practically implies for research agenda and priorities. I do not mean to suggest that all values operative in agricultural research have this ideological function; for instance, personal or even professional values may not. However, the main agreed upon values or orientations offered as constitutive of the value context of agricultural research have this ideological dimension.

In support of this view, I wish to highlight two of the broader values that have been seen as particularly relevant to agricultural research. Rosenberg (1976) suggests that near the top of any list of values in public agricultural research would be something we might refer to as "Scientism," a belief in the goodness of scientific progress. Our own study (Busch et al., forthcoming) of the increasing move into biotechnological research in public agricultural research confirms Rosenberg's point that the practice of science is valued in and of itself: scientists and administrators, in both the public and private sector, indicate that as a further "tool in the toolbox" for scientific progress, biotechnology is a good thing. The institutional implication is that whatever conflicts over the increased use of biotechnology in agricultural research there might be, these can be resolved by an appeal to the "scientistic" basis for the move. I will expand on this point below.

The second value that is an important part of the value context of agricultural research is "utilitarianism." Hadwiger (1982) maintains that agricultural scientists are "utilitarians," by which he means that scientists and the research institutions are motivated by a concern for "useful results." Indeed, the nature of public, mission-oriented research suggests this practical, utilitarian orientation: utilitarianism is generally definitive of the value orientation of public agricultural research. Our own research confirms that the agricultural sciences, particularly plant improvement, but others as well, are influenced by concerns about producing "more good." Scientists and administrators have repeatedly indicated that their goal is to serve "the public" in the establishment of research agendas and even in the choice of particular research problems. It is rarely noted that it is *particular publics* who are in fact served by particular research agendas, particular programs, particular projects. However, everyone seems to agree that public agricultural research should serve the "greatest good for the greatest number."

These two value orientations, scientism and utilitarianism, are currently the dominant ones affecting discussions about the future directions of agricultural research. While this is not a particularly original point, it is important enough to be reiterated here. Issues such as "basic" vs. "applied," teaching vs. research, research vs. extension, regional vs. national, and so forth, can be seen as direct implications of differing interpretations of what the "pursuit of science" really means. Moreover, in public agenda setting, service to the "greatest good for the greatest number" is the basis for deciding what "pursuit of science" should practically mean. Most scientific issues could be resolved if we could agree on what this value really means. The philosophical problem is that even though everyone agrees that utilitarian criteria should help resolve "scientistic" value questions, not everyone holds the same interpretation of even this value. It is nonetheless appealed to by various interest groups as justifications for their particular views of the proper direction for agricultural research. Hence, its ideological nature is apparent.

Let me return to the example of the institutional and value dynamics of the use of the "new" biotechnologies in plant improvement programs. There is currently an issue over the legitimacy of increased movement by public sector research institutions into biotechnological research (NA-SULGC, 1984). Everyone, from traditional plant breeders to microbiologists, to public and private administrators, agrees that whatever furthers the progress of science should be pursued. This common commitment implies that in presenting plans for program development or funding priorities, etc., "scientific progress" is invoked as the justification for these plans or their new directions. Each further agrees that the final arbiter of conflicts over particular projects or even programs is whether the public is served by moves in this direction. The problem is that each individual, or better, certain groups of individuals have very different things at stake in moves to increased biotechnological research. For plant breeders, it may mean the constriction of, or even the demise of, their programs. For microbiologists, it is a way to open their discipline to new subject matter. For public administrators, there are greater opportunities for extramural funding. Private corporations see the opportunity to use university talent to develop marketable products. Appeals to scientific progress for the public purpose by each of these different, competing, or at least potentially diverging, groups reflect their interests. Any or all of these, and other, interests may be legitimate, i.e., consistent with the public good. However, the important point is that by appealing to the utilitarian nature of increased biotechnological research, the real importance of conflicting interests or the legitimacy of certain interests never gets fully assessed. Furthermore, somebody's interests *are* being served, even if no one actually decided that benefitting that group constitutes service to "the public."

It should be noted here that I am not saying whether the operative interests are legitimate or illegitimate ones. The question of legitimacy is a normative one, and one to which I will return. My point is that for whatever values we observe or reconstruct through a descriptive analysis of agricultural research institutions, we must ask who is promoting those values and who stands to gain or lose from a particular understanding of what that value entails for the agenda or priorities. With this perspective on the current value dimension of agricultural research, we can begin to see why it is that some values and interests probably cannot expect to be considered in the future value directions of agricultural research without a significant change in the criterion.

New Values, New Interests: Other Possibilities?

Part of the difficulty in assessing the proper course for public agricultural research at the present time is that there are a number of new client groups or potential client groups who might be benefitted or harmed by specific projects and programs. An important element in decisions about priorities is thus to consider the range of alternative values. What interests, that is, are legitimate contenders for receiving benefits from public agricultural research? Since the interests presently operative in the "value-establishment" are such that resolving conflicts among them is complicated, the consideration of alternative research is even more complex. However, this task is both philosophically and practically necessary. Practically so, since new interests are becoming increasingly vocal critics of agricultural research policy and must be dealt with in some fashion. Philosophically so, since even though these new groups represent "special interests," as part of the larger public, they must be considered in the mission orientation of public research.

The number of new values, new interests, in agricultural research is growing. Already, observers of the research establishment such as Ruttan (1982), Danbom (1979), and Buttel (1984) have noted the environmental interests increasingly becoming important in connection with particular research agendas; processing companies' interests have come into the fore as well; to these we should now add the values offered by the alternative agriculture movements and values associated with the lifestyles of new potential constituency groups whom the research institutions might serve, e.g., backyard gardeners. These groups generally subscribe to the broader values of scientism and utilitarianism. However, they also understand these values differently on the basis of different interests. Furthermore, they have interests regarding specific programs not associated with those of any other group. I do not wish here to catalogue the alternative values or "new interests" that have been offered. Instead, I will mention only three main ones, in order to suggest that without the current interpretation of the utilitarian criterion being used in decision making, it is understandable how some interests are *a priori* important, while some are not. The latter will ultimately be underrepresented in institutional practice.

Let us first consider consumer interests. Consumerism may not be a totally new value orientation. It does, however, have a certain new twist if we consider the increased demand on AESs in states with growing urban populations to engage in research more suited to the "agricultural" needs of urbanites, for example, research on lawn grasses or household pests. In any case, it is clear that consumers' interests should be considered in setting the direction that public agricultural research is to take, not only in specific programs like those mentioned above, but also in more general orientations such as the nutritional quality of food, its availability and dependability, and the like. Examples of service to consumer interests abound, so I will not repeat them here.

An important question is how this or any other interests find their way into the research priorities established for the SAES and ARS regarding both overall directions and particular programs and projects. There are two ways: either legislators for the particular districts serving mostly urbanites introduce those values as political pressures on the AES, or scientists and administrators decide themselves that the urban "public" would desire, and indeed eventually pay for, research products developed out of programs oriented toward consumer interests. In both cases, there is a judgment that, because of the political and economic dimensions of giving this value orientation some high priority in the research agenda, it should be considered if not ultimately pursued. I am not suggesting that it should not be; rather, I am suggesting that it is *not* a matter of a systematic weighing of these values over and against any other values, but, instead, a determination of the need for serving particular, *important* interests.

Alternative agriculture should also be considered. This, too, represents a new interest contending for its place in the hierarchy. This orientation calls for research priorities stressing, even more than urban consumers might, environmental safety of the products of agricultural research, community quality of life, and, more specifically, research on intercropping systems, renewable energy resources, and agricultural management systems better suited to small, labor intensive farming conditions. The study by Busch *et al.* (forthcoming) suggests that researchers and administrators are for the most part not aware of alternative agriculture. When they are, they do think that it should be included in the research agenda-setting process. Once again, however, decisions about the relative importance of this orientation are being made with reference to the political and economic forces operative on the research decision-making apparatus.

Similar points can be made about another "new" interest that is to be considered in making judgments about research priorities. This is the orientation being introduced, particularly in the area of biotechnological research, of service to corporate interests in having marketable agricultural products. I suggest that this is a new value in the agricultural research system, since prior to the recent formation of university-industry collaborative efforts, corporate profits or potential marketability were only indirectly values to be considered in decisions about the public research agenda. Services to farmers' interests and to the interests of inputs suppliers have been part of the mission orientation of the public institution. Recently, however, large multinational corporations have been included as well. The same point applies here about how an interest becomes an important part of the public sector research agenda: political and/or economic considerations bear on these decisions. Given this, it is fairly clear that service to this "public" will become more dominant.

Since comparable statements can be made in reference to any aspect of the new agenda affecting agricultural research, I will not pursue more examples here. The major point is that it is both philosophically and practically important that we consider as many of these new interests in agenda setting as possible. Decision makers, from scientists at the bench level to legislators and USDA officials, should be alerted to all potentially important values and the interests of all those potentially affected by decisions about priorities. This would seem to be a necessary implication of the institutional commitment to utilitarianism, a fundamental orientation of public agricultural research.

The difficulty with the introduction of "new data" into the decision-making machine is that in order to manage the data effectively, i.e., decide on the relative weights to attach to various values, a criterion for ranking values is necessary. At the very least, a unit of measurement for comparison is required. That unit, as I suggested above, has become an economic one, or more precisely, a political economic one. Given this, even with a commitment to service to the general public, certain interests will be discounted. Alternative agriculture is one that *might* be considered, but it would probably not be *seriously* considered; values relating to the quality of life for farm labor, particularly unskilled labor, is another. The list of potential noncandidates for importance or even inclusion in the value orientation of future agricultural research is a long one. The exception is those corporate interests actively promoting the use of the criterion that is in use in public decision making. I am not saying that this is illegitimate; certainly, weighting interests is necessary. However, weights are illegitimate if they do not rest upon an understanding of "greatest good" in terms of the satisfaction of human needs. This is what I take the public purpose in public agricultural research to be all about, and given this, some corporate interests are probably illegitimately intruding on the public mission.

Human Needs and the Public Interest

As stated earlier, the criterion according to which interests and values affecting agricultural research are weighted is a utilitarian one. This needs to be clarified further, since even in the philosophical literature on the subject, the nature of utilitarianism is not always very well specified (e.g., Lyons, 1965). There are a number of varieties of the utilitarian criterion, from the vague "greatest good for the greatest number" variety to more technical cost-benefit analysis. Technical cost-benefit analysis is the species of utilitarianism most often cited in characterizations of institutional or bureaucratic decision making, so I will briefly describe it here, if only to suggest that cost-benefit analysis is not exactly what is dictating the weighing of particular value interpretations or interests. There are, however, some important connections between the utilitarian criterion being used and cost-benefit analysis.

Cost-benefit analysis typically is employed in decisions about the desirability of a high capital outlay, long term investment. In particular, major public works projects have been and are being subjected to an analysis in which the "present discount value" (PDV) of an investment is calculated. Specification of the actual formula for these calculations is not necessary here; the main point of PDV calculation is that future costs and benefits are to be successively discounted by an assigned rate of interest, so that the farther into the future the projectible costs and benefits, the less significant they become.

The crucial factor in PDV cost-benefit analysis is that all projectible costs and benefits must be decided upon in advance so that the complex "program" can be run. In this regard, the utilitarian criterion operative in decisions about courses of action in agricultural research is not precisely cost-benefit. There is some superficial resemblance in the fact that administrators and scientists and others involved in the decision-making process speak of benefits and burdens or costs; there is also an after the fact resemblance in the sense that accounting procedures indicate "bottom lines," the *ex ante desideratum* of cost-benefit analysis. Procedurally, however, costs and benefits are not actually "discounted" in any formal, mathematical sense, or at least it is not apparent that they are.

The important similarity between the utilitarianism and formal cost-benefit analysis is that, in both cases, *some* interests or values are systematically underrepresented in the decision-making procedures. This is basically because the "unit" or criterion upon which benefits or burdens are judged is still a mathematical one; indeed, a monetary one. In calculating the "greatest good for the greatest number," "small numbers," or nonfinancial interests, cannot be given as much weight in the utility calculus.

Despite the intuitive appeal of monetarily measurable costs and benefits as a unit for decision making, as well as its practicality, this is, in the judgment of many philosophers, ultimately unacceptable. Indeed, despite the best intentions of many decision makers to find ways to consider all present and future interests in the assessment of actions or institutional priorities, as long as monetary interests are the sole ones considered, the interests of marginally affected powerless individuals cannot be regarded as having much importance in overall prioritizations and value directions. It might be argued that this is not the result of the monetary unit; instead, it is just the inevitable result of having to weigh the relative benefits and burdens of a given course of action (Rawls, 1971). This, however, is not exactly so, since if we could devise a unit to assess benefits and burdens that would count as the "good" and would not automatically rule out the interests of particular individuals or groups, we might still be able to use a "greatest good for the greatest number" procedure in decision making. In practice, this amounts to maximizing some other criterion as "the good." This, I believe, is an important issue for priority setting in public agricultural research, since we are, after all, attempting at least ideally to maximize the "public good" or the "public interest" in decision making there. In other words, the public purpose would be better served by utilizing a different criterion. Where is this to be found? The first logical place to look is at the *underlying* notion of "good" that governs those interests operative in the history of public agricultural research.

The Hatch and Morrill Acts were originally enacted, as historians tell us (e.g., Knoblauch *et al.*, 1962), to bring the best results of the natural and mechanical sciences together to benefit agriculture. What this value orientation means, of course, is that those acts and legislative action subsequent to them were established to serve the particular interests involved in agriculture: farmers, input suppliers, seedsmen, and local and regional consumers. Over time, the clients and constituencies served by public agricultural research have changed: small to larger farms, rural to urban populations, family to corporate farms, and, now, multinational chemical corporations and machinery manufacturers.

What I suggest is that there is one interest, common to each of these "special interest groups": human needs. Whatever other interests exist are based upon the supposition that needs fundamental to human life have been or at least can be met. Such needs include: (1) adequate, affordable, or at least available, nutritionally adequate food; (2) adequate, affordable, or at least available, clothing and shelter; (3) a liveable environment; (4) secure means to provide for one's livelihood; and (5) accessible educational opportunities. Though the interests vying for input in the decisions about the "proper" value orientation of public agricultural research have changed over time and vary in terms of their understandings of the values of agricultural research, there can be little disagreement that the one interest they share, at base, is human need. Thus, I suggest that this is what the "public interest" must mean. And indeed, to the extent that the utilitarian principle fails to direct itself toward the satisfaction of these needs, any reference to the "greater good for the greater number" is simply ideological. Human need must be our criterion of "the good."

I will not pretend here to give any detailed account of what "human needs" should be interpreted to mean. There are, however, a few points that might make clear that this "public interest" will entail some very different value interpretations for governing agricultural research.

First, human needs are objective: they are determinable, scientifically, often by the very sciences integral to agricultural research. Perhaps a clear determination of what counts as human needs is not immediately at hand or forthcoming; however, by focusing on this idea of "what counts," research can be tailored toward the further understanding of objective human needs.

What follows from this is that a distinction must be made between needs and wants. Wants are subjective; they vary from person to person and from culture to culture. What people want or what they take to be in their interest are often based upon "felt needs." However, the main point about human needs is that they do not have the arbitrary and variant character of wants or perceived interests. With a clear understanding of what this criterion objectively means, the ideological aspect of both scientism and utilitarianism can be reduced and even eliminated. No one's interests are better served by adherence to the greater good of the greater number if good *means* satisfaction of objective human needs.

Second, even without that clear understanding of what human beings need, we can still know that some kinds of research should not be performed. Even if consumers or industry would be willing to pay for some kind of processes or products, we must make the judgment that these kinds of research do not serve the "public good."

Third, since each individual human being has needs such as those mentioned above, failing to include the human needs of any individuals in the assessment of research priorities violates concern for the greatest social good. What follows from this is that since future generations of human beings are equally human beings, to focus solely on short term interests is illegitimate.

The public interest in the satisfaction of human needs may be compatible with much of the research presently conducted in agricultural research institutions, even that performed under the financial auspices of private corporate grants and contracts. The principle, or criterion, that human needs should bear greatest weight in the determination of research agenda and priorities will, however, dictate that those corporate interests be assessed relative to their contribution to the satisfaction of human needs. Indeed, the criterion provides a way of determining whether or not some of the corporate interests are *legitimately* a part of public agricultural research.

I have thus far spoken of human needs as if this were a necessary and self-evident criterion for the assessment of priorities, that is, one in need of no demonstration or proof. Indeed, I believe that it is, at least insofar as the burden of proof is upon one who would deny that the point of public agricultural research, at base, is to satisfy human needs. There is a certain compellingness in the criterion that demands the research agenda, programs, and projects be designed and evaluated in accord with their contribution to human welfare in its most basic sense, and not whether they further the interests of particular economic, political, or even "moral" constituencies. More formal "proofs" of this principle are available (see, e.g., Braybrooke, 1979). My point here, however, is that with regard to public agricultural research, they are unnecessary. In virtue of our being members of the human species, each one of us has a clear need for food, clothing, shelter, a liveable environment, employment opportunities, etc. This said, the only real question is the practical one: How do we institutionalize this criterion according to which interests will be weighed and which value directions will be articulated in priorities and agenda?

This is not the place to give a complete answer to that question. However, what I will suggest is that proposals that have recently been offered in regard to institutional priorities and public-private collaborative efforts have not adequately addressed this issue, even when the opportunity has arisen. Despite calls for "social impacts statements" (Friedland and Kappel, 1979), scientists, administrators, and "new agenda" interests have not looked hard enough at possible implications that may exist for particular kinds of research or institutional arrangements concerning human needs, present and future. Changes in the institutional structures for priority setting in agricultural research may be necessary (Lipman-Blumen and Schram, 1984). Similarly, better legal instruments protecting scientists' professional interests and specifying rights and duties of corporate interests regarding particular products of research are important (NASULGC, 1984). However, the underlying "philosophy" of public agricultural research is what ultimately needs to be addressed: Whose needs will be served by these kinds of research, these research agenda, these institutional forms? This is *the* major question confronting us in assessing the value dimensions of agricultural research, and one to which I give an unqualified answer: Ours, not as consumers, farmers, scientists, corporations, etc., but as people. This is the best meaning to be given any utilitarianism that might be thought to undergird our public institutions.

Although the value issues confronting agricultural research are complex and the conflicts transparent, what is ultimately called for is for us to "raise the level of discourse" from description and new considerations of agenda to the normative one. We should resume the discussion not about what is or is not possible. The real issue is what *must* be done for people. As many of us recognize, much is at stake. Indeed, human life is the issue.

References

Braybrooke, D. "Skepticism of Wants, and Certain Subversive Effects of Corporations in American Values." Pp. 224–39 in Sidney Hook (ed.), *Human Values and Economic Policy*. New York: New York University Press, 1967.

Busch, L.; Lacy, W.; Burkhardt, J.; and Hansen, M. *Plant Breeding and the New Biotechnology: Conflict and Change*. Forthcoming.

Buttel, F. "Biotechnology and Agricultural Research Policy: Emergent Issues." Ithaca, New York: Cornell University Rural Sociology Bulletin Series, 1984.

Danbom, D. *The Resisted Revolution*. Ames: Iowa State University Press, 1979.

Friedland, W., and Kappel, T. *Production or Perish: Changing the Inequities of Agricultural Research Priorities.* Santa Cruz: University of California Press, 1979.

Hadwiger, D. *The Politics of Agricultural Research.* Lincoln: University of Nebraska Press, 1982.

Knoblauch, H. C.; Law, E. M.; and Meyer, W. P. *State Agricultural Experiment Stations: A History of Research Policy and Procedure.* USDA miscellaneous publication 904, 1962.

Lipman-Blumen, J., and Schram, S. *The Paradox of Success: The Impact of Priority Setting in Agricultural Research and Extension.* Washington, D.C.: Science and Education, Office of the Assistant Secretary, U.S. Department of Agriculture, 1984.

Lyons, D. *The Forms and Limits of Utilitarianism.* Oxford: Clarendon Press, 1965.

National Association of State Universities and Land Grant Colleges (NASULGC). *Emerging Biotechnologies in Agriculture: Issues and Policies.* Progress Report III. Washington, D.C.: National Association of State Universities and Land Grant Colleges, 1984.

Rawls, J. *A Theory of Justice.* Cambridge, Massachusetts: Harvard University Press, 1971.

Rescher, N. *Introduction to Value Theory.* Englewood Cliffs, New Jersey: Prentice-Hall, 1969.

Rosenberg, C. E. *No Other Gods.* Baltimore, Maryland: Johns Hopkins University Press, 1976.

Ruttan, V. *Agricultural Research Policy.* Minneapolis: University of Minnesota Press, 1982.

4

The Moral Factor
in Innovative Research

Stan Dundon

The Violation of "Moral Orthodoxy" in Applied Science

Our fundamental "metaphysical" assumptions about the nature of matter form a kind of orthodoxy that cannot be violated by those who wish to work in the scientific community. For example, before the current orthodoxy was fully formed, respected contributors to the formation of modern science believed in material substances of negative gravity (Priestly) or zero gravity (Lavoisier). But what would we think today of a scientist, who, in weighing a sample that seemed lighter per unit volume than expected, wondered aloud whether the sample might be adulterated with an absolutely light substance (negative gravity)? If we thought he/she was serious, even for a moment, and the person quickly recovered with a laugh and said, "Just kidding, people," we would still never be too sure about working with the person.

It is this kind of fear about basic "scientific" sanity that is encountered by radical innovators in applied sciences. It is not in entertaining doubts about metaphysical assumptions that they stir up this fear, but in harboring questions or worse, conclusions, about ethical assumptions.

Applied Sciences as Profoundly Ethical

Two agricultural scientists and I have been developing a curriculum in ethics and human values for agricultural students at our university. The agriculturalists were impressed with the strength of the initial resistance to the work on the part of some agricultural faculty colleagues. The evident seriousness and competence of persons involved, the continuity of the resistance and its failure, in some instances, to dissolve in the face of thorough knowledge of the program and the personalities disposed of trivial explanations for the resistance. Eventually, we all had to agree that the resistance was not imbedded in a lack of concern with ethics, but in an abundance, even an excess, of concern: the agricultural professionals were

39

well aware that their work was profoundly rooted in networks of assumptions about goals, service, clients, and ways (well-defined classes of technologies) in which they were expected to serve those clients. They distrusted meddling with these deep-seated values by outsiders or "activist" colleagues. In spite of occasional slights about ethics, they know that these values are ethical in nature and that their firm embrace of these values has a name: *commitment*. They are commitments to persons, institutions, and ways of serving both. Like the basic scientist who needs his/her metaphysical assumptions but is not trained to examine them and who cannot afford seriously to question them anyway while working, the applied scientist does not feel trained to question ethical commitments and could scarcely re-examine them each day without a kind of paralysis of practical motivation.

Ethical Character of Changes Sought in Agriculture

If we can grant that the two questions "Who ought we to serve and how ought we to serve them?" are ethical in nature, then the many studies of the agricultural research system done in recent years are at least implicitly based on the concern that we may need some changes in how or in whom we serve. Ethical reflection does not itself imply need for reform, but expensive studies are not funded nor are prestigious commissions appointed to prepare reports if there is not a sense of need for change. While it is most often imagined that the change sought will be managerial-institutional, technological, or concrete policy, in reality the changes sought will be in the commitments. Yet, rarely will mature persons who are living lives of energetic devotion to respectable commitments change those commitments.

Obstacles to Refurbishing Commitments

Busch and Lacy (1983) did an excellent study of the way in which the principal actors in agricultural research see their commitments and the constraints that they feel in reaching them. Like most of the studies of the agricultural system, the authors see that there is need for change both in the actual commitments, usually in the direction of broadening of the constituency served, and the service by which those commitments are carried out.

They locate the obstacles to this broadening in institutional reward systems, in disciplinary narrowness, in lack of communication with constituents and/or other professionals, and in devotion to traditional classes of technology. They advise removal of these obstacles to provide improved flow of change in the system. Such a policy would certainly allow for the agents of change to function more freely. But I feel something more must be asked about the agents themselves whom we expect to take advantage of the more permissive atmosphere.

The Innovator and the Profession

During the years 1981 to 1983, I was doing a historical study on obstacles to innovation in agricultural research. I decided to add contemporary experiences of these obstacles by interviewing innovators and asking questions aimed at testing my thesis that there is something I call a professional paradigm that constricts innovation and that must be ruptured by the innovator (Dundon, 1983). Had I been able to read Busch and Lacy I would probably not have done any interviewing at all, since I imagined that I was collecting the kind of sociological/historical data that is amply contained in Busch and Lacy. But my interviews turned up something I think is difficult to detect in a survey, namely, a severe tension between the innovators and their peers.

This tension is due to a belief by the peers that the innovators are not "good" innovators, i.e., what they do does not fit the mold of expected innovation. Agriculturalists who have heard the histories I relate below have repeatedly asserted that belief. The innovators themselves suspected that the tension or discomfort that their work created was due to the fact that their innovation involved questioning some fundamental commitments. These commitments are of two sorts—the commitment to a professional image of the constituency and a professional concept of the real needs of that constituency. Given that the constituency ought (ethical overtones intended) to include farmers, any questioning by the innovators would suggest that the profession had lost touch with some part of its legitimate constituency and their needs. The potential for, and perhaps even a sense of regret over, such loss of contact with farmers is amply documented in Busch and Lacy (1983).

But my concern with the professional paradigm caused me to focus on the question of whether there is a kind of interweaving of what it means to be an agricultural professional and what kinds of tools one uses. This interweaving can gratuitously, but inevitably, cause a painful dilemma: either the innovators, who advocate different tools, are deficient as professionals, or the pursuers of the accepted tools are.

Innovators Are Not Really Innovating

This is a corollary of the tension between the profession and the innovator. Are they really innovators or not? If any profession is wedded to tools that work by mere application of the tool to the task, without much need for the human client to interact with the professional, without much need for the professional to learn about the peculiar circumstances of the client (environmental or economic, in the case of agriculture; family or emotional life, in the case of medicine), then "true" innovations will be new tools and new procedures that fit the professional mode of practice. Thus, an innovation in alcohol treatment would be antabuse, but not social intervention in family structure and relationships. Laser clearing of arteries for heart disease would be an innovation, not reorganization of diet, exercise, and reduction of job and family stress. The profession of medicine, of course, learns to embrace these "nonmedical" tools, and agriculture is able to embrace social management concepts into its work. But initially, the innovator will not be seen as doing agriculture at all.

Another way of seeing this difficulty of the innovator is to try to be sympathetic to the image of personal professional responsibilities and competence that the applied scientist can derive from a common view of basic sciences. If the applied scientist can work in a well-defined disciplinary area, then at no greater cost than perhaps energy inputs to overwhelm environmental differences and a certain distance from the actual outcomes in the farmers' fields, the professional can see him/herself as possessing a universal body of knowledge with universal application. With enough energy to overwhelm the environment, the body of knowledge is universally applicable. A single model of farm economics, a single model of soil fertility, and of pest control, all fit the practice of professional specialization. Without this universally applicable skill, the professional has a greatly reduced sense of ability to carry out his/her responsibilities and be of service. A requirement of interdisciplinarity, consequently, seems to question the ethical quality of a person's current work. In the face of these factors, therefore, it should be clear that an innovator who questions current practice and fails to put in its place a new practice that the professional can simply add to his/her list of competencies is going to appear at best as a meddler, at worst as subversive of the fundamental responsibility and competence of the profession. Given that competence is the most basic morality of a profession, as well as its title to respect, the potential for a highly charged "moral" atmosphere surrounding innovation should be clear.

Short Stories of Innovation

In compiling the following short histories, I intended to search the special characteristics of certain innovators, their work, background, and motivations that contributed to their work. But given the inevitably "moral" character of changes in "what we ought to be doing," I will focus on the source of moral conviction that enables the innovator to persevere in the face of peer opinion that they are professionally deficient.

George Hellyer

In 1976, while the 1902 Reclamation Act's 160 acre per family member limitation was being hotly disputed, Hellyer had his land appraisal class at University of California, Davis, do a study of the profitability of irrigated farms. His conclusion: over a twenty-year period, the average income on 320 acres would be $40,000 net per year with 25 percent down or 100 percent financing. Although less than 10 percent of California farmers were not in compliance with the 320 acre limitation for a married couple, Hellyer and his department head were called on the carpet by the Chancellor at

Davis. Did they have permission to publish the offending evidence that modest farms were quite profitable on irrigated land? Efforts to get Hellyer fired from his teaching post were courageously resisted, but his whole department was aware of the tensions.

Hellyer had also become Governor Brown's direct marketing program director, an effort to improve the profitability of smaller farms by providing direct access to the retail customer. Then, Brown moved Hellyer's protector, Rose Bird, to the Supreme Court of California and subsequently informed Hellyer that in his second re-election effort he could not continue to protect Hellyer's position in direct marketing. He was promptly fired.

An innovator of nonheroic proportions, Hellyer's simple data collection and the simple measures he defended cost him a disproportionate amount of grief. Why did he do it? Hellyer became interested in farm size because his initial interest in agriculture was world food problems, derived in part from Peace Corps experience and international agriculture, the area in which he earned his M.A. He also had a distrust for the land ethic of giant corporations, since he experienced as land manager of such a corporation a decision to destroy by use of brackish water large acreages in order to avoid the acreage limitation laws. Hellyer saw that only by preservation of small farms in the third world could those immense rural populations be saved from poverty and dependency. From that came both his innovative (iconoclastic) research and application of farm economics.

Stephen Kraten

In the bibliography of the USDA's *Report and Recommendations on Organic Farming* (1980), you will find a reference to an "unpublished Master's Dissertation" by Stephen Kraten, of Washington State University, Pullman. In it, Kraten documents that in 1978 organic grain farms had achieved greater economic returns than conventional (chemical) farmers. Kraten stated that in part the greater profitability was due to the dryness of the year (1978).

This interesting study attracted so little attention that a symposium sponsored by his university on the USDA report failed to notice or include him. But during the conclusion of his master's studies, he was noticed by his dean, who suggested that his interest in these organic farmers was antiquarian. The dean was unmoved by Kraten's response that his sample were all "big-tractor" farmers selling on the regular markets and not to organic food stores. Perhaps, the dean was not unmoved, because he put in an unusual visit to Kraten's defense of his thesis.

Kraten went on to become an extension agent for "limited resource" farmers. He found that there was little the current extension system could offer these largely Filipino farmers. He had been quite successful with well-attended workshops for conventional farmers. But the "limited resource" farmers did not attend because the topics and tools did not fit their needs.

When he would point out to his colleagues the radically different resources available to these farmers, he would get the response: "Those people should not be farming that way; they should get bigger or get out." To discover the economic and farming objectives of the Filipinos, Kraten began to seek out the farmers. When a picture appeared in a local newspaper showing Kraten helping lay out the foundation of a greenhouse for a group of farmers, using his surveying skills, he was lectured by his superior: "You are an extension agent, not a construction company." That this kind of work was both related to an agricultural endeavor and a strategy to improve his ability to serve the farmers was not accepted as a justification.

There is a clear connection between his interest in the "limited resource" farmer and low-input (organic) farming, since it reduces the credit exposure of the farmer by the substitution of inputs of labor, which was abundantly available in the extended family and cooperative approach typical to them. Additional research on the profitability of organic farming, including data on wet years, would be a natural topic for Kraten's Ph.D. research. When I pointed this out, he shook his head. "Yes, but to what department would I apply for a teaching post after getting a Ph.D. on such a topic?" Kraten will do safe research after this, another modest hero of innovation.

But what caused this foray into innovation? He felt that it was the influence of a professor of agricultural economics who was reputed to be a Marxist but whose actual inspiration came from third world experience and interest. There, the professor had seen how inadequate the limited categories of farm types are for economic modelling. To render genuine service to poorer farmers, it is important to know a wider variety of viable patterns. Upon his return to teaching at Washington State, he impressed Kraten with the importance of viewing farms as belonging to many different economic types with distinctly different appropriate survival strategies. The organic farmers were a type who had received scant attention and help from the research establishment. They were, however, not "limited resource" farmers at all. In addition to neglected constituencies, Kraten's teacher had inspired him with the desire to help the poorer farmers, which led both to his seeking the "limited resource" post in Extension and to the use of fresh learning processes to reach the new constituency.

William Liebhardt

Trained as an agronomist, Liebhardt worked as a salesman of fertilizer and fertilizer production equipment to farming operations large enough to be able to formulate their own fertilizers. Upon taking a teaching and research post at the University of Delaware, he continued his interest in the actual field experiences of local farmers in their use of fertilizers. He was aware of research from the experiment stations in Ohio, Nebraska, and Kansas showing habitual overprescription of fertilizers by commercial soil-testing labs. His own research showed that many local farmers could mine the available P and K for fifteen to thirty years without loss of production. He attacked one theoretical justification for overprescription (Basic Cation Saturation Ratio) in research and publication (1981). His activities attracted the attention of the Trustees of the University. The farmers on the board were interested, but the DuPont representative was more than interested. He admitted that he feared that Liebhardt's advice would lead to zero prescriptions. Liebhardt was pressured to be less aggressive. Although his position was secure at the university, he felt that his goals of service would be too restricted. He left and went on to do research and direct the well-known series of articles in New Farm (1982) on costly overprescription of nearly every type of nutrient for farmers across the country. Particularly relevant was the fact that most labs showed no ability to capture for farmers the tremendous savings in reduced nitrogen costs due to leguminous crops grown in years previous to the tests.

Many readers of this history will experience a little shudder upon realizing that Liebhardt left a land grant university post in agronomy to work for Rodale Press, the publishers of New Farm and supporters of the private experiment station where Liebhardt continued his work. Liebhardt experienced more than one shudder in making his choice, and he was well aware of the reaction of his peers. It was an extremely difficult choice for him. I sought for explanations of why he would run this kind of risk and accept this kind of alienation from his peers. I could find none except the fact that from their earliest years together, Liebhardt and his wife had planned to do some kind of third world technical "missionary" work in agriculture and that Liebhardt himself had seen the importance of innovative agriculture for the poor farmers of the third world.[1] But there was the additional closeness to the local farmers in his work at Delaware and the realization that many fertilizer salesmen send soil samples halfway across the country to commercial labs known to give generous prescriptions.

Jerome Gaspard and Professor X

In 1981 Professor X, a young researcher in nematology at the University of California, Riverside, responded to questions about replacements for the recently banned nematicide DBCP on perennial. crops (orchards). "Well, the replacement chemicals have acute toxicity problems, and there are some management [nonchemical] approaches." I asked what kind of management would be possible for perennials. "I don't know, we only do chemicals here." Objectively, that was not true, since Ivan Thomason had long researched nematode resistant varieties for perennials. But with fumigants at $10 an acre, the pressure from the constituency was not there. Thomason did not participate in the hearings to defend DBCP, which included claims that California orchards would become deserts without DBCP. When Telone rose in price from $1 per gallon to $8 to $10 per gallon, his work became more noticeable as the growers began to request the resistant root stock for their vineyards. There was also in the department a long-term research program under Dr. Mankau dealing with nematode trapping fungi. This work, however, had not made commercially relevant progress in many years. In spite of its factual error, the social reality of Professor X's remark is more important. In his perception, they only "did chemicals" there. He would certainly know what to do to fit in.

In 1984, Jerome Gaspard, a graduate assistant for Dr. Mankau, had begun energetic work on two somewhat new forms of fungal attack on nematodes, egg and larval parasitism. The original discovery of these new forms of nematode control was made by another Mankau student, Graham Sterling, in 1979. His work had been made possible by funds from commodity groups interested in alternatives to the banned DBCP. Gaspard was aware that the commodity groups would rarely fund any long-term plant pathogen research. This meant a bias toward chemical solutions. He was also aware that the commodity or other external support was almost indispensable for any work in the experiment station. Mankau himself had made so little progress that his very presence was ignored by Professor X. Yet, Gaspard heard about Mankau and came to Riverside to work on the biological control of nematodes.

Gaspard is a city boy, and his arrival at Riverside to do this innovative work is a revealing history. He was originally a liberal arts student but became interested in "solving mankind's serious problems." Access to sufficient food supplies is the problem that affected Gaspard most acutely. He changed to agriculture and went to University of California, Davis, to obtain an M.A. in Agricultural Development Management, with a focus on third world problems. But to have breadth of tools, he also studied plant pathology. His initial work with Dow, screening fungicides and herbicides, impressed him with the marginally scientific and almost random process of searching for chemical pathogen control.

He took time off to travel and work in Kenya where he became impressed with the threat to environment and health caused by the lack of science and careful management in the use of agricultural chemicals. Although he knows that structural changes are needed to protect the farmers of Kenya, he feels that his work in the U.S. will ultimately have a favorable impact on those farmers. Gaspard is working in an area that he is well aware is basically stacked against him. Yet, he goes on.

Richard Harwood

Although Harwood had as a freshman attempted to escape the farm via a degree in engineering, fun and football led to a change to the military. While in the service, he discovered a love for science through training in meteorology. An uncle, a long time agriculturalist with Rockefeller, inspired him to take an interest in third world food problems. He did not want simply to make marginal improvements in American agriculture. He continued his education and graduated from Cornell, eighth among several hundred, with a specialty in vegetable production. Michigan State University offered him an opportunity to pursue his Ph.D. Eventually, his career at Rockefeller led to his selection as head of IRRI's multiple cropping systems program. During his tenure, this program expanded to become a major part of IRRI's budget. Under Harwood, the multiple cropping system devised by his predecessor at IRRI, Richard Bradfield, was improved to overcome its unportability. Bradfield's precise control of the resources, inputs, and environment proved impossible to carry to a working farmer's field. Due to this and other difficulties, IRRI's farming systems program was threatened with the same kind of serious curtailment or closure which was the fate of farming systems programs at other CGIAR institutions. Harwood and his associates realized that farmer-assisted design was needed. Interaction with the farmer and attention to the resources at his/her command led to the low input orientation for early stages of development intervention.

Low input orientation is a given condition of the poor farmer's practice. Its continuation during the initial stages of developmental intervention is a consequence of the well-demonstrated fact that the farmer will not invest his/her first increased gains in agricultural inputs but in family necessities or even "luxuries." Even if the goal is a development path leading to significant production of crops for urban or export markets, an at least transitory stage of successful increases in production while maintaining low input technologies is necessary. It was a perfectly rational design component.

Never happy with bureaucratic management, Harwood decided to fulfill a service commitment to his church by teaching at a religious college in Southern California with a view to preparing students for "missionary" agricultural work overseas. There, Robert Rodale found him and persuaded him to take on the direction of the Rodale low input agricultural research.

When interviewed, Harwood was in charge of the Rodale research aimed at determining the biological mechanisms involved in the gradual recuperation of productivity on fields previously farmed with intensive chemical inputs. He was also an aggressive cultivator of Kuhnian paradigms as an explanation of the nature of his own innovative work and of the intense alienation and unreasoned resistance he found in proponents of conventional agriculture. He felt that there was a positive preference for technologies that are intrusive and nature-environment dominating rather than accommodating. Many well-established peers showed curiosity and came somewhat cautiously to Emmaus to see where the research was leading, but their very caution underlined the distance between Harwood's work and what was professionally acceptable. Harwood himself revealed a kind of tension over the lack of on-paper precision and predictability that characterizes the low-input systems even though he knew that more precision could only be bought by domination of the environment with inputs and elimination of the information-based and farmer-interactive elements so important for input reduction.

Harwood explicitly justified the distress that his situation caused him on the grounds that unless we can demonstrate low input agriculture as a successful tool in our country, third world agricultural advisors will continue to ape destructively our energy intensive approaches. Still working on a consultancy basis with Rodale, Harwood is now with the International Agricultural Development Service with responsibility for Asian programs and low input and farming systems programs. It is clear that the rationality of his work in low input systems is now being recognized as the "obvious" route to go. But a variety of reasons, from the requirement of farmer-interaction, to interdisciplinary work, to change in habitual tools and information-gathering procedures and the lack of on-paper precision and predictability, made the "obvious" invisible to the profession.

What Makes the Innovator Innovate?

Research and writing on problems of innovation in applied sciences show that the institutions of applied science become significantly anti-innovative. This is true even if the institutions are devoted to research and development in search of new products (Burns, 1969). This is in part traceable to the fact that applied research institutions are captured by "paradigms" that limit what is an "acceptable" innovation (Johnson, 1972). These anti-innovative tendencies exist in agricultural sciences (Busch and Lacy, 1983; Dundon, 1983). The problems are exacerbated when the innovations are in the service of a nontraditional constituency (Busch and Lacy, 1983; Bradfield, 1981).

Given these obstacles and the aphorism of Burns (1969:11–13) that innovation is done by agents not agencies, we must see what history tells us of the sources of their innovative potential. If we divide the sources roughly into intellectual and moral, we find that the general literature on innovation and the histories I have recounted above contain ample evidence that technological breakthroughs do require a kind of interdisciplinary intellectual fertilization. Somehow, the agent of innovation must be aware of, and either competent in or capable of drawing on competence in, sciences and technologies outside the field in which the innovation is going to occur. But what I discovered is that in the agricultural sciences, the moral aspect is preeminent, because it does appear that the nonconventional scientific (or other cognitive) materials were deliberately sought out by the innovator because of a desire to serve either neglected needs of traditional constituencies or to serve neglected constituencies.

Conventional Training and Socialization

Each of the innovators received advanced degrees in land grant university agricultural schools, showed considerable talent, and manifested a very strong desire for the good opinion of their professional peers. Anger, embarrassment, or disappointment with respect to their peers seemed clearly related to the desire to be well thought of by them. They showed pride in professional recognition, invitations to read papers at conventional institutions, etc. They were not rebels or misfits by preference.

Great Personal Cost Involved in Innovative Ruptures

The decision to make a final break with a prominent college or foundation to research "unacceptable" topics caused the innovators significant distress, which was remembered with acute emotion during my interviews. At a large meeting of innovators (OTA, 1981a), which included some of my subjects, the sense of unsought alienation was covered by jocular references to each other as "crackpots." Busch and Lacy (1983:213 and passim), Bradfield (1981:25, 31), and Seastrunk (1981:94) recount every sort of obstacle and painful cost to innovators, especially those working at interdisciplinary projects and service to nontraditional constituencies, such as small farmers.

My subjects experienced them all—from job loss to administrative effort to censor or denigrate their publications, in the tradition noted in Hardin (1955:86). Given that none of my subjects showed an inclination to seek this kind of suffering, it is a wonder that they persevere, and not a wonder that some did not. But since the costs are clear and acute from the beginning, the question is, "What is the source of their innovative vision and strength?"

Outside Learning Experience and Maverick Teachers

The cognitive content of the innovation, as noted in Burns (1969), comes from unusual experiences, such as Peace Corps service or other experiences with nontraditional agriculture. Contact with teachers who also had such unusual experiences and whose teaching was changed to accommodate the lessons of that experience were noted as significant factors in the interviews.

Special Moral/Motivational Elements

These elements are the most difficult to uncover because the interviewees deliberately hid them, even falsifying their motives outrageously so as not to seem "sanctimonious" as one subject admitted when I caught him in an inconsistency. But often, a remark about a "desire to do significant work" would slip out and be elaborated to indicate a discontent with a life spent simply adding a small increment in science and technology when significant human needs might be served instead. In addition, a custom or circumstance of more intimate contact with a nontraditional constituency operated in affective ways. When the innovative work was being conducted in the standard experiment station environment, far from the neglected constituency, several of the innovators expressed hopes that its benefits would reach the distant constituency. I found that if I would recount the story of the researcher who deliberately hid his motivation and revealed it inadvertently by objecting to the opulent life-styles of certain researchers amidst third world poverty, I would get affirmations of agreement, which showed the deep desire to identify with the needs of the poor. Given the high cost and acute professional discomfort of the innovators, I believe some such deep motivation would be almost essential.

Practical Recommendations

All the recommendations made by Busch and Lacy (1983), Ruttan (1982), Hadwiger (1982), and the Office of Technology Assessment (1981a and 1981b) on the opening of the agricultural research system of this country to a broader range of innovative directions are extremely important. At least two of my histories conclude with a probably permanent derailment of an innovator due to institutional obstacles. But it is unlikely that institutions will ever be significantly permissive of innovation. The creative process is such that its inherently invisible goal is difficult for the rational and relatively distant administrator to distinguish from the equally invisible goals of the

goldbricker and dilettante. But innovators have been able to break through
those obstacles of bureaucratic rationality. With some reduction in those
obstacles, more breakthroughs can be anticipated, provided that the motivated
persons are there.

There are measures that can be taken to assure that they are there. The
experience of religious orders, which had both a conventional and a
"missionary" constituency, taught them that early experience of several years
serving in the far more arduous work of the mission field permanently
conferred an appetite for that kind of work on otherwise undistinguished
persons. Peace Corps returnees have that same special appetite. Efforts to
bring these returnees into the agricultural system would produce a great
deal of ferment. Also requiring an adequately rewarded two-year internship
overseas for recent Ph.D.s would have much the same effect. But my
examples, when placed against the present perceptions of reward systems
shown by Busch and Lacy, would suggest that adequately rewarded extension-
like internships in this country would improve the quality of research for
those entering the experiment station system.

Notes

1. Liebhardt (and his wife) subsequently worked in Honduras for two years where
they experienced third world poverty firsthand.

References

Bradfield, S. "Appropriate Methodology for Appropriate Technology." Pp. 23–34 in
Noble R. Usherwood (ed.), Transferring Technology for Small-Scale Farming.
Madison: American Society of Agronomy, 1981.
Burns, T. "Models, Images and Myths." Pp. 11–23 in W. H. Gruber and D. G.
Marquis (eds.), Factors in the Transfer of Technology. Cambridge: MIT Press, 1969.
Busch, L., and Lacy, W. B. Science, Agriculture, and the Politics of Research. Boulder,
Colorado: Westview Press, 1983.
Dundon, S. "Hidden Obstacles to Creativity in Agricultural Science." In R. Haynes
(ed.), Proceedings of the Agriculture, Change and Human Values Conference.
Gainesville: University of Florida, 1983.
Hadwiger, D. The Politics of Agricultural Research. Lincoln: University of Nebraska
Press, 1982.
Hardin, C. M. Freedom in Agricultural Education. Chicago: University of Chicago
Press, 1955.
Johnson, R. D. "The Internal Structure of Technology." Pp. 117–30 in P. Halmos
(ed.), The Sociology of Science. Keele, Staffordshire: University of Keele, 1972.
Liebhardt, W. C. "The Basic Cation Saturation Ratio Concept and Lime and
Potassium Recommendations on Delaware's Coastal Plain Soils." Soil Science
Society of America Journal 45:544–49, 1981.
Office of Technology Assessment (OTA). Background Papers for Innovative Technologies
for Lesser Developed Countries. House Foreign Affairs Committee. Washington,
D.C.: Government Printing Office, 1981a.
———. United States Food and Agricultural Research System. Washington, D.C.:
Government Printing Office, 1981b.

Ruttan, V. W. *Agricultural Research Policy.* Minneapolis: University of Minnesota Press, 1982.

Seastrunk, D. H. "Technology Transfer Programs Designed to Assist Small-Scale and Part-Time Farmers in the United States." Pp. 89–100 in Noble R. Usherwood (ed.), *Transferring Technology for Small-Scale Farming.* Madison: American Society of Agronomy, 1981.

USDA. *Report and Recommendations on Organic Farming.* Washington, D.C.: Government Printing Office, 1980.

5

Policy Science in the Land Grant Colleges: Implications of Recent Developments in Public Choice Theory and the Philosophy of Science

Alan Randall

Introduction

Social scientists had infiltrated the land grant college/USDA complex by the 1920s, and their enquiries into policy issues had made them conspicuous and controversial by the 1930s (Busch and Lacy, 1983). Public policy education, as an extension program, was well under way in the 1940s. In 1949, the director of the Federal Extension Service called a conference to review public education programs in agricultural policy and to suggest directions for further expansion of such programs, and representatives of eighteen land grant colleges attended (Timm, 1956).

In those days, there was a tendency to view research and education in the natural sciences as discovering and disseminating warrantable facts with no important emotional or political significance. The myth of value-free (perhaps, even, impartial) natural science had proven reassuring to a land grant complex that was aware of its need to maintain broad-based support or, at least, acquiescence. On the other hand, the involvement of social scientists in research and education directly addressed to issues of public policy was potentially threatening to both the prevailing notion of what constituted science and the understandable desire of administrators for insulation from political storms.

Busch and Lacy (1983:21–22) briefly review the experience of the 1930s and 1940s, as the land grant and related institutions attempted to resolve these concerns. They list, as exemplars, some of the better-known instances in which programs and organizations have been abolished or reoriented in reaction to experienced or feared political pressures and cases of individuals who have resigned under pressure rather than submit to redirection of their efforts and/or censorship of their reports. An institutional debate ensued as to whether the land grant college complex should assume an activist or quietist posture in public policy research and extension.

Eventually, broadly accepted models emerged identifying the appropriate posture of land grant professionals in policy research and extension. My purpose here is to identify these models and their intellectual and political roots and to examine them in the light of recent developments in the philosophy of science and the theory of how policy processes work. It turns out that the conceptual foundations of the traditional model for policy science are becoming less secure, and the consensus legitimating that model is becoming uneasy. I propose a rather different model that is more consistent with current thinking in the philosophy of science and public choice and consider its implications for the land grant complex. In keeping with the theme of this volume, my focus is primarily on research. Nevertheless, there is also some appropriate reference to public policy education.

The Traditional Model

As Blaug (1980) indicates, the typical textbook model for the ideal behavior of the analyst as technocrat (I prefer "humble technician") in the policy arena sees the analyst as providing value free information to the Decision Maker (DM) about the possibility function, that is, about the outcomes, of alternative resource allocations and the foregone opportunities each entails.

This model posits that the DM exists, that is, that there is an individual empowered to make policy decisions and to make them stick. Is the DM a bureaucrat or a politician? In many familiar renditions, the traditional model finesses that point. My impression is that it may not be considered a very important question, so long as it is always assumed that the DM's position is legitimate and that the DM is attuned to public opinion. One version of the traditional model recognizes three distinct levels: elected officials, senior bureaucrats, and expert analysts. Then, the ultimate DM would be an elected official, while, for routine decisions, senior bureaucrats would assume DM status.

The DM identifies the policy issues and specifies the goals of policy and the operative constraints. That is, the DM asks the questions and bounds the scope of the enquiry. Then, having considered the objective and impartial information—all the facts and nothing but the facts—provided by the analyst, the DM decides the appropriate course of action.

This model is unabashedly normative in that its adherents believe that it specifies the ideal relationship between the public, DM, and expert analyst. It is intended to be a serviceable ideal in that its adherents believe it is attainable, and, in a well-ordered world, it would be not merely ideal but also descriptive of reality.

This traditional model is founded in the positivist school of philosophy of science and the rational planning model of public administration. From positivism, it gets the notion that a value-free, objective and impartial science is attainable and desirable. From the rational planning model of public administration, it gets: (1) the sharp separation of functions among elected officials, senior administrators, and the expert analysts in their employ; (2) the idea that communication channels are linear and vertical (communications run up and down the hierarchy, and taking outsiders into one's confidence is bad form); (3) the concept of the analyst as the obedient servant of both truth and his/her senior administrator; and (4) the belief that rational and scientific policy decisions are possible and desirable.

In order to evaluate more perceptively the traditional model, one must now consider the current status of positivism within the philosophy of science and the rational planning model in the context of public choice theory.

Positivism and the Philosophy of Science

There is a long tradition of attempts to distinguish between: (1) those activities that are concerned entirely with reason and fact and to call them science, and (2) all other intellectual activities such as literature and metaphysics and to call them nonscience. Early Enlightenment notions of materialism (physical matter is the only or fundamental reality, and all phenomena, including thought, feeling, and will, can be explained as manifestations or results of matter) and objectivism (meaningful knowledge must be based on observations about physical objects) paved the way for positivism and empiricism; and these latter philosophies enjoy the allegiance or, at least, lip service of many of today's working scientists.

For my present purposes, it is enough to start the discussion with a relatively recent development, logical positivism. This was the most ambitious of the modern attempts at demarking science from nonscience, and much subsequent writing in philosophy of science was directed toward resolving some of the problems inherent in logical positivism.

The logical positivists set for themselves an ambitious agenda: to unify science and to rid it of all metaphysical elements. They posited four basic tenets:

1. All complex propositions can be derived from atomic propositions, and for each atomic proposition there should correspond an atomic fact.
2. Atomic facts are elementary sense observations.
3. The distinction between science and nonscience is identical to the distinction between sense and nonsense or meaningfulness and meaninglessness.
4. A statement is meaningful if a method for verifying it can be described.

Logical positivism, then, insisted that there is no meaningful distinction between science and reasoned discourse but at the enormous cost of claiming that reasoned discourse is limited to statements that are constructed entirely from observables and are, at least in principle, verifiable. This claim was, of course, insupportable.

Karl Popper in *The Logic of Scientific Discovery* (1934) made not one but two major breaks with the logical positivists. First, he argued that it was not essential that all scientific propositions be derived from simple observable facts. Scientific statements could be based on (at least some) premises about unobservables, so long as consequences that are observable could be rigorously derived therefrom. Second, Popper demonstrated that verification of empirical propositions was logically impossible. Since there are an infinite number of potential observations, the absence of a contrary event in any finite sequence of observations cannot be taken as verification. On the other hand, a contrary observation would unambiguously refute the proposition. Thus, verification is impossible, but refutation of false propositions is entirely possible.

Together, these two Popperian insights permitted a new demarcation of science. Scientific statements were those from which it was possible to derive refutable consequences. It was acceptable, for example, to base a scientific theory of inheritance upon nonobservables such as genes, so long as certain observable events were forbidden as rigorously derived consequences. Observation of the forbidden events would constitute a refutation of the theory. Thus, a meaningful test could be described, and the theory could be called scientific.

Since scientific theories need no longer be constructed from elementary statements about sensible (i.e., material) objects, Popper's methodology required a new definition of the venerable notion of objectivity. For Popper (1957), scientific objectivity consisted of the freedom and responsibility to: (1) pose refutable hypotheses; (2) test them with relevant evidence; and (3) report the hypothesis, the nature of the test, and the results in a manner accessible to all interested persons. Thus, objectivity remained linked to an interpersonal test of the evidence. However, theories were not to be tested directly by examining their component premises; rather, the test was by attempting to refute their consequences.

While Popper's methodology was a clear improvement on that of the logical positivists, it was not without its own problems. First, the Duhem irrefutability thesis held (correctly) that a pure test of a theory by the attempt to refute a derived conjecture was logically impossible. To derive a conjecture refutable by observation, it is necessary to apply a series of auxiliary assumptions (about the conditions under which the theory might be expected to hold, the appropriate domain for observations, the effectiveness of the devices and instruments used for observation and measurement, etc.); and it is always logically possible to attribute a refutation to a problem with the auxiliary assumptions rather than with the theory itself.

Second, while Popperian refutation remains an excellent way to rid the conventional wisdom of false theories, it is difficult to see how a body of knowledge can grow under a refutationist methodology. Strictly speaking, all that can grow is the list of refuted (i.e., failed) theories; and this list conceivably could grow indefinitely large and still fail to identify a finite residuum of unrefuted theories. Further, the possibility is always present that subsequent events may refute a currently unrefuted theory. Therefore, it makes little sense to claim that the body of knowledge consists, at any time, of currently unrefuted theories.

In his later writings, Popper (1958) attempted to soften his refutationist methodology with the notion that theories that had survived many attempts to refute them could be considered "highly corroborated" and possessing of substantial verisimilitude or "truth-likeness." These attempts are not so convincing, since Popper himself (1934) had shown the logical fallacy of verification not only of absolute statements but also of probabilistic statements. Accumulated failures to refute could not, then, make a theory probably true.

Third, Popper's demarcation of science from nonscience must be considered a failure. As Popper himself admits, the history of science contains relatively few crucial experiments that refuted important propositions. Popper's demarcation simply made science too exclusive.

Lakatos (1970) has made important amendments to the Popperian scheme of things, developing a theory of the growth of knowledge that nevertheless retains an important place for attempts to refute conjectures derived from theories. Other modern methodologists go further in dismantling the Popperian scheme. Feyerabend (1975) argues, with some plausibility, that Lakatos's amendments lead logically to the complete abandonment of the essentials of the Popperian scheme. McCloskey (1983), with his concept of a rhetoric of science, and Toulmin (1972), who finds some scientific merit in the way lawyers approach the notion of evidence, may be interpreted as attempting to lead the philosophy of science back toward the notion of reasoned discourse.

This time, however, reasoned discourse is used as a broadening concept. Rather than insisting that all reasoned discourse must satisfy a narrow definition of science (as the logical positivists had done), McCloskey, Toulmin, and others are arguing that the attempts at a restrictive demarcation of science from nonscience have failed, and the scientific enterprise differs only in degree (if at all) from other learned undertakings such as literary criticism and jurisprudence.

It is possible to read Popper (1957) as giving some support to this view. While Popperian scientific objectivity consists of three elements, it is the third that is far and away the most important. Frank and open reporting of the scientific enterprise permits criticism, and it is criticism that provides the interpersonal discipline of science. It is notable that while others have found in Popper support for various kinds of positivist and empiricist philosophies, Popper refers to himself as a critical rationalist.

In summary, the Popperian refutation test represents a useful ideal for science and occasionally permits the elimination of false theories from the conventional wisdom. Nevertheless, it provides an unsatisfactory demarcation of science from nonscience, since it would exclude the great majority of the activity that is generally regarded as scientific. Further, modern philosophy of science raises considerable doubts whether a strict and simple demarcation is possible and whether it can ever be helpful or even meaningful to prescribe a few simple rules that, if followed faithfully, will assure that one's activities are scientific. Rather, the distinctions between science and reasoned discourse are, if anything, a matter of degree, and criticism appears to be the fundamental element of reasoned discourse.

Reasoned discourse about values and ethics, as well as about relationships among phenomena, is entirely possible. Since David Hume demonstrated that it is logically impossible to derive conclusions in the value realm from statements confined to the realm of "is," criticism itself is sufficient to ensure that value statements cannot for long masquerade as "is"-statements.

The sharp distinction between science and nonscience proposed by the positivists cannot be supported. The fundamental element of scientific discourse is criticism, an element that is common to all forms of reasoned discourse. Ethics, values, and instrumental goals, in addition to fact statements, may be the subject of reasoned discourse. Further, the public has adequate defenses, in criticism, against being misled by an analyst who attempts to endow statements of personal belief about ethics, values, and preferences with respect to policy goals or outcomes with the "scientific" label or, for that matter, with respectability derived entirely from their author's prestige as a scientist or expert. Positivistic science is not generally attainable, and no great public harm follows from its unattainability.

Rational Planning and Public Choice

The rational planning model is based on a belief that a comprehensive planning process leading to rational and scientific policy decisions is possible and desirable. Clearly, this model has a strong element of technocracy or, if you will, policy engineering. It is by no means true that all rational planners are economists or that all economists are rational planners. Nevertheless, the rational planning tradition is substantially compatible with the "new welfare economics" of Pigou, Kaldor, and Hicks.

To reconcile a fundamentally technocratic planning model with the precepts and institutions of democracy, there was proposed a sharp separation of functions among the various levels of the planning process. Elected officials in close touch with the mood of the public were actually to make the big decisions and to be held responsible for the small decisions made by their subordinates. Senior administrators were to hold an intermediate position between elected officials and the scientific analysts. They were to be managers: that is, policy managers in general *and* managers of the analytical staff. The managers' responsibilities were to include defining and operationalizing the subject matter for analysis, narrowing the alternatives to be analyzed, and sifting and winnowing the analysts' output into a manageable number of well-defined choices and predicted consequences for consideration by the DM. Managers may well be called upon to make routine decisions but always subject to review by elected officials. To perform their functions adequately, the managers need to be cognizant of society's goals and values. However, the managers were expected to stay at arm's length from the political process itself (Box, 1982).

The analysts were expected to be dedicated exclusively to the standards of their disciplines or professions and to the rational and comprehensive planning process itself. They were expected to perform objective, impartial, and value-free analyses as directed by their superiors and, having done so, to turn over the results to the same superiors for use as the latter saw fit. The analysts were expected to be insulated from the political process and from amorphous public opinion and, within their own heads, to insulate their analytical processes from their own value systems.

As one moves down the hierarchy from elected officials to analysts, the permissible pattern of communications narrows. For the analysts, communications are linear and vertical: Questions and scopes of inquiry come down through channels, and the results of analysis go up through the same channels.

In the rational planning model, the state is a monolith, and everyone in the state apparatus (elected officials, managers, and analysts) is dedicated exclusively to serving the state in his/her special role.

By the 1950s, the rational planning model had begun to lose credibility. Observers questioned first its correspondence with reality, then, its attainability as an ideal, and, finally, its appropriateness as an ideal.

Recognition spread that the state is not a monolith; that influential individuals in government disagree on social goals, and the goals that emerge depend on who is ascendant; that value freedom is an attribute neither of people nor of propositions; and that truly comprehensive planning is impossible.

Ironically, at the time public administration specialists were beginning to lose faith in the rational planning model, there came an explosion of newly developed operations research techniques that promised operational, quantitative tools for comprehensive planning. Operations researchers, engineers, and planners became enamored of these tools, and the rational planning model got its second wind. In the 1970s, the Forest Service's FORPLAN model was completed, providing a state-of-the-art example of the use of operations research techniques in comprehensive planning. As Behan (1981:802) writes, this model and the planning process in which it is used are:

> . . . as close to the classic, rational and comprehensive model, and as close to perfection, as human imagination can design and implement. . . . We have adopted an idealized planning process and blessed it with all the force and power and rigor of statutes that a law-based society can muster.

Regardless of this explosion in developing computerized tools for rational and comprehensive planning, the rational planning model went into eclipse among students of political processes and public administration. Braybrooke and Lindblom (1963) proposed an incremental model of policy decision making. Policy decisions are made by teams, not a single Decision Maker, and policy objectives and outcomes depend on which team members are in the ascendancy at a given moment. Further, the policy team starts not with defined objectives but with existing policies and operates via a disjointed process in which both ends and means are adjusted piecemeal.

The incremental model departs from the rational planning model in important ways. The sharp separation of functions in the rational planning model is here obliterated, as are the sharp distinctions between ends and means, and values and facts; the planning process is seen as not quite so rational nor comprehensive; and the myth that personalities don't matter (that is, any group of people faced with the same information would arrive at the same decision) is abandoned. Nevertheless, the incremental model retains the premise that individuals involved in the planning process are dedicated exclusively to serving the state and society. For that reason, I tend to characterize the incremental model as "rational planning with noise."

An alternative model has been gaining favor in recent years. In various forms, it has been called public choice theory, rent-seeking theory, interest group theory, and, more generally, theories of endogenous government. These models depart from the rational planning and incremental models in two fundamental ways. First, all who operate the institutions of government (elected officials, administrators, analysts, and others) are perceived as utility-maximizing individuals dedicated neither to the public interest nor to the search for objective truth. Thus, the interests of the broader society can be protected only by institutional devices that bring social costs and benefits to bear directly on the well-being of individual "public servants." Second, in place of rational planning with its sharp separation between government and the governed, public choice theorists see government as emerging from the disorganized and independent activities of myriad citizens and interest groups. In public choice models, then, policy decisions emerge from processes that bear more resemblance to the "invisible hand" than to a rational and comprehensive planning process.

The endogenous policy process is visualized as very diffuse with a wide variety of interests involved and a large number of different arenas offering themselves as loci for conflict resolution: electoral politics; legislative and administrative institutions at the federal, state, and local levels; quasi-governmental organizations; the judicial system with its courts and professional advocates; the public information media; and markets, large and small, but all subject to law.

In such a system, no one is entirely above self interest. Even within government, different agencies may pursue conflicting goals; and individual public servants may pursue individual goals not always congruent with those of their department or the administration as a whole. Individuals within and without government will allocate their endowments—and endowments are broadly defined to include, for example, political contacts and information-media skills in addition to income, wealth, education, and technical skills—

across the various decision loci to achieve their objectives. They may invest in order to maximize within existing institutions or to maximize via institution changing behaviors. Different individuals will perceive their best strategies differently and behave accordingly.

The distinction between government and the rest of society becomes blurred. Individuals will seek some things through markets and others through a variety of government institutions. Individuals will seek to use the power of government institutions to modify market behavior and market outcomes.

Channels of communication are diffuse rather than linear. It is not always possible to predict in advance which individual(s) will make the final decision or, for that matter, which of the various arenas will be the locus for the final decision. In fact, few decisions are truly final. Most kinds of decisions—the exceptions including, for example, the irreversible destruction of natural environments—may be later reversed often at some tolerable cost. This being the case, individuals and coalitions that are disappointed with particular decisions will continue to seek reversal of those decisions in the same arena and in others.

This diffuse public decision process has a voracious and omnivorous appetite for information, which is not merely accepted at face value but interpreted, criticized, defended, and evaluated. Many divergent kinds and qualities of information—fact oriented and in varying degrees accurate, inaccurate, or intended to mislead; goal oriented and in varying degrees conventional or revolutionary—compete for attention. Participants in the policy process continually add to the stock of information: evaluating it; promoting the validity of some of it, while disputing other parts of it; and deleting that which fails to withstand critical examination.

The rational planning model is viewed by many of its proponents as a valid description of the ideal if not the typical policy process. On the other hand, it is not clear that the endogenous policy model, which on superficial examination may look like a mere babble of discordant voices, has any demonstrable optimality properties. Nevertheless, there are persuasive defenses of such a system. Defenders have ranged from Benjamin Franklin (who argued that, if forced to choose, he would have chosen an independent press and no government rather than a government unscrutinized by an independent press) to Karl Popper (1950) with his spirited defense of *The Open Society*. It is notable that criticism, the fundamental element common to science and other forms of reasoned discourse, emerges here as the essential source of public protection in the endogenous model of government.

The Demise of the Traditional Model

The traditional ideal model for the policy analyst (the analyst provides value free information for the Decision Maker) is based on the rational planning model of the policy process and the positivistic view of science. It is dependent upon the following notions: rational and comprehensive planning; the sharp separation of the public and the state; the separation of functions among the elected officials, administrators, and analysts who serve the state; the dedication of all individuals in the policy process to the service of the state in the role that each fulfills; the positive/normative distinction; and the belief that individuals and propositions can achieve the status of value freedom. Modern views of science and of the public policy process deny each of these premises. By now, this is familiar ground. But there is more.

The traditional model exalts the rational and comprehensive planning process and, thus, the analyst as technocrat. However, if the analyst is accorded technocratic powers, it is important that there be restraints on the use of these powers. This is why the traditional model allows the DM (who is in contact with the public mood) to ask the questions, identify the constraints, and define the scope of the inquiry. This is why the analyst is obligated to perform value free analyses and to eschew the making of recommendations. Perhaps, even, this is why the analyst is obligated to maintain a dutiful silence if it seems that his/her analyses are being ignored or misused by those higher in the hierarchy.

Popper's post-positivist philosophy makes clear that these proscriptions on the analyst's behavior in no way enhance the objectivity of his/her research. To the contrary, objectivity requires the freedom and responsibility of the scientist to pose refutable hypotheses, to test them with relevant evidence, and to report the results so they will be available to any interested person. The traditional model violates Popper's concept of objectivity by requiring that the analyst submit to the DM's authority to define the scope of the inquiry and to use the results as he/she sees fit. The traditional model may require the analyst to go along with a DM who asks the wrong questions, places the wrong constraints upon the scope of inquiry, makes decisions that seem to ignore the best available research findings, and/or publishes distorted analyses to support the decisions he/she has made. The traditional model may allow a DM to scorn the analyst and the public.

On the other hand, the traditional model may allow the analyst to abuse the DM and the public. With respect to the analyst, the traditional model reduces to an exhortation to abide by its rules. It has little in the way of institutionalized protections for the DM or the public against an incompetent or biased analyst who violates its rules. Direct public scrutiny is eliminated by the linear communication structure inherent in the traditional role model. The integrity of the system at this point relies entirely on the personal ethics of the analysts.

Toward a New Model for Policy Science

An alternative model must recognize that the premises of positivism have been systematically undermined by modern philosophy. The post-positivism of Popper is now seen as representing an ideal that may be achieved in a few of the great moments of science rather than a meaningful line of demarcation between science and nonscience. Increasingly, science has come to be seen as a form of reasoned discourse, and recognition has spread that reasoned discourse is possible about values and ethics as well as more tangible phenomena. In reasoned discourse, quality control is accomplished through social institutions that encourage free information flows and criticism. Where feasible, a potentially refuting experiment represents a particularly effective form of criticism; nevertheless, less definitive forms of criticism provide considerable quality control in discourse about matters of fact and normative matters.

An alternative model must abandon the dream of rational and comprehensive planning, the notion of a single Decision Maker with power to make decisions stick, the sharp and artificial separation of the value and fact realms, and the quaint idea that science can be made to serve the public interest by placing scientists subordinate to the DM and requiring them to take vows of impartiality and value neutrality.

If, as I have argued, the public is best protected from high-handed government and technocratic policy scientists by institutions that promote open information flows and criticism, it follows that fewer restraints need be placed upon participants in the process of generating and critiquing policy-relevant information. With unrestrained criticism, incomplete analysis will be identified, errors will be discovered, fact-oriented work will be distinguished from value-related argument, and biased and partisan analyses will be exposed. The public is little harmed if overt advocates coexist with analysts who make every effort to be impartial. No important public harm is done when, as so often occurs in real life, prominent scientists seek to express themselves on matters of ethics, values, and policy choices. To the contrary, reasoned discourse about such matters is of great social value, and an ethic that excludes some of the best intellects from such discourse performs a public disservice.

The advancement of knowledge and the functioning of an open society both work best when generation, flow, and evaluation of policy-relevant information are not controlled by a central administration but, instead, emerge from the independent efforts of myriad thinkers, advocates, and critics.

Policy Science in the Land Grant Complex

It is not merely inevitable but also desirable that there coexists a great diversity of individuals, interest groups, and institutions, each playing a little different role in the generation, flow, and evaluation of policy-relevant information. The land grant college complex with its research and extension functions is one participant in this process. Arguments in favor of a broad diversity among participants in the process at large do not necessarily translate into a denial that the land grant system's role should be more specialized. Arguments that the restraints upon policy scientists, which are inherent in the traditional model, are inessential and even counterproductive for the public protection do not translate into a denial that the traditional model is helpful to the institutional survival of the land grant system. Perhaps the land grant system has a specialized function, and the traditional model is serviceable to the survival of that system. Let us consider these possibilities.

For policy scientists in the land grant complex, the traditional technocratic role model is frequently endorsed. However, it enjoys more lip service than obedience. The predominant research ethic in the land grant colleges is much broader than the technocratic model. From positivism it gets the exaltation of value freedom and objectivity, and from pragmatism it gets the belief that research ought to be a conscious response to a felt need existing among the clientele and that the ultimate result of successful research is always real-world application. These things are consistent with, but not exclusive to, the technocratic model. In addition, the land grant research ethic draws from the broader scholarly tradition a strong belief in the desirability of scholarly publication. This is clearly at odds with the technocratic model in which the scientists' output becomes the property of the DM. Thus, we systematically depart from the technocratic model while maintaining its fundamental myth that it is the role of the policy scientist to provide value-free information to the Decision Maker.

If this myth is believed serviceable, it must be because of its emphasis on value-freedom and the notion that neither decisions nor recommendations fall within the purview of the policy scientist. Perhaps the myth of the DM is maintained only to emphasize this latter restriction on the role of the policy scientist.

The public policy extension education model is consistent with the research model in that its purposes are pragmatic, and its methods require the strict avoidance of any attempt to impose the educator's values upon the clientele. However, the clientele is seldom the DM; usually, the clientele is drawn from among public opinion leaders. Accordingly, the policy education model includes a goals clarification component. The educator assists members of the clientele in clarifying their own goals and understanding the relationships between goals, policy instruments, and the outcomes of policy.

The inclusion of goals clarification in the policy education model is not an especially adventurous step. Teachers of values and ethics tend to regard goals clarification as the least assertive of the various things they might undertake to do (Morrill, 1980). The traditional public policy education model emphasizes that the educator should be extremely circumspect about his/her own value system. The educator is thought to have done well if, at the end of the education process, no one among the clientele is really sure what it is that the educator personally values and what policies he/she would recommend. The traditional public policy extension model departs from the technocratic model in that it encourages its practitioners to work directly with public opinion leaders and to seek broad publication of their work. Again, the technocratic model is treated as a serviceable myth rather than a rigid guide for action.

The functional components of the land grant ethic with respect to public policy research and education are the pragmatic direction of effort, the appeal to positivist methodology, and the conscious avoidance of controversy. Positivism, with its doctrine that the fact and value realms can be meaningfully separated, lives on here—after its demise among serious philosophers— because it is thought to be a useful ideology in an institution that seeks the avoidance of controversy.

Does the public benefit from adherence to a positivistic ideal in the land grant complex? I have argued that the process of criticism well equips the public to protect itself from any harm that might arise when values become intermingled with facts. Nevertheless, it could be argued that criticism is itself a resource-consuming and expensive business. General adherence to a positivistic ethic in the land grant complex may serve, according to this argument, as a signaling device that reduces public transactions costs. The public would need to invest less effort in critiquing information that emerges from the land grant complex if it already knows that such information is prepared by individuals who adhere to a positivistic ethic requiring concentration on the fact realm and a sharp separation from the realm of values. However, there are counter arguments. The fact/value distinction is insupportable. Value-freedom is logically impossible, and the institutional attempt at value-freedom results only in the systematic application of values inoffensive to the mainstream of society. Given the impossibility of value-freedom, we become value-chameleons. While we may often avoid controversy, the public is deprived of our contributions to reasoned discourse about values and policy choices.

On the question whether our lip service to the traditional technocratic model and our persistent attempts to apply positivistic methodology are useful for the institutional survival of the land grant complex, I am undecided. Given some of the personal and institutional upheavals of the 1930s and 1940s and the perception that these resulted from controversy, it is not surprising that our institutions have opted for a noncontroversial stance. On the other hand, avoidance of controversy often means avoidance of the front-burner issues of the day or avoidance of the really hard questions associated with those issues. This kind of posture has us backing away from controversy and into irrelevance. Irrelevance is surely not of instrumental value for institutional survival.

Conclusion

The traditional ideal for the policy scientist in the land grant complex is examined and found insupportable because its conceptual bases are unsound. It serves no useful and effective public purpose as a "serviceable myth." The glue that maintains the integrity of policy research and education is not value-freedom and the sharp separation of the realms of "is" and "ought." Rather, it is criticism, the guiding principle of scholarship that tends to unify rather than differentiate the learned disciplines, which is the great protector of the public in the policy arena. Replacement of the traditional model with the critical model would tend both to liberate and expose the policy researcher and educator. The public would benefit by elimination of unnecessary barriers that exclude some of the brightest and most knowledgeable from discourse on ethics, values, and policy choices.

While I can sympathize with the reasoning that led land grant institutions into a posture of controversy avoidance, I believe a shift toward the "critical, reasoned discourse" model may enhance the relevance and public esteem of these institutions. There are risks involved in such a shift, but there are also risks in maintaining the traditional model.

References

Behan, W. "RPA/NFMA—Time to Punt." *Journal of Forestry* 79(December):802–05, 1981.

Blaug, M. *The Methodology of Economics: Or How Economists Explain.* Cambridge: Cambridge University Press, 1980.

Box, T. "Professionalism, Politics and Land Managers." Presented to symposium on "Politics vs. Policy: The Public Lands Dilemma." Logan: Utah State University, April 21–23, 1982.

Braybrooke, D., and Lindblom, C. *A Strategy of Decision.* New York: Free Press, 1963.

Busch, L., and Lacy, W. B. *Science, Agriculture, and the Politics of Research.* Boulder, Colorado: Westview Press, 1983.

Feyerabend, P. K. *Against Method: Outline of Anarchistic Theory of Knowledge.* London: NLB, 1975.

Lakatos, I. "Falsification and the Methodology of Scientific Research Programmes." Pp. 91–196 in I. Lakatos and A. Musgrave (eds.), *Criticism and the Growth of Knowledge.* Cambridge: Cambridge University Press, 1970.

McCloskey, D. N. "The Rhetoric of Economics." *Journal of Economic Literature* 21(2):481–517, 1983.

Morrill, R. L. *Teaching Values in College.* San Francisco: Jossey-Bass, 1980.

Popper, K. R. *The Logic of Scientific Discovery.* New York: Harper Torchbooks, 1934 (translated 1959, 1968).

_____. *The Open Society and Its Enemies.* London: Routledge and Kegan Paul, 1950 (4th edition, 1962).

_____. "Philosophy of Science: A Personal Report." Pp. 155–91 in C. A. Mace (ed.), *British Philosophy in Mid-Century.* London: George Allen and Unwin, 1957.

_____. *Conjectures and Refutations: The Growth of Scientific Knowledge.* London: Routledge and Kegan Paul, 1958.

Timm, T. R. "Progress in Agricultural Policy Education." Pp. 3–5 in *Increasing Understanding of Public Problems and Policies.* Chicago: Farm Foundation, 1956.

Toulmin, S. *Human Understanding.* Oxford: Clarendon Press, 1972.

PART TWO

Research Priority Setting

6

The Dynamic Tension Between the Scientific Enterprise and the Political Process: Priority Setting in Agricultural Research

Jean Lipman-Blumen

Introduction

In recent decades, Congressional and other critics have been demanding that the agricultural research community establish research priorities linked to long-term national goals. Publicly funded agricultural programs face special dilemmas in setting research priorities. The purposes of this paper,[1] based on a two-year study of the agricultural research system, are twofold: first, to examine several key factors in the dialectic between the scientific enterprise and the political process; and second, to suggest several strategies for addressing these issues.

In earlier decades, agricultural budgets were robust, protected by a strong "farm bloc." Priority setting in agricultural research ordinarily meant adding "new initiatives" to an already substantial "wish list." In a bottom-up process, agricultural scientists generated the wish list. The list would then weave its way through various institutional levels and advisory groups, eventually reaching legislative budget and appropriations committees.

Priority Setting: A New Definition

For many years, this bottom-up priority setting constituted the agricultural research system's *modus operandi*. Critics, however, began to demand a new, more rigorous priority-setting process. The new process required articulating goals and implementation strategies, critically ranking and pruning the wish list, while eliminating less critical or completed programs. The system, however, responded initially simply by augmenting its usual process. Eventually, the confusion generated by this "new definition" of priority setting was clarified, but not without unrelenting pressure from the system's critics.

Other changes were occurring. The dramatic demographic shift of rural population into urban centers weakened the traditional "farm bloc's" juggernaut. Now, it became necessary to forge a new urban/rural coalition to ensure legislative clout and to entice urban legislators with priorities fashioned to fit their constituent's needs.

These were not inconsequential changes. They required the system to: (1) accept the new definition of "priority setting"; (2) confront unprecedented budget competition from other federal departments; and (3) incorporate new, unfamiliar groups (i.e., urbanites, consumers, environmentalists, etc.) into the traditional agriculture clientele.

Responding to Demands
for Long-Term Planning

Demands for more long-term planning accompanied the overall call for improved priority setting (e.g., GAO, 1981; OTA, 1981). What long-range national goals should be articulated? How should they be implemented?

In addition, the Farm Bill of 1977, later amended by the Farm Bill of 1981, established two new advisory and coordinating structures to address priorities: (1) The Joint Council on Food and Agricultural Sciences (hereafter, the Joint Council), and (2) The National Agricultural Research and Extension Users Advisory Board (hereafter, the Users Advisory Board, or UAB). The Secretary of Agriculture was to "consult [both] . . . in the formulation of basic policies, goals, strategies, and priorities for programs of agricultural research, extension, and teaching" (Subtitle B, Sec. 1405).

These two new structures were designed specifically to increase coordination and generally to assist long-term planning in the highly decentralized agricultural system. Given the revised definition of "priority setting," this need for coordinating structures intensified.

The Central Question

One central question frames the issues surrounding priority setting in agricultural research and extension: *How is it possible to set and maintain priorities that are subject to perturbations, or disturbances, caused by: (1) the cyclical political process; (2) nature-based agricultural emergencies; and (3) social change?* More specifically, what factors facilitate or impede the maintenance of priorities guiding publicly supported programs? How does the political context affect the process? How can the system adapt priorities to changing societal needs without losing scientific and programmatic integrity? How can the tension between science and politics be managed productively?

Political Perturbations

Three types of political perturbations often impede scientists' and administrators' efforts to establish and sustain priorities: (1) broad, cyclical, political changes in the Administration and Congressional committees; (2) interventions by individual legislators on behalf of their own scientific concerns or their constituents' interests; and (3) intermittent shock waves from critical, if often contradictory, government and private sector reports. Research priorities are caught in the tension between the scientific enterprise and the political process (Lipman-Blumen, 1979). The processes of politics and research are often "out of synch."[2] Science administrators, therefore, try to encourage research that somehow will sustain budget support across successive and divergent political administrations.

Legislators frequently intervene on behalf of their own strongly held scientific concerns or their constituents' interests. Individual legislators, particularly chairpersons and members of key Congressional committees, may subvert established scientific priorities by injecting line items or earmarking funds for special uses. Occasionally, they restore previously rejected projects. And, of course, the familiar ritual of administrators cutting certain programs they expect Congress (sometimes OMB) to restore is one strategy for protecting other programs and possibly even ensuring a slightly larger overall budget.

Legislators may use these strategies to promote new research they believe is truly important. Occasionally, however, narrower political motives may lead to what observers regard as pork barreling. Political trade-offs between Congressional members or their staffs also may inadvertently upset long-term priorities.

The disquietude some legislators express toward esoteric "basic" research may limit funding of specific projects, but rarely derails major research priorities. In addition, the fluctuating importance of basic vs. applied research across successive administrations complicates the individual legislator's response by raising issues of party loyalty.

Program duplication is a long-standing Congressional bugaboo. Yet, unlike other fields where definitive experiments in one laboratory may be replicated elsewhere, site-specific agriculture often requires parallel research efforts in several locations. Agriculture necessitates a broad-based continuing research effort simply to keep abreast of the adaptive, evolutionary changes in nature.

Even though they are less pervasive than the shifts brought about by changes in the White House, perturbations created by Congressional committee members are not inconsequential. Given the well-publicized interests of key legislators, certain interventions represent anticipated setbacks or welcome support for long-standing priorities. (They also provide the garden-variety "give and take" of politics.)

Reports by groups with formal or self-appointed oversight responsibilities represent a third source of potential disturbance for research priorities. The system, constrained to address all reports, may respond by: (1) denial of the "problems"; (2) immediate structural reorganization, with downgrading or elimination of criticized programs; and/or (3) reassessment and careful response to the issues raised.

Agricultural Emergencies and Preemptive Priorities

Agricultural emergencies can disrupt dramatically organizational priority-setting efforts, as well as substantive priorities themselves. Despite their inevitability, the exact time and place of agricultural emergencies are difficult to predict. Until resolved, agricultural crises establish preemptive priorities. Nevertheless, the decentralized nature of the agricultural research system permits flexible and immediate response to localized agricultural emergencies.

Social Change

Large-scale social trends clearly alter agricultural research priorities. The rise of environmentalist and consumer movements eventually influenced at least a portion of the agricultural research agenda. The conservative resurgence of the eighties has led to the elimination or reduction of many programs created in the more socially conscious sixties and seventies.

The Scientific Enterprise and the Political Process

The Scientific Perspective

Classically conceived, the scientific enterprise seeks knowledge for its own sake, without reference to political or social consequences. In the American context, agricultural research was characterized from the outset by "logical positivism," the belief that science inevitably produces salutary societal results.

The esoteric nature of basic research tantalizes and frustrates policymakers who would control the expenditure of public funds. It also renders basic research virtually invisible to the general public, thereby depriving it of a broad-based, informed vocal constituency. The long time period required for basic research results often obscures their ultimate value, thereby undercutting still other potential political/popular support. In addition, most researchers, immersed in their scientific work, are unlikely candidates to make the political case for basic research.

The unforeseen, long-term negative consequences of scientific breakthroughs (dramatized clearly in the nuclear energy case) have shaken the public's previously unquestioning belief in scientific research. Certain initially heralded advances (e.g., yield-enhancing chemical pesticides and herbicides) have created unanticipated, longer-term negative effects, dimming the scientist/hero's halo. Consequently, spectres of unmonitored scientific research activities cast uneasy shadows across the public consciousness, evoking caution and concern among policymakers.

Still, the perception of science as a creative process tends to moderate the growing public predeliction to control research. Many observers argue that the creative dimensions of science cannot be managed, merely nurtured. They suggest that growing demands for accountability and evaluation of publicly funded research make it impossible to encourage the uniquely creative scientist. True originality, they suggest, defies both accurate judgment by peer review panels and management by science administrators.

Most scientists, as well as some legislators, contend that the bench scientist is the most qualified judge of scientific needs. Only the bench scientist, they insist, is qualifed to identify researchable questions and critical research gaps. These are just a few of the dilemmas that science contributes to the dialectic between the scientific enterprise and the political process.

The Political Perspective

Nonsynchronized Political and Research Cycles. The political process generates its own set of tensions. First, the relatively short political cycle rarely coincides with the basic research time frame. Consequently, scientific initiatives of one political administration may have difficulty sustaining substantive and budgetary support in the next. Stigmatized by the previous administration's sponsorship, research projects often see their funding evaporate.

Political Shuffling and Trade-Offs. The defeat or retirement of key legislators and the reshuffling of committee responsibilities have serious consequences for agricultural research priorities. Such changes can derail research efforts before their successful completion or, alternatively, clear the way to previously blocked research initiatives. Daily trade-offs, constituting the warp and woof of Congressional life, suggest still another way in which the political process impinges upon the scientific enterprise.

Policymakers' Scientific and Public Relations Concerns. Elected policymakers' scientific concerns, as well as their need to please the electorate, are additional terms in the "science and politics" equation. In some instances, these concerns may reflect a broad view of the national interest. In others, they may represent the specific need of the legislator's district. Like other publicly funded programs, the agricultural research agenda is fair game for legislators eagerly demonstrating their fiscal marksmanship.

To garner broad-based Congressional support, legislative champions must demonstrate the utility of agricultural research. Basic research, however, rarely produces rapid results. Pragmatic politicians frustratedly ask, "What has basic research done for us lately (i.e., with last year's appropriation?)."

To complicate matters, emerging constituencies raise new research issues. Policymakers, caught between lay constituents and the scientific community (some of whom also number among their constituents), worry about reelection. The still evolving rural/urban coalition contributes additional tensions as it gropes toward a new consensus. The inevitable push and pull of different constituencies—commodity groups, professional scientific associations, land grant institutions, consumers, environmentalists, and more recently ethicists—gradually adjust the scientific agenda to address emerging societal problems.

The Site-Specific Nature of Agricultural Research and "Duplications." Cost-conscious legislators, sensitive to duplicative research efforts, face special problems arising from the site-specific nature of agricultural science. Investigating similar problems under varying environmental conditions can appear both duplicative and "old hat" to budget-minded legislators more excited by "high tech" research. Still, multiple research groups studying the same problem commonly produce solutions more quickly and economically than one group working alone.

The Impact of Critiques. Critical reports by government oversight groups and private sources create additional political tensions for agricultural research. The agricultural research community's recent priority-setting efforts were sparked largely by Congressional demands for long-term planning, embodied in Congressionally requested reports (OTA, 1981; GAO, 1981). Oftentimes, various forms of political oversight move the research community to consider potentially negative consequences of scientific advances.

Scientists, Science Administrators, and Policymakers: Different Traditions, Values, and Objectives

The difficulty in establishing and sustaining priorities for agricultural research flows partially from the divergent traditions and objectives of agricultural scientists, science administrators, and policymakers. Agricultural scientists, themselves, represent a diverse group. Traditional agricultural scientists with farm backgrounds have tended to pursue mission-oriented research, guided by the utilitarian and positivistic ethic of science designed to improve life. Recently, a new breed of agricultural scientists, drawn from various scientific disciplines, have introduced a strong basic research orientation (Busch and Lacy, 1983).

In earlier decades, legislators who shaped agricultural research policy shared a rural, utilitarian, and positivistic orientation with scientists from similar backgrounds. The more recently created rural-urban Congressional coalition binds together policymakers with divergent constituencies and issues. This fragile coalition has emerged during a period marked by increasing concern over long-range national goals and dwindling economic and natural resources.

Agricultural research's recent articulation with long-term national goals has highlighted the importance of agricultural science. This connection has tended to polarize policymakers' priorities and strategies for accomplishing national goals, while subjecting agricultural research priorities to intensifying review. With increasing "belt tightening," the need to make the budgetary case for agricultural vs. other kinds of research escalates. The result of these intertwined conditions is heightened tensions between the scientific enterprise and the political process.

Not infrequently, USDA science administrators have been caught in these crosscurrents. Many agricultural research administrators from farm backgrounds share the traditional agricultural science values: utilitarian knowledge leading to cost-effective productivity. Nonetheless, their role as intermediaries between the bench scientist (usually represented by the land grant institutions) and the Congress has heightened USDA administrators' sensitivities to priority setting in agricultural research. Their greater proximity to the federal budget process has impressed USDA administrators with the necessity of setting both short- and long-term priorities. But their structural position—

trapped betwixt the scientific community, the Congress, and the White House—often leaves them without the organizational or political leverage to implement priority-setting strategies.

While science, per se, may be sacrosanct, the management of science has become a ready target for political attack. Beginning with the Pound Report (National Research Council, 1972), USDA administrators have taken the brunt of priority-setting attacks unleashed by political oversight bodies and other public critics. Since this baptismal experience, USDA administrators have developed considerable expertise in negotiating the tensions arising between the scientific community and its political environment.

Disagreements between agricultural administrators and the White House are influenced further by the scientific orientation of key figures in the Office of Science and Technology Policy (OSTP), particularly the President's science advisor. The President's science advisor, too, must balance the norms and values of the scientific community from which he/she comes against political allegiance to the President. Occasionally, presidential science advisors have felt deliberate pressures from their chief executive, who sought more their public validation than their scientific judgment.

Many USDA administrators worry that political usurpation of the scientist's priority-setting autonomy threatens research whose promise is evident only to the scientific eye. They are equally aware of pragmatic political imperatives. It falls to the scientifically knowledgeable and politically sophisticated science administrators to interpret each side to the other without losing their own heads in the process.

Staff to USDA science administrators also find themselves caught in political cross-winds. Oftentimes, staff live between the "rock" of scientific results and the "hard place" of the current administration's ideology. Staffers involved in policy formulation may discover their own work or field research they have supported yields results inimicable to the current administration. To complicate matters, these same research findings may be welcomed by the states, particularly their land grant and Congressional representatives.

Science administrators and staff seek various ways to keep research priorities "on track." Long-range program plans conceived in the very broadest terms provide an umbrella under which old and new initiatives can fit with reasonable comfort. Redescribing existing research projects with the current rhetoric or "buzzwords" is another strategy for protecting their integrity. Including a new segment that addresses the administration's priorities may shift the goals and/or enlarge the scope of the original program or project. These various means of protecting old and integrating new scientific concerns provide some minimal continuity.

Mediating Structures

In the highly decentralized agricultural research system, mediating structures perform several critical functions. First, they link together the decentralized components in a communications network. Second, mediating structures orchestrate the tensions generated by the formulation and conduct of publicly funded agricultural research. Depending upon the circumstances, the interventions of these mediating structures exacerbate or facilitate the dialectic between the scientific enterprise and the political process.

Mediating structures, which constitute the policy environment of agricultural research, span the public and private sectors. Congressional committees and oversight agencies (e.g., OMB, OSTP, and various USDA budget and planning offices, etc.) intervene in research priority setting, primarily through the budget process. Advisory groups, representing both the producers and users of agricultural research (i.e., the Joint Council and Users Advisory Board), participate in priority setting, most specifically through various Congressionally mandated reports. In addition, the Experiment Station Committee on Organization and Policy (ESCOP) and the Division of Agriculture Executive Office in the National Association of State Universities and Land Grant Colleges (NASULGC) influence the formulation of agricultural research priorities. Professional scientific associations and scholarly bodies (e.g., the American Association for the Advancement of Science (AAAS) and the National Academy of Sciences (NAS)) work both formally and informally with science administrators in the field, the White House, Congressional members and their staffs, as well as with USDA officials to shape research priorities.

Not infrequently, the picture becomes exceedingly complicated. These groups collaborate in a complex set of interactions to develop consensus regarding research priorities, expressed concretely in the federal budget. The substantial 1985 budget increase for biotechnology research in the USDA Competitive Grants Program was the result of such coordinated effort.

Quasi Checks and Balances:
Changes at the Margin

This interplay of scientists, science administrators, and policymakers, connected and influenced by many of their members acting through mediating structures, constitutes a system of "quasi checks and balances." This dynamic creates marginal change, ideally directing attention to new problems without completely undermining important ongoing research.

Despite the difficulties generated by these seemingly contradictory forces, many seasoned observers suggest that the key priorities in agricultural research have changed only at the margin. Productivity has been the guiding priority through many administrations, with the exception of consumer and environmental priorities highlighted during the Carter years. While farmers' recent financial difficulties attract major media coverage, overall agricultural research priorities remain relatively impervious.

This is not to imply that change never occurs or that science administrators and their constituencies are not alert to possibilities for expanding the research agenda. At times, an exciting topic—such as biotechnology—catches the Congressional imagination. Those more politically attuned members of the scientific community move swiftly to package a new research agenda in wrapping they hope will attract Congressional support.

Nonetheless, productivity remains a key priority. In fact, new agenda items are particularly likely to succeed if they represent novel and more efficient means of increasing productivity. Recognition that diminishing natural resources will require new plant and animal varieties able to thrive under resource-depleted conditions confers a new meaning on "productivity."

Marginal and incremental policy changes reflecting shifting priorities characterize democratic societies (Lindblom, 1980). Recent negative examples of centrally planned economies suggest that "muddling through" is not without its virtues. Large, decentralized systems, such as the agricultural research system, commonly take an incremental approach to changing and implementing new priorities. Not surprisingly, a society composed of heterogeneous constituencies is unlikely to respond favorably to dramatic shifts in science policy that might obliterate key groups' priorities.

The Culture of Agriculture: A Key Variable

Embedded in the culture of agriculture are values and structures that help to mitigate tensions evoked by priority setting. Agricultural scientists form a relatively small, congenial town stretched taut across the fifty states. Family and professional kinship lines stretch from county to federal level. Generations of agriculturists share common values imbued through a rural upbringing and a land grant education.

The core agricultural science community remains surprisingly homogeneous, despite new entrants from divergent backgrounds. It reflects an impressive array of traditional American values: respect for independence, initiative, cooperation, hard work, usefulness, pragmatism, education, science, nature, age, experience, and tradition. Clearly, the very interplay of certain values creates distinctive tensions (e.g., tradition vs. science). The culture of agriculture integrates these conflicting values through a structure of complex partnerships within local, state, and federal agricultural institutions.

In some ways, the agricultural science community resembles the currently heralded Japanese firm. Long-term personal and work relationships and common social, political, and religious heritage generate shared values. In the traditional agricultural community, implicit priorities enjoyed strong consensus. These shared values, particularly cooperation and partnership, have facilitated adjustment to the seismographic shifts evoked by recent priority-setting demands. Thus, the culture of agriculture helps to alleviate tensions sparked by the flint of agricultural science striking the steel of political process. Despite this strong cultural background, adapting to the realities of dwindling economic resources has not come easily to this community of congenial, pragmatic scientists and policymakers.

Organizational Issues and Possible Strategies

To function effectively, large, complex, mature, and decentralized systems must resolve the organizational issues inevitably generated by the intricacies of priority setting. The agricultural research system is no exception. What are the key structural issues, and what mechanisms or strategies can be used to deal with them? Here, the discussion is limited to several critical structural issues that affect the system's capacity to set and maintain long-term agricultural priorities linked to national goals. In addition, possible alternatives for addressing these issues are presented. (For more detail see Lipman-Blumen and Schram, 1984.)

The Need for a Mechanism to Articulate and Sustain Priorities

There is an obvious need for a stable mechanism to articulate and sustain long-term priorities that are coupled with national goals. Such a mechanism ideally should be articulated with other system components involved in priority setting and implementation. Although certain existing structures, such as the Joint Council, the UAB, and ESCOP, participate in priority-setting activities, no existing structure has both the national and scientific stature, as well as the policy experience, to sustain national research priorities across successive administrations.

Ordinarily, the impeccable scientific credentials of the National Academy Board on Agriculture (NAS) would make it a natural candidate for this role. As currently structured, however, the Board's responsibility to conduct studies on specific topics does not lend itself to this purpose. Moreover, most NAS board and committee staffs are required to seek their own study funds from nonNAS sources, a condition that tends to drive the actual topics studied.

Concern for Components' Independence and Power

Perhaps the major barrier to creating a mechanism for tracking priorities is the system's concern about its own power. Each system component attempts to preserve its autonomy within the larger context of a cooperative, decentralized system. Currently, there is little recognition of the greater total system benefits to be gained by each component relinquishing some small amount of power. Only a superordinate, priority-evaluating mechanism, respected by all "partners" in the process, offers hope for ensuring the continuity of long-term priorities linked to national goals. Otherwise, the agricultural research system can expect continual buffeting by its external policy environment.

A National Agricultural
Issues Commission (NAIC)

One possible mechanism for alleviating the priority-maintenance problem is a National Agricultural Issues Commission (NAIC) within the National Academy of Sciences (or a similarly apolitical entity). Such a commission would be composed of approximately fifteen members, whose responsibilities would be to identify the emerging national and international agricultural issues and assess the scientific possibilities for dealing with them. The Commission (NAIC) would articulate and define new research and educational priorities. It would not represent an additional bureaucratic layer for the system, since no system component would report to it. The Commission would, however, insulate the system from scientifically indefensible disruptions emanating from its policy environment.

The Commission's membership would consist of the most highly regarded and relevant members of three primary groups: natural scientists whose work centers or impinges on agricultural issues (i.e., including agricultural and life scientists, as well as scientists from related physical and medical sciences); social and behavioral scientists whose research concerns related key sociological, political, economic, psychological, and ethical problems; and elder statespersons not currently in office, who are recognized for their global and long-range agricultural and societal perspectives. In addition, representatives from the National Board on Agriculture, the Joint Council, and the UAB would serve as ex-officio members, providing two-way channels of communication between the Commission and these other priority-relevant structures.

A Search Committee, appointed by the President of the National Academy of Sciences in consultation with the NAS Board on Agriculture, would nominate members to staggered terms. This mix of members' professional expertise and backgrounds would ensure the integration of scientific problems, social issues, and geopolitical realities.

The professional stature of the members and the sponsorship of the National Academy of Sciences would grant the Commission virtually automatic credibility. The legitimacy of the Commission would ensure that no administration, nor any other political or bureaucratic entity or individual, would casually disregard its pronouncements. The Commission's publicized conclusions would have the pervasive impact of a Carnegie Report (e.g., A Nation at Risk, 1983).

Insulated as much as possible from external and internal political pressures, the Commission would identify long-term, national, even international, agricultural issues and knowledge needs. It would issue a major report through the National Academy of Sciences in January of the years in which national elections are held. This timing is designed to maximize freedom and effectiveness.

More specifically, in an election year, a first-term administration would be unlikely to try to offset its pronouncements. The Commission's recommendations could shape the administration's second-term agricultural research agenda or the initial agenda of a new administration. This timing also would provide input for the Farm Bill, which is passed in the year following the national election. During each of the three subsequent years, the Commission would issue a minor report to reaffirm previous priorities and/or make course corrections.

Coordinating the Joint Council and the UAB

The *Joint Council's and the UAB's functions should be reshaped* to mesh with the Commission's and the USDA Science and Education Division's activities. In the year the Commission's major report is issued, the Joint Council could develop a four-year strategic plan for the Science and Education Division. The strategic plan would identify those parts of the Commission's priorities appropriate for S&E. To address this four-year plan would provide the framework for annual budgets developed by USDA agency administrators, with the assistance of ESCOP. The UAB's responsibilities should be similarly coordinated with the priorities identified by the Commission.

The Joint Council also could handle agricultural emergencies that impinge on long-term priorities. In addition, the Joint Council could develop innovative approaches to meet enduring scientific issues confronted by the USDA Science and Education Division and its stateside partners. It would also be the Joint Council's responsibility to delineate the implications of its four-year strategic plan for various types of funding mechanisms (i.e., formula funds, competitive grants, etc.).

The Joint Council's annual priorities report is a contradiction in terms, since no significant national scientific priority can be fulfilled adequately within that time frame. Moreover, the considerable effort required to produce the annual priorities report is incommensurate with its limited utility. Its current use as a budget justification document could be better met by a four-year strategic plan, supplemented with a streamlined annual assessment of S&E's previous year's strategy development and implementation. This annual assessment would replace the annual accomplishments report.

Implementing Mechanisms Within the USDA

Within the USDA, a *Federal Science and Education Executive Committee on National Priorities*, composed of the Assistant Secretary and the relevant S&E administrators, would then design and coordinate a set of strategies for meeting the objectives articulated by the Joint Council. An *Implementation Task Force (ITF)*, composed of deputies to S&E agency administrators, would be responsible for implementing these strategies. The Joint Council, in its annual assessment, would make recommendations regarding which areas should be strengthened or reconceptualized in the coming year. The Implementation Task Force should have a liaison to the Federal Science and Education Executive Committee on National Priorities (FSEECNP).

Federal Interdepartmental Coordination: Interorganizational Discontinuities

At present, various federal departments engage in agricultural research without any systematic articulation of their respective programs except through OMB review. These interorganizational discontinuities impair each department's capacity to set meaningful priorities.

Some structural mechanism is required to reduce these discontinuities and facilitate distributing the National Agricultural Issues Commission's priorities across the federal research system. At the present time, no regularly convened interorganizational forums exist where key federal planners concerned with research priorities meet (1) to develop joint plans for agricultural research, and (2) to deal with the interorganizational tensions generated in the science and politics dialectic. As a result, many Congressional and Executive Branch policymakers and administrators involved in priority setting, planning, and budget processes work in compartmentalized—if not clearly contradictory—ways.

These system participants ordinarily meet only "after the fact" of planning and in structured adversarial forums, such as budget and appropriations hearings. Moreover, as noted above, the different traditions, value systems, and agenda of science administrators and policymakers create a hot-house environment for misunderstanding and even total lack of communication. An ongoing forum of key policymakers and science administrators also would go far toward creating a more coherent process for drafting and promulgating the Farm Bill, as well as for developing annual budgets.

To meet this need, it would be useful to create an ongoing *Federal Interorganizational Planning Group (FIPG)*, composed of planners from USDA, OMB, relevant Congressional committees, other executive agencies that conduct agricultural research, as well as GAO, OSTP, and OTA. This planning group would conduct an ongoing dialogue to identify, discuss, and negotiate those issues and specific programs deemed important by both the scientific community and the political system. Since these are also the system members who formulate legislation and budgets, their ongoing interaction within a cooperative but nonbinding milieu should have a positive effect on both processes.

Another strategy for addressing interorganizational discontinuities involves specifically *authorizing the Assistant Secretary for Science and Education to take the lead in coordinating the research priorities of the various federal departments engaged in agricultural research.* The language of recent Farm Bills has left somewhat ambiguous the Assistant Secretary's leadership role vis-à-vis agricultural and food research programs in nonUSDA federal agencies.

Section 1404(3) of the 1985 Farm Bill designates the USDA as the "lead agency of the Federal Government for agriculture and research." Although the 1985 Farm Bill still assigns USDA lead responsibility for coordinating food and agricultural research across all federal agencies, it does not provide an adequately explicit leadership mandate to the Assistant Secretary for

Science and Education. The next Farm Bill should give the Assistant Secretary explicit lead responsibility for bringing the considerable resources allocated to agricultural research by other federal agencies under the national priorities established for the USDA.

Giving the Assistant Secretary for Science and Education an explicit mandate through unambiguous language in the next Farm Bill would empower his interorganizational leadership role. Undoubtedly, the implementation of this interagency leadership role is a delicate task. The priorities articulated by the National Agricultural Issues Commission and the Joint Council's strategic plan for USDA activities should help clear the way for interorganizational turf allocation. Within this context, the Assistant Secretary could seek to engage his nonUSDA counterparts in cooperatively mapping the specialized, but coordinated, foci of all federal agencies engaged in such research. This coordinated approach would provide a more coherent U.S. food and agriculture research program.

*Public-Private Sector
Priority-Setting Coordination*

One last structural issue remains: the lack of any ongoing mechanism for systematic public-private sector priority setting. At the present time, the federal government has only a very general sense of private sector priorities. Thus, the USDA is obliged to prepare its Science and Education budget without any systematic knowledge of where and if there is duplication with private sector budgets.

In this era of renewed public-private cooperation, a mechanism fostering cooperative priority setting among public and private research planners seems appropriate. One possibility is a *Public-Private Agricultural Research Policy Task Force* (PPARPTF) to enable high-level policymakers in both sectors to plan as cooperatively and openly as various legal constraints and proprietary concerns allow.

Conclusion

The issues and dilemmas, as well as the strategies, discussed in this chapter represent merely the tip of the iceberg. Other structural, as well as communication and human resources, concerns remain. Nonetheless, these issues are basic. Further discussion and agreement without implementation is an empty exercise. It is not surprising that the highly autonomous, but coupled, components of a traditional, decentralized system should have serious reservations about relinquishing power—even for the good of the larger system. It will take strong and creative leadership to convince the system that it has nothing to lose but its annual browbeating at the hands of its critics.

Notes

1. For a complete report of the findings, see Lipman-Blumen and Schram, 1984.
2. Some observers suggest that basic research projects often take from seven to 25 years or longer to yield results, compared to four- to eight-year presidential cycles.

References

Busch, L., and Lacy, W. B. *Science, Agriculture, and the Politics of Research*. Boulder, Colorado: Westview Press, 1983.

General Accounting Office. *Long-Range Planning Can Improve the Efficiency of Agricultural Research and Development* (CED-81-141). Washington, D.C.: General Accounting Office, July 1981.

Lindblom, C. E. "The Science of 'Muddling Through'." In H. Leavitt, L. Pondy, and D. M. Boje (eds.), *Readings in Managerial Psychology*, 3rd edn. Chicago, Illinois: University of Chicago Press, 1980.

Lipman-Blumen, J. "The Dialectic Between Research and Social Policy: The Difficulties from a Policy Perspective—Rashomon Part I. The Difficulties from a Research Perspective—Rashomon Part II." In J. Lipman-Blumen and J. Bernard (eds.), *Sex Roles and Social Policy*. Beverly Hills, California: Sage Publications, Inc., 1979.

Lipman-Blumen, J., and Schram, S. *The Paradox of Success: The Impact of Priority Setting in Agricultural Research and Extension*. Washington, D.C.: USDA, 1984.

National Commission on Excellence in Education. *A Nation at Risk*. Washington, D.C.: U.S. Government Printing Office, 1983.

National Research Council. *Report of the Committee on Research Advisory to the U.S. Department of Agriculture* (The Pound Report). Springfield, Virginia: National Technical Information Service, 1972.

Office of Technology Assessment. *An Assessment of the U.S. Food and Agricultural Research System*. Washington, D.C.: U.S. Government Printing Office, 1981.

7

The CSRS Scientist:
A Role in Transition

Robert L. Christensen and Roland R. Robinson

Introduction

Beginning with the Hatch Act in 1887, the federal government has provided research funding to the land grant universities. In 1888 the Office of Experiment Stations (OES) was established to administer the provisions of the Act. Subsequent legislation and occasional administrative interpretations modifying and extending that original mandate have defined the responsibilities and functions of the agency currently known as the Coöperative State Research Service (CSRS). Accordingly, the roles of individual staff member/scientists within CSRS have evolved over the nearly one hundred years of legislative history. Other factors influencing the role of the CSRS scientists have included changes in administrative and political philosophy and budgetary cycles within the federal government. Less obvious, but perhaps also important, have been disciplinary influences as the CSRS scientist reflects his/her discipline in the internal processes of the agency.

This chapter first presents a historical overview of major legislative acts providing federal support of experiment station research as well as significant administrative actions that have shaped the agency known as CSRS. Particular emphasis is given to those aspects that bear a relation to the role of the CSRS scientist. Second, the chapter addresses the processes currently used at the national level for problem identification, prioritization, and budget development. Third, a brief analysis of funding sources and trends and their implications for the scientist's role in CSRS is presented. Fourth, the chapter discusses the current responsibilities of the CSRS scientist as well as his/her potential for enhancing university research in process and content.

Historical Overview: Legislative Acts,
Organizational Function, and Scientist Role

The Hatch Act of 1887 provided the initial federal investments to assist the states in the establishment of a nationwide system of agricultural experiment stations. Four basic functions for the administrative organization created by the Hatch Act of 1887 are implicit. These are fiscal accountability, research coordination, research prioritization, and service in an advisory role. These basic functions were reaffirmed by virtually all subsequent agricultural legislation between 1887 and 1955 (Robinson, 1978). (The following summary of legislative acts and administrative interpretations is drawn from Robinson's 1978 report.)

The original Hatch Act embodied the purposes of promoting research in the agricultural sciences and the dissemination of useful and practical information on agricultural subjects. Coupled with the land grant college concept, it appears obvious that the intent was to develop research capabilities oriented to the needs of the individual states. Further, while predating the Smith-Lever Act (which created Cooperative Extension), the wording implied a strong orientation to applied research. The original Hatch Act objectives called for both the production of useful and practical information (research) and for its diffusion among the people (extension). However, subsequent interpretations held that use of Hatch monies for extension purposes was inappropriate.

The duties and responsibilities of the OES, as described in the Hatch Act, and the letter to directors from A. C. True stressing financial accountability required little science capability on the part of OES personnel. In fact, the OES personnel visiting the stations in early days were called "federal investigators," implying an auditing function. These periodic on-site visits have evolved into the present day research review, a process almost entirely devoid of financial accountability content.

The Adams Act (1906) provided additional federal support for experiment station research. However, these funds were specifically designated for support of *basic research* in the agricultural sciences. The Act also specified financial accountability activities and the Secretary of Agriculture subsequently sent a letter to the station directors establishing procedures and requirements. The OES was also charged under the Adams Act with *promoting* effective work (research). Thus, the charge to promote effective research and to make a distinction between basic and applied research placed greater demands on the science capabilities of the OES staff.

The necessity for making a distinction between basic and applied research probably marked the beginnings of a significant division of labor within the organization. The two categories were: (1) administrative/managerial functions concerned with policy and procedural matters largely related to financial accountability, and (2) science functions increasingly concerned with the research performance of the experiment stations. The credibility of the organization began to depend on the science competency of its staff.

The Purnell Act (1925) again stressed financial requirements for the expenditure of federal funds. The OES, representing the Secretary of Agriculture, assembled these financial reports from the SAES and (1) prepared a certification statement for each station enabling it to receive its share of annual federal appropriations, and (2) prepared a report for Congress on the work, receipts, and expenditures of the SAES.

The Purnell Act purpose statement included the goal of conducting research to promote the development and improvement of the rural home and rural life. This act also called for sociological and economic investigations to produce the knowledge and information needed to achieve this goal. It thus gave substantial impetus to social science research at the stations. Between 1920 and 1935 the number of social science research projects increased dramatically. This act was the first specifically to define research needs by discipline. In later legislation other specific disciplinary research needs were identified, and specialization became more prevalent among the OES staff.

The original Bankhead-Jones Act, passed in 1935, provided federal funds to support research, extension, and teaching activities conducted by the land grant universities and the SAES. The legislation also introduced the "matching requirement" and the formula method for the distribution of federal funds to the SAES.

Because of the increasing complexity of financial requirements involved in the use of federal funds and the funding of multiple functions under the Act, in 1935 Secretary Wallace elaborated the financial requirements of the stations in using federal funds and the responsibilities of the OES in administration of the various acts. The letter identifies six major items related to financial requirements to be met by the stations in the use of federal funds and validated by OES and five items with a bearing on the OES scientist's role. These five items included: (1) coordinating research among the SAES; (2) determining the eligibility of projects on the basis of a coordinated program basic to the major problems of agriculture; (3) assisting the stations in the selection of projects and the organization of research in order to coordinate SAES research on a regional basis with USDA research; (4) developing a uniform research classification scheme to categorize research expenditures from all federal sources—Hatch, Adams, Purnell, and Bankhead-Jones; and (5) since the act provided federal funds for not only research but also extension and teaching, the OES was charged with the responsibility of ensuring that research funds were used for research purposes.

The amended Bankhead-Jones Act and the Agricultural Marketing Act (1946) contained several new features affecting support of SAES research programs, the allocation of research resources, and the role of the OES science staff. Title I provided additional federal support for basic agricultural research. Not less than 20 percent of Hatch funds were to be expended for marketing research, and Title II (204b) also provided research funds to support competitive projects to improve the marketing and distribution of agricultural commodities. The new legislation also revised the formula for the distribution of federal funds to the experiment stations. In addition, not more than 25 percent of the funds appropriated were to be used for cooperative regional research in which two or more states cooperated to investigate problems that concerned the agriculture of more than one state. At least 20 percent of regional research funds also had to be expended on "marketing" research.

The following appears to be some of the major impacts of the 1946 legislation on station programs and the OES science staff. First, the "earmarking" of funds for marketing and regional research designated funds for specific uses and imposed constraints on the allocation of research funds at the station level. Second, the regional research requirement effectively mandated a major role for the OES scientist in the planning, coordination, and management of regional research projects. Third, the social goals embedded in the purpose or mission statement of the legislation and the expansion of the research agendas of the SAES required greater specialization among the OES staff. Science capabilities in plant sciences, animal sciences, food science, human nutrition, social sciences, etc., were now required. The marketing aspects of the 1946 legislation not only affected station research programs and the OES staff, it also established major precedents in funding procedures and research management.

A significant feature of the 1946 legislation was the introduction of the competitive project concept as a funding mechanism. To administer the marketing provisions of the Act, the Experiment Station Marketing Research Advisory Committee (ESMRAC) was formed. This group of individuals from the stations with training and expertise in marketing and related fields and OES personnel were to develop guidelines and criteria to be used by OES in differentiating marketing research under Title I and to assist in the evaluation and selection of marketing projects for funding under Title II (204b). Thus, station scientists were brought into research management at the national level.

The 1946 legislation compounded the accountability problems. The stations and OES had to maintain separate accounts and make separate reports for the use of Hatch, Adams, Purnell, and Bankhead-Jones funds in accordance with the specific requirements and conditions for their use. Moreover, the matching, marketing, and regional research requirements had to be accounted for and monitored by OES. A special regional research office was established in the organization to administer the regional research program at the national level.

The amended Hatch Act of 1955 consolidated the several laws providing federal funds to support experiment station research. Goals were virtually unchanged from earlier legislation. The new act did include a statement giving responsibility to the Secretary for encouraging cooperation and coordination of research and also enabled the use of federal funds for planning and coordination of cooperative research among stations and between the stations and the USDA.

Title XIV of the National Agricultural Research, Extension, and Teaching Policy Act of 1977 and the 1981 amended Act had a major influence on federal support of SAES programs and funding mechanisms. However, the impact on the role of the organization's scientists has been minimal. The Competitive Grants program, Animal Health and Disease program (Sec. 1433, PL 95-113), and the Rangeland Resource Grants (Sec. 1480, PL 97-98) came into existence under Title XIV. The Special Grants Office is autonomous of, but ancillary to, CSRS. The Special Grants, Animal Health, and Rangeland Resource programs are administered by CSRS, while the Competitive Grants program is administered by a special office established for this purpose. Growth in these granting programs administered by CSRS will increasingly involve the CSRS scientist in program and project management, since the proposals are screened and selected in the competitive process.

Title XIV did not explicitly state the functions of the responsible administrative organization representing the Secretary in carrying out the provisions of the Act. However, the responsibilities described for the Secretary of Agriculture, the Joint Council on Food and Agricultural Sciences, and the National Agricultural Users Advisory Board have significance for both CSRS and the organization's scientists.

Under the 1977 and 1981 Acts, the Secretary of Agriculture was delegated the leadership role in the federal government for research, teaching, and extension in the food and agricultural sciences. Several responsibilities relate to coordination or the development of coordinating structures, policymaking, and accountability. Two responsibilities involve: (1) establishing review procedures to assure completion of federally funded research projects, and (2) promoting multidisciplinary research on major agricultural research problems. Both have implications for the role of CSRS and its science staff.

Many of the responsibilities and activities of the Secretary of Agriculture, the Joint Council, and the Users Advisory Board, as described in Title XIV, are already built into the functions of the existing administrative agencies—CSRS, ES, and the Higher Education Programs brought to USDA from HEW. Therefore, the staff of the existing agencies indirectly serve the Secretary, the Joint Council, and the Users Advisory Board.

Problem Identification, Prioritization, and Budget Development

Title XIV of the 1977 Food and Agriculture Act changed the institutional framework within which agricultural research directions are formed. Three entities were created by the Act. The Committee on Food and Natural Resources includes representatives from twelve federal agencies (not limited to agriculture) and is charged with bringing about better planning and coordination of research in food, renewable resources, and nutrition at the federal level. In the 1977 Farm Bill the Congress created two additional groups charged with assisting in research planning and prioritization. The Joint Council on Food and Agricultural Sciences was established with the intent of improving regional and national planning and coordination of agricultural research, teaching, and extension activities. The Joint Council has responsibilities largely in the area of communication, information dissemination, program analysis, and management. Specifically mentioned among the charges to the Council are determination of high priority research areas and the analysis and evaluation of the impacts of teaching, research, and extension programs.

The 1977 Act also created the National Agricultural Research and Extension Users Advisory Board. This Board represents an attempt to obtain citizen participation in the policy formation and evaluation process. It is composed of twenty-five individuals who represent users and those impacted by agricultural research and extension activities. The responsibilities of the Users Advisory Board largely relate to policy formation and program analysis (Neilson and Brazzel, 1980).

Both the Joint Council and the Users Advisory Board have assumed an active stance in identifying research needs and priorities. Illustrative is the Joint Council's report entitled "FY 1986 Priorities for Research, Extension, and Higher Education" and the Users Advisory Board review of the 1985 budget entitled "New Directions for Science, Education, and Agriculture." These reports receive careful attention in the budget formation process. The considerable overlap in functions of the Council and Board have the potential for producing conflicting statements of needs and priorities.

Another influential group in the problem identification and prioritization process for research funding is ESCOP (Experiment Station Committee on Organization and Policy). It, too, produces occasional reports on research direction and priorities (in addition to its direct input into the budget process). For example, a 1981 report entitled "Research and the Family Farm" contained recommendations for an "aggressive agenda of research to increase agricultural productivity" and "increased emphasis on policy research," among other topics (ESCOP, 1981:ii). A 1984 report entitled "Research and Agricultural Trade" concluded that efforts devoted to research on trade in agricultural products is extremely limited (ESCOP, 1984). The report calls for sizable investments in building the research capability needed in the area of agricultural trade. It is significant that a subcommittee of ESCOP works closely with the administration of Science and Education and CSRS in budget development.

In spite of these efforts to plan, coordinate, and prioritize research at the state and national levels, critics find the system lacking. For example, in 1981 Phillips asserted that, "There is a lack of well-defined and agreed-upon national goals for U.S. Food and Agriculture." He attributed lack of funding for research as due to the research system's failure to make its case. Finally, he stated, "Research continues to lack prominence within USDA as witnessed by inadequate funding requests to Congress, the continuing decrease in number of positions assigned to agricultural research, and the lack of young scientists" (Phillips, 1981:2,6).

Funding Sources and Trends and Their Implications for the Scientist's Role in CSRS

Table 7.1 presents a summary of SAES research support (in current dollars) by funding source for 1970 and 1983 and the relative importance of these sources (in percentage terms) in the respective years, the growth in support (current dollars) from these funding sources between 1970 and 1983, and the percentage increase from the various sources.

TABLE 7.1   Changes in Funding Sources of SAES Research, 1970 and 1983

Funding Source	1970 Amount (000)	1970 Per-cent	1983 Amount (000)	1983 Per-cent	Changes 1970-1983 Amount (000)	Changes 1970-1983 Per-cent
Federal	($ 89,465)	31.7%	($280,706)	28.2%	($191,241)	214%
CSRS Administered	56,200	19.9	174,207	17.5	118,007	210
Hatch/RRF	51,887		141,355	14.1	89,468	172
McIntire-Stennis	2,988		9,177		6,189	207
Special grants	1,325		12,858		11,533	870
Competitive grants	0		6,040		6,040	
Other funds [a]	0		4,777		4,777	
NonCSRS Administered	33,265	11.8	106,499	10.7	73,234	220
USDA (CGCA)	6,825		33,149		26,324	386
Other federal agencies [b]	26,440		73,350		46,910	177
Nonfederal	192,329	68.3	715,601	71.8	523,272	272
State appropriations	152,276		550,044		397,768	261
Product sales	19,606		61,893		42,287	216
Industry	13,719		61,008		47,289	345
Other nonfederal	6,728		42,656		35,928	534
Total all funds	$281,794	100%	$996,307	100%	$714,513	254%

[a] Animal Health Sec. 1433; 1890/Tuskegee Sec. 1445; Nature PL 95-592; Alcohol Fuels Sec. 1419.
[b] NSF, D&E, AID, DOD, WIH, PHS, HHS, NASA, TVA, and others.

In 1970 the largest source of support for SAES research was nonfederal (68.3 percent), followed by CSRS administered sources (19.9 percent) and nonCSRS administered federal funds (11.8 percent). By 1983 there was a change in the relative importance of these major categories of SAES research support. Nonfederal sources of funding increased to 71.8 percent of total support, while CSRS administered funding declined to 17.5 percent of total support, and nonCSRS administered federal support declined to 10.7 percent.

The absolute and relative importance of growth in SAES research support by funding source are shown in the last two columns of the table. Between 1970 and 1980, nonfederal sources of support increased the greatest extent (272 percent), followed by nonCSRS administered federal sources (220 percent), and CSRS administered funding (210 percent). While it has long been recognized that nonfederal sources of support for SAES research were increasing to a greater extent than federal sources, it has not been generally recognized that growth in support for SAES research from nonCSRS administered federal sources exceeded that of CSRS administered federal funds. Funding from the sources administered by CSRS is very important to researchers in the land grant universities. It is relatively stable and dependable and is used in many universities as the primary funding support for graduate research assistantships.

Within the nonfederal category of support sources, "other" nonfederal increased the greatest extent (534 percent) followed by "industry" (345 percent). Within the nonCSRS administered federal category, USDA support increased by 386 percent. Within the CSRS administered category, "competitive" and "special grants" were the fastest growing funding sources. The percentage increase in competitive grants and other funds could not be computed because there were no funds available from these sources in the 1970 base year.

The competitive grants concept has received strong support from several quarters in recent years, although there is a mixed reaction among some state experiment station directors. While the debate will continue with respect to the merits of competitive grants, some significant points may be noted. First, it is currently the belief in the administration that competitive grants are an effective means of accomplishing research directed to national needs. Second, the nature of those national needs appear to be, at least in part, a result of inputs from the Joint Council and the Users Advisory Board. For example, both groups identified biotechnology as the highest priority area for research in their recent reports, and the Users Advisory Board was particularly supportive of the competitive and special grants programs (Joint Council, May 1984; Users Advisory Board, February 1984; July 1984).

Implications for the CSRS Scientist's Role

As already indicated, the increasing ratio of grant to formula funds administered will likely shift the scientist's role in the direction of project management.

The trends would also suggest that the organization examine its mandated and nonmandated functions. For example, the review process, usually carried out in disciplinary departments at the land grant universities, is nonmandated. The review process grew out of the on-site visits by OES personnel in the early 1900s that were part of the financial accountability responsibility. The purposes of the review process are to assist in the planning, evaluation, and prioritization of departmental programs and generally to promote the more effective use of resources in achieving departmental goals and objectives. Because of the close interaction of research, teaching, and extension functions in most departments, all three functions are generally reviewed and evaluated in the same process. Because of the increasing support of SAES research programs from nonCSRS administered sources, the review process increasingly covers research projects and programs supported from these other sources. Those other agencies and organizations (both federal and nonfederal) capture the benefits of the review to the extent that the review promotes more effective use of all research funds, without making any input to that process. This, of course, excludes the inputs of the departments being reviewed since they devote considerable resources in preparing for the reviews and in carrying them out. For example, we have conducted reviews in departments of agricultural economics where CSRS administered funds made up less than 10 percent of total departmental funding.

In summary, the CSRS scientist is carrying out a function that is not specifically mandated and at the same time evaluating programs that are increasingly supported from nonfederal sources. It should be added that because of the severe shortage of CSRS staff for other reasons, the land grant universities are often found to be conducting their own internal reviews. In contrast, the participation of the CSRS scientist in the planning and coordination of regional research is a mandated function. Also, the regional research program receives a higher level of CSRS administered support than station research programs in total. In 1984, CSRS administered funds provided 30.6 percent of total support for regional research projects.

Finally, the increasing size of station programs serviced by a declining CSRS science staff has greatly increased the workload/scientist ratio over time. In 1965, CSRS had about forty scientists. The staff serviced 180 regional projects and 6,845 scientist years (SYs) of station research effort. By 1983, the CSRS science staff had been reduced to about twenty-five persons. This staff has the responsibility of servicing 230 regional projects and about 7,500 SYs of station research effort (CSRS Personnel records, 1983; CSRS Regional Research Office records, 1963 and 1983; Agricultural Handbook No. 305, 1965, 1983; USDA and Association of State Universities and Land Grant Colleges, 1966; Inventory of Agricultural Research, FY 1983).

Current and Potential Roles for the CSRS Scientist

Obviously, the legislation cited earlier does not specifically define the role and tasks of the CSRS scientist. These have evolved in response to the responsibilities of the Secretary of Agriculture specified by law and as interpreted by successive administrations. As mentioned earlier, a consistent responsibility of CSRS has been that of financial accountability. This, however, is not a role of the CSRS scientist. The role of the CSRS scientists in recent years has evolved from the responsibility for assisting and encouraging the cooperation and coordination of research as first mentioned by Secretary Wallace in 1935. Thus, in the last decade, CSRS scientists have had a major role in connection with development and monitoring of cooperative regional research. In addition, they have represented CSRS in reviews of agricultural research programs in disciplinary departments in the agricultural experiment stations. A third important role also stems from the responsibility for assisting and encouraging the planning and coordination of research. The scientist assists, in a staff role, the administration of CSRS and the experiment stations in the identification of research program needs, articulation, and rationale for programs, prioritization among competing program demands, and recommended program funding levels.

It is in the internal processes of the organization that the CSRS scientist has a subtle, yet very important, role in defining program areas, developing justifications, and exerting influence, both orally and in writing. CSRS scientists sit in on budget discussions. They also have specific assignments to develop background materials and to write justification statements to accompany budget materials. Disciplinary biases, whether conscious or not, condition perceptions of problems and weighing of priorities. Such biases permeate the groups and institutions involved in the entire process but become more critical within the relatively small circle dealing with priorities and budget allocations.

A 1982 external review report on CSRS contains the following statements that relate to the scientist's role:

> Providing the access point for effective research planning, coordinating, and prioritization of the States' effort into the Federal-State partnership is an essential function to CSRS.

> The State and Regional planning of research and the NASULGC-ESCOP activity, with augmentation by the scientific staff of CSRS provide this interaction between Federal and State administrators.

> The process of Budget Development, Program Justification, and Monitoring during the budget negotiations . . . for cooperative states' programs is a function of CSRS. This function should receive first priority on a continuing basis by the administrators and scientific staff . . . to ensure that budget requests reflect priority research needs.

> Staff work by competent scientists is essential to ensure appropriate budget justifications. . . . To fulfill this function necessitates broad competencies among scientific support staff and a climate of partnership among complementing administrators working on budget adjustment (CSRS Special Panel Report, 1982:6).

The CSRS scientist has, in recent years, played a major role in the regional research process. This role has included advice in project definition and development, review and recommendations to the Committee of Nine with respect to approval, and continuing contact with the regional technical committees as the research project progresses toward completion. The extent of the CSRS scientist's influence upon the character of regional research is largely dependent on two factors. The first is the scientist's personal conception of his/her role in the process. Some see their role as that of ensuring that the protocols for regional research are followed along with providing a technical advisory role to ESCOP and the administrative advisors of the committees. Other CSRS scientists, in varying degrees, assume an advisory role in a disciplinary as well as administrative sense. This leads to the second factor influencing the character of regional research. To the extent that the CSRS scientist is recognized for his/her disciplinary competence, he/she may be able to exercise leadership in the definition of regional research problems and approaches. If this latter characteristic of disciplinary leadership is accepted as a proper role for the CSRS scientist, it is apparent that scientist staff must be selected for this characteristic.

Making this whole area of disciplinary competence even more difficult are the increasing degrees of specialization within disciplines. A scientist acknowledged as an expert in one aspect of animal science may be relatively unknown in another aspect. This, coupled with the static (and in some disciplinary areas decreasing) staffing levels in CSRS, often results in the CSRS scientist having little to contribute in terms of technical knowledge leadership. All of these factors have combined to cause a lack of clarity in individual role perceptions on the part of scientists. In addition, differences in leadership capacities have created a substantial ambiguity with respect to the disciplinary role of the CSRS scientist.

Most CSRS scientists would agree that a major part of their role is the furtherance of research excellence in their discipline. However, most are no longer directly involved in the research process. Their influence must come through the indirect means of their functions on regional research committees and the occasional research and comprehensive reviews of university departments. It would seem that more direct and active contributions could be made through the professional associations. By this we mean that the CSRS scientist's role might be expanded to include a more pro-active role in professional affairs. CSRS scientists might well be encouraged to advocate CSRS sponsorship of symposia on selected topics at professional meetings. This is a means by which CSRS could focus disciplinary attention on research problems and priorities of national significance.

For the most part, CSRS has failed to utilize the professional associations as vehicles for the development of research agendas. At the same time, the professional associations have shown little appreciation of the importance of CSRS scientists to disciplinary research. Perhaps a process could be institutionalized that would enable greater interchange between the associations and CSRS. Recently, an ad hoc committee of the American Agricultural Economics Association recommended formation of a standing committee that would annually make recommendations to the administrator of CSRS and to ESCOP concerning research needs and priorities in the social science areas (AAEA, 1984).

Summary Statement

The foregoing discussion leads to certain conclusions and questions regarding the future role of the CSRS scientist and the use of the resources of the organization in support of science.

First, the increasing workload/scientist ratio will continue to move the scientist into a generalist/managerial mode as opposed to a specialist mode of operations. This has significant implications for future staffing policies of the organization. It also raises questions with respect to the CSRS scientist's credibility with disciplines characterized by increasing specialization.

Second, because of the growing importance of the federal budgetary process, the CSRS scientist must not only become more involved but develop greater capacity to contribute effectively to that process. At the same time, greater involvement in the budgetary process means greater potential for exerting influence for disciplines in the program development, prioritization, and budgeting processes.

Third, changes in funding sources and trends not only have effects on the scientist's role but also raise important questions about the future. The increasing importance of competitive and special project funds relative to formula funds will by necessity move the scientist in the direction of competitive program and project management. Next, CSRS administered federal funds are a diminishing proportion in total SAES research funding. Will this create pressures over time for the organization to shift its limited science resources: (1) in the direction of institutions, programs, and projects more heavily supported with CSRS administered funds, and (2) toward mandated and away from nonmandated functions?

Fourth, CSRS has a major mandated responsibility for promoting cooperation and coordination of SAES and USDA research. The financial support of SAES research by the research agencies of USDA and the involvement of USDA personnel in regional research projects are becoming increasingly important over time. These trends place greater significance on the SAES-USDA coordination responsibilities of the CSRS science staff. With dwindling CSRS science resources, will this coordination role increasingly drift toward the research agencies of the department?

Historically, the administrative agencies of the department have formulated their functions around the responsibilities of the Secretary described in legislative acts providing federal support for institutional research. At this point, the responsibilities of the Secretary, the Advisory Board, and the Joint Council, as described in Title XIV of the 1977 Farm Bill, have minimal influence on the role of the CSRS scientist. The implications of these responsibilities for the functions of CSRS and the scientist role have never been consciously and systematically examined. The important question is: Will the future role of the CSRS scientist be significantly influenced by the responsibilities of the Secretary, Advisory Board, and Joint Council?

Notes

The views expressed are solely those of the authors and should not be attributed to the University of Massachusetts or the U.S. Department of Agriculture.

References

AAEA, Ad Hoc Committee on CSRS. "Agricultural Economics Representation in the Cooperative State Research Service (CSRS)." Report submitted to the Executive Committee of the American Agricultural Economics Association, June 1984.

Agricultural Handbook. *Professional Workers in State Agricultural Experiment Stations and Other Cooperating Institutions.* Agricultural Handbook No. 305. Washington, D.C.: CSRS, USDA, 1965 and 1983.

CSRS Personnel Records. Washington, D.C.: Cooperative State Research Service/ USDA, 1983.

CSRS Regional Research Office Records. Washington, D.C.: Cooperative State Research Service/USDA, 1965 and 1983.

Experiment Station Committee on Policy (ESCOP). "Research and the Family Farm." Washington, D.C.: USDA, February 1981.

————. "Research and Agricultural Trade." Washington, D.C.: USDA, December 1984.

Inventory of Agricultural Research, FY 1983. Washington, D.C.: CSRS/USDA, 1984.

Joint Council on Food and Agricultural Sciences. "Five Year Plan for the Food and Agricultural Sciences—A Report to the Secretary of Agriculture." Washington, D.C.: USDA, May 1984.

————. "FY 1986 Priorities for Research, Extension, and Higher Education—A Report to the Secretary of Agriculture." Washington, D.C.: USDA, July 1984.

National Agricultural Research and Extension Users Advisory Board. "New Directions for Science, Education, and Agriculture." Washington, D.C.: USDA, February 1984.

————. "Science and Policy Issues: A Report of Citizen Concerns and Recommendations for American Agricultural Research." Washington, D.C.: USDA, July 1984.

Neilson, James M., and Brazzel, John M. "Evaluation as an Aid to Decision Making in the Food and Agricultural Sciences." Special publication entitled, "Federal Funding Philosophies, Policies, and Procedures." Berkeley, California: Western Association of Agricultural Experiment Station Directors, 1980.

Phillips, M. J. "Research and Technology—OTA Assessment of the Research System." Paper presented at the 1982 Agricultural Outlook Conference, Washington, D.C., November 4, 1981.

Robinson, R. R. "Administration of Federal Agricultural Research Funds by the Science and Education Administration/Cooperative Research (SEA/CR)." Unpublished. Washington, D.C.: CSRS, USDA, September 1978.

Special Panel Review of the Cooperative State Research Service. "Meeting the Expanding Need for Agricultural Research." Unpublished, restricted distribution. Washington, D.C.: CSRS, USDA, February 1982.

USDA and the National Association of State Universities and Land Grant Colleges. *A National Program of Research for Agriculture.* Washington, D.C.: U.S. Government Printing Office, 1966.

8

Research Funding and Priority Setting in State Agricultural Experiment Stations

James J. Zuiches

Introduction

Agricultural science is in the midst of a revolution concerning expectations of administrators, funding sources, and researchers. It has been criticized for being excessively oriented to short-term, incremental, production-oriented applied research. Recommendations for increases in funding for basic research, for more peer review of programs and competition for funding, and for a shift in the balance of basic and applied agricultural research have been made. The responses of the agricultural research establishment have been multiple—from reorganization and redirection of programs to a clear definition of priorities and an organized effort to achieve funding for highest priority research needs.

Even as the system adjusts to criticisms and initiates its own responses and new directions, one must recognize the ongoing tensions in the management of agricultural research. These tensions are reflected in the continuing debates over the balance in funding for basic and applied agricultural research, the autonomy that is accorded scientists, the relative roles of disciplinary, subject matter, and problem-oriented research, and the necessity of research results that can contribute to profitability in agriculture.

This chapter is concerned with these issues from the perspective of the directors of the State Agricultural Experiment Stations (SAES). Although the SAES represent only one aspect of the federal, industrial, and state research programs in agriculture, they have the mission under the Hatch Act (1955):

> To conduct original and other researches, investigations, and experiments bearing directly on and contributing to the establishment and maintenance of a permanent and effective agricultural industry of the United States, including researches basic to the problems of agriculture in its broadest aspects, and such investigations as have for their purpose the development and improvement of the rural home and rural life and the maximum contribution by agriculture

to the welfare of the consumer, as may be deemed advisable, having due regard to the varying conditions and needs of the respective States (U.S. Congress, 1955).

The interpretation and implementation of these duties are the responsibility of the director of the State Agricultural Experiment Station.

This chapter summarizes and assesses the perceptions and responses of the directors to a series of questions about research management in the SAES. These questions address fundamental values concerning philosophy of research funding and the operationalization of this philosophy in the decision making of directors and research activities of station scientists. It is the result of an informant survey, with the informants holding a key role in the agricultural research establishment. In addition to the general overview of responses, a review of the activities and philosophy of the Cornell University Agricultural Experiment Station as a case study of research management and decision making is provided.

Funding, Politics, and Science

The history of agricultural research is one of continuing "endemic ambiguity" (Rosenberg, 1976:145) as the scientific community strives for disciplinary development and advances, the rural production sector presses for rapid solution to problems to increase profitability, and the two groups compete for funds, personnel, and priority. Station directors have historically mediated the pressures from each community reflecting, on the one hand, the values and norms of the university and its scientific and educational missions and, on the other, the needs of the society supporting the university activities. These fundamental pressures on directors and the system have not changed within the last century, even though the agricultural research system has grown from an underfunded and understaffed infancy to a maturity reflected in the land grant system with its ability to accommodate the extraordinary diversity in research, instructional, and extension programs.

The historical analysis of the early pioneers in agricultural research organization and administration makes fascinating reading (see Rosenberg, 1976, and Rossiter, 1975). One insight gained from such analysis is the close interaction of station administrators with the agricultural producers and the associated pressures for immediate results, beneficial to the users. Lay expectations have been countered with arguments on the value of basic and applied research to understand and then solve client problems. Balancing the autonomy of the scientist and the goals of the station with the needs of the farmers has meant a constant communication flow to explain, inform, and defend the institutional activities.

This presentation is derived from a contemporary concern to inform a citizen advisory group, the National Agricultural Research and Extension Users Advisory Board (UAB), about research management issues and the responses of SAES. The UAB's membership includes representatives of the food and fiber production industries, consumers, agricultural suppliers and marketing participants, environmental specialists, rural development officials, human nutritionists, and other interest groups. The UAB issues annual reports appraising budget plans and research priorities and making recommendations to USDA from a "citizen's" perspective.

A survey of directors was originally undertaken by James E. Halpin, director-at-large for the Southern Region at the request of the chairman of the UAB. The questions related to the role of federal grant funds (other than USDA) in the SAES program and the relationships between scientists in the SAES and in general science departments of the land grant universities. Only thirty-one stations replied to the initial request in 1983, representing slightly more than half the SAES programs and funding. A summary of correspondence was prepared by Dr. Halpin and submitted to the UAB. This chapter extends that initial summary report, provides additional detail on the responses of directors, and discusses in greater depth the Cornell response.

In December 1984 a follow-up letter was sent to stations that had not responded to the initial letter. The directors were urged to respond by providing a comprehensive survey of the different strategies for organizing research programs, the Station philosophies with respect to research funding, and the relationship of Hatch formula funds and non-USDA federal grant funds. Concerns about priority setting, the balance of applied and basic research and coordination of interdisciplinary research, and suggestions for system improvement were to be part of the response. The specific questions were the same in both the initial and follow-up surveys.

The initial and follow-up requests went to all fifty-seven stations in the United States, which include each of the fifty state land grant universities; the experiment stations at Geneva, New York, and New Haven, Connecticut; the District of Columbia; Puerto Rico; Guam; Virgin Islands; and Samoa. Only four Stations did not respond: Idaho, Utah, Virgin Islands, and Samoa.

The responses of fifty-three stations reflect nearly complete coverage of the state agricultural research programs in 1983: 98 percent of the 6,381 scientist years in research, 97 percent of the $127 million in Hatch-appropriated funds, 99 percent of the $72 million in non-USDA federal funds expended in 1983 on SAES research, and 98 percent of the $531 million in state appropriations.

Since the results of this informant survey are not amenable to simple numeric summarization, the strategy for analysis involves content analysis and summarization, but without coding the number of stations answering "yes" or "no" or weighing station responses by scientist years (SYs) or Hatch, State, or other federal dollar volumes. The directors' responses are taken at face value, and interpretations of emphasis and significance of results are based on multiple readings of the letters.

Conceptually, the answers are organized with respect to the general and specific questions. Practically, the responses often interweave rationales, explanations, and straightforward answers, so the synthesis is clearly imposed on basically fifty-three letter responses to each question. Some subtle, but easily described, differences are mentioned in the analysis. The general themes may do some injustice to the clarity, impact, and emphasis of specific state responses, but these themes represent the diversity and, yet, to a high degree, a set of consistent responses across the SAES to these questions.

Directors' Responses

What is the role of non-USDA federal grant money in the program of your SAES? How important is it? With one exception, the directors indicated that non-USDA federal funds (NIH, NSF, DOE, EPA, etc.) provide a valuable and in some cases essential augmentation of federal formula funds for agricultural-related research, both basic and applied. Responses ran the gamut and included such statements as (1) augments/supplements/complements a base level of state and Hatch funds, (2) extends scope and collaboration in domestic and international areas, (3) increases the depth and breadth of research activity and productivity, and (4) demonstrates the excellence of Station scientists in the national, competitive peer review process.

The essential criterion applied by the directors in explaining the role of such external federal funds is the "fit" to ongoing programs. In every case the encouragement and support of such efforts lay in underpinning, strengthening, and stimulating projects conceived of and implemented within the mission and objectives of SAES.

One quote exemplifies the sentiments of nearly all the SAES directors:

> As a general statement, research programs that have had access to non-USDA federal funds have tended to progress more rapidly than research programs that have not. Effective research teams have been assembled more easily; essential equipment otherwise beyond our means has been acquired; our scientists have become integrated into a second network of productive investigators, i.e., the scientists competing for the non-USDA federal funds; the need to develop a competitive edge tends to sharpen research "instincts" (Storrs Agricultural Experiment Station, University of Connecticut).

The contrasting argument, espoused by only one station director, is that non-USDA federal grant money plays only a small role and is unimportant in his station programs. This position is justified by an array of alleged disadvantages and a philosophical position on scientific advancement, which argues that the marginal dollar determines the mission; grants are designed for purposes of grantors; seeking grants dissipates effort, disorganizes the program, and leads to "the chaos that evokes pleas for interdisciplinary research." Such a position represents the opposite end of a continuum on which all directors fall; but it is my judgment that no other directors, even those with no grant funds, are as philosophically opposed. As indicated above, given the criterion of contribution to mission, most directors are supportive and encouraging.

How do such funds augment the Hatch/state/McIntire-Stennis "hard money" program? The responses all reflect the flexibility of grant funds in association with project activity. Grant funds provide regular salary, summary salary, equipment, training funds, technician support, postdoctoral and graduate student support, travel, instrumentation, operating expenses, and overhead or indirect costs. This last item has both positive and negative connotations: in some instances, it further strengthens the research program by contributing to the payment of the indirect costs, real costs of conducting sponsored research; and in others, where overhead monies return to the university general fund or the state budget offices, the loss of these funds is perceived to lessen the research support. Many directors emphasized the necessity of external grant funds for sophisticated, costly equipment for research laboratories being brought into the age of modern biology.

The augmentation process is clearly a two-way action with respect to Hatch funds. In many cases, Cornell included, the Hatch funds often serve as the seed money for pilot, demonstration, or feasibility studies that provide the scientific basis for successful pursuit of external funds for a major programatic effort. In other situations, Arizona for instance, the grant funds frequently provide support for high-risk research, perhaps on nontraditional crops. When these are demonstrated to be viable alternatives for state agriculture, formula funds for longer term efforts are assigned to the projects.

How do you determine which non-USDA funds your scientists seek? This question implicitly was asking directors how priorities are set for research. The consistent response was that if projects are approved within the mission orientation of SAES, encouragement and support is the norm. It is difficult to rank order the responses, but a clear emphasis on two elements does appear. First, funds and projects must be consistent with the goals and mission of the Station, college, or department; and second, scientists make the decision and choice, keeping in mind state and station priorities, and disciplinary priorities.

The relative consistency of responses concerning the choice and decisive role of the scientist is reflected in much earlier judgments by the department, administration, and advisory bodies at the time of hiring a new scientist. The specific orientation of a research program is decided when faculty appointments are made. Over time, continued discussion within the institution, department, Station, and state advisory groups plays an essential role in determining what funding will even be perceived as appropriate. The work by Lipman-Blumen and Schram (1984) contains an extended discussion on priority-setting processes in SAES.

What are the advantages? Many of the advantages have already been cited as explanations of the role such grants play in program funding, but five common advantages were mentioned: (1) major source of funds for basic research efforts, (2) establishes agricultural research in national context, (3) opens up new intellectual avenues for scientists, (4) demonstrable evidence of quality of agricultural scientist and science, (5) pays for full costs of research.

What are the disadvantages? The most frequent answer was "None." The caveat on that answer, however, reflects the directors' assessment of their responsibilities: there are no real disadvantages if research administration does its job in the selection of staff and issues; management of scientists and projects; and administrative follow-up concerning productivity, application, and knowledge transfer to the user. This last element may be from the basic scientist to the applied scientist as well as the more typical situation to the end-user. Directors were often concerned about maintaining the appropriate balance between basic and applied research, but with a variation across states from 0–50 percent basic research, the appropriate balance must of necessity be state-specific in its management and achievement.

Some disadvantages cited represent significant concerns to all scientists and research administrators: time invested in proposal preparation, excessive accountability, and restrictions; lack of timeliness for emergency needs; short duration, one to five years, which limits long-term employment and does not address long-term goals; stress of "soft money" appointments; breakdown of peer review—"old boy" network funding decisions.

They also cited lack of continuity in funding, either as a result of disruption in a pattern of awards or a shift in federal policy or priorities, because such erratic funding affects morale and the ability to maintain research teams together, to support students, and to continue productive efforts. Other substantively relevant disadvantages included the limited nature of many funding sources that exclude agriculture or even agriculturally related basic research, as well as the potential for grant funds to divert, bias, or influence the direction of research or to accentuate research at the periphery of the station mission.

Overcoming each of these concerns requires a different strategy. The lack of continuity in funding and the limited willingness of some agencies to fund agricultural research are national concerns that appropriate national agricultural research committees must address. Controlling the negative influence of external funds on station priorities and mission, however, is part of the responsibility of the director. Although many directors raised this issue as a "potential" disadvantage, only one felt so strongly about it that a clear signal was given to his scientists not to consider application for external funds. Another admitted that funds were declined when they were considered to be outside the mission of the Station. Clearly, most directors encouraged external funding of projects and were satisfied that the potential biassing effects could be mitigated or overcome by sound management: internal administrative and peer review and conscious decision making prior to encouraging submission or approving submission of a proposal for non-USDA federal funding.

To quote one director, "The rare individual who can compete successfully for NSF or NIH grants and still make significant contributions to agriculture is a definite asset on any SAES faculty." Although the number of individuals combining such talent is rare, the number of stations possessing individuals complementing one another in their respective contributions, via basic NSF-funded projects and Hatch-funded basic and applied research, is clearly an asset of the agricultural research system.

Relationship of SAES
and General Science Programs

An extraordinary amount of criticism has been leveled at the agricultural science effort over the past decade. It has ranged from the Pound Report in 1972 to the Rockefeller Winrock Report in 1982. Rather than repeat again the charges of these critical assessments, it is valuable to remember the cycles of political support and political conflict associated with agricultural research since its organizational inception. Whether one reads Rosenberg's historical discussion of "Politics and Scientific Research" (1976, Chapter 10) or a history of SAES (Knoblauch *et al.*, 1962), the issues are the same: the need for better trained staff, more scientific research rather than inspection or regulatory activities, more basic understanding of fundamental mechanisms than of applied research, intellectual freedom for the scientist, and a longer-term perspective for research than that demanded by the farmers' organizations and agricultural leadership.

The conclusion of the early political struggles, albeit a continuing struggle, was the creation of new applied science disciplines, the strengthening of basic disciplinary efforts in genetics, biochemistry, and bacteriology, and the invigoration of general science at the land grant institutions. Legislation, in particular the Adams Act (1906) and the Purnell Act (1925), reinforced the research programs of SAES. The project system provided a new management tool to review, monitor, and control research activities. The next section discusses the current relations of SAES and general science.

What are the relationships of SAES programs with general science departments? Directors responded to this question with varying degrees of detail, so one cannot determine precisely the numbers and names of general science departments within the SAES; but two conclusions are clear: (1) fewer than a quarter of the Stations have *no* general science departments in the SAES, but even these often provide joint appointments or summer employment for general science faculty collaborating with SAES scientists or conducting SAES-funded research; (2) the vast majority of SAES have from one department to over 50 percent of their faculty located in numerous general science departments. These departments cover the entire range of general science subjects from botany, biochemistry, or genetics to seventeen different disciplinary units.

The funding of research in general science departments is widespread and includes direct funding, joint appointments, collaborative team project funding, and funding through intercollege institutes. Administrators and scientists relate through seminars, workshops, interdisciplinary institutes, and Ph.D. programs, and in administrative coordination of research programs. Projects are typically developed through faculty initiative within and outside the SAES. The norm and willingness of directors to fund general science faculty who propose appropriate projects is not universal; in at least one Station, the tradition of not funding projects in general science departments still operates.

What are federal mechanisms to improve linkages? Obviously, the most common and likely response is more federal resources. Such new resources, however, need to be targeted to improve effective linkages. Directors suggested increasing formula funds for allocation at the state level to fund basic science in line with the mission of the SAES, requiring federal support for basic science to address issues with agricultural potential, and requiring in federal competitive grant programs an integration of agricultural and general science.

In each case, the federal agencies would have to take responsibility for the appropriate allocation of funds to targeted arenas. Within USDA, the Cooperative State Research Service (CSRS) should serve as a lead agency to improve interagency efforts in bringing together general science and agricultural science. As one director noted, the competitive grants program in USDA has drawn more general science expertise to agricultural issues.

The above comments reflect a majority view; but one director felt that no federal action was necessary; a second believed that more impediments existed within the university system than at the federal level; a third argued that just as the federal dollars would draw general scientists to agriculture, such federal support could draw agricultural scientists away and detrimentally affect the SAES mission. Again, this last concern is not commonly held.

Are SAES scientists doing basic research? According to a recent CRIS analysis, 38 percent of the research funding in 1983 was addressing basic research questions. This varies from none in smaller stations to over 50 percent in larger stations. In 1982 scientists of SAES obtained over $57 million in research funding from the National Science Foundation and National Institutes of Health. This is clear evidence of the capability of SAES scientists to conduct basic research within the approved missions of SAES.

What are some ideas to stimulate increased participation of general science faculty in agricultural research efforts? The responses to this question represent an array of mechanisms currently being used by individual stations. In effect, these suggestions provide a summary of multiple, local brainstorming efforts to achieve such participation. Some are general ideas such as allocation or reallocation of funding for interdisciplinary, collaborative research and new programmatic thrusts requiring cooperation, e.g., biotechnology, acid precipitation, environmental toxicology, groundwater quality, with joint participation in state initiatives. More specific recommendations included extending regional research activity to include nonstation participants, establishing joint SAES/general science search committees for new faculty, and providing summer salaries for nine-month faculty.

In each case, the emphasis is on increased communication of interests and potential mutual contributions to a joint effort. Improving access to funding for mutually beneficial projects is an operational necessity.

What limitations exist for such involvement across SAES and general science departments? The principal limitation for involvement is the availability of funds in view of the wide range of research problems to be faced. Inadequate resources and no real increases in Hatch funds force the careful evaluation of all proposals and determination of congruence with station priorities. As noted above, even with limited resources, many directors are supporting projects in general science departments that address agricultural problems, especially when the focus is on "why" the problems exist.

Three serious perceptual problems do exist that seem to inhibit involvement. First, on the part of general science faculty, many still equate agricultural research with the stereotypes of an earlier era. These perceptions, often similar to those of the critics of the last decade, do not recognize the quality of new scientists, the willingness of directors to consider basic research projects, and the overall system concern with high quality science. Second, on the part of general administration, there is likewise a serious concern about the quality of agricultural science. As one director noted, his faculty were considered station scientists until the state's biotechnology initiative was successfully underway; at which point they became "university scientists." Third, on the part of directors, real concerns were expressed about the effect on morale of station researchers if traditional allocation of resources were shifted to general science departments and, importantly, the likely political consequences within the state agricultural and legislative leadership.

Resolution of these limitations is not achieved merely by additional resources and funding. The continual strengthening of SAES programs and communication across the university is essential to overcome the perceptual hindrances to involvement.

The Cornell Response

This effort at synthesis means that the detailed discussion of particular directors is submerged in the process of abstraction. To provide the flavor of one station response, the materials for the Cornell University SAES are included. Cornell University SAES cannot be claimed to be representative of any station except itself; but these issues have been discussed extensively in the director's office during the tenure of Theodore L. Hullar, director until June 1984, and Norman R. Scott, the current director.

Non-USDA federal funds are exceptionally important in the overall research program of the Cornell University Agricultural Experiment Station. In FY 1983 these funds amounted to $8.1 million, which is 19 percent of the total research budget for that year. This percentage has been increasing relative to the formula funds and remains steady as a proportion of all funds (e.g., 19 percent in FY 1978). These non-USDA federal funds play many roles and include support for basic research components of agriculturally important topics (e.g., environmental stress physiology, bovine reproductive physiology, disease mechanisms, acid precipitation, renewable energy resources and methods, and all manner of social and economic questions), as well as almost total support for many of our faculty whose emphases are so strongly in basic research that USDA grant programs are not applicable to them. We do not determine which non-USDA funds our scientists and faculty seek. They make that determination. Faculty members at Cornell are responsible for the conduct, direction, and quality of their own programs. We administrators assist that initiative. We point out sources of non-USDA funds for faculty and then provide assistance to them in applying for the funds.

The non-USDA federal funds augment the traditional USDA formula funds by providing the additional support needed for basic research (see above comments). The formula funds at our Station are generally used as support for start-up funds for new faculty, for pilot studies, for new directions for current faculty, for applied research that is regional or commodity oriented, for very long-term studies, and for developmental research at the research-extension interface.

The major advantages of non-USDA federal funds are that they are more plentiful for us than the formula funds (e.g., in FY 1982 formula funds were only 10 percent of total research funds) and provide an invaluable augmentation to formula funding. The major disadvantages of non-USDA funds are that the characteristics of their funding categories may be such as to direct a scientist's attention away from major state or agricultural commodity research into an interest for which funds can be obtained. Also, the lead time for grants from agencies such as NSF and NIH does not permit rapid redirection of research as results become available.

In our view the funds available for agricultural scientists (either USDA or non-USDA funds) should be dramatically increased so as to provide additional funding opportunities for faculty in all our disciplines. For example, competitive grant funds are needed, preferably within a USDA competitive grants program (to supplement the NSF, NIH, DOE, and other programs), for at least the following areas: biotechnology, environmental stress, animal reproductive physiology, animal nutritional biochemistry, plant biochemistry and physiology, agro-ecosystems, major increases in the current categories for biological stresses and human nutrition, soil and root system phenomena, food science and technology, postharvest technologies, chemical communication, and social and economic phenomena. If it is not possible to get competitive funding for such programs through the current USDA competitive grants program, then we all should seek them from other federal sources, harsh as that viewpoint may be. Until such USDA sources are available, the faculty at Cornell and many other locations will use all aspects of the non-USDA federal system to seek such funds to the extent that they are available.

The formula funds, of course, provide invaluable long-term support for many research efforts across the country, particularly those that (1) require very long-term studies, (2) are not easily accommodated by competitive grant categories, and (3) may be regional or commodity in nature. Such funds should continue with increases at least to meet inflation costs.

At Cornell the general science departments are called sections and they comprise the Division of Biological Sciences. Faculty in the sections are on budget lines in the College of Agriculture and Life Sciences, College of Arts and Science, and College of Veterinary Medicine. As such, the deans of these colleges are integral to the budgeting and personnel decisions for the sections and the division. (Two of the three colleges are intimately connected with the SAES and the missions of the USDA, of course.) Thus, we consider the faculty in the sections to be just as integral to the colleges (and the SAES) as faculty in traditional agricultural departments. Indeed, the traditional view of our SAES is that any faculty member in the university who wishes to do research on topics relevant to our mission should be encouraged and assisted in doing so to the extent that funds are available.

Any mechanisms for improved linkages between general science and agricultural departments must be incentive based. And incentives usually translate into money. Several mechanisms seem possible such as increased competitive grant programs inside or outside USDA that relate to the agricultural mission and grant programs (competitive, special grants, formula) that require multidisciplinary approaches in which both basic and applied researchers address the same problem. A number of program areas are obvious: plant biochemistry and physiology in relation to insect, disease, and environmental effects; animal nutritional biochemistry and reproductive physiology; social and economic factors, theories, and effects involved in the "demographic reversal"; biotechnology in the food industry, environmental enhancement, and production of chemicals; soil physics and chemistry in relation to fertility, porosity, and movement of nutrients and pesticides through soil; agro-ecosystems studies that, perforce, must involve researchers from a variety of disciplines; dry-land agriculture and unimproved pasture studies that similarly must involve plant succession and reproduction ecologists along with others; food science and technology wherein the chemical and physical properties of food are crucially important to its commercial use; human nutrition in relation to biochemical and physiological mechanisms and disease and health effects; social and economic factors affecting technology transfer from laboratory to field or production use; and many others of similar type.

Nonincentive based possibilities could also be considered. For example, annual reports from each SAES director could include a brief discussion as to who, how, why, and to what effect general science faculty have on agricultural programs. Although reports are onerous and may not be taken as seriously as the requester may intend, such a topical report would draw attention to the contributions of general science faculty to agricultural research. There could also be a requirement for each SAES director to earmark (allocate) formula funds to general science faculty for work on agriculturally related programs. Such a fundamental policy change concerning allocation of funds would clearly require extensive consultation with ESCOP and directors' associations.

Are our general science faculty doing research within our agricultural departments? Yes. The structure of our sections and divisions makes this easy. In addition, we have a number of basic-oriented scientists in all our agricultural departments who do such research and collaborate with others outside their departments.

What means can stimulate faculty in general science departments to participate in agricultural research efforts? Funding is the best way, both for agriculturally related topics and through programs requiring multidisciplinary approaches.

The second way is more psychological and perceptual. It requires each SAES director individually and the directors as a whole to think of "we" rather than "us-them." The contributions of collaborative, multidisciplinary research may not be as immediate as a targeted applied project, but a balanced program of funding is necessary.

What limitations exist for general science faculty being involved in SAES research programs? Few, if any. Funding helps. Collegiality works even better. Being sought after and welcomed probably works best of all. General science faculty members are intrinsically interested in how the world works, and because of that can get as interested in an agriculturally related problem as in any other. But we must begin to make the linkages and encourage the conversation.

Discussion

The criticisms of the agricultural research establishment have not been taken lightly by the Agricultural Research Service, the Cooperative State Research Service, or the State Agricultural Experiment Stations. Even when the criticisms have been unjustified, the misperceptions of critics have created a reality of myths that needs to be challenged and debunked by solid information about programs, philosophy, and actions taken to strengthen the science of agriculture.

One myth often expressed about SAES faculty and scientists is the applied nature of the research and the inability of SAES scientists to compete successfully in the national funding arena for non-USDA federal research support. The results of the Experiment Station Committee on Organization and Policy surveys concerning biotechnology research and NSF-NIH federal funding in 1982 of $57 million clearly demonstrate capability and success in this arena. The results of this survey of directors provide an administrative perspective on the significance and use of such non-USDA funds for research programs. One clear conclusion is the value and major role such funds play in station research. Although the dollar volume of these non-USDA federal funds varies by station, a nearly unanimous positive assessment by directors can only be interpreted as positive reinforcement for the efforts of scientists.

The advantages outweigh the disadvantages of such funds. Again, although many directors sensed the potential of such funds to divert scientists from the mission of the station, alert and conscious administrative management will protect the station from such biassing effects.

One subtle, yet major, contextual difference does appear in responses concerning who determines which non-USDA grant money scientists seek.

In stations with diverse and large programs, with heavy investments in basic science, and extensive linkages with general science departments, directors indicate that the key factor in seeking external funds is faculty initiative. In smaller stations, with a more applied and state-oriented research program and few or no general science connections, a closer administrative oversight seems to operate between director's office and faculty. The faculty typically still must exercise the initiative; but the normative structure of oversight, review, and close congruence with mission may inhibit the aggressiveness of such efforts.

Directors are typically supportive of basic science and fund research in general science departments given the limited resources available. Positive reinforcement of collaborative, interdisciplinary interaction and research is a commonly expressed norm. Importantly, mechanisms exist and others have been suggested to strengthen such intellectual linkages.

Active efforts to increase political support for Hatch formula funds and competitive grant funds as well as support for other agency science-funding programs are implied by the affirmation of value of such funds for basic and applied research. Demonstrable and successful integration of such research is a key ingredient in achieving the mission as defined by many directors. Such successes would also contribute to overcoming the misperceptions and stereotypes of the past.

The research reported here is another effort to debunk the myths about attitudes of SAES directors toward non-USDA federal funding of SAES research and the linkage of general science programs and SAES. Even with the extraordinary diversity in the system as a consequence of state and commodity specific orientations, a set of common themes was apparent in these responses. Are these responses congruent with the future needs of agriculture in the U.S.? A definitive answer may not be possible; but the awareness of these issues, the thought given to their resolution, and the actions of directors in management and research leadership, particularly rigorous control of quality and relevance of science in agriculture, are signs of the health and vigor of the system.

Notes

The discussion in this chapter is based on survey responses of individual directors, associate directors, and assistant directors of State Agricultural Experiment Stations throughout the United States. The conclusions and interpretation, however, are solely those of the author, who takes full responsibility for any errors of interpretation in the synthesis of the directors' responses.

References

Knoblauch, H. C.; Law, E. M.; and Meyer, W. P. *State Agricultural Experiment Stations, A History of Research Policy and Procedure.* Miscellaneous Publication 904. Washington, D.C.: USDA, 1962.

Lipman-Blumen, J., and Schram, S. *The Paradox of Success: The Impact of Priority Setting in Agricultural Research and Extension.* Washington, D.C.: USDA, 1984.

Rosenberg, Charles E. *No Other Gods.* Baltimore: Johns Hopkins University Press, 1976.

Rossiter, Margaret W. *The Emergence of Agricultural Science—Justus Liebig and the Americans, 1840–1880.* New Haven, Connecticut: Yale University Press, 1975.

U. S. Congress. Public Law 352. An Act to consolidate the Hatch Act of 1887 and laws supplementary thereto relating to the appropriation of federal funds for the support of agricultural experiment stations in the states, Hawaii, and Puerto Rico. 5 pp. (U. S. Congress, 84th, 1st session, Ch. 790, S. 1759), 1955.

9

The Emerging Role of the Computer in Managing for Excellence

Don Holt

Introduction

Colleges of agriculture and state agricultural experiment stations are very large complex organizations. The managers of these public research and educational programs range from nonacademics with managerial responsibility to deans and university-level administrators. Their ultimate goal is to produce a unique research and education program to serve a constituency or group of constituencies. They address both general and specific subjects and questions and establish a certain balance between basic and applied research and education. This involves authorizing individuals to make decisions, exerting effort to attract outside resources, and holding back a certain proportion of resources for contingencies. Much of the administrative decision making involves allocating resources to reward excellence and productivity and promoting promising lines of endeavor.

Some questions about the unique research and education program of the University of Illinois College of Agriculture have come to my mind since I joined the organization as an administrator. Are the characteristics of our program the result of conscious policy making? If so, how is that policy implemented? To what extent are the characteristics of our organization merely the result of a great number of individual transactions among faculty, administrators, and others, each pursuing specific goals and operating under his/her own philosophy? Have the goals and philosophies of strong-minded, unusually persuasive persons, or persons with positions of power, had disproportionate influence on the nature of the program? How much are the circumstances of the past and traditional philosophies and patterns of thought controlling present operations and planning? If it becomes evident that some major operational changes or shifts in emphasis are needed, how quickly and efficiently can we change? Can faculty and administrators, who are by nature independent thinkers, rugged individualists, articulate spokesmen, and who, by virtue of tenure, are immune to virtually any pressures to conform, actually develop a coherent, detailed, overall research and

111

educational policy and implement it? Would the capacity to develop and implement such a policy be good, or would it be better and less risky to let a more or less random process of reacting to individual situations structure the organization and shape its program?

The principal mechanism by which research policy is implemented in agricultural experiment stations and colleges of agriculture is the process of allocating resources to various research efforts. To make sure that this process is working to implement desired policy, it is necessary to do several things. First, it is important to identify the critical decision points. Sometimes, faculty feel frustrated, thinking that they have relatively little input to the decision-making process. They may not realize that as they seek outside support for their programs, as they serve on committees identifying new positions to be filled and on search committees, promotion committees, and research policy committees, and as they allocate resources within their own research programs, they are indeed implementing research policy.

The people (positions) who have important input and decision-making authority at the critical decision points should be identified. When the critical decision points, their importance in the overall allocation process, and who has the principal decision-making authority in each case have been determined, the power structure is defined and can be systematically modified to achieve certain goals.

It is obviously important in managing a research operation to have adequate and accurate data to support decisions. Thus, another step in designing a system to implement research policy through allocation procedures is to identify and develop the necessary data bases to support decisions at each of the critical decision points. Agricultural experiment stations within colleges of agriculture in land grant institutions generate vast amounts of internal data. The decision-making process could easily become mired in data. Thus, it is essential not only to develop the data bases but to develop appropriate computer software to analyze the data bases. The data bases should relate directly to the criteria for decision making. The decision-making process can be refined by describing as quantitatively as possible the formulae by which various items of data are integrated to arrive at a decision. It is important to determine and specify how various items are weighted in the decision-making process.

Decision makers in experiment stations and colleges of agriculture are constantly frustrated by the problem of translating subjective information into quantitative decision support data. In many situations, such as decisions on salary increments, a great deal of subjective information is reviewed, but the final decision is a number. Thus, in real life, qualitative information becomes quantitative. Individual decision makers should elucidate as clearly as possible the decision-making procedure, identifying the input variables and describing how they are quantified and weighted to arrive at the final quantitative decision. Such an exercise has great potential value because, when the model is revealed to the people affected by the decisions, it shows them how they should operate to maximize their benefits from the decision-making process. Thus, by creating such a model, decision makers can in fact shape a program and implement desired policy.

We are trying to envision a coordinated, systematic decision-making process for the College of Agriculture at the University of Illinois. We have not as yet formally developed the models except in a few specific situations but have identified critical decision points, decision makers, criteria for decisions, and some of the necessary data bases. In the following discussion, each of the critical decision points, not necessarily in order of importance, is described. When the system has been more clearly defined, it will be possible to analyze historic data bases to find out which decision processes have been most important in implementing research policy in the past, and whether or not the research policy implemented was that desired by various decision makers in the institution.

Critical Decision Points, Decision Makers, Decision Criteria, and Data Bases

Decisions on Hiring New Faculty

In general, the most important budget lines in most departmental and college of agriculture budgets represent faculty positions. Faculty positions are ordinarily described in terms of subject matter. A faculty member is a soil physicist, an animal nutritionist, a gerontologist, etc. In the institutions with which I have had experience, namely, the University of Illinois and Purdue University, there has been considerable historic continuity in the general subject matter expertise in faculty lines. Decisions to be made on faculty lines are often of the form, "Do we replace this person with a person in the same subject matter area or shall we shift in another direction?" Such decisions are made by ad hoc faculty committees, formally elected faculty advisory committees, department heads, directors, deans, and campus administrators. In most institutions the final decision rests with the Board of Trustees or a comparable governing body. Ad hoc faculty committees, faculty advisory committees, and department heads have the principal decision-making power in this situation, with directors, deans, and higher administrators tending to sign off on most decisions.

The criteria for faculty line decisions include the centrality of the subject matter in the university's role, the importance of the subject matter to society or some branch of society, such as farmers, agribusiness people, etc., the teaching and other needs of specific departments, and the perceived availability of support in various areas. Decision makers try to take a long range view on faculty line decisions, because, with the tenure system, the decision will influence the program for many years in most cases.

It is readily observed that departments that are most effective in identifying and attracting highly talented, aggressive, productive individuals set the stage for a disproportionate allocation of resources into their programs. Such a person will attract more grants, generate more compelling requests for internal funds, receive a higher salary, attract more attention, and otherwise benefit the program of the department more than someone less talented, productive, and aggressive. The faculty line decision, therefore, becomes extremely important for colleges and departments as they compete for both internal and external resources. Realistically, the decision on subject matter in that situation is not as important as identifying the appropriate individual for the position and allocating adequate resources to attract and keep the person in the position.

In some institutions, when a faculty position is vacated by retirement or other termination, the support for the position reverts to the college or the university and is reallocated to faculty lines according to some set of priorities. This, of course, shifts the relative influence of faculty, department heads, and college- and university-level administrators. This approach has some advantages in that it creates great flexibility, permitting relatively drastic changes in direction and restructuring. For example, resources freed by retirements and terminations can be redirected to totally different subject matter areas to address new needs or recently emerging themes. An institution might decide it needed more support personnel or more funds for supplies and expenses and can reallocate regularly recurring resources for those purposes. Thus, a substantial restructuring can occur.

Centralized decision making on faculty lines has some disadvantages, depending on how much input is solicited from faculty, department heads, deans, etc. The decision makers may be too far removed from the disciplines to make good decisions. Soliciting and processing input from faculty, department heads, etc., is time consuming and often frustrating, at least in those situations where there are wide differences of opinion.

Nevertheless, there are great potential advantages in deliberately interrupting the historic continuity of position lines. Ideally, each department should maintain a prioritized list of position lines and other needs. Presumably, department heads sitting with directors and a dean, as an administrative committee, could meld departmental priority lists into college-level lists. The prioritized items could be obtained as funds are freed by retirements and terminations or as new recurring funds become available. Thus, the structure and program of a college would develop according to a unified plan with a minimum of influence of past history. It probably isn't surprising that when decisions on faculty positions involve historic continuity considerations, they are sometimes influenced by whether or not the incumbent's feelings will be hurt if his position is not filled by someone working in the same subject matter area. Under our present circumstances, most institutions cannot afford to be strongly influenced by such concerns. The problem is avoided when the decisions about filling faculty lines are separated in time and space from decisions on retirement and termination.

The data bases required for effective decision making relative to faculty lines and other positions include a list of existing lines with projected retirements and terminations for some period of years into the future and a prioritized list of needed faculty lines, other positions, and other needs for funding. It should be extremely helpful to have a subject matter analysis of each existing and proposed line, perhaps according to the categories identified in the CRIS system. Analysis of such data bases would yield a step by step description of the transition from the present program to one envisioned for the future, thus, allowing decision makers to see if the specific decisions are leading to the coherent overall program desired in the future, if the program is addressing the important themes of the future, and if the organization is going to have the desired structure. Other information in the faculty line data base and prioritized list should include division of the faculty member's effort among research, teaching, and extension and proposed rank of a new faculty member or other employee.

It is harder to describe the data bases needed to assess the centrality of various positions in the university's, college's, or department's role, their importance for meeting societal needs, and the projected availability of support in various areas. Some of this information is quite subjective. One approach is to seek many opinions, perhaps, through computer-administered questionnaires. Data on the consensus or lack of consensus of views of various groups could be assembled. Their views could be quantified and weighted and included in a data base. More objective analyses might stem from assessing the economic and social importance of various activities in terms of value added, numbers of workers involved, social benefits, etc. I believe agricultural institutions have tended to avoid such analyses because they are obviously enormously complex and will lead predictably to considerable controversy. Nevertheless, there is little hard evidence that the way institutions are now structured relative to subject matter is the best way to serve the needs of agriculture and the rest of society. Possibly, some of the precepts of portfolio theory would be applicable to investment in agricultural research and development.

Decisions on Salary Increments

There are two important aspects to salary change decisions. First, decisions are made as to how much of a total allotment will be allocated to "across the board" increments (or cuts) and how much to merit increases. These decisions may be made at any one of several levels. Directives may come from higher administration or even from state governments as to what standard increases will be approved. In most institutions, department heads have considerable influence on salary increments and, of course, department heads differ considerably in their philosophy regarding merit increases and in their ability to deal with the inequities created by merit increments.

Criteria for determining across the board increases include salary levels relative to those in comparable jobs outside the institution and peer positions in other institutions, internal perceptions of where the institution should rank salary-wise, and most important, the level of resources provided by funding agencies, primarily state governments. Criteria for merit salary decisions include productivity as evidenced by publications, innovative nature of teaching and extension programs, national and international activity and recognition, cooperative attitude and activity, grant-attracting ability, etc.

Most departments and colleges require individual professors to supply activity reports detailing their publications, committee activities, awards, recognitions, and other evidence of quantity and quality of scholarly production. This information lends itself particularly well to computerized data bases. It would probably be relatively efficient to maintain these data bases at a college level. Information could be keyed into the data base by secretaries as the activities occur and as the publications and assignments are generated, thus avoiding the time-consuming, inefficient, once-yearly, desperate attempt to assemble the data. Appropriate programs could be developed for analyzing these data bases, making comparisons, and determining appropriate increments. Some institutions already have mechanisms for soliciting subjective information on the quality of publications, presentations, teaching, and other activities of faculty members, and on their general cooperative attitude, willingness to help students, etc. Of course, such subjective information has political overtones. An appropriately designed questionnaire, administered, analyzed, and secured by a carefully planned piece of interactive computer software, should maximize objectivity.

Decisions on Promotions

Promotions serve to allocate resources, at least in those situations where a salary increment accompanies the promotion. Even if a salary increment is not involved, the person being promoted is moved to another salary range in which both general and merit salary increments will probably be larger. Thus, a department that gets more faculty promoted will have more resources allocated to its program.

The principal decision makers on promotions include any faculty member who is solicited for information on the productivity and quality of work of his/her colleagues, ad hoc and regular committees from which such information is solicited, formally constituted promotion and other evaluation committees at department, college and university levels, directors, deans, and campus or university administrators. These decision makers must obtain information on productivity as evidenced by publications, innovative teaching and extension programs, national and international activities, recognitions and awards, and other information similar to that used in determining merit salary increases. The same data bases used for merit salary increases are helpful in making decisions on promotions.

Decisions on the Quest for Gifts, Grants, and Contracts

The quest for gifts, grants, and contracts is becoming more important in the total funding effort of most agricultural experiment stations and colleges of agriculture. The primary decision makers in this quest are individual faculty members who decide what funding agencies to approach and thus select at least the general and in some cases the specific subject matter to be researched. Those decisions are driven in many cases by the quantity of funds available for various efforts within the range of the individual's expertise. Faculty teams may decide to seek support from an agency or group of agencies. Administrators likewise develop proposals. These tend to be broader than those of individual faculty members because they seek support for a wide range of activities involving many people.

The criteria for decisions concerning the quest for gifts, grants, and contracts include subject matter interest and expertise of individual faculty groups and administrators, perceived availability of funds, individual goals and missions, departmental goals and missions, college and university goals and missions, and perceived societal needs. From this, it follows that data bases on funding sources, criteria of funding agencies for selection of proposals to be funded, procedures and formats for proposals, names and backgrounds of persons on selection committees, and success ratios in past experiences with agencies would be useful in the decision-making process.

Each investigator and administrator should have a clear knowledge of his/her position responsibilities, so that the quest for gifts, grants, and contracts does not lead him/her too far astray from certain institutional objectives. This concern becomes somewhat academic as institutional funds become increasingly difficult to obtain. The scientific literature constitutes an extremely valuable data base in the quest for gifts, grants, and contracts. Thus, highly automated systems for accessing the scientific literature make it possible for those developing proposals to have the latest and most comprehensive information available, to summarize it most effectively, and to generate the ideas most likely to capture the imaginations of grantors, contractors, and benefactors.

Obviously, as more and more of the funding of a university comes through competition from outside the state institutional framework, greater decision-making ability relative to research subject matter passes to the givers, grantors, and contractors who supply the money. This is not a bad situation as long as the givers, grantors, and contractors have the same goals and wish to serve the same clientele as the university. In agricultural research, the trend toward greater support from national competitive grants is causing a shift in focus from our historic farmer and agribusiness clientele toward our peer scientists in other institutions, who serve on proposal review and selection committees.

Other Decisions on Allocation
of State and Federal Funds

Deans, directors, and department heads are involved in allocating state-supplied, regularly recurring funds for nonacademic personnel and supplies and expenses. They make these decisions, presumably, according to their perception of the importance and needs of specific programs. Deans and directors allocate to departments and departments to specific programs. Useful data bases include the numbers of professorial and professional people in each department, some data on relative costs of doing research

PART THREE

Disciplinary and Interdisciplinary Research

10

The Pretechnology
Agricultural Sciences

Robert E. Evenson

Introduction

The conventional distinction between applied and basic research is misleading in many ways. It suggests that a strong division exists between basic science, which is only generally influenced by economic considerations, and applied research, which is strongly influenced by economic considerations. The agricultural sciences are often simply classed as applied research even though within the agricultural sciences, classification of research into basic and applied categories is attempted. In this chapter I argue that explicit recognition of a category of scientific activity termed "pretechnology science" is required for a more complete basis for understanding the contemporary agricultural research system in the U.S.

The Organization and Structural
Relationships of the Agricultural Sciences

It is useful to think of the structure of scientific and technological research activities in much the same way that one thinks of the structure of economic activities. There are many parallels. First, a high degree of specialization is apparent in research activities. The counterpart of firms producing consumer goods in the economy is the applied research organization producing new technology for a clientele. In the private sector most R&D conducted by private firms is directed to the invention of new technology. Some public sector applied research organizations such as medical schools and agricultural experiment stations also specialize in the production of technology for a clientele.

There are also counterparts in the research world to industrialized firms specializing in the production of "intermediate" goods from basic materials (e.g., a firm producing ball bearings from basic metals). These are the "pretechnology sciences." Relatively little pretechnology science is conducted in the private sector. A number of pretechnology science research programs

121

exist in the public sector, but as will be noted presently, not all are efficiently structured. The counterparts of the basic materials industries are the basic or general sciences in the scientific world.

Figure 10.1 provides a schematic picture of the structure of research programs of relevance to agriculture. Four vertical levels of research activity are depicted. Level IV activities (portrayed here as the furthest downstream) are described as technology screening and subinvention. They are the activities required to "adopt" and to a minor degree "adapt" new technology produced at Level III. The firms and organizations engaging in Level IV activities are agribusiness firms dealing directly with farmers, extension services, and farmers themselves. These Level IV firms and farms form the clientele for the agricultural research system. Both preharvest and postharvest industrial firms are engaged in Level IV activities.

Level III activities are those research efforts directed toward the invention of new technologies. This includes mechanical, chemical, biological, managerial, and policy technology. Agribusiness firms engage in both Level III and IV activities. Indeed, most mechanical and chemical invention is actually produced by private firms. Increasingly, the private sector is producing more biogenetic technology as well (Evenson, 1983). Most of these private sector inventions are entitled to intellectual and property right protection under U.S. patent and copyright law and under the terms of the U.S. Plant Variety Protection Act (1970 as amended in 1980).

The public sector USDA-SAES research system also engages in Level III invention. In many cases it does so in direct competition with the private sector (as in soybean breeding). Much of its invention, however, is in technology fields where intellectual property rights are not sufficient to stimulate private invention. Much plant and animal breeding and managerial and policy technology (produced by economists) falls into this category.

The truly special feature of the USDA-SAES research system (at least of parts of it) is that it engages in research designed to produce "pretechnology" science products or knowledge (Level II). The distinction between pretechnology science and invention is important because the products of pretechnology research are not subject to intellectual property protection, while much invention is. Pretechnology science means research directed specifically toward producing discoveries that enable and assist technology invention. That is, pretechnology science is specifically an intermediate product supplied to invention-producing firms. This intermediate product is critical to both public and private invention producers.

Level II activities are the most critical to an effective research system, particularly over a long time period. Level II research is by and large beyond the range of influence of existing intellectual property right laws, and, hence, little of it is undertaken by the private agribusiness sector. It is also generally not conducted in institutions specializing in general science research (for reasons discussed below). Unless this type of research is specifically institutionalized with strong links to Level III research, it tends not to be done effectively. The USDA-SAES system has achieved some success in pretechnology science by specifically developing agricultural science disciplines and supporting research programs to undertake pretechnology research (Evenson, 1983; Bonnen, 1983).

Scientific Exchange

This structure of research specialization is, as noted, roughly parallel to the organization of an economy with units specializing in basic materials production, intermediate goods production and final (consumer) goods production. Low cost and efficient exchange mechanisms are the key to specialization in a normal economy. The same is true for a research economy. The exchange mechanisms in an economy are prices and associated transactions costs. Efficient prices are those that reflect consumer demand preferences in final consumer goods markets. For intermediate and basic goods markets, efficient prices reflect demands derived from consumer preferences. Prices also reflect the supply or cost side in each market.

There is not extensive pricing in technology and scientific knowledge markets. Intellectual property rights (patents), however, do provide a basis for pricing of a certain range of inventions by allowing an inventor to exclude others from practicing his invention for a period of time. Patent law is instructive regarding the importance of credible information. The patent is awarded to an inventor only on the condition that the invention is accurately and credibly described. Indeed, a patent is not valid if it can be shown that it did not meet the requirement that it fully "disclose" the nature of the invention.

The exchange of knowledge between different specialists is not efficient if it does not meet standards of credibility accepted by all parties. To facilitate this exchange, scientists have developed specialized language and measurement procedures to achieve more exactness and hence credibility. In the inexact sciences this language is the language of statistics, experimental design, and accepted measurement techniques.

Researchers generally specialize in particular research problems within one of the levels depicted in Figure 10.1. For example, plant breeders specialize in the invention and development of improved varietal technology in a particular commodity (Level III). They exchange information horizontally, i.e., within Level III, with other specialists working on similar problems. Similarly, a research specialist in plant physiology (Level II) exchanges information horizontally with other plant physiologists. Vertical intellectual exchange, however, is required for effective functioning of a research system. The Level III plant breeder must communicate and exchange knowledge with both upstream (Level II plant physiologists) and downstream (Level IV extension workers) specialists in the system if the economies of specialization are to be realized.

Scientific communication systems were developed primarily to facilitate horizontal exchange in the general or basic sciences. The journal paper, the specialized language, and elements of style are chiefly designed to allow

124

FIGURE 10.1 Structural Relationships in Agricultural Research Programs

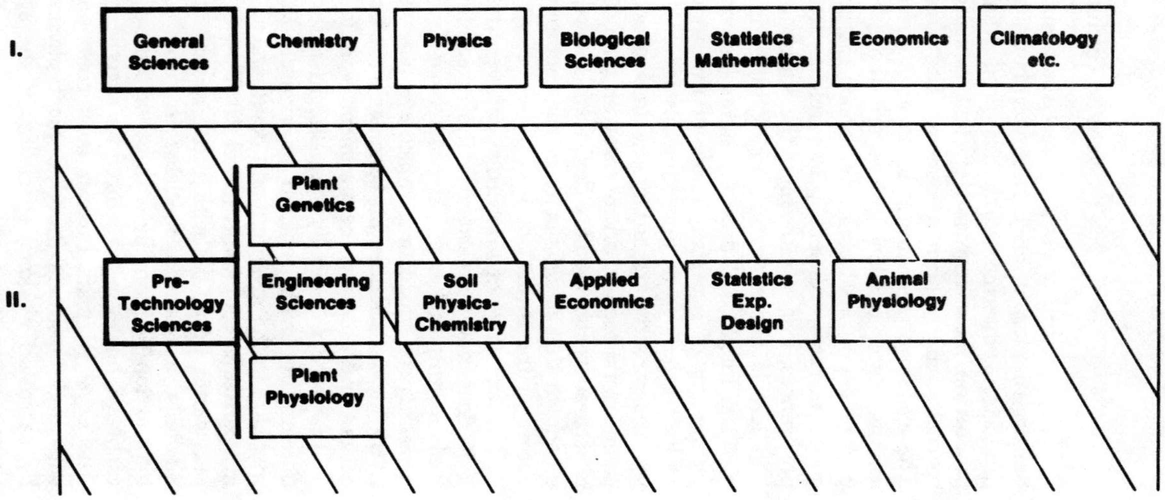

I.

| General Sciences | Chemistry | Physics | Biological Sciences | Statistics Mathematics | Economics | Climatology etc. |

II.

Pre-Technology Sciences

Plant Genetics

Engineering Sciences

Plant Physiology

Soil Physics-Chemistry

Applied Economics

Statistics Exp. Design

Animal Physiology

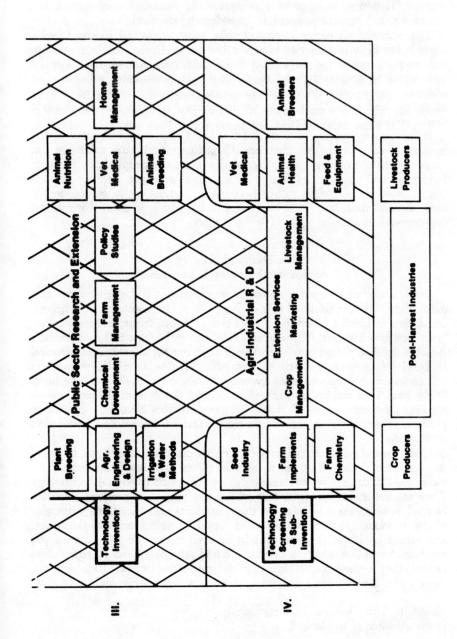

scientists working on similar problems to disclose findings quickly to one another. This disclosure process facilitates the cumulation of verified hypotheses that constitutes scientific knowlege in the field.

The scientific exchange apparatus that really originated in the Level I sciences has been modified and used in the Level II pretechnology sciences and even to some extent in Level IV activities. Knowledge must be communicated and exchanged to facilitate the cumulation process. The scientific paper with its specialized language, usually associated with a discipline, and with "standards" set by scientists themselves has been a useful vehicle for horizontal exchange at all levels.

It has also served as the vehicle for vertical exchange, but some of the features of scientific papers that actually facilitate horizontal exchange can hinder vertical exchange. Language and style, for example, can facilitate horizontal communications within a field but seriously hamper vertical communication. Indeed, as will be noted later, vertical exchange is generally more difficult than horizontal exchange, and unless it is given institutional support and incentives, little of it takes place.

The Demand Side of
Agricultural Research Systems

Vertical exchange from a demand perspective calls for upstream communication. We can think of this exchange in an economic sense. The real demanders of Level III inventions are Level IV firms, farms, and institutions (including governments). They demand technology because it is economically valuable. Intellectual property rights such as patent rights enable this demand at Level IV to be articulated to Level III. That is, Level III researchers will endeavor to supply technology because they can actually sell it to Level IV buyers. This market is quite efficient, and the correct demand signals are sent upstream. Level III researchers or inventors have an incentive to produce inventions that are of maximum value to downstream consumers or clientele.

Unfortunately, intellectual property rights don't work well for much of the output of Level III research because rights have not been defined for most managerial and policy technology or for much biological technology. They are generally not defined at all for the output of Level II research. Normal markets do not exist for these products. Yet, the basic principles of the economic market remain valid. Level III inventions are demanded and valued by Level IV firms and farms even if they do not have to pay for them. Level II products are demanded and valued by Level III researchers because they are intermediate goods in the production of Level III inventions. Hence, the demand for Level II products is a derived demand.

How Can This Demand Be Articulated
in the Absence of a Market?

The general science establishment holds what might be termed a supply side view (see the following section). It essentially contends that Level I (science) and Level III (technology) research are independent of each other in terms of their production processes. The argument is that science builds on past science not on past technology. Technology in turn builds on past technology not on past science directly. It is further argued that leaders and administrators of science are well aware of the ultimate value of scientific findings but that the process by which these findings work their way into the invention processes is long and complex. This view then holds that there is little scope for pretechnology science per se and that the attempt to conduct pretechnology science will be unproductive and that the effort to consider explicitly and directly pretechnology economic value in research problem choice and conduct "contaminates" the process of science. This view is in contrast to the current critical perspective on the USDA-SAES system as reflected in "Science for Agriculture" (Rockefeller Foundation, 1982). If one accepts this view, there would be only two main forms of research activity, general science (Level I) and invention (Level III) induced by intellectual property rights.

The USDA-SAES system demonstrates that effective Level III invention can be undertaken in the public sector. The demand articulation mechanisms are partly due to the integration of USDA-SAES research with extension and partly due to the political support mechanism in the states. Extension staff play an important role in conveying technological information to farmers, but they are also important in conveying information from farmers to researchers. They, in effect, facilitate exchanges of intellectual property in both directions in the absense of a market. They also facilitate exchange between public sector researchers and private sector researchers to some extent. This form of exchange conveys information to the public sector inventor as to the value of his or her invention.

The political support process, particularly at the state level, is critical because it reinforces the exchange process. Interest groups (e.g., dairy farmers) find that they can influence both research spending and conduct. They can, in a sense, buy inventions from public sector research firms. They can offer more support for particular types of research that they see as important and valuable and less for research that they see as being of little relevance. Research administrations, of course, do not act entirely on these demand side signals. They consider supply side signals as well. Nonetheless, this mechanism of demand articulation is very important to the conduct of Level III research.[1]

Demand articulation in the USDA-SAES system is also important to the establishment of Level II research programs within the USDA-SAES institutional structure. This type of research is generally not supported from "above." It is developed only within an institutional structure where a strong derived demand exists. The USDA-SAES system has used two devices to institutionalize Level II research. First, it has created specialized disciplines—agricultural science disciplines—which maintain much of the form and process of the general science disciplines but are differentiated from them along explicit technology production lines. Second, it has reinforced the research-extension marriage by adding teaching—notably graduate teaching—as an institutional function. These agricultural science disciplines generally attempt to span both Levels II and III research. In some institutions, departmental structure is used to integrate Levels II and III research programs. In almost all cases, Level II research programs are institutionally embedded in the USDA-SAES system (see Ruttan, 1982).

The Supply Side of the
Agricultural Research System

The essential issue on the supply side is that intellectual property is produced in a "sequential building block" process. Most research projects or invention projects attempt to add an incremental improvement to an existing "core." A technology core is typically incorporated or embedded in past inventions such as machines and materials. Technology can also be described as a form of intellectual property. A scientific core may also be related to materials, plants, and animals, but it is typically in a more abstract intellectual property form. The scientific paper is the medium of exchange for this knowledge.

One often finds clusters of cores existing and expanding in parallel fashion until some are revealed as inferior at which point they tend to die out. New cores are continually being initiated by pioneering research efforts, but these are usually spin-offs from older cores. It is seldom the case that science cores spin off new technology cores. New cores do not always thrive and grow.

This building block process is reinforced by the procedure of science. The scientific paper is designed to allow efficient horizontal exchange of intellectual property between researchers working around the same core or cluster of cores. It is not always necessarily well-suited to facilitate exchange between researchers working to expand a scientific core and researchers working to expand a technology core (i.e., vertical exchange). Researchers in the general sciences do not see a strong need to devise better exchange mechanisms between themselves and researchers in distant cores, particularly technology cores. They do not support the establishment of pretechnology science cores because many of these cores do not have high growth potential, i.e., high growth potential in a purely quantitative sense. Since the general sciences are largely immune from demand side pressures, they tend to choose research problem areas on strictly supply side grounds. They work on problems that are promising regarding the rate of core expansion. They rightly recognize that pretechnology problems often do not have high growth potential. In many cases a long period of work is required simply to establish the materials and methods of a pretechnology science before it can become productive.

Yet, as the agricultural sciences have demonstrated, pretechnology sciences can be highly productive in an economic sense because they form a bridge between science and technology. As they develop they respond to both demand and supply interests. Pretechnology science sacrifices pure knowledge growth potential in favor of economically valuable growth potential. It modifies the forms of communication to facilitate vertical exchange with downstream (Level III and even Level IV) researchers as opposed to simple horizontal exchange.

From an economic efficiency perspective, the pretechnology sciences should give weight to both demand and supply factors. They should produce a mix of products that are of maximum economic value downstream for any given level of resources invested. A general science research program usually does not ignore the downstream value of increments to scientific knowledge. Horizontal citations of scientific papers tend to be given more weight than downstream (or upstream) citations. To the economist these weights are wrong because they should reflect the economic value of the research. Downstream citations are, on average, probably more valuable than horizontal citations because they reflect the fact that inventors with economic interests valued the research in question. Upstream citations are also valuable because they indicate that the upstream researcher is interested in the economic value of the knowledge produced. Effective pretechnology science generates downstream citations and upstream (to Level I) citations. It also tends to cite downstream and upstream research papers and inventions.

Level III invention itself has a different economic value depending on the number of economic units affected by an invention and the cost-reducing or value-enhancing effect of the invention. Efficient allocation of research resources requires that the expected value marginal product of each research component in a portfolio of research projects be equalized. For Level III components, this will be based on the probabilities of achieving a given invention or inventions and on the expected economic value of the invention.

For Level II components, the value marginal product depends on the probabilities of achieving or discovering new scientific information and on the expected increase in the downstream inventions made possible. While these values may be difficult to measure, they are nonetheless real. Furthermore, these values are enhanced by scientific credibility because this improves the likelihood that downstream supply effects will occur and that upstream demand effects will be recognized. With higher levels of scientific credibility, more specialization can take place. It is in this sense that one can argue that scientific credibility is more important in the agricultural sciences where both vertical and horizontal exchange is critical than in a general science where only horizontal exchange is valued.

Evidence for Efficient Exchange:
Citation Data

So far, the theme has been developed that scientific credibility and the associated standards of clear communication facilitate intellectual property exchange and allow for specialization of research effort. From a casual knowledge of departmental and disciplinary organization in agricultural research, it is clear that a great deal of specialization exists. However, it does not follow from this that a great deal of exchange, particularly between pretechnology research and invention research, takes place. Three studies that have some bearing on the matter are reviewed here.

The first study is based on patent citation data (Wright and Evenson, 1980). The intent with these data is to measure intellectual property exchange between a special type of USDA-conducted, pretechnology research and downstream invention by both public and private inventors. The research in question is postharvest research on foods and textiles and related materials by the USDA. Most of this research is conducted in the USDA's regional research centers. The second study is based on scientific paper citation data related to USDA-SAES postharvest technology (PHT) research. The third study is a study of the relationship between research investment (including pretechnology science) and agricultural productivity.

The USDA patent data are of special interest because much of the research on utilization of farm products is designed to produce "pilot-inventions," a special type of pretechnology research. This pretechnology work is expected to lead to a pilot invention that will lower the cost of downstream private invention. One test of whether real intellectual property exchange takes place is provided by data on subsequent citations of USDA-patented inventions. When applications for U.S. patents are examined by patent office examiners for determination of validity, the examiner (not the inventor) cites prior inventions (usually a prior patent) as "next best art." In effect, the examiner is citing pretechnology inventions. In some fields of pretechnology research, the patent citation data are also of interest in this regard.

Citation patterns for the sixty-four and 102 textile patents granted to the USDA in the 1967–1969 period and the thirty-one and fifty-one textile patents granted to the USDA in the 1977–1979 period were examined. A comparable sample of forty-eight food and thirty-two textile patents granted to U.S. inventors and thirty food and thirty-one textile patents granted to foreign inventors was drawn for the 1977–1979 period. Regarding the prior patents cited, in both periods the USDA patents cited a higher proportion of USDA patents than the USDA proportion in the "citable pool." USDA patents in both food and textiles were less than 5 percent of U.S. patents granted. Nonetheless, USDA citation predominated over prior private patents. Of more relevance is the fact that the private U.S. origin patents cited prior USDA patents to a much greater extent than the citable pool would indicate. Roughly 20 percent of the private U.S. patents (drawn from the same patent class) in this period cited prior USDA art.

The 1967–1969 USDA patents were also compared with a 1967–1969 sample of private patents to see whether they generated comparable numbers of subsequent citations. By 1980, 78 percent of the USDA food patents and 6 percent of the USDA textile patents had generated subsequent citations. The comparable figures for the private sample were 70 percent for food and 81 percent for textiles. The average numbers of citations were roughly comparable, indicating that USDA pilot invention does stimulate downstream invention.

The second study examines the scientific publications in 1976–1979 and the citations generated by these publications in 1979 of 456 principal investigators in two postharvest technology fields (RPA 403, new and improved fruit and vegetable products; RPA 406, new and improved food, textile, and industrial products from field crops). The principal investigators were located in the USDA regional laboratories and in state experiment stations.

Regression methods were utilized to analyze the factors determining the number of publications, the number of citations generated, and the proportion of "horizontal" citations generated. The study found:

1. Institutional affiliation (USDA or SAES) did not significantly affect publications, citations generated, or the horizontal proportion of citations.
2. Publications and citations generated were lower in RPA 403 than in the other two fields.
3. Size of the research unit did not affect publications or citations but was inversely related to the horizontal proportion of citations. Larger research units tend to produce more vertical citations.
4. Experience of the researcher does not have a large impact on the number of publications or citations, but it does affect the horizontal proportion. Young researchers generate predominantly horizontal citations. As researchers age, the proportion of vertical citations rises.
5. Researchers with early (pre-1970) histories of high citation generation and high horizontalness of citation produce more current citations (1976–1979), and their current citations are more horizontal. That is, researchers with records of high citation generation in the past generate higher levels of publication and citation currently, and those are less vertical. This suggests a trade-off between the quantity of citations and the verticalness of citations.

The final study of relevance is a study of productivity change in U.S. agriculture (Evenson, 1982). This study proceeded in two stages. In the first stage a total or multi-factor productivity index was computed from farm income and related data for each U.S. state for the period 1949 to 1972. This index is a measure of the change in the efficiency of farm production in the state. It is, of course, measured with error. The second stage entails a statistical analysis of the factors determining productivity. It explicitly recognizes that productivity is measured with error.

The determinants of productivity growth include previous investments in extension, schooling of farm operators, business cycle effects, and past investment in both applied technology invention (Level III) research and pretechnology science research (Level II) in the state and in other states.

A procedure was utilized to estimate the "time-shape" of the research-productivity relationship and the spatial transfer pattern of this relationship.

Pretechnology science in this study was somewhat arbitrarily defined to include the following categories of research undertaken in state agricultural experiment stations and USDA work in the states: botany, zoology, genetics, plant physiology, animal physiology, phytopathology, and soil science. (Recent research data can be more accurately classified.)

The study concluded:

1. The number of years between research spending and maximum impact on productivity was five to seven years for Level III research and eleven to fifteen years for pretechnology Level II research.
2. The proportion of state research produced impacts realized in states other than the investing states was .43 for Level III research and .68 for Level II research.
3. A $1,000 investment in year T in Level III research was associated with a maximum productivity gain valued at $12,000 in the 1948–1971 period. The comparable value for a $1,000 investment in pretechnology science Level II research was $4,500. Thus, investment in pretechnology science yielded a high rate of return to investment. The specification was that Level II research impact was realized entirely through its enhancement of Level III research. Thus, pretechnology science was shown to raise the productivity of Level III research.

Concluding Comments

In this essay, the case for demand-induced pretechnology science as part of applied research systems has been argued. Evidence is reported indicating that the pretechnology sciences have been a productive component of the agricultural research system in the U.S. Further study is required to understand better the institutional arrangements required for effective management of pretechnology science in agricultural research systems. The incentives for vertical intellectual exchange, for example, appear to be critical to effective system development.

The growth of private sector Level III agricultural research makes an understanding of intellectual property exchange processes even more important. This is because private firms generally invest little in Level II research because they usually cannot capture a high proportion of the benefits from this research. There is an important public sector role in conducting Level II research because of this. Effective Level II research in the public sector, however, requires effective intellectual exchange with downstream private sector firms. The public sector must receive demand signals from downstream, and it must communicate its research findings effectively downstream.

There is also reason for concern in the USDA-SAES system with Level I to Level II exchange. The biological sciences, largely organized as Level

I sciences have, in fact, produced a substantial body of Level II scientific knowledge of high value to Level II researchers. The USDA-SAES system has been slow to respond to these developments, and Level II research in critical microbiology areas has not expanded as rapidly as it has in the private sector.

Thus, the USDA-SAES system, while pioneering in the development of effective pretechnology sciences, is currently under considerable stress from developments both upstream in the Level I sciences and downstream in private firm research. Its response to this stress will be an important determinant of its productivity in the future.

Notes

1. See Wright and Evenson for an analytic argument as to why pretechnology science will grow less rapidly than general science.

References

Bonnen, James T. "Historical Sources of U.S. Agricultural Productivity: Implications for R&D Policy and Social Science Research." *American Journal of Agricultural Economics* 65(5):958–66, 1983.

Evenson, Robert. "Agriculture." Chapter 5 in R. Nelson (ed.), *Government and Technical Progress: A Cross-Industry Analysis*. Elmsford, New York: Pergamon Press, 1982.

————. "Intellectual Property Rights and Agribusiness Research and Development: Implications for the Public Agricultural Research System." Yale University, Economic Growth Center, Discussion Paper #350, 1983.

Rockefeller Foundation. "Science for Agriculture." Report of a Workshop on Critical Issues in American Agricultural Research. Jointly sponsored by the Rockefeller Foundation and the Office of Science and Technology Policy, Executive Office of the President, held at the Winrock International Conference Center, Morrilton, Arkansas, 1982.

Ruttan, Vernon W. *Agricultural Research Policy*. Minneapolis: University of Minnesota Press, 1982.

Wright, Brian, and Evenson, Robert. "An Evaluation of Methods for Examining the Quality of Agricultural Research." In *An Assessment of the United States Food and Agricultural Research System*, volume II, Office of Technology Assessment. Washington, D.C.: Government Printing Office, 1980.

11

A Century of Periodic Research on Soil Conservation

Louis Swanson

Introduction

Periodically, soil erosion is determined to be at a crisis level. In fact, a strong argument can be made that it is a persistent resource crisis in the United States (cf., Batie, 1982; Rasmussen, 1982; Sampson, 1981). Much of the burden for both basic and applied soil conservation research has fallen upon the experiment stations of America's land grant universities. Both technical and socio-political factors have tended to determine the scope and priorities of soil conservation research. The bulk of this conservation research has occurred during three general historical periods when the adverse effects of soil erosion have been considered to be particularly unacceptable or visible. These periods and concomitant policies are (1) the progressive era with the Country Life Commission, (2) the Great Depression and the agricultural policies of the New Deal, and (3) the past decade and the move toward a supposed "free market" agricultural policy.

Research scientists in each of these periods have approached the problem of soil erosion differently. The progressive era researchers appear to have spent much of their efforts in defining the problem in terms of soil exhaustion. New Deal researchers were primarily concerned with the introduction of agronomic conservation techniques such as contour plowing and structures (e.g., terraces) in conjunction with supply-control programs. The present period emphasizes research on supposed technical solutions such as conservation tillage with the hope that such technical panaceas will be rapidly adopted by farmers.

This study examines selected experiment station publications from around the country in an effort to document the generally shared research focus on soil conservation research for each of these periods. However, it is necessary to note at the outset that only general tendencies are discussed. Each period, including the present, has important exceptions that may serve either to modify or eclipse the dominant conservation research assumptions of their period. Unfortunately, the breadth of the general tendencies discussed here precludes an examination of such important anomalies.

Role of the Market

During the past century, experiment station scientists have developed a myriad of technical and agronomic options for conserving the nation's soil. Indeed, impressive amounts of intellectual and capital resources have focused upon effective management of soil erosion. However, economic realities often have meant that the great majority of farmers have not adopted these techniques. Agricultural economists, and more recently rural sociologists, have proposed that without favorable market conditions or federal policies, the mere existence of effective conservation techniques will not assure their adoption. Instead, these experiment station social scientists believe market conditions may be the most important determinant in the use or nonuse of soil conservation practices.

Historical analysis indicates that economic and social factors may be associated with the relative inability of farmers to practice soil conservation during the past century. Margolis's (1977:43) examination of resource exploitation among frontier societies, including areas of the United States during the nineteenth century, identifies the following minimum of five economic factors that favored resource degradation among frontiers:

(1) demand for a valuable cash crop, (2) the presence of free or inexpensive virgin frontier land, (3) unstable market conditions affecting the price received for the crop, (4) the accessibility of markets, and (5) the availability of credit.

Margolis also notes that the quality and slope of the land and the influence of unpredictable natural conditions such as draught will also contribute to soil erosion.

The central assumption of Margolis's work is that short-term benefits will outweigh long-term benefits for future generations under conditions of economic stress. In particular, uncertain natural conditions, price fluctuations, and scarce labor and capital resources may each militate against the adoption of nonprofitable conservation technologies. It is not difficult to apply Margolis's argument to present commercial farming conditions. Rasmussen (1982:14) offers the following assessment of how current economic uncertainty and debt have contributed to soil erosion.

As the cost-price squeeze began to make itself felt in the late 1970s, farmers sought to produce more on the same land and with the same equipment. Many had to do so because notes were due this year, not five years from now. One way to meet the note was to cash in on previous soil conservation practices, to plow up grasslands, to stop strip cropping, to give up contour plowing. . . . The result? Land more subject to rain and wind erosion, powdery soil more likely to be washed into the streams.

Rasmussen is not alone in his assessment. Batie (1982), Wessel (1983), Sampson (1981), and others point to the pressures for farmers to put scarce capital resources into production rather than conservation and to recent incentives to increase grain production in response to the expansion of farm export trade in the mid 1970s.

Pre-Progressive Conservation Efforts

Soil erosion was a serious social and environmental problem during the colonial period. Henretta's (1974) review of New England social histories includes numerous references to the association among increased population pressure on the land, low levels of capital accumulation by yeoman farmers, and high rates of soil erosion. Similarly, southern historians document the socially and environmentally exploitive character of tobacco and cotton agriculture (Eaton, 1961; Genovese, 1967; Hahn, 1984). Even Thomas Jefferson "appealed for conservation of the soil" (Rasmussen, 1982:4). In 1841 agronomist Chitwood Allen told the Kentucky State Agricultural Society that the areas with the best soils were deteriorating rapidly (Genovese, 1967:98). Unsurprisingly, the colonial period and the early decades of the nineteenth century were characterized by the emergence and proliferation of conservation societies. Agricultural and geological societies throughout the country performed rudimentary agricultural research (Genovese, 1967:Ch.4). Among these antebellum agricultural historians is the common theme that soil erosion was less the result of careless or unwitting farmers than the consequence of economic pressures similar to those discussed by Margolis.

The Civil War marked an important divergence from notable concern with soil erosion. Rasmussen (1982:5) states:

> Post Civil War pressures on many farmers to increase production in order to pay debts as farm prices fell encouraged soil exploitation rather than conservation. . . . [The] Civil War, westward expansion, and the pressures of commercial agriculture diverted attention from soil conservation for almost three-quarters of a century.

Concern for soil erosion ebbed as recessions and depressions follow one after another during the final decades of the century. An initial federal government response aimed at helping commercial farmers increase their productivity in the face of unfavorable markets was the passing of the Hatch Act in 1887, which provided federal support for a national system of agricultural experiment stations. "There were, of course, some agriculturalists, particularly in the new colleges of agriculture and the USDA, who [also] urged care of the soil" (Rasmussen, 1982:5). But their few voices seem to have been overwhelmed by unfavorable political and economic conditions. It was at this time that the political confrontation between agricultural producers and urban elites was fueling the emergence of the Populist and Progressive movements, respectively, neither of which was particularly conservation oriented (the Progressives were quite conservative in political orientation).

The Progressive Period

Perhaps the most significant political movement for rural people during the early years of the twentieth century was the urban-based Country Life Movement (Danbom, 1979). This movement was made up of social and physical scientists, educators, businessmen, and other urban elites. They were primarily concerned "with raising rural America to a twentieth-century standard of social and economic organization and efficiency" (Danbom, 1979:vii). They were convinced that farm production and rural people were lagging behind the rest of the nation. The types of structural changes these urban-oriented professionals wished for rural people were extensive. Danbom argues that these reformers, while well meaning, believed a renovated agriculture would more adequately serve the needs of an urban-industrial society, the most important of which was the need for cheap food. Consequently, a primary interest was in increasing farm productivity, a chief obstacle to which was soil exhaustion.

The Country Life Movement was associated with the Progressives (Danbom, 1979:46-47). Both movements were interested in the industrial, social, and economic advancement of the nation based upon the social and economic assumptions of capitalism tempered by a unique form of corporate liberalism.

Soil conservation was defined by researchers in terms of reducing soil exhaustion. However, this term was primarily associated with soil fertility and not soil erosion. This distinction underlies an important perception of soil management that demarcates the research of this period from later research. It is a perception that was tightly bound to the primary goal of the Country Life Movement, i.e., increased agricultural productivity. Not inconsequentially, many of the leading institutions and corporations politically underwriting the Country Life Movement stood to benefit directly from increased farm productivity. Danbom (1979:40) documents the formation of business organizations such as the National Fertility League as well as extensive local-level publications and lectures aimed at helping farmers utilize the knowledge emerging from the agricultural experiment stations. Conservation, though, was not a visible dimension of the productivity message. Furthermore, Danbom (1979) argues this urban-based movement did not fully assess all of the consequences of their proposals including increased landlessness, tenancy, and poverty among disfranchised farm families not owning the necessary skills and capital.

During this period soil scientists "held that soil damage and lack of fertility were caused largely by chemical processes involved in plant growth and that erosion was of minor consequence" (Rasmussen, 1982:6). The first University of Kentucky Extension circular based upon experiment station research reported that the "greatest single problem confronting the farmer is soil exhaustion" and that this was primarily a threat to "soil fertility"

(Smith, 1981:296). A 1910 Missouri publication on soil management contained a passing note that "A feature which should be given greater attention in this region [the Ozarks] is the prevention of washing on these rolling hills" (Miller, 1910). However, even this comment only pertained to winter cover crops, and not the prevention of soil erosion during the cropping season.

By 1924, concern for soil erosion appeared to be increasing. Another Missouri Experiment Station bulletin reported that the loss of nutrients due to soil erosion might be more serious than the loss of nutrients due to the raising of crops (Duley, 1924). However, only sod and crop rotations are mentioned as methods of controlling soil erosion. Among the bulletins examined between 1900 and 1923, most soil management articles mention methods of increasing soil fertility without significant comment on either soil erosion or washing. Significantly, among these same bulletins there is a clear understanding that a decline in soil fertility can be associated with economic conditions.

While soil erosion was not a central issue in most of the bulletins, one 1919 Iowa State College bulletin stands out as an example of future concerns. In their article entitled "Soil Erosion in Iowa," Eastman and Glass (1919) examine a multitude of methods for controlling gullying, sheet erosion, and hill erosion. They directly tie erosion to economic conditions, even concluding that continuous erosion may eventually significantly decrease soil fertility and the value of the land.

Other scientists also were becoming concerned with soil erosion. Two USDA bulletins entitled Soil Conservation and Corn Cultivation argue that farmers must control soil erosion if their farms are to maintain production (Rasmussen, 1982:5). One such enlightened soil scientist was Hugh Hammond Bennett, who was a leader in arguing that sheet erosion, though less obvious than gullying, was just as great a threat to the continued high productivity of the land. His 1928 paper Soil Erosion: A National Menace served as a bridge between the laissez faire progressive approach to soil erosion and the federal programs of the New Deal. The research vehicle for this transition was the 1930 Agricultural Appropriations Act.

New Deal

The public and scientific interest in soil erosion increased with the double crises of the Great Depression and the Dust Bowl. The combination of economic and ecological crises provided the necessary political legitimacy for agricultural economists to investigate the association between socioeconomic conditions on the farm and soil erosion. The introduction of social science research into the farm problem represented an important policy innovation. For the first time, government planners were not only making a connection between economic conditions and soil loss, but they were advocating direct state intervention.

The New Deal represented a particular perspective of the political economy that radically departed from the market-oriented views of the Progressives and later administrations. For example, Rexford Tugwell, a key agricultural adviser:

argued that for [soil erosion control programs] to be effective they must deal not only with erosion but also with such intertwined problems as farm tenancy; unplanned urban growth, which took farmland out of production; low farm income, which made conservation practices uneconomical for many farmers; [and] more general economic problems caused in part by a weakened agricultural economy (Roeder, 1982).

The conservation assumptions of the New Deal planners were relatively straightforward. It was reasoned that soil conservation could not occur until the farm economy improved. Even President Roosevelt, who campaigned for soil conservation along with his agricultural program, stated that the root problem of the Dust Bowl was a depressed farm economy. Roosevelt's advisers argued that farm income was low due to depressed urban incomes and farm overproduction. Their diaries, reports, and policies indicate a perceived contradiction between what was rational economic behavior at the farm level and what was rational at the national level. They also imply that economic rationality at the farm level may be ecologically irrational. It was proposed that while it was apparently rational for a farmer to expand his or her scale of operation, the aggregation of such farm level decisions at the national level, given relatively inelastic demand, would create a situation in which supply would greatly exceed demand, thus forcing farm prices down. Since demand was more difficult to manipulate, it was argued that supply-control programs were necessary. By reducing the amount of agricultural products on the market, the price for farm commodities would rise. Furthermore, Roosevelt's advisers assumed that by reducing production while raising prices, farmers were more likely to practice soil conservation. In terms of soil conservation, it was concluded that the primary conservation problem was understanding how physically to control erosion and then diffuse the information to the farmer. The experiment stations picked up much of the new demand for conservation research.

Soil erosion was treated as both an agronomic and social problem. New Deal planners linked soil conservation with agricultural programs designed to protect small farms, augment farm income, and establish regional planning. This linkage is particularly evident in the following quotes from the 1937 Report of the President's Committee on Farm Tenancy, which include such statements as "Erosion of our soil has its counter part in erosion of our national society. . . . The one wastes natural resources and the other, human resources" and "Tenancy has contributed to soil erosion" (Roeder, 1982:21–22).

Perhaps, the clearest indication of the New Deal's simultaneous concern for soil conservation, its association with the farm economy, and the long-term undesirable consequences of soil erosion was Roosevelt's warning that "the nation that destroys its soil destroys itself" (Rasmussen, 1982:8).

The New Deal triggered the first great surge in land grant conservation research. The primary foci of the agronomic research during this period were either on the characteristics of soil structure or on farm-level techniques such as contour plowing, strip cropping, terracing, etc. What is interesting is that Thomas Jefferson and Edmund Ruffin had made similar proposals during the colonial period (Rasmussen, 1982:4). It took almost 150 years to resurrect these soil conservation practices.

By the 1930s agronomists were making a clear distinction between soil exhaustion and soil erosion. The 1935/36 Annual Report for the Agronomy Department at Ohio State states:

> That the maintenance and improvement of soil productivity depends first of all upon the cropping system is supported by steadily increasing evidence. This seems to be true whether exhaustion or erosion is the chief factor causing soil deterioration (Salter, 1937:18).

The rate of soil erosion was being monitored on a national level for the first time. Agronomists were beginning to search for economic thresholds above which soil erosion was deemed intolerable. They were also carefully researching various agronomic techniques such as terraces, contour plowing, and other conservation structures for various types of soils and slopes. A 1937 bulletin entitled *Soil Erosion in Ohio* provides an excellent example of how the erosion crisis was perceived and the conservation strategies necessary to abate it. Selections from this bulletin include the following (Cunrey et al., 1937:23):

> Accelerated erosion has been a major contributing factor in the depletion of soil resources in Ohio.

> Control of erosion is largely a matter of proper land use in combination with such soil conserving practices as crop rotations, contour tillage, field stripping, strip-cropping, terracing, pasture improvement, and protection of woodland from fire and grazing.

However, agronomists were not as concerned with the economic and social dimensions for soil erosion as is evident in the absence of any mention of farm structure among the causes of soil erosion in the bulletin cited above. This concern was the domain of agricultural economists.

A landmark social science study was Reed and Falconer's *The Effect of Land Use and Management on Erosion* in 1937. The purpose of their detailed examination of 100 Ohio farms "was to determine in a limited area some of the factors within the control of man which had contributed to erosion" (Reed and Falconer, 1937:18). They report a strong association between the extent of soil erosion and the type of farm. For example, they note that the "less eroded farms had more livestock and less cash crops" (p. 18). In addition, they note that soil erosion was correlated with the amount of land devoted to clean-cultivated crops, close-grown crops, and woods. On these points, their research was highly consistent with the work of agronomists. However, the most important findings deal with the relation of the farms' social and economic structure and soil erosion. They register the following conclusions (Reed and Falconer, 1937:19):

Erosion is associated with land tenure. There were a lower percentage of tenancy, a longer period of occupancy per tenant, and a longer period of ownership per owner on the less eroded farms than on the more severely eroded farms.

Erosion is associated with the owner's financial condition. A smaller percentage of the less eroded farms were mortgaged, and the mortgage indebtedness per acre was smaller on the less eroded farms than on the more severely eroded farms. A lightening of the mortgaged indebtedness would evidently assist in the solution of the problem.

It was experiment station social science research such as this that provided the scientific evidence in support of the New Deal's assumptions about political economy. Experiment station social science research on the social and economic correlates of soil erosion provided the necessary empirical legitimacy for the New Deal conservation programs.

As social science experiment station research progressed, it became more sophisticated in its farming systems models. A particularly troublesome question first posed during the New Deal was the extent to which economic and social factors were farm or national problems. A particularly good study conducted at Iowa State College in 1951 by Heady and Allen (1951) was entitled "Returns From and Capital Required for Soil Conservation Farming Systems." The intent of the article was to determine the extent to which farms could take on conservation practices without depending upon the larger society for help. They argue that given the profit goals and short-term planning horizons of farmers and the external costs of soil erosion to society, both farmers and society must confront two questions: (1) At what economic threshold is conservation profitable? and (2) How should society provide help to farmers when conservation is not profitable? They answer the first by noting that conservation practices that are profitable merely require educating farmers of their worth. However, they answer the second by proposing that public assistance is necessary for farmers when conservation practices cost more than they return in the short-term.

Heady and Allen (1951:358) provide evidence from an extensive survey from which they infer that the virtual absence of conservation practices on Iowa farms was in order of importance due to "(1) [a] lack of capital (including related risks), (2) adjustment to varying economic conditions, (3) limited remaining period of farm operation, and (4) lack of technical knowledge." Heady and Allen go on to state that farmers are not necessarily irrational in their decision not to adopt conservation practices. They propose that farmers with limited capital may be making a sound decision not "to borrow additional capital, lower [their] equity position and hence endanger the survival of [their] farm business (1951:358)." They conclude that farmers with large debt to asset ratios often cannot put scarce capital into conservation practices. The more recent assessments of Margolis (1977), Rasmussen (1982), and others on economic causes of soil erosion resemble old wine in new bottles.

The transition to the present period of research is not nearly as well defined as the change from the Progressive period to the New Deal. Many of the New Deal supply-control policies were gradually modified or, in many cases, discarded during the Eisenhower administration. However, it was in 1956 that the Eisenhower administration experimented with the Soil Bank. This was a new USDA program that was designed to combine soil conservation with price support programs. The program ended in 1958. Since then, public incentives for soil conservation have declined slowly. Probably, the most clear demarcation between the declining programs of the New Deal and the move toward a market-oriented agricultural economy was the rapid development of conservation tillage in the late 1960s and early 1970s, coupled with the expansion of agricultural trade abroad.

The Market-Oriented Conservation Program

Between the New Deal and Nixon's New Federalism, assumptions about farm change and soil conservation underwent a transformation. A key delineator of this change was the simultaneous emergence of arguments against massive federal intervention in the farm sector and for unregulated farm commodity markets. Increased production and not conservation became the policy theme. By the early 1970s Secretary of Agriculture Earl Butz was exhorting farmers to increase the size of their operations as well as their productivity. Presently, the Reagan administration is calling for a sharp decline in the federal government's role in farming (i.e., a departure from the New Deal legacy) and movement toward a "market-oriented agricultural economy." Uncoincidently, this call for reductions in the farm program occurs at a time when farm payments are at an all-time high and the fiscal crisis of the State is deepening. With the exception of some of the Carter administration proposals, the Executive branch for most of the last two decades has emphasized increased farm productivity and reduced government involvement in commodity markets.

Such assumptions concerning the role of government in farming are not dissimilar from those of the progressive era. However, there are important differences. Given the legacy of the Dust Bowl and conservation research during the New Deal, the control of soil erosion has remained a part of the research agenda. Evidence of the continuing concern for conservation includes the Resource Conservation Act of 1977 and more recently the fledgling steps toward the establishment of a conservation reserve in the 1985 Farm Bill. The emphasis in conservation research has tended to focus on developing conservation techniques that will not significantly hurt productivity such as the various forms of conservation tillage systems. It is assumed that market forces will create incentives for long-term financial benefits from soil conservation such that farmers will practice conservation if the information is diffused properly and the market is allowed to work freely.

This market-oriented approach represents a clear departure from the policy assumptions of the New Deal. Overproduction is no longer considered to be a problem. Instead, the problem is one of increasing farm productivity, locating new markets abroad, and changing food consumption habits at home in order to increase domestic demand. In short, this approach attempts to manipulate demand rather than supply. The years following the Russian Wheat Deal saw this principle work as farm prices rose. However, by the late 1970s, farm production had expanded beyond international demand, and the U.S. dollar had begun to increase greatly in value. Consequently, farm prices dropped, and international markets shrank as U.S. agriculture became the supplier of last resort.

Social science research after the New Deal was highly influenced by the adoption and diffusion model. The hegemony of this model reflected the conservative politics of this period. An important consequence was the virtual abandonment of macroeconomic and social structural explanations of soil conservation behavior similar to the work of Heady and Allen. This social-psychological model divided farmers into the dubious categories of "innovators" and "laggards." Laggards were either simply misinformed about the benefits of soil conservation or too traditional in their value orientation. It was concluded that erosion control was primarily a matter of educating farmers. By the early 1970s there was evidence that soil erosion was once again approaching historically high rates, thus indicating that the model was limited (see Batie, 1982; Sampson, 1981; Wessel, 1983). While educating farmers is a necessary dimension of any conservation effort, the limitations of this approach suggest that it is not a sufficient condition.

There is a remarkable similarity between the assumptions of the progressive era and those guiding conservation research and policy over the past two decades. The Country Life Movement was characterized by an emphasis on farm productivity and was led by agribusinesses—who would directly benefit from overproduction through reduced farm prices and increased farm dependency on factor inputs. While there is no equivalent to the National Fertility League set up by agribusinesses in the 1900s, the Nashville symposium on conservation tillage in October 1984 represented a similar agribusiness effort to encourage farmers simultaneously to increase productivity, practice conservation, and purchase agricultural inputs, especially agricultural chemicals.

It is not surprising, then, that experiment station conservation research of the past decade has increasingly emphasized the development of conservation-, reduced-, and minimum-tillage and chemical agriculture. Conservation tillage represents a major effort to develop a technological panacea for the control of erosion that will not reduce productivity, will not require federal programs to implement, and can be diffused to farmers easily. Indeed, it is very difficult to argue with these characteristics. However, experiment station research also suggests that conservation tillage may have significant ecological and economic limitations that could reduce its overall effect in reducing soil erosion. Of particular concern is the increased use of agricultural chemicals that compensate for reduced cultivation. It may be that conservation tillage will substitute one ecological crisis for another. If the goal of conservation is to reduce resource degradation, then, it is possible that conservation tillage, which requires increased chemical application, may not be the universally viable option that it first appeared to be.

Recent social science research suggests that the adoption of conservation tillage technologies is probably more a consequence of labor-saving characteristics than either farmer conservation altruism or the result of complicated long-term computations by farmers of discount rates for conserving soil (cf., Buttel and Swanson, 1986; Swanson et al., 1986). In other words, the assumption that the market will provide incentives for soil conservation continues to be unsupported.

Conclusions

Undoubtedly, experiment stations have made enormous contributions to understanding the causes of soil erosion and the development of conservation practices to control erosion. Indeed, the experiment station system is the primary contributor to the accumulation of knowledge on soil management during the past century. However, social science research at experiment stations also provides considerable evidence that the mere existence of effective erosion techniques does not mean that farmers will practice ecologically and economically sound farming systems. Such social science conservation research strongly suggests that investment in most conservation practices is an allocation of capital that does not contribute to short-term profitability in an industry constantly posed on short-term needs. There is little to no evidence that the marketplace provides the economic incentives necessary for the adoption of most conservation practices. The major exception is conservation tillage.

During the past century, soil erosion has risen and fallen as a widely perceived crisis. A recurring criticism directed toward conservation research is that, if such research is so good, why is erosion still a nemesis? The answer is quite simple. Research can help provide conservation practices to reduce soil erosion. But an economic environment favorable to the short-term profitability of conservation practices appears to be necessary. If economic conditions are not favorable to the widespread use of the practices developed by experiment station research, then soil erosion will continue to occur.

The experiment stations have been remarkably sensitive to changing perceptions of both farm structure and soil erosion. The New Deal researchers were quick to distinguish between declining soil fertility and soil erosion and to associate erosion with socioeconomic conditions. More recently, agronomists, agricultural engineers, and social scientists have picked up on conservation tillage. The public can expect the experiment station system to be a leader in developing new conservation practices. However, it cannot expect experiment stations to create the economic and social conditions that promote voluntary use of soil conservation methods or to pursue research that is contrary to the dominant public policy. For example, regenerative agriculture is not politically popular at this time, yet, there is evidence that by reducing costly factor inputs, a medium-sized farm can maintain and even increase profits while practicing conservation. However, various approaches to regenerative agriculture are not a high research priority; apparently because they do not increase total production (i.e., do not contribute as much to overproduction).

A consistent finding of land grant social scientists since the New Deal is that most farmers are economically hard pressed and consequently are not likely to invest scarce capital on the possibility of long-term profitability. As Heady and Allen (1951) have noted, it may be economically rational for farmers to ignore the advice of the experiment station researchers. Experiment station agronomists and agricultural engineers have provided the farmer with a myriad of excellent techniques for controlling soil erosion, but few farmers are able to incorporate them into their farming systems. Technological panaceas are unlikely to reverse current resource degradation in American agriculture (Office of Technology Assessment, 1986).

In each of these eras, a dominant theme has been the promotion of increased efficiency of farm labor and capital while maximizing production and profits. Until recently, it was almost unquestionably assumed that increased efficiency meant the top of the production curve for biological transformations. However, some agricultural scientists and economists are now proposing that the point of diminishing returns on the profitability curve may occur well before the point of diminishing returns on the production curve. It may be that farmers can maintain their total profits by cutting back on increasingly expensive factor inputs. Such a strategy would reduce overall production, which in turn might reduce aggregate supply and thereby increase the prices received. The farmer, then, might benefit from both decreased costs of production and increased farm prices. While this example is speculative and may offer only temporary relief, it does indicate an alternative to a key assumption influencing research priorities of experiment stations during the past century. It also provides an example of experiment station research that would unlikely be conducted by the private sector since it would not enhance agribusiness profits. In short, it is an example of public research in agriculture—research that the private sector may either be unable or unwilling to perform. Conservation research at the experiment stations historically has been a leading and exceptional example of such public research.

References

Batie, Sandra S. "Policies, Institutions, and Incentives for Soil Conservation." Pp. 25–40 in Harold G. Halcrow, Earl O. Heady, and Melvin Cutner (eds.), *Soil*

Conservation Policies, Institutions, and Incentives. Ankeny, Iowa: Soil Conservation Society of America, 1982.

Buttel, Frederick H., and Swanson, Louis E. "Soil and Water Conservation: A Farm Structural and Public Policy Context." Pp. 26–39 in Stephen B. Lovejoy and Ted L. Napier (eds.), Conserving Soil: Insights from Socioeconomic Research. Ankeny, Iowa: Soil Conservation Society of America, 1986.

Cunrey, G. W.; Cutler, J. S.; and Pascall, A. H. "Soil Erosion in Ohio." Bulletin No. 589. Wooster: Ohio Agricultural Experiment Station, December 1937.

Danbom, David B. The Resisted Revolution. Ames: Iowa State University Press, 1979.

Duley, F. L. "Controlling Surface Erosion of Farm Lands." Bulletin No. 211. Columbia: University of Missouri Agricultural Experiment Station, April 1924.

Eastman, E. E., and Glass, J. S. "Soil Erosion in Iowa." Bulletin No. 183. Ames: Iowa State College Agricultural Experiment Station, January 1919.

Eaton, Clement. The Growth of Southern Civilization, 1790–1860. New York: Harper and Row, 1961.

Genovese, Eugene. The Political Economy of Slavery. New York: Vintage Books, 1967.

Hahn, Steven. The Roots of Southern Populism. New York: Oxford University Press, 1984.

Heady, Earl O., and Allen, Carl W. "Returns from Capital Required for Soil Conservation Farming Systems." Research Bulletin No. 381. Ames: Iowa State College Agricultural Experiment Station, May 1951.

Henretta, James H. "The Morphology of New England Society in the Colonial Period." Pp. 191–210 in Theodore K. Rabb and Robert I. Rotberg (eds.), The Family in History. New York: Octagon Books, 1974.

Margolis, Maxine. "Historical Perspectives on Frontier Agriculture as an Adaptive Strategy." American Ethnologist 4(1):42–64, 1977.

Miller, M. F. "Soil Management in the Ozark Region." Bulletin No. 88. Columbia: University of Missouri Agricultural Experiment Station, July 1910.

Office of Technology Assessment. Technology, Public Policy, and the Changing Structure of American Agriculture. Washington, D.C.: Government Printing Office, 1986.

Rasmussen, Wayne D. "History of Soil Conservation, Institutions and Incentives." Pp. 3–18 in Harold G. Halcrow, Earl O. Heady, and Melvin L. Cotner (eds.), Soil Conservation Policies, Institutions, and Incentives. Ankeny, Iowa: Soil Conservation Society of America, 1982.

Reed, E. H., and Falconer, J. I. "The Effect of Land Use and Management of Soil Erosion." Bulletin No. 585. Wooster: Ohio Agricultural Experiment Station, July 1937.

Roeder, George H., Jr. "A Discussion." Pp. 19–24 in Harold G. Halcrow, Earl O. Heady, and Melvin L. Cotner (eds.), Soil Conservation Policies, Institutions, and Incentives. Ankeny, Iowa: Soil Conservation Society of America, 1982.

Salter, Robert F. "Crop Rotation as the Foundation of Soil Conservation." Fifty-fifth Annual Report of the Ohio Agricultural Experiment Station. Wooster, Ohio: Experiment Station Press, 1937.

Sampson, R. Neil. Farmland or Wasteland: A Time to Choose. Emmaus, Pennsylvania: Rodale Press, 1981.

Smith, J. Allan. The College of Agriculture of the University of Kentucky. Lexington: Kentucky Agricultural Experiment Station, 1981.

Swanson, Louis E.; Camboni, Silvana M.; and Napier, Ted L. "Barriers to Adoption of Soil Conservation." Pp. 108–20 in Stephen B. Lovejoy and Ted L. Napier (eds.), *Conserving Soil: Insights from Socioeconomic Research.* Ankeny, Iowa: Soil Conservation Society of America, 1986.

Wessel, J., with Hantrian, M. *Trading the Future.* San Francisco, California: Institute for Food and Development Policy, 1983.

12

Development of an Interdisciplinary, Interagency Integrated Pest Management Project in the Western United States

Gary A. McIntyre

The Evolution of Integrated Pest Management in Crop Protection

Traditionally, control of pests on crops was based on a firm foundation of biological principles that predicted the interaction between host and pest in the agroecosystem. After World War II, however, development of organic pesticides (e.g., 2,4-D and DDT) caused a marked shift in the philosophy of pest control. The broad foundation of control based on biological principles was essentially abandoned for a pesticide-oriented system in which a specific pest or group of pests were controlled by a pesticide with little regard to the impact on the total agroecosystem. Increased reliance on pesticides for control has produced a substantial change in the varieties of individual crops developed and how they are grown. Current crop varieties were developed to respond to greater usage of pesticides, more fertilizer, and increased irrigation (NAS, 1975a). This has led to an increasingly homogenous cropping system in which the crop has a narrower gene pool and is more susceptible to attack from pests (e.g., corn to southern corn leaf blight) (NAS, 1972, 1975b). This genetic vulnerability has, in turn, created higher demand for use of pesticides at higher concentrations and greater frequency. This practice has reduced the number of natural predators and parasites of pests normally found in the cropping system, thus allowing, in some instances, rather minor pests to assume a new, major importance.

More recently, evidence has been gathered (NAS, 1975b) that shows that pesticide resistant races of pests have developed in response to the intensive use of certain pesticides. Both reduction in natural enemies and development of resistance of pests to pesticides have created a situation whereby either new methods of control must be developed or still more pesticides used. As the latter is neither cost effective nor environmentally safe, it is clear that new, economically sound means of controlling pests must be developed.

This calls for the integration of control procedures into a management system based on the understanding that pest species are single components of a complex agroecosystem[1] and that the interactions of these components transcend the artificial barriers created by the traditional, taxonomically oriented crop protection disciplines (Glass, 1976). While such a system may require utilization of pesticides, use is incorporated into an overall system that will ensure that pesticides are applied strategically in appropriate quantities to assure control with minimal adverse effects upon the environment.

Development of such systems is referred to as Integrated Pest Management (IPM). IPM, as originally conceptualized, dealt with one pest or complex of similar pests (boll weevil–cotton or boll weevil and bollworm complex–cotton) on a single crop. While this approach provided significant progress toward control of pests in these rather narrowly defined systems, it did not address the impact of these control measures on an entire agroecosystem. This has led to a redefinition of IPM as a procedure that integrates pest control in an economically and ecologically sound manner within the total cropping system. Clearly, integrated pest and agroecosystem management (IPAM) must be expanded and refined if we are to maintain economic crop production. The IPM approach utilizes multitactics in a compatible manner to maintain pest damage below economic thresholds (Intersociety Consortium for Plant Protection, 1979). To establish IPAM programs, interactions such as those between pests, pests and parasites, pests and predators, pests and antagonists, or pests and hosts and the effects of cultural practices, soil type, irrigation practices, microclimate, and surrounding fauna and flora in a specific geographical area must be considered. Development of an approach that recognizes the large number of interactions occurring within the system calls for an interdisciplinary effort incorporating not only traditional crop protection disciplines but also disciplines not ordinarily involved in agricultural sciences such as systems analysis, microclimatology, and hydrology. This interdisciplinary effort must provide current information on pests to be controlled, their natural enemies, crop phenology, weather, etc., and the interaction of each of these with the others. The ultimate measure of success of such a program will be the ability of the IPAM research component to provide to the extension component a cost-effective, environmentally safe program that will be acceptable to the farmer and rancher. In addition, this program must expose and train students in these new philosophies and technologies to assure that they are qualified to play a significant role in the future of agriculture.

The Need for IPAM in the Western Region

The western region of the United States can be divided into five major agroecosystems. These are:

1. Arid and semiarid irrigated: once desert or semidesert lands, economically the largest agronomic production base

2. Semiarid dryland, winter rainfall: wheat-fallow and range
3. Semiarid dryland, summer rainfall: wheat-fallow and range
4. Subhumid, winter rainfall: annual crops and orchards
5. Subhumid, summer rainfall: annual crops

Of the five agroecosystems mentioned above, numbers one, two, and three are common to all of the western states, include most of the land in the region, and are essentially unique to the region and the most important economically.

The semiarid, irrigated agroecosystem (one) includes over 12 million acres and produces an annual cash income of $3.7 billion to the farmers of the western region. The semiarid, dryland system includes over 19.8 million acres in small grain production and over 462 million acres classified as range (two and three). The annual cash income for small grains exceeds $2.3 billion (USDA, 1979a; 1979b). While these two systems are dissimilar in many ways, both can be used for small grain, alfalfa, and livestock production.

Undisturbed soils within these regions are low in organic matter and have a simple, fragile biological community when compared to the rich soil flora and fauna associated with soils of eastern forests and prairies. The more complex biological community of eastern soils is far more stable than that found in western soils. Cultivation and irrigation of these soils containing unstable biological complexes create a dramatic shift in species found within the community and previously unavailable niches. These niches are rapidly colonized by introduced organisms that are often serious pests to introduced crops. The high initial yields associated with crops grown on lands recently brought under cultivation for the first time drop rapidly as the soil is colonized by introduced pests. For example, high yields of potatoes can only be maintained through the rigorous application of soil fumigants, a practice in which the West leads the United States. Terms such as "spudded out" and "potato decline" are used by growers to describe the ever-growing problem of dramatically lower yield associated with the spectacular increase in pests on these lands. Growers are confronted with either fumigating, a control system that is expensive, to maintain production, abandoning the land and moving to a new area where the previously described cycle is repeated, or accepting lower yields that often make farming economically unfeasible (McIntyre, 1982).

The arid climate of the western states greatly limits airborne pathogens and insect pests. This has placed much of the West in a favored position regarding production of disease-free seed for other regions of the United States where summer rainfall and high humidity provide an optimum environment for development of numerous leaf spots, blights, fruit rots, insects, and weeds despite the rigorous application of pesticides. However, this advantage is rapidly being lost in the West. The advent of the modern, center pivot sprinkler irrigation system that can deliver overhead moisture to every plant in a field as frequently as every six to twelve hours has created a local environment with the high humidity associated with the eastern agroecosystem. Consequently, foliar pests are rapidly becoming major problems to crops grown under irrigation.

Usually, soilborne pathogens are immobile and thus remain confined to fields. Unfortunately where irrigation canals are used, soilborne plant pathogens and weed seeds in particular are becoming widely distributed from field to field and throughout the irrigation districts by one of the most efficient means of dissemination known. Quarantines become academic in this situation. One grower's problem is transformed in a single season to every grower's problem.

For dryland agriculture and more specifically dryland wheat, water stress and associated soilborne disease problems are more evident in the western states than in any other wheat-growing area of the United States. Unlike the Great Plains states, dryland wheat in the western states must head and mature on stored summer fallow moisture because there is no effective rainfall after April or early May. Plants often grow luxuriantly during early stages when moisture is abundant. However, the production of many tillers with the concomitant increase in leaf area may become a liability to the plant when moisture becomes marginal and it is too late to abort the tillers.

Identification of Commodities
Included in Project

Substantial numbers of scientists in the West in experiment stations, ARS, and extension are involved in activities related to the management of the semiarid dryland and semiarid irrigated agroecosystems. The initial western regional (W-161) project was developed because of an appreciation for the economic and geographic importance of these systems to the West and for the commodity linkages that tie the two together. The project was limited in numbers of crops included and pests studied but recognized the diversity of management systems used on the range-dryland system and the diversity of crops incorporated in a rotation on irrigated, arid lands within the region. The commodities currently identified within these agrosystems as most important in the region are range in the semiarid dryland agroecosystem and tree fruits and potatoes in the semiarid irrigated agroecosystem.

Alfalfa and small grains form a natural link between the systems in that these two crops are often produced on former range, are important export commodities, are grown in dryland or irrigated cropping systems, or are consumed by livestock. These crops relate to the row crops in a fundamental way. Historically, crop rotation has been a cornerstone of pest management. By rotating crops, one not only influences the edaphic factors of soil but more importantly can influence populations of weeds, soil insects, and pathogens. In the irrigated West, alfalfa and cereals are a key component of many rotational schemes. Beyond that, alfalfa potentially provides a stable habitat for the development of many beneficial parasites and predators.

Deciduous tree fruits, which have been added to the project recently, are important crops in the semiarid West. Apples, peaches, pears, and cherries, which were selected for intensive study in the project, account for almost 50 percent of the total fruit production in the region (USDA, 1982). One or more of the states included in the West consistently ranked from first to fifth in production of these fruit crops in the United States. In total, the region produces about 80 percent of the value of the national fruit and nut crop.

Beyond marketed value, there are additional features that make western deciduous tree fruit crops appropriate systems for developing IPAM methods. They are highly diversified and complex agroecosystems and have more in common with natural ecosystems than most other crops. This diversity usually includes mixed plant varieties, highly varied ground cover communities with distinct successional factures, and a highly diverse and relatively permanent litter and soil fauna. In addition, there is appreciable interaction of orchard-inhabiting species with associated irrigated crops, range plants, and other wild plant communities.

Although a commodity approach will often be used to address IPAM, an additional thrust is focused on development of research, extension, and teaching materials that recognize semiarid agroecosystems as a component of larger, more regional agroecosystems. In these cases, the project commodities form the subelements for individual program development. However, understanding and management at the regional level involve the larger, combined mosaic of crops and their surrounding environments.

Relationships Between Commodities/Pest Complexes and Surrounding Environments

"Pest complexes" include a broad range of individual pest problems or conglomerates of pest problems that lend naturally or logically to a focus within a commodity or across commodities. For example, barley yellow dwarf is a virus transmitted by insects from a number of plant hosts. The many insect pests, predators, pathogens, nematodes, and weeds are constituents of a definable agroecosystem in which a crop is grown and can be considered a pest complex.

The overall relationship between selected commodity/pest complexes and the variety of surrounding environments identified for study is illustrated (Figure 12.1). Commodity research, extension, and teaching programs are focused on the five previously mentioned major commodity areas. These commodity areas can be viewed along a continuum of management intensity from intensively managed plant communities (e.g., greenhouse crops, potatoes, tree fruits grown under conditions of intense management) to the almost natural ecosystem (e.g., rangelands, forest communities). Within a subregion, the relative placement of these commodities on the continuum scale shown will vary appreciably (Figure 12.1). For example, alfalfa might be managed more intensively than potatoes within a given area, or fruit orchards in a nursery might be less like a natural ecosystem than small grains grown in an area of less intensive management. The important point is that each

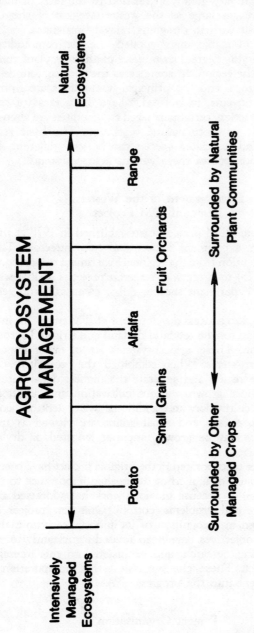

FIGURE 12.1 Regional Agroecosystem Dynamics

commodity system can vary greatly in relation to the level of management applied across an area as large as the western region of the U.S. This diversity must be dealt with in designing relevant programs.

Beyond the level of management applied, the five commodity systems are surrounded to varying degrees by mosaics of different plant communities in different areas of the region. In some cases they are surrounded wholly by other managed crops, and the principal interactions are from crop to crop. At the other extreme, in isolated valleys or in areas of continuous rangeland-forest production, certain managed commodities are almost wholly surrounded by native or more natural vegetation. The basic regional interactions of pests and associated species can be very different depending on the type and conditions of these various agroecosystems.

Development of the Western Regional IPM Project

The western regional IPM project was established in 1978 at the request of regional extension, experiment station, and ARS directors. The project followed a natural evolution from the regional experiment station coordinating committee (WRCC-25) to a regional research project (W-161) with strong representation from experiment station, ARS, extension, and resident instruction personnel.

W-161 was designed to address development of IPM programs in teaching, research, and extension for the semiarid dryland and irrigated agroecosystem of the western region. These agroecosystems are of major importance to all contiguous western states. When combined, they constitute the largest agroecosystem in the region and generate the highest dollar return. Commodities included those grown without cultivation and additional water (rangeland) or with cultivation and additional water (cotton, corn, sugar beets, and potatoes). Alfalfa and small grains are viewed as transitional commodities, as they may be grown in either irrigated or dryland agroecosystems.

Three commodities incorporated in the original project have been dropped from the project because of limited or diminished importance to the region (sugar beets and corn) or because previous work has addressed and solved many of the IPM related problems (cotton). One new project area, tree fruits, has been added in recognition of its importance within the region. In addition, project objectives have been revised significantly to reflect the integration of teaching, research, and extension into this interagency, interdisciplinary project. These changes reflect the incorporation of agroecosystem management into the program (IPAM).

Project Organization

Commodity Coordinating (CC) Subcommittees

The organization of the western regional IPAM project is a significant departure from the more traditional format for supervising regional projects.

This interdisciplinary, multicommodity program requires a substantial cooperative effort from administrative units in ARS, extension, experiment stations, resident instruction, and agribusiness. There is no one administrative structure within the region that satisfies that closely coordinated effort outlined herein. While the three semiarid dryland and irrigated agroecosystems and commodities grown in each will provide the confines for operation of the project, our emphasis is on controlled pest complexes that are impacted by the entire management system within a rotation, between cropping systems, or between native vegetation and cropping systems.

To this end, we have established multidisciplinary, commodity coordinating (CC) subcommittees within the region to identify those pest complexes that are most important to that commodity and most suited to an IPAM approach for control. Different pest complexes may be identified as most important within different subregions of the West. These committees play a major role in fulfilling the objectives of the project. The CC subcommittees are charged with providing data on the current status of pest control for the commodity and prioritizing the importance of pests and pest complexes attacking the commodity within the region. In some instances, regional coordinating committees such as WRCC-29, Diseases of Cereal Crops, may be in place and provide such data. In other instances, the western directors may wish to consider establishment of coordinating committees charged with the responsibility of obtaining these data. As appropriate, other means of obtaining such data will be considered. In all instances, care will be taken to provide input from extension, industry, resident instruction, and ARS.

An additional activity of the CC subcommittees has been to evaluate the need for first order manuals that will integrate pest management into the cropping cycle. These manuals are aimed at extension personnel, farmers, agribusiness, and pest control advisors. In addition, the manuals will be used as supplements to resident instruction programs in pest management. Manuals for cotton, potatoes, and small grains are at various stages of completion. A manual for alfalfa will be developed by modifying the current California IPM manual to make its content regional in scope. The range subcommittee will develop a series of publications derived from state-of-the-art symposia that will be held during the duration of the project.

Pest Complex (PC) Subcommittees

Some members of the CC subcommittees as well as other scientists will serve as members of appropriate pest complex (PC) subcommittees. The PC subcommittees are charged with identifying data gaps and prioritizing research and extension needs within the individual pest complexes identified by the CC subcommittees for incorporation into the project. The PC subcommittees identify research, extension, and resident instruction needs for the individual pest complexes and recommend priority areas for grant solicitations. The PC subcommittee is visualized as an equilateral triangle with disciplines, commodities, and agroecosystems of the semiarid West representing the sides (Figure 12.2). The participating units are listed below

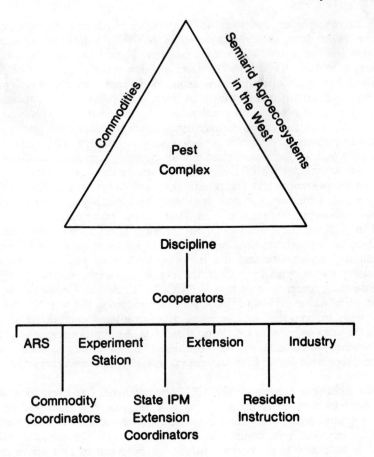

**FIGURE 12.2 Illustrated structure of Pest Complex (PC)
Subcommittee**

the triangle. It is recognized that participation will vary depending on the commodity, discipline, geographical subregion, and point in time within the project.

Master Coordinating Committee (MCC)

The chairman of each CC subcommittee will serve as a member of the master coordinating committee (MCC). The MCC will be charged with assuring overall completion of the entire project and, with the project coordinator, will review recommendations of the CC subcommittees regarding review of competitive proposals, allocation of resources, and review of project funding.

IPAM Coordinator

The position of IPAM Coordinator is staffed on a temporary, part-time basis using combined support from ARS, experiment stations, and extension within the western region. The IPAM Coordinator is responsible to a steering committee consisting of administrative representatives from resident instruction, extension, experiment stations, and ARS in the region. The steering committee assures that all participating administrative units have maximum input into project coordination and development.

Ultimately, the position of IPAM Coordinator will be a full-time position with an appropriate staff and travel budget. Not only will the coordinator be charged with maintaining communication with the CC and PC subcommittees to assure that the entire program stays on schedule, but the coordinator will also be expected to develop and maintain liaison with those federal and state agencies that are responsible for IPM programs. This effort will be accomplished, in part, through development and enhancement of appropriate state and national contacts within the previously mentioned agencies.

Financial Support

The western regional project is fortunate to receive a modest level of support from western regional ARS and experiment station and extension directors. This support has provided some salary and secretarial support for a part-time regional coordinator, travel funds for the coordinator and committee members, "seed money" for manual development, and a small amount of support to initiate a regional research effort on barley yellow dwarf, one of the high priority pest complexes identified within the project. Recently, additional support has been obtained through the CSRS special grants program.

Problems Associated with Development of an Interagency, Interdisciplinary Project in IPM

Preceding sections have identified the constraints in which the western regional IPM program operates. The committee structure with representatives from experiment stations, extension, ARS, resident instruction, and agribusiness has provided a forum that maximizes scientist input into development of overall program thrusts and a mechanism to modify or change program priorities. There appears to be little problem in assuring data exchange and program coordination. However, the fact that resources are allocated from a multitude of agencies and institutions creates competition between the regional IPM project and other local, regional, and national priorities. Such competition provides unusual challenges in assuring program continuity and compatibility. However, these problems, while challenging, are not insurmountable and are solved by involving all representatives in development, modification, and administration of the program.

Notes

1. An "agroecosystem" is used here to mean any managed agricultural cropping system that may be applied to an individual field or orchard subjected to a specific combination of management practices, a combination of contiguous fields within a specific geographic area, or a broad expanse of managed ecosystems such as range.

References

Glass, E. H. "Pest Management: Principles and Philosophy." Pp. 39–50 in J. L. Apple and R. F. Smith (eds.), *Integrated Pest Management*. New York: Plenum Press, 1976.

Intersociety Consortium for Plant Protection. *Integrated Pest Management: A Program of Research for the State Agricultural Experiment Stations and Colleges of 1890*, pp. 1–190. USDA, SEA/CR. Washington, D.C.

McIntyre, G. A. "Development of an Integrated Pest Management Program for Wheat in the Semiarid Regions of the Western United States." *Proceedings*. The National Wheat Research Conference, 1982.

National Academy of Science (NAS). *Genetic Vulnerability of Major Crops*. Washington, D.C.: Committee on Genetic Vulnerability of Major Crops, National Academy of Science, 1972.

_____. *Agricultural Production Efficiency*. Washington, D.C.: National Academy of Science, 1975a.

_____. *Pest Control: An Assessment of Present and Alternative Technologies*, Volume I. *Contemporary Pest Control Practices and Concepts*. Washington, D.C.: National Academy of Science, 1975b.

United States Department of Agriculture. *Crop Values (1976-1977-1978)—Season and Average Prices Received by Farmers and Value of Production*. Cr. Pr. 2-1(79), 1979a.

_____. *Crop Production, 1978 Annual Summary—Acreage, Yield, Production*. Cr. Pr. 2-1(79), 1979b.

_____. *Noncitrus Fruits and Mites, 1974 Ann. Surv., Prod., Use and Value*. SPS Bulletin. FrNt 1-2(75) USDA. Washington, D.C., 1982.

PART FOUR

Commodity Studies

13

A Comparative Study of Rice Research in California, Texas, Arkansas, Louisiana, and Mississippi

Cornelia Butler Flora and Jan L. Flora

Introduction

Research on rice (*Oryza sativa* L.) production in the U.S. cannot be understood without viewing the interaction between state policy and ecological factors. It is the thesis of this chapter that much of the difference between rice production in California and in the South is due to the differential roles of state governments, which are in turn related to the distinct structures of agriculture in California and the South, the organizations that are fostered in each setting, and their different degrees of mobilization. This mobilization affects commodity programs, controls on production, and also research.

Because it is a self-pollinating grain that can be saved by farmers rather than a hybrid that "self-destructs" after each season and must be repurchased, the bulk of the research on rice has been carried out in the public sector. Berlan (1983) discusses the importance of hybrids for the creation of private seed research organizations. Yet, the division between public and private research is not a dichotomy but a continuum. A comparative analysis of rice research strategies helps define the differential role of a variety of commodity-based research organizations including, but not exclusively, the state experiment station.

Rice differs from other small grains in a number of other ways:

1. Rice can be grown only in rather limited areas—on soils that are quite dense or are underlain by a hard pan, which allows for flooding of the crop during a major portion of its growth cycle. The limited number of suitable areas in the U.S. has important political implications.

2. While it is a staple food, relatively little rice is eaten in the U.S. For example, about ten pounds of rice (both direct and processed foods and brewing) per capita is consumed annually (Holder and Grant,

1979:25) compared to 118 pounds of wheat per capita (Heid, 1980). In most of the rest of the world, however, rice tends to be grown in the countries where it is eaten, and in many countries it is the staple grain of choice. While the U.S. produces less than 2 percent of the world's rice, nearly one-third of the rice that passes in world trade is grown in the U.S., although that share has recently declined. As much as 75 percent of U.S. rice is exported. This has significant implications regarding potential growth in rice production, which peaked in 1981, and for the stability of U.S. rice prices. Because of fluctuating climatic conditions worldwide, U.S. rice prices have become increasingly unstable as dependence on world markets has increased. Previously, U.S. rice was sold to neo-colonial markets such as Cuba.

3. Rice is a cash crop par excellence. It significantly outyields other small grains and is generally more valuable per bushel than feed grains, which approach or surpass it in yield. It is less perishable than most other crops that equal or exceed it in dollar value per acre. Because rice has been historically profitable in the U.S., it was the first grain to be cultivated with a highly mechanized input, including land leveling, land cultivation, planting, applying nutrients and pesticides, as well as harvest. It requires less labor than other crops with high product-to-land ratios. These facts have important implications for cultural practices and the type of research related to them.

These three sets of facts suggest two broad topics that will be used to organize this discussion of why the rice industry and, therefore, rice research have evolved as they have in this country: (1) domestic geopolitics of rice production and research, and (2) constraints in cultural practices that feed back as constraints on research.

Domestic Geopolitics of Rice Production and Research

Rice is presently produced in two socio-political regions in the U.S.: (1) four southern states—Arkansas, Louisiana, Mississippi, and Texas (with a small amount produced in the Missouri bootheel on the Mississippi River delta); and (2) California. The two areas are quite different both ecologically and politically. The southern regions are warmer than California, with more rainfall over a greater portion of the year. In addition, the political differences between the two areas have important implications for rice production and research.

Historically, the South has been dominated by agrarian interests, and this is still true today to a large extent. Thus, the healthiness of the rice (or cotton, sugar, or tobacco) industry tends to be equated with the well-being of the entire state or region. Those who disagreed with that interpretation had little political power. In California, although its agricultural production exceeds that of any other state, agricultural interests do not consistently dominate but must compete with other interest groups regarding the use of resources. This is increasingly the case in Texas as well. That difference has important implications for both state and federal policy and regulation with respect to the rice industry.

On the national level, because of the existence of the seniority system in Congress and because the South has been and continues to be in large part a single party region, southern rice interests have had their own representatives on important agricultural committees. The California people whom we interviewed could name only two representatives out of thirty-two who could be counted on to go to bat for the rice industry; neither of their senators would. While there was some grumbling about too liberal senators and representatives from Arkansas, there has been strong support of the rice industry by rice state congressmen from all the rice-producing southern states. This is reflected in regular federal appropriations from the Cooperative State Research Service of USDA, which form a higher proportion of the nonspecified research budget of the land grant system in the southern states than in California.

The South has historically had a low budget ideology regarding state and local government. While in general that ideology has also applied to the federal government, the New Deal farm programs have been particularly good to the South. Because of the political power of southern congressmen, the South has received preferential treatment at the hands of the Department of Agriculture. This is illustrated in the rice research program, which has located many more USDA rice scientists in the South than in California. The presence of a considerable number of USDA researchers has in the past allowed southern legislatures to spend relatively little on rice research and still maintain quite respectable rice research programs. Louisiana is an exception to the southern generalization. It has recently invested heavily in rice research, spending more than double what California spends, with a relatively low federal contribution. In 1981, Louisiana's extension service hired an outstanding research extensionist with solid research skills from California to head its program.

Because the cost of the rice subsidy program was rather small compared to that for wheat and major feed grains, support prices for rice have been maintained at a higher level than is true for any other grain. Action by southern senators delayed the removal of acreage allotments from rice three years beyond that of other grains. Further, rice farmers received an unusual concession—allotments without quotas, providing continued price and income protection beyond that provided to other grain farmers. The farm program for rice producers in the South also benefitted those in California.

In the early 1970s, a number of factors came together to reduce sharply the importance of government's role in keeping rice prices high through production limitations and direct payments. First, the increase in the cost of imported oil and the decline of the competitiveness of American manufactured goods in the world market made it necessary to look to other sectors for export growth. The two areas most readily available for such expansion were agriculture and military sales. Both increased as sources of foreign exchange because of decreased concessionary sales or grants (shifting them to commercial sales) and by an absolute increase in the amount exported. Years of shortfall in world grain production, including rice, were 1973 and 1974. This made it politically easy to suspend or dismantle the system of acreage limitations and price supports. (In the case of rice, allotments were suspended until 1976 when they were legislated out of existence.)

In the 1970s, the congressional seniority system, although not totally dismantled, was dealt a serious blow. Decline in the number of farmers, coupled with the emphasis on exports as a way of solving farmers' income problems, contributed to a serious decline in power of the farm bloc. By 1981, the farm bloc was in disarray. Inflation played a big role in pitting farmers against consumers, the latter historically having been rather sympathetic to the farmers' plight. By 1985, shifts in factor costs of production and the strong dollar further pitted farmers against consumers in terms of policy. Farmers are heavier users of credit than the rest of the population, and real interest rates are at an all time high, benefitting savers, not borrowers. Farmers are exporters, while consumers find themselves benefitting from cheap imports of consumption items.

Initially, the role of government for rice producers was the same as for other U.S. industries: market protection and market penetration. Tariffs early imposed on rice importation allowed a protected market for rice production in the United States. However, this market was always relatively small, limited early in our history to people of French and African origins (Littlefield, 1981).

Government activity was crucial in market penetration as well. Beginning with the Spanish-American War, the rice market followed military expansion. It is instructive to see the bursts in the rice industry and rice growing at the turn of the century with the conquest of Cuba and the Philippines in the Spanish-American War; with World War I and the immediate postwar period; with World War II when Japan, a major rice-eating country, was conquered and its rice production temporarily halted; with the Korean War when another important market developed during the armed struggle there; and with Vietnam, the rice bowl of Asia, which was systematically destroyed, increasing for a relatively short period of time U.S. rice exports to that area.

Market penetration with rice, as with other grains, was aided not only by armed intervention of the United States overseas, which in the cases of both Korea and Vietnam had major impacts on important rice-producing areas, but by such programs as P.L. 480 and its Food For Peace variant that served as an initial penetrator of certain foreign markets. These gifts later shifted to subsidized sales and ultimately to cash sales. The greatest expansion of concessionary rice programs took place during the Vietnam era, when government sales represented about 40 percent of exports. There was a major decline in government concessionary rice exports from 1972 to 1983, with a large increase in P.L. 480 sales and soft credit through the Commodity Credit Corporation for overseas buyers from developing countries.

Rice farmers have lobbied hard for more P.L. 480 sales because of an alarmingly large rice surplus and alarmingly low prices. They now have achieved that objective despite the Reagan administration's early emphasis on increasing trade on cash terms.

In international trade, the rice industry feels itself disadvantaged by government action and regulation. The Corrupt Practices Act, which makes it illegal for U.S. companies overseas to bribe local officials or potential buyers, is seen by several of the people we interviewed in the rice trade as particularly disadvantageous to U.S. rice sales. They point out that most rice sales are made to government entities in countries they view as traditionally using bribery. As they see it, U.S. rice sales abroad are hurt by the unwillingness of the United States government to accept local cultural patterns. Thus, market penetration is affected directly by U.S. interventions and U.S. subsidized sales, and market penetration is impeded by state action, which passed and enforces the corrupt practices law.

By the mid-1980s, dependence on concessionary sales and P.L. 480 rice allocations had again increased. The contradictory goals of P.L. 480—as a lever for U.S. foreign policy as well as an enhancer of U.S. farm exports—again aroused the wrath of the U.S. rice industry as P.L. 480 sales of rice to Liberia, the Philippines, and Kenya were delayed in order to pressure for economic policy reforms in those countries (Webster Communications Corporation, 1985).

Another important way the state can be active in an enterprise is through subsidizing technology development. The kind of technology developed for rice seeks to decrease the risk of production, decrease labor costs, and allow for the use of a mobile labor force—one that can be hired for specific tasks at specific times and then can be dismissed. The thrust of this technological development increases the potential for high formal rationality—and high capital accumulation.

Decreased dependence on labor has been an implicit goal directing technology development in rice as in other U.S. crops (Ruttan and Hayami, 1984). The rice industry, particularly in California, involves the most highly technologized grain production in the world today. The state has been very important in evolving this kind of technology by subsidizing its creation. The organization of technology generation and the division of labor between the state and the private sector mean that the public sector absorbs the risk and the private sector appropriates the profit. For this to occur best in a free enterprise environment, there must be an understanding by the providers of capital of the degree to which technology generation is necessary for the generation of profits. Technology shifts are necessary to achieve a comparative advantage through formal rationality—by decreasing production costs and increasing profits. Agriculture in the United States has set a goal of high productivity rather than reducing cost of production. This choice has been particularly evident in breeding rice in California.

The state is active in the rice agro-industry in providing subsidized credit, guaranteed prices, subsidized storage, subsidized inputs, quality control standards through grading, tax breaks, export subsidies, acreage limitations, and a market of last resort. These are the traditional, direct government activities.

The role of the federal government with respect to agriculture has thus shifted from an emphasis on improving agriculture's lot by increasing its terms of trade with the rest of the domestic economy (through government payments or purchases) or by limiting supply of staple agricultural products that, because of the price inelasticity of demand, results in greater farm income. The policy has shifted to expansion of exports, encouragement of production increases, and some effort at stabilization of major price swings. The precise role that government will play in this strengthened emphasis on exports is still in a state of flux. The implication for research is to help produce more with less cost in contrast to producing more of higher quality.

Rice Research Organizations

The most important impact of the ecological differences between California and the South is that the same varieties cannot be produced in both zones due to climate. Traditionally, each has had its own breeding program (*indica* or *indica*-like long and medium grain in the South, *japonica* short to medium grain in California). Public and proprietary breeders in California are working on *indica* varieties to develop a grain that is adapted to that climate and that retains flavor and cooking quality. Lack of pests in California has allowed for a focus of research on yield, while pest resistance, along with grain quality, has had to be part of the breeding strategy in the South.

The breeding programs in the two areas have developed quite differently. At least until the late 1960s, the South had a better developed rice research program: more rice breeders on the three principal state-run rice experiment stations, interchange of information and new varieties among the stations, and a greater presence of USDA research on rice than in California.

However, beginning with the rice "marketing order" first voted by California rice farmers in 1969, California began to catch up with and surpass the South in rice varietal research. California rice growers had the advantage of a 1938 law establishing procedures for implementing marketing orders for promotion, research, and orderly marketing of commodities. They could take advantage of the experiences of other commodity groups (mostly in perishable commodities) in developing their own marketing order and in obtaining grower acceptance.

The marketing order was developed specifically for research. It established the California Rice Research Board, which received checkoff money collected by the mills and directed it to specific research projects. The growers took over the struggling University of California rice experiment station at Biggs. In subsequent years, the research station (run by a separate foundation, whose board is also composed of rice growers) and the University of

California at Davis have been the principal recipients of rice research funds. A rather simple division of labor exists: the university does basic and intermediate research and the experiment station does adaptive research only on varieties developed elsewhere. The basic genetics work of varietal development is done by a USDA geneticist, and the final crosses are carried out by the three rice breeders at the growers' research station. The varieties are then tested by the University of California Cooperative Extension Service in field situations. Varietal development has had top priority and has paid off handsomely in the last few years. In 1976 the first short stature or semi-dwarf rice was released. In the four subsequent years, average yields for the state have grown by over 25 percent.

In the South, while new varieties with increased yield capacity are regularly released, few short stature varieties have been introduced, and yields have shown little increase. In Arkansas, yields have actually declined slightly because of the sowing of rice on new land, neophyte farmers going into rice following the suspension, and elimination of allotments.

The most important difference between California and southern rice production and research is the linkage between researcher and grower. In California, there is a secure and bountiful source of funding—the growers themselves (the checkoff is obligatory and increases with increasing production). The farmers through their elected representatives control both boards that set research priorities. They are willing to tax themselves because they control where the funds go, and the benefits that accrue to them as rice growers are visible and tangible.

In the South, the low budget ideology plays an important role in limiting state appropriations for rice research. That ideology relates to the historical locus of power. Because of the disproportionate power of southern congressmen, the place where things got done with respect to agricultural policy was Washington, not Little Rock, Baton Rouge, or Austin. State and local governments were conceived of as limited—doing what must be done but cannot be done by either the private sector or the federal government. The federal rice program involved spending other states' money for the people of Arkansas, Louisiana, or Texas. Since results from the experiment stations in the South are largely transferrable to the other southern rice-growing states, the mechanism for state-funded programs is the reverse: spending the state's own money partially for the benefit of rice growers in another state. Establishment of the marketing order concept in one state would be even more difficult, since the rice growers of state X would be spending *their own money* (not the state's taxpayers' money), part of the benefits from which would accrue to rice growers in other states. California growers didn't have to contend with that problem when establishing their market order since there is little transferability of varieties, and there are significant differences in disease problems from those of the southern states. (However, a California long grain variety, L201, is being produced in the South to some extent. Ironically, this is the "unacceptable" California long grain, which may be acceptable when produced in a southern climate.)

While southern state governments are not as active in rice research as members of the rice industry might like them to be, neither are they very active in regulating the rice industry. That is due to both the "limited government" concept and to the view that what is good for agriculture is good for the state as a whole. In contrast, California, being a large cosmopolitan state, finds its state government a focus of many competing and often conflicting interests. Environmental regulation, which complicates the lives of those in the rice industry, is much more prevalent in California than in the southern rice-growing states. A point of contention has been the burning of rice straw; the smoke floats over Sacramento, which, by unfortunate coincidence for the rice growers, is the seat of government where environmental legislation is written. The response of the growers— albeit under pressure—has been an active one because of the existence of the Rice Research Board. When a bill was introduced that would have taxed the growers on a per acre basis for the development of an independent research fund to provide data on alternative means of disposing of rice straw, the growers headed off that effort by voting to double the per hundred weight assessment under the marketing order and with that money com- missioned studies on straw disposal.

In the South, different cultural practices, as well as a different political climate, mean that rice straw removal has not developed as a political issue. Because of a specific weed problem, red rice, rice cannot be grown more than two seasons in a row in most of the South. Weeds are more of a problem in the South because of the higher heat and humidity anyway, but most can be treated by broad leaf specific herbicides. Red rice, however, is physiologically very similar to the commercial rice being grown; thus far, no herbicide has been developed that is able to differentiate between them. Therefore, fields must be rotated and different crops planted. Currently, the rotation crop is soybeans for two years. While previously soybeans were simply plowed under as a green manure, they are now harvested and sold through the same marketing channels (the cooperatives) that handle the rice. The levees are not permanent in southern rice fields, and the rice stubble is plowed under when cultivating for soybeans. Also, some say the straw of the taller southern varieties decomposes more easily than the straw of the semi-dwarf varieties grown in California.

Perhaps a more revealing issue is the use of powerful herbicides. Weeds are the major problem in rice production, and, with growing environmental concern over the use of toxic chemicals, herbicides must be federally approved for use. In general, farmers feel that chemical restrictions are too severe and aimed disproportionately at them. A residual pre-emergent herbicide, included in such products as Bolero, Prowl, and Machete, was approved by the Environmental Protection Agency's Section 18 emergency exemption permit. Southern farmers applied it with excellent results. In California, however, the farmers then had to have it approved by the California Division of Food and Agriculture Pesticide Division in a long and complex battle. Although they got permission for one year's use of Bolero, the political struggle to keep it legal in California continues. In the South, the federal government was the relevant body with whom the farmers had to deal; in California, it was both state and federal governments.

The southern states are approaching a point of transition regarding the organization of rice research. A voluntary checkoff has been implemented in Arkansas. The possibility of strengthening state support for rice research exists. However, it is not likely that federal support for rice research can be augmented significantly. Whether this increasingly important industry opts for grower-supported or state-supported research (or something in between) will be most interesting to watch.

Constraints in Cultural Practices

Cultivation practices not only account for variation of productivity for a given rice variety, but the introduction of new technology allows the development of new varietal strains. For example, the short and semi-dwarf rice varieties sometimes show less seedling vigor than do the tall varieties. Thus, too deep water leads to a poor stand. In the South, the problem of seed implantation is dealt with by flushing the field after drilling the rice or after seeding by air. With the development of laser leveling, which allows a high degree of precision to be introduced in the degree of slope of a field between levees, a water depth of from two to four inches is achieved. This allows for (1) better seedling rooting for all rice varieties, and (2) the introduction of the more vulnerable semi-dwarf varieties.

The semi-dwarfs also create an increased problem with weeds because less shading occurs and because water management suitable to semi-dwarf seedling vigor tends also to increase the vigor of grass weeds. Weed control has been defined as the number one production constraint for rice for quite some time, and both cultivation practices and herbicide application have shifted to meet the problem. New rice varieties require new water management and herbicide application practices. Farmers exert political pressure to increase pesticide use at the same time that environmental controls from government are increased. With the help of applied research, the California growers have derived a water-holding strategy to dissipate the pesticides before the water is released to irrigation channels.

Somewhat different cultural practices have been developed in California and in the South largely because of differences in ecology. The Sacramento and San Joaquin valleys of California, with a Mediterranean climate, have very little rain during the growing season, which means it has been less important to breed for resistance to a number of diseases that are a problem in the more humid South. In addition, the more valuable land of the California valleys (and historical settlement and cultural patterns) has contributed to a somewhat more mechanized, and certainly more capitalized, rice farm in California than in the South. (Eleven California rice farmers, of whom all but one were incorporated, were among the fifty-one U.S. growers who netted at least $1 million from USDA in deficiency payments and in-kind commodities for participation in the 1984 acreage reduction programs.)

The work of the California Crop Improvement Association has been particularly important in eliminating the red rice problem through annual certification of rice seed, thus allowing rice to be continuously cropped. The high value of California land means that inputs represent a smaller proportion of costs per acre than in the South. The value of annual seed renewal, which implies yearly purchase of certified seed, was recognized more readily in California. Similarly, the higher land values in California have probably contributed to the fact that nearly all rice is sown by plane, while in the South, the majority is drilled. Up to three times as much seed is needed when broadcast seeding is used, but the additional cost is relatively minor given land values and levels of production in California. Similarly, the additional nitrogen requirement of new higher yielding varieties is not of great concern, since fertilizer, even at today's prices, is a small portion of total costs of production. (That is true for California and the South.)

In the early 1930s in California and the 1940s in the South, when there was a shift in harvesting technology from the binder-thresher to the combine-drier method (which greatly reduced labor requirements), new varieties were required with shorter, stiffer straw, more resistance to lodging, more even ripening, easier threshability, smoother hulls, and capability of being successfully dried (The Rice Journal, 1947).

In the South, the existence of rice allotments was an impetus to increase production per acre planted to rice but not to increase the productivity of a particular piece of land by planting it to a high-yielding crop every year. It was only the late 1970s, when land inflation was higher than general inflation, that there was strong pressure to increase the productivity of rice land, whether it was planted to rice or another crop in a particular year. It is for that reason that many southern rice farmers are double cropping with fall-planted wheat. In California, precisely because of the more intensive use of the land, double cropping is not practiced except in the San Joaquin Valley. This valley is south of and warmer than the Sacramento Valley, so if rice is planted later to accommodate the wheat harvest, the likelihood of blanking because of cold is not so great as in the Sacramento Valley.

In the South, where fall-planted wheat is followed by soybeans, which can be planted later than rice, double cropping is easier because of a less intensive rotation regime. The less intensive methods in the South also contribute to less conflict over disposal of rice residue. Since rice is generally followed by two years of soybeans, the straw can be worked into the soil over that period of time. There is also a residue problem if rice is followed immediately by winter wheat. Hence, wheat is usually planted between the two crops of soybeans. Once farmers deal with the red rice problem in the South (the enhanced value of the land, particularly in Texas, suggests that there will be impetus to develop a more carefully controlled system for seed rice, which will include annual renewal of the seed), there will be greater problems with disposal of straw. It will be more difficult to double crop, but total value of production per acre will increase significantly.

The crops with which rice is rotated in the South, principally soybeans, do not provide nearly as much income as does rice, e.g., soybean yields are much lower. The allotments were much smaller than the total land apt for planting to rice. In California, because of the high value of land and because a significant portion of land planted to rice was only suitable to rice, there was a greater push toward mechanization of rice production, including eliminating the red rice problem through a pure seed program. In the South, where capital was relatively scarce, research lagged behind California where land was the scarce factor of production. With the shift in factor costs increasing the costs of capital, a change in research strategy may occur in California. Analysis of recent CRIS/USDA reports suggests a research focus on lower input alternatives now in California.

Agricultural Programs and Rice Research

The rice industry provides us with clues as to future trends in other grains produced in the U.S. The role of government in rice production, research, and marketing is in transition. With the growth in farm size and the concern of the federal government for improving the balance of payments with agricultural exports, there was a shift from concern for price to an emphasis on volume produced. Because a large majority of rice is exported, there is no close linkage between volume of U.S. production and price; this means traditional subsidy programs and even innovations like PIK have become quite expensive for the government. Acreage reductions have only limited effectiveness in bringing up market prices. Thus, rice farmers seek to expand production, since volume is the major source of profit. There is negative incentive for choosing quality over quantity (Greenwalt and Greenwalt, 1984).

It is in the interest of the government (for balance of payments reasons) and of the growers that the government play a more active role in export promotion. However, the strong dollar makes U.S. grain uncompetitive. The impact of aggressive sales efforts by major agricultural-exporting countries on developing countries seeking greater food self-sufficiency and improved balance of payments needs to be examined. Currently, dramatically expanded P.L. 480 famine relief exports are absorbing some of the rice that cannot be marketed commercially.

The long-term trend in rice research appears to be toward more grower financing. Given the structure of the industry—large, highly capitalized farms with increasing separation of land ownership from management—this would seem appropriate. It is probably not appropriate for taxpayers to subsidize what one Arkansas informant called the "Cadillac of grains." Within the framework of grower financing, important questions remain to be resolved. Foremost among these is the question of who owns new varieties that are developed. The California growers jointly release new varieties with USDA and the University of California. They are adamant that after paying directly for development of new varieties, they do not want to have to pay individually for the right to use those varieties. The public is not entirely relieved of the costs of rice research. The University of California does more rice research now than before grower financing was introduced. University-based rice research is basic and intermediate, not applied, which may have indirect benefits to a number of commodities. Rice tends to be a good species for experimentation in another tissue culture and other forms of cloning. However, examinations of the CRIS reports suggest that, particularly in California, grower funds are leveraging public dollars toward more applied, problem-oriented research.

Grower-financed research still involves a subsidy to growers, for their grants do not cover the entire cost of doing research—much of the overhead or infrastructural cost is covered by the taxpayer. Perhaps, this is an appropriate exchange in return for cheap rice for the consumer, a contribution to alleviating the nation's balance of payments problems and increasing the base of knowledge about plant science and crop production. In any case, grower financing of research would appear to be superior to the traditional model of having commodity research financed entirely by the public. Still, the question of degree of flexibility of the land grant system in choosing research topics must be carefully monitored as we move to greater private financing and, hence, control of commodity research. The implications of such a shift for the role of the land grant experiment station system need to be examined. It will be particularly interesting to see how the southern rice-growing states handle the question of public vs. private financing of rice research. The traditional low tax ideology mitigates against complete and adequate state financing; the overall support for agriculture as the dominant industry within those states implies that state support would gain in importance as federal support for research becomes more inadequate to the task of massively increasing yields. Which of these tendencies will become dominant is an open question.

Conclusion

It is clear that the development of improved varieties, improved cultural practices, resistance to disease, etc., have developed differently for rice in the South compared to California. We would argue that the more highly organized California rice interests, in a place where land ownership is separated from management, have resulted in a more rational understanding of the relation of private and public sectors in the production of research. A hierarchical research arrangement has evolved there. The USDA funds basic research, the University of California funds intermediate research, and the rice farmers themselves fund applied research and variety adaptation. This division of labor in plant breeding has maximized rice varietal development in California and has most closely linked varietal development to cultivation practices, increasing production at lower per unit costs.

Differential sources of funding facilitated this division of research labor in California. This has evolved because agriculture in California relates to a much stronger and activist state than is the case in the South. In the South, the famous call for states' rights basically meant "federal government, keep out." It did not mean that the state would enter into the process. The states in the South have traditionally had a rural orientation dominated by a low tax ideology. In that setting, the emphasis is on doing things as cheaply as possible to keep taxes as low as possible (Vidich and Bensman, 1958). A more sophisticated state, as exemplified by California, even with the recent moves there to decrease taxes, understands that higher taxes can result in more benefits to the private sector as the state serves to maintain the labor force, train it, and provide the basic technological development that the private sector can then appropriate.

In the case of agriculture, the more activist state, the stronger state with higher taxes and a higher budget, has served to help the agricultural interests. It has also provided a more formidable opponent when, as in the cases of burning rice stubble, water use, land use, and pesticide regulation, agricultural interests are seen to conflict with urban or general welfare interests. Willingness to be taxed and to tax oneself differentiates the farmers of California from those of the rice sector in the South. Nevertheless, rice is the U.S. grain crop that, particularly in California, most nearly approaches conditions of an industrialized crop. This has come about by close interaction of the rice industry with both state and federal levels in a struggle to decrease regulation, increase profitability through both tax incentives and subsidized sales, and through analytically looking at the research process and allowing high risk research to be performed by the state sector and high profitability research by the semi-public sector. However, once the states ceased to maintain price stability in the 1970s, the profits from this research accrued increasingly to millers, not growers. The result was to disadvantage farmers with a low capital base, particularly tenant farmers (Grant et al., 1984).

Because of the organization of rice farmers in California, the results of this have not accrued to the suppliers of technology but to the rice farmers themselves. In the case of the South, there is more disarticulation in the research process. Owners of smaller farms, who are more apt to be indirectly linked to the land and to the work force, particularly through some traditional tenant arrangements, have a much less rational research production system. The accrual of advantages through increase in technology would not revert to the producers but to the suppliers of inputs and the marketers of the grain, particularly rice millers and shippers.

Neither of the two should be viewed as redistributing income between workers and owners. Rice production is in the hands of favored farmers and is moving more toward that direction over time. Research is a key to maintaining production. To this point, the emphasis has been on productivity. With increasing capital costs, growers may influence researchers to focus on input reduction. Basic research on the rice plant will change little, at least initially. This research is protected from public pressure and thus can carry out the long-term research necessary as a base for applied innovations. However, adaptive research, which is more directly responsible to rice growers, will change both in qualities sought in the varieties being adapted and in the cultural practices tested to grow them.

In rice research, a continuum of public and private funding and control exists. On the one hand, rice is the most expensive grain to produce in the U.S. today. On the other, it is the most profitable. As the factor costs of production change, we can expect the research organizations connected with the rice industry to be particularly responsive to these changes.

Notes

Contribution Number 86-83-B of the Kansas Agricultural Experiment Station.

References

Berlan, Jean-Pierre. "Les Semences: Economie et Politique." *Revue Francaise d' Economie Rurale* 158:18–28, 1983.

Grant, W. R.; Richardson, J. W.; Brorsen, B. W.; and Rister, M. E. "Economic Impacts of Increased Price Variability: A Case Study with Rice." *Agricultural Economics Research* 36:4, Fall 1984.

Greenwalt, B., and Greenwalt, E. "Differences in Net Income Between Four Rice Varieties." Paper presented at the Rice Technical Working Group. Lafayette, Louisiana, 1984.

Heid, Walter G., Jr. *U.S. Wheat Industry.* Economics, Statistics, and Cooperatives Service, U.S. Department of Agriculture, Agricultural Economics Report No. 432, 1980.

Holder, Shelby H., Jr., and Grant, Warren R. *U.S. Rice Industry.* National Economics Division, Economics, Statistics, and Cooperatives Service, U.S. Department of Agriculture, Agricultural Economics Report No. 433, 1979.

Littlefield, Daniel C. *Rice and Slaves: Ethnicity and the Slave Trade in Colonial South Carolina.* Baton Rouge: Louisiana State University Press, 1981.

The Rice Journal 50(10):8–12, October 1947.

Ruttan, Vernon, and Hayami, Y. "Induced Innovation Model of Agricultural Development." Pp. 59–74 in Carl K. Eicher and John M. Staatz (eds.), *Agricultural Development in the Third World.* Baltimore: The John Hopkins Press, 1984.

Vidich, A. J., and Bensman, J. *Small Town in Mass Society: Class, Power and Religion in a Rural Community.* Princeton: Princeton University Press, 1958.

Webster Communications Corporation. *Rice + Plus* 1(2), August 16, 1985.

14

Tradition and Innovation in Agriculture: A Comparison of Public and Private Development of Hybrid Corn

Deborah Fitzgerald

Introduction

In his address before the hybrid corn division of the annual American Seed Trade Association meeting in 1955, Henry A. Wallace reflected on the difference between public and private development of hybrid corn. Wallace argued that there was a natural division of labor between the experiment stations and USDA on the one hand and the private seed companies on the other. The division was between pure and applied science; while the public sector was responsible for theoretical developments in corn breeding, the private sector made advances in production-related areas. "In the minds of the majority of the Public," Wallace claimed, "including even better than average informed farmers, all corn breeding is being done by the private sector." Nonetheless, he pointed to the widespread use of hybrids by farmers as "one of the outstanding examples of close and practical cooperation between private individuals, the state experiment stations, and the USDA" (Wallace, 1955). But Wallace's reliance on the pure vs. applied science dichotomy is neither very useful nor very apt in describing hybrid corn development. While there was a measure of cooperation between public and private institutions, competition played a more critical role. In this context, competition refers not to commercial or even intellectual wrangling but rather to an intangible dispute over which kind of institution could claim scientific authority in the broader agricultural arena.

Both the agricultural experiment station and agribusiness derived their strength from an ability to appear authoritative on agricultural matters. For the station, authority implied two things. First, it referred to the staff's expertise on a broad range of agricultural topics, from dairy herds to orchard pests to marketing, from abstract mathematical formulations to basic farm accounting methods. Second, authority referred to their perceived impartiality in judging the assets and liabilities of agricultural innovations, their interpretation of rumors and advertisements. For agribusiness, authority implied integrity, an equally elusive term but one that usually referred to a company's longevity, product reliability, and the perceived honesty of its owners. By the early twentieth century, authority also implied scientific methods for both the station and agribusiness. For the station, scientific activity was the basis of both its expertise and impartiality; for agribusiness, it became a necessary ingredient of the competitive process.

In the 1920s and 1930s, three seed companies in Illinois linked their commercial authority and success with their scientific research programs in hybrid corn. DeKalb Agricultural Association in northern Illinois and Pfister Hybrid Seed and Funk Brothers in central Illinois developed sophisticated programs that resembled those undertaken by the experiment stations. They conducted hybrid research and studied corollary farm practices, invented mechanical farm equipment, compiled facts and figures attesting to their achievements, compared different strains and made recommendations, and in general bombarded farmers with scientific explanations for everything.

Role Differences

This chapter compares the roles played in hybrid corn research by the University of Illinois experiment station and Funk Brothers Seed Company during the 1920s and 1930s. Both groups were strategically involved in the early hybrid research and frequently cooperated on projects, shared experimental findings, drew on each other's expertise, and publicly commended each other's work. But they also competed in ways that reflected the different goals each played in Illinois agriculture. As impartial expert and judge, the university was an advocate for Illinois farmers, teaching them how to farm in a manner congruent with farmers' needs and interests. In exchange for the university's attentiveness to their concerns, farmers deferred to the university, relying on the latter's judgment. Funk Brothers, however, had no such obligation to farmers. Their relationship was more direct, relying on mutual satisfaction in an agreed-upon trade.

This difference in roles became more pronounced when hybrid corn development shifted from the experimental to the commercial arena. While the university taught traditional methods of corn improvement, Funk Brothers urged farmers to switch to hybrids. When the company began conducting university-type research on hybrids, its own role and authority in Illinois agriculture was enlarged. No longer just a seed house, it became a dispenser of scientific knowledge. With this expanded scientific authority, Funk Brothers destabilized the university's balance of authority, calling into question their relationship with one another and the proper role each should play.

Neither the university nor Funk Brothers faced particularly difficult technical requirements in hybrid corn research (Hayes, 1963). The corn plant is monoecious, carrying the male parent on the tassel and the female on the ear silk. In an open field, pollination was a random affair with the windborne pollen resting arbitrarily on available silks. In open-pollinated corn, only the female parentage could be known with certainty. Hybrid techniques controlled both male and female parents. In the first step, inbreeding, a corn plant was carefully self-pollinated for several generations until it approached a homozygous state in which its dominant features were isolated. In the second step, an inbred with favorable characteristics, such as strong roots or drought resistance, was cross-pollinated with another inbred. In commercial production, two single crosses were combined into a double cross that, with luck, exhibited the best characteristics of each parent: In 1930 the entire process took from five to seven years to complete.

Participants in this research did not depend upon complex instrumentation, Ph.D. degrees, or sophisticated theoretical abstractions. Rather, the major prerequisite was a lengthy commitment of land and labor. Controlled pollinations required manipulating each corn plant individually throughout the season, bagging shoots and silks as well as detassling. Researchers kept painstaking records on each strain tested, noting its vital statistics, the changing field conditions, and its final assets and liabilities. The most critical problem of corn research, and the stage at which bottlenecks were most likely to occur, was adapting promising hybrid combinations to particular regional variations.

The agricultural problems introduced by hybrid corn were in large part a function of the dramatically different farming requirements of hybrids and open pollinates, and these problems were exacerbated by the different research and extension agendas of the university and Funk Brothers. While their research fundamentally reflected their differing roles—that is, Funk Brothers used science for profit while the university used it for public service—their behavior did not reflect such simple ideals. Indeed, the similarities between the two are striking. (Both groups had been studying corn breeding and nomenclature since at least the 1890s.)

At the Illinois station chemist Cyril G. Hopkins invented the ear-to-row method of selection, which allowed for identification of parents, and demonstrated that the chemical composition of corn could be altered by selecting for particular characteristics such as high or low oil or protein content. These studies were of little direct benefit to farmers but helped identify the commercial limits of breeding (Alexander, 1959). Perry Holden and A. D. Shamel began inbreeding studies in 1895 in an effort to understand inheritance patterns, and in the first decade of the twentieth century, L. H. Smith studied hybrid vigor and the transmission of unit characters in corn, a fairly typical scientific response to the rediscovery of Mendel's laws in 1900. In the 1920s and 1930s, George Dungan and C. M. Woodworth examined inheritance of characteristics and, particularly, chemical composition of hybrids (U.I., Agronomy Department, 1941).

Eugene Funk was also active. In 1892 he developed a specialized varietal cross called "Funk's 90-Day" that was designed for late planting or short growing seasons. In that year, too, he began using Hopkins's ear-to-row method of corn improvement by which he developed smooth, utility type corn, a minor revolution that ultimately redefined standards in open pollinated corn (J. D. Funk, 1903; Holbert, 1945).

Both groups were involved in Illinois farmers organizations such as the Illinois Corn Breeders Association, which Dean of the Agricultural College Eugene Davenport created in 1901 and in which Eugene Funk was a prominent member and officeholder (Cavanagh, 1959; Moores, 1970). Funk also sat on the Field Crops section of the university's Agricultural Advisory Committee. While one expects university agronomists to have been well acquainted with contemporary scientific trends, it is notable that Eugene Funk was also corresponding with early geneticists such as Donald Jones and George Shull and hosting Hugo deVries on the latter's tour of American agricultural centers (Funk Brothers Seed Company, 1940; Jones, 1921; Shull, 1914).

The differences, however, between Funk Brothers and the university more readily account for their divergent concerns in corn research and development. First, despite the university's impressive array of scientists, technicians, laboratories, and equipment, their commitment to hybrid corn was mediated by their multidisciplinary nature. Corn farmers and producers were not the only clientele clamoring for attention, and the college and station had other priorities. Soil surveys occupied the lion's share of research time at the station, followed closely by cultural studies of other new crops such as alfalfa, clover, and soybeans (UI, Agronomy Department, 1941). Nor did the university possess the experimental fields necessary for full-scale corn research. In the 1910s, its available farmland was both sparse and of marginal quality.

Funk Brothers, on the other hand, owned over 22,000 acres of prime Illinois farmland, constituting a field laboratory of unmatched scale. And while the company continued to produce and sell open-pollinated corn as well as other crop seed, its attention to hybrids was complete and uncompromised. Funk Brothers's research projects on corn extended beyond the standard inbreeding studies and gave the company the appearance of a hybrid corn experiment station unfettered by the usual demands from farmers. Its catalogues from the late 1920s through 1941 were testimonials to scientific experimentation and research, describing in detail the procedures used in hybridizing. The company also sponsored its own yield contests, modeled on those of the university's experiment station, for farmers growing Funk Brothers's strains.

The most fundamental difference between the two groups, however, was reflected in their very different organizational structures, which provided distinct opportunities as well as constraints on the kind of science each could develop. At Funk Brothers, the commercially oriented research program was given a substantial boost by long-term support from the USDA. In 1913 Eugene Funk decided that corn disease was the greatest problem of Illinois farmers and the greatest obstacle to permanent corn improvement. He spent three years studying the problem with the assistance of James R. Holbert, then an agronomy student at Purdue who spent summers working with Funk. In 1916 Funk went to Washington for help, arguing that Funk Farms would be a good place to establish a federal field station for the study of corn diseases. The following year the station was in place and Holbert became a USDA employee in charge of station work (E. D. Funk, 1938).

During the twenty years the station was in operation, it contributed more to the accelerated pace of hybrid production than any other single farm or station, and, by Funk Brothers's own admission, distinguishing between USDA and Funk Brothers's contributions to the work was virtually impossible (Steele, 1984). While the USDA did not provide the company with much in terms of capital and equipment, it did provide it with unusual advantages. Most importantly, the USDA supported Holbert who, by the 1930s, was easily one of the most sophisticated and experienced corn breeders in the country. This linkage also provided access to the research findings of other breeders, both public and private, which were not as available to small-scale breeders. And, of course, the prestige Funk Brothers gained from the association undoubtedly enhanced its business and commercial integrity and was useful in attracting university scientists such as Earl Sieveking who, in 1928, left the University of Illinois for a research position at Funk Brothers. Not surprisingly, university scientists and administrators were less than thrilled with federal stations such as the one at Funk Brothers, and in 1931 an Alabama experiment station employee called them "one of the most embarrassing features of federal-state relations" (Funchess, 1931).

While the university had a formal relationship with the USDA via the federal appropriations, its corn work commanded no special attention, and in fact relations between Eugene Davenport and the federal government were strained at best. In 1916, two years after the Smith-Lever bill was adopted setting up extension work, Davenport threatened to abrogate that agreement because he felt it seriously undermined university autonomy (Davenport, 1916). He was, in general, highly suspicious of federal involvement with state programs and accused the government of sending field representatives into Illinois whom farmers identified as university men but who were untrained and incompetent (Davenport, 1913, 1916). It seems plausible that this tension explains in part why the USDA overlooked the University of Illinois in selecting a state experiment station to cooperate with the field station; the lucky winner was Purdue, Holbert's alma mater.

The university's research and extension efforts were most clearly shaped by their commitment to the needs and interests of Illinois farmers. While university scientists conducted a significant amount of theoretical research and published in professional journals, the experiment station publications tended to concentrate on routine farm issues. In corn research especially, the station's practical work was dominant. Between 1903 and 1928 there were a dozen projects aimed at systematizing farm practices compared with four concerned with hybrid research, two of which were cooperative projects instigated by Funk Brothers (U.I., Agronomy Department, 1941).

The practical studies involving corn were of two types. One concentrated on familiar farming concerns and included studies of the effect of frequent and infrequent cultivation on yield, the effect of varying distances between corn stalks on yield, the differing effects on corn of planting according to the checking method and the drilling method, the effect of time of harvest on yield, and so forth. The other type of corn work focused on systematizing traditional methods of corn improvement, that is, identifying and selecting good seed from the field for planting. When the Division of Crops Extension was established in 1922, its director, J. C. Hackleman, concentrated his efforts on teaching farmers how to distinguish visually between good and bad seed corn, how to increase their yields through such selection, how to construct and use seed germinators, and he encouraged them to enter the annual statewide ten-acre corn yield contest sponsored by the university (Hackleman, 1922-1938). Hackleman emphasized the extension ideal of self help by attempting to educate farmers in a way that enabled them to manage their farms in a productive and scientific fashion. In addition, he created an agency called the Illinois Crop Improvement Association (ICIA), whose goals of identifying seed types and increasing supplies of pure seed were achieved through an elaborate system of inspecting and certifying corn destined for sale as field seed (Lang, 1973). While the ICIA enjoyed a certain popularity among pure seed enthusiasts, and in fact grew both in terms of membership and acres certified, its excessively complicated requirements for certification alienated the largest seed companies who, while sitting on its board of directors, did not certify their own seed (Woodworth, 1934). The university ultimately waived its requirement that entrants in the yield contest certify their entries providing they had a corn breeder on staff, a reluctant recognition that the university could not control large companies' research or success (U.I., Agronomy Department, 1938).

By the mid-1930s, when hybrid corn became commercially available, the university and Funk Brothers had built up momentum in quite different directions, and this was reflected in their approach to extending results to farmers. Funk Brothers's interest in getting its hybrids on the market before the competitors led the company to claim, rather optimistically, that it had produced the first commercial hybrid as early as 1916 (Funk Brothers Seed Company, 1941). The company introduced its first "true double cross hybrid" in the 1928 catalogue, prefacing the particular description with a lengthy discussion of scientific corn breeding. While they did not recommend that farmers plant only the new hybrids, and in fact charged double the price of premium open-pollinates, their enthusiasm for hybrids was entirely uncritical. They hoped to induce farmers to adopt hybrids with such incentives as a seed package containing both hybrid and open-pollinated corn, free hybrid seed for buyers of open-pollinates, and even free hybrid seed to boys entering the yield contest in exchange for names and addresses of farmers (Funk Brothers Seed Company, 1929-1932). Although Funk Brothers continued to sell open-pollinates until 1940, they received less and less attention in the catalogue.

The real problems at Funk Brothers, however, centered not so much on convincing farmers to try hybrids but rather on creating hybrids appropriate to regional variations. In 1929 the company shipped nearly 1,000 bushels of hybrid seed to growers in thirty-five states, Canada, and Cuba. Much to their chagrin, all the seed failed except that grown in Bloomington (Funk Brothers Seed Company, 1944). While in a good year most hybrid corn yielded at a higher rate than open pollinates, a year of drought, early frosts, late rains, chinch bugs, rootworms, or any particular natural disaster would claim the specialized hybrids and leave untouched the more "experienced" open pollinates. The process of research and development was consequently an ongoing process. By 1939 Funk Brothers offered over thirty of its own specialized hybrids plus nearly thirty hybrids developed by agricultural colleges (Funk Brothers Seed Company, 1938).

For the university, the commercial appearance of hybrid corn presented a number of problems, and their approach until about 1940 was characterized by conservatism, caution, and frustration. First, while their research contributed substantially to hybrid development, their extension efforts had successfully promoted a system of farm practices fundamentally incongruent with hybrids. For example, although farmers could modestly improve their open-pollinates' yields by selecting good seed from the field as Hackleman taught them, such a practice had disastrous consequences with hybrid corn. Since second generation hybrids were substantially less vigorous than first generation ones, farmers who used the hybrids two years in a row suffered a much decreased yield. Farmers repeatedly tried selecting seed for planting from their hybrid fields, either unable or unwilling to believe that they needed to buy new seed each year (Hackleman, 1934, 1938). In addition, in the early years when available hybrids were not adapted to specific conditions, a farmers' local open pollinate would often perform better than hybrids (Hackleman, 1935). This problem in adaptation led to many exaggerated claims both for and against hybrids, leaving experts at both Funk Brothers and the university at a loss to predict the performance of any single strain.

Second, university officials were unclear how to proceed with their own inbreds and single cross seed. While in 1931 it seemed plausible for farmers to do their own hybridizing with university inbreds, by 1940 the idea was all but dead (Corn Belt, 1937; U.I., Agronomy Department, 1921). Once the university began disseminating inbreds for crossing, it became difficult to ensure that participating farmers bred them properly and responsibly. Some farmers received inbreds and single cross seed and sold them as true hybrids, a practice that confused everyone and reflected badly on the university (Hackleman, 1936). By 1937 the university had developed a program in conjunction with the ICIA for distributing inbreds and single cross seed that catered to established seed producers. While the large producers obtained station inbreds for crossing with their own lines, the program also made a serious attempt to supply the smaller seed houses that did not have breeding programs and were therefore entirely dependent on the station (Blair, 1938).

By the late 1930s the hybrid corn juggernaut was rolling. Where in 1933 hybrid corn acreage in the United States was only 0.4 percent, by 1945 it was 90 percent (Sprague, 1978). While the virtues of hybrids—their higher yield and resistance to environmental problems—offered persuasive reasons for switching from open pollinates, there were two more compelling incentives. First, the adoption rate was hastened by several bad crop years, especially the drought in 1936, when seeds of all kinds became scarce. Not only were farmers anxious to obtain high-yielding seed corn during a period of high prices, but they were also more receptive to advertisements for hybrid corn bred especially for drought resistance (Hackleman, 1936). In addition, the Agricultural Adjustment Administration launched their restricted acreage program in 1934, whereby farmers were encouraged to take land out of production. For many farmers, the prospect of reduced output was the ultimate incentive to try hybrids, whose higher yield per acre allowed farmers to produce as much as ever, if not more (Klinefelter, 1938).

For the university, the success of hybrid corn signalled the end of an era. With the creation and growth of private agricultural research centers such as Funk Brothers, scientific authority was claimed by both private and public sectors. During these years, the university's role as the farmers' advocate became tangled in conflicts between tradition and innovation, public and private, caution and enthusiasm. As an advocate, the university attempted to "put a brake on" early adoption of hybrids when it became clear that adaptation was incomplete, and through the ICIA it tried to regulate the distribution of station inbreds in a way that gave small producers a chance to compete (Hackleman, 1937:20). The university also continued sponsoring and publishing the results of state corn yield contests, which attempted to evaluate fairly the assets and liabilities of different hybrids throughout the region.

Despite these efforts, however, the concentration of authority, if not expertise, shifted unmistakably to commercial firms such as Funk. The farmer could no longer select his own seed and was obliged to follow the seed company's advice on appropriate seed selection. When in doubt, Funk reassured farmers, "let us choose the corn that is best for you" (Funk Brothers Seed Company, 1935). And, indeed, all hybrids looked virtually identical, making visual selection impossible. Only those who understood the mysterious pedigree system could make such important decisions. By 1938, the university advised farmers to rely on the integrity of big seed companies (Klinefelter, 1938). The university was no longer the sole proprietor of agricultural expertise, and in fact private centers could often claim broader familiarity with both practical farming and research trends. But while some argued that universities should concentrate on theoretical science and leave practical matters to private researchers, the university's public service function demanded a more activist role (Wallace, 1955). It should come as no surprise that in the wake of hybrid corn, the university shifted its attention from hybrid corn production to corn marketing and by-product conversion, issues the private firms were content to ignore.

Conclusion

Beyond the hyperbole that surrounds the notion that hybridization techniques have increased the world's food supply, this case of hybrid development raises thorny questions about the role of the land grant system in commodity production and its responsibility to those engaged in agriculture as farmers and seed producers. Clearly, hybrid corn did not benefit both groups uniformly. While large seed companies were enormously strengthened, smaller seed producers often were absorbed by large producers or squeezed out of the market entirely. The benefit to farmers, moreover, has been mixed. The ability of hybrids to withstand a wide range of adverse field conditions has made corn growing a more stable and predictable venture, but the social and economic costs have been considerable. Not only must farmers buy new seed each year, hybrid corn has introduced an array of corrollary farm products such as fertilizer; insecticide, pesticide, and herbicide; the equipment used to apply these chemicals; and the enormous (and enormously expensive) machinery used to plant and harvest corn. In the past thirty years such additional "inputs" have attained the status of farming necessities to all but a minority of agriculturalists. Further, the higher yielding capacity of hybrid corn, which initially increased farmers' yield and income, has had the overall effect of sustaining chronic overproduction and declining farm prices.

For the land grant university, this history of hybrid corn development provides a useful lesson in the politics of agricultural research. At issue is the way in which the university identifies its primary responsibilities and clientele. The Illinois agricultural population represented a broad spectrum of needs and interests and benefitted unevenly from hybrid development. As Hightower (1973) has pointed out, the increasing interdependence of agribusiness and the land grant university on research and development matters often has a negative impact on farmers and consumers and undermines the "good faith" understanding between the farmer and the university by which the university is perceived as a public servant that acts in the best interests of the farmer. Despite this, the relationship between farmers, seedsmen, and the university has always been ambiguous, and the research and development choices made by the university have rarely been guided by long-term policy commitments. Whether or not this ambiguity has worked to the advantage of American agriculture is unclear; in the case of hybrid corn, it seems that only the seed companies emerged from the turmoil unbruised.

References

Alexander, D. E. "Early Work in Corn Experimentation at the University of Illinois." Urbana, Illinois: Unpublished manuscript, Alexander Collection, March 20, 1959.

Blair, Joseph C. "Annual Report of the Agricultural Experiment Station." Urbana: University of Illinois Archives, 8/1/2, Box 120, 1938.

Cavanagh, Helen. *Seed, Soil, and Science: The Story of Eugene D. Funk.* Chicago: Lakeside, 1959.

Corn Belt Regional Workers Meeting. Urbana: University of Illinois Archives, 8/ 1/2, Box 32, March 12, 1937.

Davenport, E. D. "Relations Between the Federal Department of Agriculture and the Agricultural Colleges and Experiment Stations." Mimeograph. Presented to American Association of Agricultural Colleges and Experiment Stations. Urbana: University of Illinois Archives, 8/1/2, Box 85, 1913.

_____. "Recommendation for Abrogation of Cooperative Relations with the United States Department of Agriculture." Urbana: University of Illinois Archives, 8/ 1/2, Box 83, 1916.

Funchess, M. J. *et al.* "Report of Committee on Federal State Relations in Agricultural Research." Urbana: University of Illinois Archives, 8/1/2, Box 83, November 17, 1931.

Funk Brothers Seed Company. Catalogues. Bloomington, Illinois: Funk Brothers Files, 1928, 1929, 1932, 1935, 1938, 1940, 1941, 1944.

_____. "Supplemental Data Pertaining to Application for Relief Under Section 722 of the Internal Revenue Code for Fiscal Years Ending June 30, 1941, 1942, 1943." Bloomington, Illinois: Funk Brothers Files, 1941.

Funk, E. D. "The Search for Better Corn." Address written for presentation in St. Charles, Illinois, but not given due to weather, October 28, 1938.

Funk, J. D. "Agronomist's Report." Bloomington, Illinois: Funk Brothers Files, May 2, 1903.

Hackleman, J. C. "Annual Reports of the Division of Crops Extension." Urbana: University of Illinois, Office of Division of Crops Extension, 1922–38.

Hayes, H. K. *A Professor's Story of Hybrid Corn.* Minneapolis, Minnesota: Burgess, 1963.

Hightower, Jim. *Hard Tomatoes, Hard Times.* Cambridge, Massachusetts: Schenkman, 1973.

Holbert, J. R. "Funk's 176A Story." Bloomington, Illinois: Unpublished manuscript, Funk Brothers Files, 1945.

Jones, D. F. Letter to E. D. Funk. Bloomington, Illinois: Funk Brothers Files, February 9, 1921.

Klinefelter, H. E. "The Coming Revolution in Corn Production." *Missouri Farmer* 5, October 15, 1938.

Lang, A. L. *Fifty Years of Service: A History of Seed Certification in Illinois, 1922–1972.* Urbana: Illinois Crop Improvement Association, 1973.

Moores, R. G. *Fields of Rich Toil: The Development of the University of Illinois College of Agriculture.* Urbana: University of Illinois Press, 1970.

Shull, G. H. Letter to E. D. Funk. Bloomington, Illinois: Funk Brothers Files, January 17, 1914.

Sprague, G. F. "Introductory Remarks to Session of the History of Hybrid Corn." Pp. 11–12 in David B. Walden (ed.), *Maize Breeding and Genetics.* New York: John Wiley, 1978.

Steele, Leon. Interview with author, 1984.

University of Illinois Agronomy Department. "Report to the Advisory Committee." Urbana: Alexander Collection, Department of Maize Genetics, January, 1921.

_____. Meeting of Agronomy Department Advisory Committee to the Illinois Crop Improvement Association. Urbana: University of Illinois Archives, 8/6/2, Box 9, April 22, 1938.

———. "Historical Data for President McKinley." Urbana: University of Illinois Archives, 8/6/2, 1941.

Wallace, H. A. "Public and Private Contributions to Hybrid Corn, Past and Future." *Proceedings of the 10th Annual Hybrid Corn Industry Research Conference* [typescript copy, Funk Brothers Files]. Washington, D.C.: American Seed Trade Association, 1955.

Woodworth, C. M. Letter to J. C. Hackleman. Urbana: University of Illinois Archives, 8/6/2, Box 9, September 4, 1934.

15

History of Wheat Research at the Kansas Agricultural Experiment Station

Jan L. Flora

Research Response to State Action

In this chapter, I examine one phase of the role of the state in agriculture, the provision of technology through agricultural research. As research in agriculture has traditionally been organized around specific commodities—principally those for which federal commodity programs have been designed—this research is specific to a particular commodity—wheat. Wheat is the major agricultural product in Kansas, and Kansas is the number one wheat-producing state in the nation. Thus, what happens to wheat farming has a vital impact on the state.

Commodity research must be seen as an advance from discipline-oriented research, which broke down the specific parts of the wheat-growing cycle into separate and often unarticulated parts. The emergence of commodity research, as opposed to disciplinary research, can be seen as a triumph of the users of research, who were seeking that their state-supported institutions be receptive to their needs and that their investments were profitable. As indicated by the shifts in the acreage planted to wheat in Kansas, farmers are indeed sensitive to changing policy decisions, responding to price and policy stimuli with relative alacrity.

Are the researchers as responsive? What constituencies mobilize to express publicly their research needs? Possible constituencies for such research include farmers and their associations, both general interest and commodity-specific; food processors; farm input producers, including international conglomerates for seed, fertilizer, and pesticides; grain traders; consumers; other scientists; and, finally, the public, as represented particularly by state legislators. Busch and Lacy (1983) have shown how, for agricultural scientists, the constituencies most directly addressed tend to be other scientists, rather than some of the other more diffuse constituencies. I attempt in this chapter to summarize the wheat research undertaken in the Kansas Agricultural Experiment Station, to examine the logic behind wheat research strategies, and to identify the constituencies benefitted.

The Development Period—
From Establishment of the Experiment Station
to the 1920s Depression

In the early period of wheat production in Kansas, farm survival and expansion was based on the expansion of wheat acreage (Flora and Stitz, 1985). The ability to increase the number of acres planted and harvested depended to a large degree on engineering technology development, which came primarily from the private sector. For the machines that brought the new lands under cultivation and then reaped the harvest, the private researcher was at the forefront, with profit and marketing closely linked to product development. At Kansas State Agricultural College (KSAC), a Farm Machinery Department within the Division of Engineering was established in 1915, but the first Professor of Agricultural Engineering was appointed only in 1921 (Willard, 1940:201, 227, 266).

For the first quarter century of the existence of the Kansas Agricultural Experiment Station (KAES), established in 1888, the year following passage of the Hatch Act, greatest emphasis in wheat research was placed on cultural practices, although testing of yields of different varieties and selection of improved strains was also important.

The early experiments in growing wheat were summarized in two important bulletins. The first, published in 1911 and written by Jardine and Call, is called simply "How to Grow Wheat in Kansas." Jardine, who was Professor of Agronomy, later became Director of the Experiment Station, President of KSAC, and, in 1925, U.S. Secretary of Agriculture. The second bulletin, "Growing Wheat in Kansas," was published in 1918. It was authored by Call and Salmon. Call later became Director of the Experiment Station and Dean of Agriculture.

In the introduction to each bulletin it is noted that, while Kansas was a pre-eminent wheat-producing state (in the interim between the two bulletins, Kansas became the undisputed leader in total wheat production [Call and Salmon, 1918:9]), its yields were not a point of pride. Kansas ranked thirty-second in yield per acre among the states (Jardine and Call, 1911:5):

> Kansas farmers are trying to operate more land than their machinery and labor will cover efficiently. They are not giving attention to the rotation of crops, the growing of livestock or the up-keep of the fertility of the soil, which facts . . . undoubtedly contribute largely to our low acre-yields (Jardine and Call, 1911:6).

The following examples are results presented in the above bulletins, which it was believed would improve those yields:

Cultivation

Winter wheat yields were from four to six bushels greater for early plowing (July or early August) than for late plowing (mid-September) in seedbed preparation under continuous cropping. Three-inch plowing was preferred to deep plowing, because the increased yield from subsoiling did not pay for the added expense of the operation. In Western Kansas, listing increased yields by protecting small plants from hard winters and spring blowing, and from winter kill when planting was late (Call and Salmon, 1918:34-40).

Summer Fallow

While research on summer fallow was considerable, the bulletins draw no clear conclusion whether summer fallowing was profitable or not. KSAC had not yet established an Agricultural Economics Department. The Director's Report of 1915-1916 is the first to list an agricultural economist as a member of the KAES (he was in the Economics Department). Only in the 1918-1919 Director's Report does an *Agricultural* Economics Department first appear.

Hessian Fly

Since no wheat varieties were resistant to Hessian fly, it had to be controlled by cultural means. Early deep plowing was deemed effective, but it would have to be practiced by the entire neighborhood, as the flies migrate considerable distance. Thus, it was concluded that the only practical solution was planting after the fly-free date (Call and Salmon, 1918:25; see Headlee and Parker, 1913 for a more complete summary of work to that date at KSAC on the Hessian fly).

Seeding Rate

Experiments conducted over five years established norms for seeding rates (Call and Salmon, 1918:31), which were consistent with those derived in the 1890s (Experiment Station, 1896:105) and which have not been significantly modified to the present.

While the greatest emphasis in KAES research during the first quarter century was on cultural practices, work was also conducted on varietal development and fertilization. What was significant was that none of the work of the KAES was reflected in significantly improved yields during this development period. So long as new land came into production, there were no great pressures for research dollars to improve per acre yields. By 1919, the amount of land planted to wheat leveled off to around eleven million acres, an average around which planted acres of wheat would fluctuate until the present. The 1920s saw expanded activity in wheat breeding.

The Era of Emphasis on Yield per Acre

With the advent of World War I and later with acreage limitations in the 1930s, concern shifted even more sharply to increasing yield per acre (Flora and Rodefeld, 1978). Investments in the 1920s and 1930s began to pay off in the 1940s with the release of important new varieties, thus undermining federal policy in the short-term interests of local producers. In the second half of the 1950s, sharp increases in yield occurred in farmers' fields. In Kansas, wheat yields increased from an average of sixteen bushels per acre (with a great deal of fluctuation due to great weather variations) from 1940 to 1956 to twice that amount by the 1970s (USDA, various dates).

Varietal Development

The first wheat breeder (also in charge of oats, barley, and sorghum breeding) at Kansas State Agricultural College, J. H. Parker, discussed wheat variety development at KSAC in three overlapping stages: (1) introduction of new varieties from other places, (2) selection, and (3) crossing or hybridization (Parker, 1934:121–22).

In the early years, the first two were carried on simultaneously. In the first year of the experiment station's existence, some fifty-one varieties were planted for yield tests (Shelton, 1888:43); by 1891, the number had expanded to 240 (Georgeson et al., 1891:19).

Both hard red winter (HRW) and soft red winter (SRW) wheat were grown in Kansas in the early days of the experiment station. For at least the first decade, SRW varieties were used as the standard against which performance of other varieties were measured in experiments at Manhattan. In 1918, SRW wheat was still recommended for approximately the three easternmost tiers of counties of the state (Call and Salmon, 1918:14).

The standard varieties of HRW wheat grown during the first three decades of existence of the KAES were various selections of Turkey red (brought by the Mennonites from Russia in 1874) and Kharkov, another Russian variety imported by the U.S. Department of Agriculture in 1900. In 1908, Experiment Station Director Burkett was commissioned by the Board of Regents to travel to Russia and Turkey "for the purposes of investigating the source of seed-wheat supply and make arrangements for importation if deemed advisable" (Agricultural Experiment Station, 1909:vii). Burkett spent four months in Europe. Upon his return he concluded, "The wheat of Turkey is inferior to Kansas-bred wheat, and it is not advisable to look in that direction for improved seed stock" (Agricultural Experiment Station, 1909:vii–ix). From Russia, he selected some twenty varieties from central Crimea and the Province of Kharkov for importation and testing. Few of these varieties were used as bases for future crosses; none was grown commercially in Kansas.

In 1891, experiments began in the selection of superior berries of a particular variety (Georgeson et al., 1891:7–9). The first new wheat variety selected in this fashion and released at Kansas State was Kanred, selected from Crimean HRW wheat by Professor H. F. Roberts, a botanist, in 1906. After considerable testing, Kanred was finally released in 1917. For the seven years it was grown at Manhattan before its release, it yielded over 4.5 bushels more than Turkey or Kharkof (Call and Salmon, 1918:17). There were two major reasons that Kanred never occupied a very large portion of Kansas wheat land: it had weak straw, particularly important with combine harvesting, and it was upstaged by the introduction of the higher yielding Blackhull (Parker, 1935:147). Blackhull, introduced by a private breeder, did not have the long testing period, which the experiment stations imposed on themselves.

Kawvale, a SRW wheat, was selected from older eastern varieties in 1918 (Parker, 1934:122). In 1931, a semi-hard pedigree (pure line) of Kawvale was released for Southeast Kansas. It was fairly tolerant of Hessian fly and leaf rust. However, Kawvale shattered easily and was therefore not adaptable to combine harvesting (Agricultural Experiment Station, 1932:34; Parker, 1935:155–56). Since the selection process involved strengthening desirable characteristics already present in the variety, breakthroughs in yield or other characteristics could not be expected. Varieties adapted climatically to Kansas, but developed before combine harvesting, were unlikely to have characteristics appropriate to the new harvesting technology. "The coming of the combine has stimulated the demand of Kansas farmers for early varieties of winter wheat with stiff straw and heads from which the grain will not shatter in the field. . . ." (Parker, 1934:124–25). Cross breeding would allow for the bringing of greater genetic diversity to new varieties adapted to the region.

The first *crossed* wheat to be released by Kansas State was Tenmarq, a combination of Marquis, a popular hard red spring (HRS) wheat grown in the northern plains states and in Canada, and a strain of HRW wheat similar to Kanred. Tenmarq was developed by Parker. Apparently, the choice of Marquis as a parent was to develop a HRW wheat that had comparable baking qualities to the HRS wheats. Marquis was one of the most popular wheats in the HRS region. In particular, HRS wheats had greater strength, i.e., made larger loaves per unit of flour, although HRW wheats had a higher flour yield (flour-to-grain ratio) (Thomas, 1917; cited in Parker, 1935:142). Tenmarq was the first successful wheat developed at KSAC for which baking quality was a primary (along with yield) characteristic bred into the new variety.

Kawvale and Tenmarq had substantially higher yields than previously available varieties. In nursery trials at Manhattan, they averaged 25 and 19 percent higher yields than Kanred (average of 1923–1929) (Agricultural Experiment Station, 1930:30).

Parker's next released cross after Tenmarq was Quivira, which he bred for less shatter proneness and for resistance to red leaf rust, as well as yield and stiff straw (Parker, 1934:124–25). While it did not turn out to be a widely adopted wheat, its development illustrates the characteristics that Parker was seeking.

The ability to breed rust resistance into new varieties derived from what was learned about rust resistance of many different crosses through their innoculation with rust cultures in the nursery beginning in 1918–1919 (Agricultural Experiment Station, 1920:32). In the early thirties, similar work was done in classifying varieties according to degree of Hessian fly tolerance (Agricultural Experiment Station, 1932:128).

Blackhull, a selection from Turkey wheat made by Earl G. Clark, a private breeder from Sedgwick, Kansas, was first distributed in 1917, the same year as Kanred. By 1927, it was grown on four million Kansas acres. About one-third of the wheat grown in Kansas during the decade ending in 1939 was developed by Clark (Heyne and Reitz, 1944:768). Clark's varieties did not go through the rigorous testing that publicly released varieties do.

According to multi-year KAES trials, Blackhull outyielded Turkey substantially and equalled Kanred. It also had a stiff straw and a tendency to ripen early, thus reducing the impact of hot winds and drought. Its main deficiencies were lack of winterhardiness (it was more adapted to South Central than Northwest Kansas), and, more importantly, it was not well accepted by many millers and bakers. While it normally tested two or three pounds higher than Turkey and Kanred, it had a thicker bran and a lower flour yield. This meant farmers liked it, for they were paid more because of a higher test weight. Millers considered it to be inferior because of a less favorable flour yield and because the gluten or protein is not as "strong" as the proteins of other HRW wheats, i.e., an equal amount of flour will not produce as large a loaf. No way existed to distinguish the threshed grain from other HRW wheats (Salmon et al., 1927). The bulletin on "Blackhull Wheat in Kansas" summarizes the pros and cons of blackhull, concluding with the following statement:

> Kansas enjoys a premium for her wheat in the world's markets, because of the splendid reputation which has been established. It would be very unfortunate for all citizens of the state if this reputation should be lost by the widespread use of a variety unsuited to the trade requirements of a large part of the milling industry. It would, therefore, seem to be the part of wisdom for a majority of Kansas farmers in the hard-wheat belt to grow varieties of the Turkey type (Salmon et al., 1927:4).

Blackhull and other varieties developed by Clark were designed with the immediate client in mind—the farmer. Not only did Blackhull have a higher test weight than its competitors, but the straw was bright and the berries attractively plump and long. Experiment stations, perhaps because they could take a long-term perspective, balanced the interests of the farmer (breeding for yield and disease resistance) and the miller and baker (breeding for baking quality).

Laude and Salmon (1932), in examining "Twenty Years of Testing Varieties and Strains of Winter Wheat at the Kansas Agricultural Experiment Station," conclude that yield differences between wheats traditionally grown in the state and the newer higher yielding varieties were due chiefly to early maturity to escape drought and high temperatures, resistance to winter kill, and resistance to disease. In the era of J. H. Parker, wheat breeding was based on the triple objectives of increased yield, disease resistance, and baking quality, the principal goals of Kansas State's breeding program to this day. Parker resigned from Kansas State in 1939.

In 1943, Kansas State released two varieties—Comanche and Pawnee (Pawnee was actually released first by the University of Nebraska in 1942). Both were the fruits of fourteen years of breeding and testing. The breeding was done under the supervision of J. H. Parker. Both had Tenmarq as one parent. Pawnee was a selection of a cross between Tenmarq and Kawvale. Comanche was a cross between Oro (a selection from Turkey) and Tenmarq (Laude et al., 1955:29–30). Thus, both varieties had a strong Turkey red ancestry. Comanche was recommended for the south-central, central, and southwestern parts of the state and Pawnee for the eastern half of the state. Both showed higher statewide yields than any existent variety.

Comanche was bunt resistant, sufficiently early to escape most rusts, and equal to Tenmarq in baking quality. It did not have Hessian fly tolerance and therefore was not recommended for Eastern Kansas. Pawnee's "superior characteristics are high yield and test weight, short stiff straw, high resistance to loose smut, and moderate resistance to leaf rust, stem rust, bunt, and Hessian fly." It had good milling qualities and was moderately winter-hardy (Reitz and Laude, 1943:8). Its baking qualities were acceptable. Its major fault was that it shattered readily (Laude et al., 1955:29).

Varietal development in the period initiated by World War I was first oriented toward stronger, stiffer straw and resistance to shattering to make the wheat more adapted to combine harvesting. Yield, of course, was also a consideration. Pest resistance and baking quality were soon factored in. By the 1940s, wheat breeding came to be based on three pillars: improved yield, milling and baking quality, and resistance to pests and diseases (KAES, 1983:3). No new variety could be introduced that did not maintain or improve yields and that was not at least as good as existent varieties in the other two categories.

Cultural Practices of the 1920s
Through the 1950s

Preventing Wind and Soil Erosion. As early as 1918, it was clear that pulverizing the soil surface was an inappropriate practice for the more arid part of the state. "Recent experiments show that for Central and Western Kansas a dust mulch is not necessary to conserve moisture, as many think" (Call and Salmon, 1918:41). It was also explained that blowing could also be prevented by cultivating at right angles to the prevailing winds. It was recommended that blowing be stopped by applying straw to the field and working it in with a disk or making occasional lister ridges at right angles to the winds.

During the 1930s, wind erosion became an urgent topic of concern. The most serious dust storms in the state's history occurred in 1935, following three years of seriously subnormal precipitation. Writing immediately previous to those dust storms, the director of the Fort Hays Branch Experiment Station (in Northwestern Kansas) stated: "The blowing of soil, excepting in the very sandy areas is a sign of carelessness. . . . Land which shows a tendency to blow cannot safely be farmed by the suitcase farmer, the city agriculturist, or the shiftless tenant" (Aicher, 1935:67–68). This statement suggests that absentee farming was a pervasive practice and a significant problem in the far western part of the state (see Hewes, 1973). The branch station director indicated that blowing could be prevented with the timely use of the proper implements. Blowing occurs because the surface is too fine. Particularly unsuitable implements for land with a tendency to blowing are the disk harrow, the drag harrow, and the one-way plow. It was strongly urged that the one-way plow should be used only when there was excessive weed growth brought on by a wet season. Stubble should not be burned off, but should be kept partially on the surface by use of implements such as the lister, the duckfoot weeder, the rod weeder, and the spring tooth harrow. Once soil begins blowing, it can be stopped only by community effort. "Unless all the land in the affected area receives protective attention just as soon as the soil begins to move, tremendous effort at a later date may prove fruitless" (Aicher, 1935:71).

Call (1936) describes a community effort at stopping soil blowing in Thomas County (where the Colby Branch Station in extreme northwestern Kansas is located) in 1914, which, because it was only getting underway when the winds came, was not successful. The blowing stopped when the rains came. However, that effort provided organizational experience, which was put to use in the 1930s.

District meetings were held in the affected territory attended by county agents, county drouth committeemen, and county commissioners. . . . As a result, a detailed survey of the condition of the land in each county was undertaken to determine the exact acreage that was eroding and in need of attention. The National Recovery Administration was asked to appropriate funds with which farmers might purchase fuel oil for tractors or feed for horses used in the work. . . .

The efforts of the farmers to control blowing were aided this season by rainfall somewhat above that of the previous four years. This increased rainfall, together with various methods of cultivation that have been used to work the soil, . . . has re-established a cover of vegetation over much of the area in Kansas that was blowing last spring. Whereas it was estimated that eight million acres were in condition to blow in March, 1935, a survey of the situation made the first of November showed this area to have been reduced to about 830,000 acres (Call, 1936:195–196).

In the 1950s a new method of reducing wind erosion was developed—stubble mulching or "trashy" tillage. A sweep or blade type implement is used to keep the residue from the previous crop on top to protect the soil from the winds (Laude et al., 1955:14). This is the modern version of spreading straw on the blowing land and partially working it in, which was practiced before the advent of the combined harvester-thresher. Shelterbelts were also recommended for prevention of wind erosion in the 1955 bulletin (Laude et al., 1955:23).

The Director's report for the biennium of 1930–1932 discusses research regarding a new conservation measure: terracing as a means of reducing soil erosion and conserving moisture. Soil loss from one torrential rain of 2.5 inches at Fort Hays was 11.2 tons per acre on summer fallow ground and 11.2 on land planted to kafir. It was .69 tons from land in wheat and .02 or less from sod (Agricultural Experiment Station, 1932:42, 119). This was the first research reported on water-caused soil erosion in station directors' reports. The 1955 bulletin on "Growing Wheat in Kansas" did not recommend terraces on wheat land but recommended them if wheat was grown in rotation with row crops (Laude et al., 1955:12–13).

Soil Moisture at Planting Time, Summer Fallowing, and Subsequent Yields. In the 1920s and 1930s, a good deal of work was done at the Western Kansas Branch Experiment Stations (Fort Hays, Garden City, and Colby), in conjunction with the Office of Dry Land Agriculture of the USDA, on the relationship between moisture in the soil at planting time and subsequent yields (Hallsted, 1937). Using data from over twenty years of experiments, results at all three stations showed that early plowing, rather than late plowing, increased soil moisture dramatically and resulted in moderate yield increases.

At the two westernmost stations—Colby and Garden City—summer fallowing increased soil moisture more than at Fort Hays and resulted in yields that doubled those of early plowing (Hallsted and Mathews, 1936:28,36). At Fort Hays, results from nineteen years of experiments indicated that summer fallowing one year in four resulted in the same yields from three crops as that obtained from four years of continuous cropping (Hallsted, 1937:13).

Regarding general cultural practices, the conclusion from time series results from three Western Kansas branch stations was:

When wheat stubble land is to be fallowed, the most practical method under most conditions is to leave the stubble of the preceding crop in the land during the winter and spring to protect the soil against wind action. The field should then be cultivated with the one-way, disk, or duckfoot as soon as weeds start to grow in the spring. As soon as the second growth of weeds starts, and not later than the middle of May, the land should be plowed or listed. Plowed land may be cultivated with the springtooth harrow, duckfoot cultivator, or rotary rod weeder throughout the summer to prevent weed growth and maintain a cloddy condition of the surface (Throckmorton and Myers, 1941:16–17; see also Laude et al., 1955:8, for similar results).

The results on early plowing and summer fallow led to recommendations for deciding when winter wheat should be abandoned:

When the initial soil moisture is deficient and the precipitation is low to April 1, it is probable that abandonment of the crop and the conservation of water in a summer fallow for a future crop will pay far better than allowing the water to be wasted by the poor crop and weeds on the land (Hallsted and Mathews, 1936:46).

Throckmorton (who later became Experiment Station Director) and Myers actually showed probabilities of obtaining specific yields based on the depth of soil moisture at seeding time (1941:10).[1] Measurement of the depth of soil moisture is much more practical for the farmer than determining the actual number of inches of water in the soil, although the relationship between the three variables varies according to the texture of the soil; whether farmers actually used these results by measuring depth of soil moisture in deciding how much wheat to plant or to plow up wheat in the spring is not reported in any of the KAES work.

Work continued through the 1940s and 1950s on soil moisture in the semiarid western part of the state. Myers indicated that approximately ten inches of moisture were necessary to produce a minimal wheat crop in Western Kansas. There appears to be a threshhold below which the plant will put all its energy into its own growth without seeking to reproduce itself (Myers, 1940:70).

The effectiveness of recommending summer fallowing for most of the period of existence of the Experiment Station is illustrated by the fact that for the period 1947-1951, about 24 percent of all cultivated land in the western half of the state was summer fallowed (Laude *et al.*, 1955:7).

Throckmorton and Myers state that summer fallow influences crop production in three ways: "It results in higher annual acre yields than can be obtained on continuously cropped land, it reduces the frequency of crop failure, and it stabilizes total production" (1941:20, 23).

Pasturing. "It seems that when judiciously pastured, the reduction in yield is seldom more than one or two bushels per acre. Often the value of the pasture is more than enough to make up this loss" (Call and Salmon, 1918:31).

Fertilization Studies of the 1920s to the 1950s

Early experiments in fertilizing wheat tended to show negative results. In 1892, the following tentative result was reached: "So far the plats continuously in wheat, without manure, have given the best return, the manured plats being so rich that the wheat lodges and does not fill out" (Experiment Station, 1892:50). Similar results were found in 1896. This may be because of the heavy fertilization (twenty tons of manure per acre), the richness of the new soil, and perhaps the varieties used did not have strong straw.

Other results in 1896 indicated the need to enrich the soil. "The acre which has been in wheat for sixteen years past is beginning to show signs of exhaustion" (Experiment Station, 1896:90, 104).

By 1907-1908, research results were showing a positive response of wheat production to fertilizers.

Fertilizer experiments were continued with wheat and oats during the past year with marked results favoring the use of barn-yard manure. However, certain chemical fertilizers or combinations of chemical fertilizers have also given increased yields, nitrates and phosphates showing a marked effect, especially with wheat (Agricultural Experiment Station, 1909:xxxv).

Call and Salmon point out that yellow berry, rather than being an inherited characteristic indicating that the farmer's seed is "running out," is an environmental response to low nitrogen content of the soil (1918:23). Experiments at Manhattan showed a nearly 50 percent increase in yields on continuous cropping wheat from the application of five tons of manure and a 15–20 percent increase in wheat yields from application of a similar amount of manure to land in a corn-cowpeas-wheat rotation (seven-year averages). However, researchers gave only a qualified endorsement to commercial fertilizers. While recommending phosphorus or phosphorus and nitrogen for certain Eastern Kansas soils, they state bluntly, "In Central and Western Kansas, commercial fertilizers never pay" (Call and Salmon, 1918:47).

The first appearance of the term "conservation of the soil" in Experiment Station Director's Report occurs in 1918–1919, which states:

One of the most important problems in Kansas is the problem of a declining soil fertility. A large proportion of the agriculture of the state in the past has been essentially exploitative, with the result that the soil in large districts of the state is much less productive now than it was 50 years ago (Agricultural Experiment Station, 1920:14).

As late as 1937, Hallsted, the branch station's agronomist who did seminal work on cultivation practices, soil moisture, and yields, states that at Fort Hays, "The application of fertilizers, on the Fort Hays Branch Experiment Station has not increased the yields of wheat. That indicates that the failures or low yields were not due to lack of fertility" (1937:1).

The breakthrough in determining that application of usable nitrogen generally increased wheat yields came from the studies of Gainey and Sewell, bacteriologist and soils agronomist at KSAC. They noted the lush green spots in wheat fields that had been pastured. The spots were found to have been caused by urine deposits from the cattle. The initial study conducted in Central and Western Kansas in 1929 showed the spots contained significantly greater nitrates in the soil and in the plant than did samples taken from nearby locations within the same field (Gainey and Sewell, 1930). Further study during four subsequent seasons revealed that the spots showed higher grain yields, grain with higher protein content, and the wheat was no more susceptible to lodging than wheat from the nearby control locations. When attempts were made to replicate the spots by application of commercial nitrogen, results were not as dramatic: yields tended to be higher, but protein content of the grain was not significantly different (Gainey et al., 1937).

Work done in the twenties suggested that cultivation practices had an impact on protein content of wheat produced and on other aspects of wheat quality. Sewell and Swanson found that early tillage resulted in more nitrates in the soil at the time of planting, which positively influenced total grain protein produced per acre (1926:9). A low percentage of phosphorus in the grain was associated with high nitrate supply in the soil. Apparently, a soil deficient in nitrates produces a low yield and small kernels, which have a high proportion of bran. Since most of the phosphorus is stored in the bran, this explains a high percent of phosphorus where the yield is low. In fact, the percent of phosphorus in the grain is used to indicate the bran-to-flour ratio of wheat. The total quantity of phosphorus in the crop varied directly with yield, showing that phosphorus was not a limiting factor (1926:5, 10–11). In summary, early tillage "produced the largest quantity of nitrates in the soil, not only produced the largest yield of wheat and the highest percent of protein, but the flour from this wheat was also of superior quality as measured by loaf volume and texture of the bread" (Sewell and Swanson, 1926:16). The linkage between cultivation practices and nitrogen production in the soil, and wheat quality was established.

Work in the 1950s, which drew on twenty years of time series experiments in Western Kansas, illustrates a complicated relationship between nitrogen fertility and available moisture. Early plowing dramatically increased soil moisture over that occurring with late plowing. This was not translated into substantially greater yields except at the Colby Station in far North-western Kansas. At the Fort Hays Station, the advantage of July over September plowing was five bushels per acre, at Garden City, one and one-half bushels. At Colby, there was actually a yield advantage for the late planted wheat. The explanation was the following:

> . . . more nitrates are made available by early tillage. In these relatively favorable areas [more humid sections of the dryland areas of the Great Plains, such as Hays], there usually is enough moisture stored by early tillage to provide water for the lush growth induced by the extra nitrates. At Colby and Garden City, . . . less moisture but ample nitrates are usually provided by early tillage. In the latter areas there may not be enough moisture in the early-tilled land for the growth caused by the abundant nitrates. *Accordingly, reduced yields may result from early tillage in drier years* (Laude et al., 1955:9).

Early plowing also had a positive impact on yields in Eastern Kansas. Experiments at Manhattan from 1913 to 1952 indicate that "an average of one bushel of wheat per acre is lost for each week's delay in plowing the land after July 15" (Laude et al., 1955:6). Since moisture is usually not a limiting factor in Eastern Kansas, the introduction of precipitation-associated nitrogen is the probable explanation for increased yields from early plowing.

Experiments conducted in Eastern and Central Kansas during the period 1948–1952 indicated that the application of 50–100 pounds of nitrogen with fifty pounds of phosphorus (P_2O_5) increased wheat yields thirteen to fifteen bushels to the acre. The addition of potash had marginal impact.

Because moisture, more than fertilizer, limits crop production in Western Kansas, response to fertilizers is unpredictable. Fertilizers on dryland wheat

will seldom reduce yields. Yields may be increased but the increase is liable
to be too small to pay for the fertilizer (Laude et al., 1955:17).

Since in Western Kansas the principal limiting factor is moisture and
since precipitation brings nitrogen, the need for nitrogen was not proven,
except perhaps in years of abundant moisture, when yields were well above
average. (The studies of Gainey et al. [1937] were carried out in 1930 and
1931, both of which were years of above average soil moisture.) The
effectiveness of fertilization of wheat in Western Kansas had to await the
development of considerably higher yields, which began in the late 1950s,
immediately after the studies cited above.

The Export Era of the 1970s and 1980s
and Its Prelude

While the beginning of export dominance in American agriculture and
for wheat in particular can be placed at 1973, the agricultural experiment
station and the entire agricultural production system were preparing the
way for an agriculture that was export oriented through the tremendous
growth in productivity and the introduction of substantially higher yielding
varieties beginning in the latter half of the 1950s.

For these decades the method of analysis shifts. The existence of more
comprehensive experiment station directors' reports from 1958 to the present
allows a more direct analysis of the presentation of the station to the public
and to its most important constituency, the researchers themselves. Annual
reports of the KAES Director, which were presented at the station conference
beginning in 1958 when the first station-wide conference was held, have
been examined. This allows a more direct examination of perceived constituencies and station responses to them than the analysis of research
findings allowed.

The first experiment station conference had the theme "Agricultural
Adjustment" and occurred at the beginning of a period of good times for
Kansas wheat farmers (1958–1962) (Beck, 1958). In the 1962 conference, in
the midst of large-scale migration from farm to city, the director discussed
the contribution of land grant education to profound structural changes
that had hastened the shift from agrarian to urban life, created new paths
of occupational mobility, and offered the world a model of the highest
export quality (Wilson, 1962). Efficiency was the watchword; adjustment
had only a positive side in this period of prosperity of the agricultural
sector as a whole.

The period from 1964 to the early 1970s was a period of low wheat
prices and, in many of those years, rather low incomes for wheat farmers.
In 1964, the director expressed the desire to have a facility for the development
of industrial uses of winter wheat and grain sorghum (Wilson, 1964). Two
years later, there was concern expressed for more efficient production of
plant proteins, suggesting a desire to expand markets for Kansas wheat by
differentiating it qualitywise from wheat produced in other states (Smith,

1966). By 1971, research was being done on improving efficiency of wheat as a swine feed through amino acid supplementation, and expanded use of wheat as a beef feed (Smith, 1971). Research at the Fort Hays branch station paved the way for utilizing 275 million bushels of wheat as cattle feed in 1972 (Smith, 1973)—immediately prior to the revealing of a large sale of grain to the Soviet Union!

In 1970, the director assessed the following research needs for the coming decade (Smith, 1970):

1. A concerted effort to improve net farm income (which except for 1966, had been mediocre since the early 1960s). Kansas had slipped from sixth to seventh in total agricultural production. The director's goal was to make it fourth by 1980. He saw increased production as a means of improving net farm income, when in reality, increased production in the short or medium term has historically brought about low farm incomes.

2. Emergence of "true commercial agriculture." The director foresaw the emergence of capitalist agriculture, with leasing of land and facilities, contracting of technical services, and price negotiation. "True commercial agriculture," he indicated, "may well account for 95 percent of total agricultural production in the 1980s" (Smith, 1970:13).

3. Emphasis on wheat research, for which efficiency gains are easier to achieve than with corn or sorghum. He predicted a 30 percent increase in yields by 1980, through development of high-yielding varieties. Since development of a new variety took twelve to fifteen years (recently shortened to seven to ten years) (KAES, 1983:7), striving for better yields occurred even in periods of overproduction. In fact, the KAES director's view of agriculture in industrial terms glossed over the contradiction between expanded production and low farm incomes.

Coincidentally with the Russian grain sales and phasing out of farm programs, four new wheat varieties were approved for release in 1973 and 1974, the first multiple releases since 1943. With soaring grain prices, there was a call for greater production and an expression of a "need to lower domestic food prices to appease the American consumer" (Smith, 1974:11). Added grain production would also help alleviate world hunger and improve the U.S. balance of payments "in the interest of national economic solvency" (Smith, 1974:11).

The energy crisis occurred almost simultaneously with the Russian grain sales. The 1974 director's report devoted ten pages to a discussion of energy use in agriculture and linkage of that to the need to deal with world hunger (Smith, 1974:13-22). It was estimated that the 50 percent of synthetic fertilizer used in Kansas, which was applied to wheat, increased wheat yields by 20 percent, which in turn was used to alleviate world hunger, a humanitarian justification of the continued use of scarce natural gas for fertilizer production. The director suggested diversion of substantial research effort in plant science projects, which were considered low priority, to research into improving protein content of wheat.

In 1975, it was stated that "future wheat research priorities were clearly indicated as a result of 1974 marketing activities. . . . It was obvious that additional resources and efforts must be dedicated to producing hard winter wheats with more acceptable bread-making qualities" (Smith, 1975:11). In 1977, Larned wheat was released. It had better bread-making qualities than Scout or Sage, built-in Hessian fly resistance, and good yields (Smith, 1977:9).

Hessian fly resistance had been sought in Kansas State's early wheat breeding efforts. Resistance to other diseases was also important. In the director's report (Smith, 1975), mention is made of research on wheat streak mosaic. The search continued for protection against soilborne wheat mosaic by attempting backcrossing with wheat grass.

The 1977 report emphasizes the difficult situation of Kansas farmers (Smith, 1977). In November 1976, wheat prices were one-third below those of the previous year and half their peak from early 1974. The 1976 wheat crop in eight northwest counties exceeded thirty bushels for the eighth consecutive year (Smith, 1977). (These data indicate the continuation of secular tendencies toward overproduction as well as a reduction of weather- and disease-associated risk in dryland farming in the semi-arid plains.) Farmers were also plagued with inflationary rises in cost of inputs, rapidly rising land prices, high taxes, and even drought. In the 1977 report, the solution offered to the farmer and to the nation (in three previous years, growth in agricultural exports had offset added costs of importing petroleum) is: "We have no choice but to increase our competitive sales position in wheat and other food grains" (Smith, 1977:5).

Concretely, the director suggested "directing as much attention in the future to improving wheat quality as we have given in the past to increasing yields" (Smith, 1977:5). Preliminary trials of one of five high protein crosses suggested the possibility of gaining 1.5 percent increase in protein with little or no loss in yield. The goal was to achieve 2.5 percent increase in protein content by 1985 without sacrificing yield. Experience with an infrared type of protein analyzer during the previous year was important in identifying high protein wheat, which might then be segregated for separate marketing from lower protein wheat. It was also used as a preliminary screening device for selecting genetic material for high protein varietal development.

With continued surpluses and resultant low prices in 1977, the director, in 1978, made a plea for support from wheat producers and others in developing a hard white winter wheat for Kansas (Smith, 1978). He explained that Kansas was at a competitive disadvantage in overseas markets since such a large proportion of its wheat production (two-thirds) is sold abroad and is of only one type. Developing a second type would give Kansas wheat access to more foreign markets. This expression of willingness to make a major shift in wheat breeding died aborning. White wheat is not mentioned in future reports. The problem of segregation of a second type of wheat in the state's marketing system was probably the principal stumbling block.

The collective view of elevator operators was undoubtedly made known to the Kansas State University administration. Only in the 1980s is basic research given a prominent position in the KAES director's report. The groundwork for such research had been laid a decade earlier. In 1969, a grant of nearly a million dollars was received from the National Science Foundation (NSF) to establish a Division of Biology (Smith, 1970:11). The basic research in genetic engineering was visibly linked with varietal improvement in the late 1970s—beginning with the research on soilborne wheat mosaic virus. In 1978, the legislature funded a special project on "Improved Disease and Insect Resistance in Cereal Crops through Genetic Manipulation and Variety Development" ($236,000).

Conclusions

Increased yields created new research agendas. The heavier heads led to more lodging, and, thus, shorter, stiffer straw to resist lodging again became a consideration. Hence, the recent movement to semi-dwarf varieties. The introduction of new strains of wheat with substantially higher yields induced planting of a limited number of varieties with a resultant vulnerability to disease and pests. Breeding then attempted to counter that vulnerability. Although currently used varieties are perhaps more disease resistant than earlier ones, vulnerability to disease still exists. In 1982, 41 percent of Kansas wheat land was planted to Newton, a semi-dwarf wheat recently developed at Kansas State University. The risk of an outbreak of leaf rust, to which it is somewhat vulnerable, would be much less if a greater diversity of varieties were planted (KAES, 1983:5).

Since the focus on higher yields per acre, brought about in part by governmental attempts to limit production, coincided with the new concern with grain as a generator of foreign exchange, there was no need to readjust research goals drastically in the 1970s. Those goals emphasized varietal development.

The new feature in varietal development is a greater concern for milling quality. Significant efforts have been made in the past ten years to introduce new varieties with high protein content. The unsuccessful effort to introduce white wheat was an attempt to improve Kansas's competitive position in the international wheat market by diversifying potential markets and thereby reducing risk.

The tremendous increase in the cost of capital, as real interest rates (the difference between the nominal interest rate and the inflation rate) have skyrocketed, land prices have plummeted, and perhaps one-fourth of farmers are in serious financial difficulty, has not had a significant impact on wheat-related research at Kansas State. This major shift in factor prices for farmers since 1981 has not been translated into research policy except for a thrust in the area of conservation tillage, which in the short run has the opposite effect for some farmers because of the need to buy new and different equipment.

The long-term orientation of wheat varietal development has in an important sense limited purchased inputs. Since the hybridization route was not chosen in wheat, varietal development remained in the public sector, for there was no way for the private sector to capture the fruits of varietal improvement. Thus, public research includes breeding for disease and pest resistance, while it is in the interest of the private sector to seek chemical solutions to those problems.

In contrast to private wheat breeders, wheat varietal research at Kansas State has attempted to balance interests of farmers, millers, and bakers by taking the view that in the medium and long term, their interests coincide, since there will be little market for wheat with inferior milling and baking qualities. On the other hand, the interests of elevator companies have been strong enough to prevent the development of a white wheat, which would have placed Kansas producers in a more competitive position in the world market.

Historically, Kansas State University and the land grant system have been best at increasing the productive capacity of farmers. That has been accomplished, in the case of wheat research, in such a way as to contain the need for purchased inputs, such as seed and chemicals, but it has encouraged purchase of fertilizers due to the quest for higher yielding varieties. If wheat research had been principally in the private sector, input requirements would have undoubtedly been higher.

Kansas State's research effort has been most effective when it tackled a long-term problem—whether it be varietal development, cultural practices, or even soil conservation measures. The experiment station has been less successful in seeking alternative uses of wheat, alternative crops, alternative sources of energy, or, in general, means of shoring up farmers' incomes during hard times. A principal reason is that the payoff time for a research effort may be eight to ten years or longer. Generally, the conditions that generated the pressure for these new research topics disappear or ameliorate in a shorter time span. An exception is the current farm crisis, which began in 1980 and today shows few signs of ameliorating.

The research advances that have been made—and they are impressive—have contributed to the improvement of farm incomes over the long term through growth in farm size, greater production per farm, and exportation (until the 1970s when a migration turnaround to agricultural communities occurred) of the "excess" population from rural communities. Land grant administrators and many scientists have tended to see only the positive side of the precipitous decline in farm numbers. The consumer, even more than the farmer or the rural community, has been the number one beneficiary of land grant research.[2]

Notes

Thanks is expressed to Marie Neher for contributing to research on an earlier draft of this paper.

1. For instance, they found that when the ground was completely dry at seeding time, the probability of crop failure was 71 percent and the probability of a twenty-or-more-bushel crop was zero regardless of future rainfall; if soil moisture was a foot in depth, the probability of a thirty-bushel crop was zero; if moisture was three or more feet deep, the probability of a crop failure was only 10 percent and the probability of a thirty-bushel-and-more crop was 23 percent (Throckmorton and Myers, 1941:10).

2. See Flora and Flora (1986) for an examination of the impact of changes in numbers of medium and large farms on rural communities in the wheat and livestock counties of the Great Plains and West.

References

Agricultural Experiment Station. *Twenty-first Annual Report.* Manhattan: Kansas State Agricultural College, 1909.

———. *Director's Report, 1918-1919.* Manhattan: Kansas State Agricultural College, 1920.

———. *Fifth Biennial Report of the Director.* Manhattan: Kansas State Agricultural College, 1930.

———. *Sixth Biennial Report of the Director.* Manhattan: Kansas State College of Agriculture and Applied Sciences, 1932.

Aicher, L. C. "Curling the Wind." *Twenty-ninth Biennial Report* 34:67-71. Kansas State Board of Agriculture, 1935.

Beck, Glenn H. "Opening Remarks" and "Closing Remarks." Pp. iii and 78 in *Minutes: Station Conference.* Manhattan: Kansas Agricultural Experiment Station, January 13-15, 1958.

Busch, Lawrence, and Lacy, William B. *Science, Agriculture, and the Politics of Research.* Boulder, Colorado: Westview Press, 1983.

Call, L. E. "Cultural Methods of Controlling Wind Erosion." *Journal of the American Society of Agronomy* 28:193-201, 1936.

Call, L. E., and Salmon, S. C. "Growing Wheat in Kansas." Agricultural Experiment Station Bulletin No. 219. Manhattan: Kansas State Agricultural College, 1918.

Experiment Station. "Bulletin." No. 1. Manhattan: Kansas State Agricultural College, April 1888.

———. "Experiment with Wheat." Agricultural Experiment Station Bulletin No. 33. Manhattan: Kansas State Agricultural College, August 1892.

———. "Experiments with Wheat." Agricultural Experiment Station Bulletin No. 59. Manhattan: Kansas State Agricultural College, 1896.

Flora, Jan L., and Flora, Cornelia Butler. "Emerging Agricultural Technologies, Farm Size, Public Policy, and Rural Communities: The Great Plains and the West." Paper prepared for the project, *Technology, Public Policy and the Changing Structure of Agriculture,* Office of Technology Assessment. Washington, D.C.: U.S. Congress, 1985.

Flora, Jan, and Rodefeld, Richard D. "The Nature, Magnitude, and Consequences of Change in Agricultural Technology." In R. D. Rodefeld *et al.* (eds.), *Change in Rural America: Causes, Consequences, and Alternatives.* St. Louis, Missouri: C. V. Mosby Co., 1978.

Flora, Jan L., and Stitz, John M. "Ethnicity, Persistence, and Capitalization of Agriculture in the Great Plains during the Settlement Period: Wheat Production and Risk Avoidance." *Rural Sociology* 50 (Fall):341-60, 1985.

Gainey, P. L., and Sewell, M. C. "The Role of Nitrogen in the Production of Spots in Wheat Fields." *Journal of Agricultural Research* 45(3):129–48, 1930.

Gainey, P. L.; Sewell, M. C.; and Myers, H. E. "Nitrogen—The Major Cause in the Production of Spotted Wheat Fields." Manhattan: Agricultural Experiment Station, Kansas State College of Agriculture and Applied Science, 1937.

Georgeson, C. C.; Cottrell, H. M.; and Shelton, W. "Experiments with Wheat." Experiment Station Bulletin No. 20. Manhattan: Kansas State Agricultural College, July 1891.

Hallsted, A. L. "Reducing the Risk in Wheat Farming in Western Kansas." *Thirtieth Biennial Report*, pages 98–111. Kansas State Board of Agriculture, 1937.

Hallsted, A. L., and Mathews, O. R. "Soil Moisture and Winter Wheat with Suggestion on Abandonment." Agricultural Experiment Station Bulletin No. 273. Manhattan: Kansas State College of Agriculture and Applied Sciences, January 1936.

Headlee, T. J., and Parker, J. B. "The Hessian Fly." Bulletin No. 188. Manhattan: Kansas Agricultural Experiment Station, 1913.

Hewes, Leslie. *The Suitcase Farming Frontier: A Study in the Historical Geography of the Central Great Plains.* Lincoln: University of Nebraska Press, 1973.

Heyne, E. G., and Reitz, L. P. "Characteristics and Origins of Blackhull Wheat." *Journal of the American Society of Agronomy* 36(9):768–78, 1944.

Jardine, W. M., and Call, L. E. "How to Grow Wheat in Kansas." Farm Bulletin No. 176. Manhattan: Experiment Station, Kansas State Agricultural College, 1911.

Kansas Agricultural Experiment Station. "Kansas Wheat Research: Producing Grain for the Staff of Life." Special Publication. Manhattan: Kansas State University, April 1983.

Laude, H. H., and Salmon, S. C. "Twenty Years of Testing Varieties and Strains of Winter Wheat at the Kansas Agricultural Experiment Station." Kansas Agricultural Experiment Station Technical Bulletin No. 30. Manhattan: Kansas State College of Agriculture and Applied Sciences, 1932.

Laude, H. H.; Hobbs, J. A.; Smith, F. W.; Heyne, E. G.; Clapp, A. L.; and Zahnley, J. W. "Growing Wheat in Kansas." Agricultural Experiment Station Bulletin No. 370. Manhattan: Kansas State College of Agriculture and Applied Sciences, August 1955.

Myers, H. E. "Soil Moisture and Winter Wheat in Kansas." *Transactions of the Kansas Academy of Science* 43 (March 28–30):69–73, 1940.

Parker, J. H. "The Romance of Plant Breeding." *Kansas State Board of Agriculture Quarterly Report* 53 (March):119–30, 1934.

———. "Wheat Improvement in Kansas, 1874–1934." *Twenty-Ninth Biennial Report* 34:139–64. Kansas State Board of Agriculture, 1935.

Reitz, L. P., and Laude, H. H. "Comanche and Pawnee: New Varieties of Hard Red Winter Wheat for Kansas." Manhattan: Agricultural Experiment Station, Kansas State College of Agriculture and Applied Science, 1943.

Salmon, S. C.; Swanson, C. O.; and Laude, H. H. "Blackhull Wheat in Kansas." Manhattan: Agricultural Experiment Station, Kansas State Agricultural College, 1927.

Sewell, M. C., and Swanson, C. O. "Tillage in Relation to Milling and Baking Qualities of Wheat." Kansas Agricultural Experiment Station Technical Bulletin No. 19. Manhattan: Kansas State Agricultural College, 1926.

Shelton, E. M. "Experiments with Wheat." Experiment Station Bulletin No. 4. Manhattan: Kansas State Agricultural College, September 1888.

Smith, Floyd W. "Director's Report." *Minutes: Station Conference*. Manhattan: Kansas Agricultural Experiment Station, 1966, 1970, 1971, 1974, 1975, 1977, 1978.

Throckmorton, R. I., and Myers, H. E. "Summer Fallow in Kansas." Manhattan: Agricultural Experiment Station, Kansas State Agriculture and Applied Science, 1941.

U.S. Department of Agriculture. *Agricultural Statistics.* Washington, D.C.: U.S. Government Printing Office, various years.

Willard, Julius Terrass. *History of the Kansas State College of Agriculture and Applied Science.* Manhattan: Kansas State College Press, 1940.

Wilson, C. Peairs. "Adapt or Be Adopted." *Minutes: Station Conference, 1962*, pages 19–32. Manhattan: Kansas Agricultural Experiment Station, January 22–24, 1962.

————. "Director's Report." *Minutes: Station Conference, 1964*, pages 38–52. Manhattan: Kansas Agricultural Experiment Station, January 13–15, 1964.

PART FIVE

The Experiment Stations and Science Education

16

The Supply of New Agricultural Scientists by U.S. Land Grant Universities: 1920-1979

Wallace E. Huffman

Introduction

The production of scientists by U.S. universities has become a major industry during the second half of the twentieth century (Harmon, 1978; NSF, 1983; Syverson, 1983). Furthermore, it has become clear that well-trained and motivated scientists are the source of most new ideas leading to advances in science and technology that are the driving force behind modern economic growth (Kuznets, 1972, 1977). The land grant universities are the primary, although not exclusive, source of trained scientists for U.S. agriculture. Most of the new agricultural scientists receive doctorates from departments that are closely affiliated with the agricultural experiment stations. A significant number of the graduate students in these departments receive station-funded research assistantships, which are a major source of student income. The assistantships also provide graduate students with an opportunity to learn valuable research skills while working under the direction of a professor.

The objective of this study is to present a quantitative summary of the Ph.D. output and major characteristics of Ph.D. recipients in science fields closely associated with agriculture and home economics in U.S. land grant universities. Much of the analysis starts in 1920, when the National Academy of Sciences and National Research Council records on earned doctorates begin and covers the sixty-year period up to 1979. Only 274 doctoral degrees were awarded in these fields by the land grant universities during 1920-1924, but the number increased to 8,958 degrees awarded during 1970-1974. Since the early 1970s, the total number of degrees awarded per year has declined. Although data are available on characteristics of Ph.D. recipients for only relatively recent years, they show some significant changes in the sex and citizenship composition of recipients.

The Production of Doctorate Degrees

All Fields

The doctoral degree is the highest recognized level of educational training. The skills associated with doctorates in the sciences are different from other areas. The Doctor of Philosophy, a research degree, is awarded in the sciences to signify excellence in the mastery of an appropriate body of scientific knowledge and in skills to perform research through application of the scientific method. Doctorates awarded in the humanities signify mastery of a body of knowledge having primarily cultural character. Doctorates awarded in education and the professions (medicine, law, dentistry, etc.) signify mastery of a body of knowledge and skills appropriate for practicing a particular profession. These latter two doctorates are nonresearch degrees.

Historically, the first doctoral degree was conferred by Yale University in 1861, and currently more than 300 universities are granting doctoral degrees. In 120 years, about 765,000 doctorates have been awarded by U.S. institutions in all fields (sciences, engineering, humanities, education, professions). About 65 percent of these doctorates have been awarded in science and engineering fields, and 72 percent have been awarded during the last eighteen years, 1965-1982. The leading universities in total number of doctoral degrees awarded have changed over time from the Ivy League private universities to the large state universities, i.e., University of California-Berkeley, University of Wisconsin, University of Illinois-Urbana, University of Michigan.

Fields Associated with Agriculture and Home Economics

In this study, nineteen science fields associated with agriculture and home economics are considered (see Table 16.1). Most of the fields are in agricultural sciences. Other fields are basic science fields that are generally administered by departments outside the colleges of agriculture, e.g., biochemistry, genetics, plant and animal physiology. These basic science fields are the mother science for the biological science component of agricultural and home economics research. Home economics fields are aggregated into two categories, nutrition and/or dietetics and other home economics.[1]

In fields associated with agriculture and home economics, eight of the land grant universities founded under the 1862 Land Grant Act—University of California-Berkeley, University of Illinois-Urbana, Iowa State University, University of Maryland, University of Minnesota, Rutgers University, Cornell University, and University of Wisconsin—awarded Ph.D. degrees in 1920[2] (see Table 16.2). Fifty years later, all fifty-one of the land grant universities were awarding Ph.D. degrees in one or more of these nineteen fields. The long-term compound average growth rate in number of Ph.D. degrees awarded by land grant universities in the nineteen fields associated with agriculture and home economics is 6.9 percent (1920-1979). Over the sixty-year period, 1920-1979, these fifty-one land grant universities awarded more than 39,095 Ph.D. degrees in these fields. Sixty-two percent of these degrees were awarded during the last fifteen years of the period, 1965-1979.

Figure 16.1 shows the pattern over time of Ph.D. degrees awarded by the fifty-one land grant universities for field groups: (1) total over all nineteen fields, (2) over thirteen fields (excludes six basic science fields), (3) in applied agricultural production science fields (field group I includes: agronomy, soils and soil sciences, horticulture, animal husbandry, animal science and nutrition, veterinary medicine, agricultural engineering, and general and other agriculture), and (4) in basic science fields for agriculture (field group II includes: food and agricultural chemistry, biochemistry, animal physiology, plant physiology, plant and animal physiology, and genetics).

The total number of Ph.D. degrees awarded in the nineteen field groups grew rapidly in the early ten-year period 1920-1929, but the Great Depression of 1929-1933 slowed this growth rate, and World War II caused a sharp reversal starting in 1942. The number of Ph.D. degrees awarded in 1946 was only 44 percent of the prewar 1940 number. The end of World War II, however, brought large enrollments of war veterans in colleges because of favorable G.I. Bill educational benefits.[3] The number of Ph.D. degrees awarded in 1950-1954 was 2.7 times larger than the previous high for any preceding five-year period. The growth in total number of Ph.D. degrees awarded in these nineteen fields slowed temporarily in 1955, turned sharply negative in 1958, and continued at a slower average annual rate of 7.1 percent for the period 1950-1971. The total number of Ph.D. degrees awarded in these nineteen fields peaked in 1971 and declined slightly thereafter.

Except for the periods 1928-1932 and 1977-1979, the number and growth in numbers of Ph.D. degrees awarded in applied agricultural production sciences (I) and basic sciences for agriculture (II) are similar (Figure 16.1). The growth rate of new Ph.D.s awarded in applied agricultural production sciences was somewhat less affected by both the Great Depression and entry into World War II of the United States compared with the growth rate for new Ph.D. degrees awarded in basic sciences for agriculture.

Some other trends, which are not included in Figure 16.1, are as follows: the plant maintenance field, consisting of entomology and phytopathology (plant pathology), awarded larger numbers of Ph.D. degrees than the applied field of agronomy (including soils and soil sciences) up to 1950, and the annual numbers for Ph.D. degrees awarded in both these fields have followed a similar growth pattern after that date. Very few Ph.D. degrees were awarded in the applied animal production field (animal husbandry, animal science, animal nutrition, and veterinary medicine) before 1946, but the increase was at about a 20 percent annual rate for the period 1944-1955; the rate was negative during 1953-1960; and the number of Ph.D.s awarded in this field group peaked in 1974. The growth pattern for the food, nutrition, and economics field group is quite irregular. Some of the sharp changes are due to either adding or dropping field classifications.[4]

TABLE 16.1 Number of Ph.D. Degrees Awarded in Fields Associated with Agriculture and Home Economics by 51 Land Grant Institutions in Selected Five-Year Intervals

Science fields	1920-1924		1950-1954		1975-1979	
	No. of degrees	No. of institutions awarding degrees	No. of degrees	No. of institutions awarding degrees	No. of degrees	No. of institutions awarding degrees
Agronomy, inc. soils & soil sciences	42	8	527	27	1,115	47
Horticulture	14	5	240	19	339	36
Forestry	1	1	17	5	306	25
Entomology	41	8	308	21	735	43
Phytopathology	48	7	171	18	428	41
Physiology--plant[a]			14	4	184	40
Physiology--plant and animal	37	10	206	18	-	-
Animal husbandry, animal science and nutrition[b]	13	5	333	23	717	44
Veterinary medicine	1	1	25	8	152	17
Physiology--animal	-	-	2	2	601	46

TABLE 16.1 (continued).

Science fields	1920-1924		1950-1954		1975-1979	
	No. of degrees	No. of institutions awarding degrees	No. of degrees	No. of institutions awarding degrees	No. of degrees	No. of institutions awarding degrees
Agric. engineering	1	1	28	5	235	28
Agric. economics[c]	-	-	-	-	761	38
Food sci. and tech.[c]	-	-	-	-	510	30
Agric. and food chem.	14	7	67	7	42	14
Fish and wildlife	-	-	13	6	225	28
General agriculture and other	7	4	117	16	388	38
Nutrition and (or) dietetics[d]	2	2	152	16	283	34
(Other) home economics	-	-	35	9	269	18
Biochemistry	28	8	425	25	1,041	49
Genetics	24	4	162	14	373	38
Totals	273		2,842		8,734	

[a] In fiscal year 1962, "Physiology" was broken into "Animal Physiology" and "Plant Physiology."
[b] "Animal Science" was added in fiscal year 1973. Field change to "Animal Science and Nutrition" in fiscal year 1977.
[c] Added as a field in fiscal year 1969.
[d] "Nutrition" (human) dropped as a field in fiscal year 1960. "Nutrition and/or Dietetics" added as a field in fiscal year 1976.
Source: National Science Foundation, Survey of Earned Doctorates, 1983; Harmon, 1978.

TABLE 16.2   Top Fifteen Land Grant Universities by Number of Ph.D.
Degrees Awarded in Nineteen Fields Associated with
Agriculture and Home Economics, 1920-1979[a]

University	Year founded	Year first Ph.D. awarded	Number of Ph.D. degrees awarded[b] 1920-1979	1965-1979
University of Wisconsin-Madison	1836	1920[a]	3,624 (9.3)	1,622 (6.7)
Cornell University	1865	1920[a]	3,154 (8.1)	1,350 (5.6)
University of Minnesota	1851	1920[a]	2,392 (6.1)	1,052 (4.4)
University of Illinois-Urbana	1867	1920[a]	2,339 (6.0)	1,314 (5.4)
Michigan State University	1855	1927	2,148 (5.5)	1,465 (6.1)
Iowa State University	1885	1920[a]	2,104 (5.4)	983 (4.1)
Purdue University	1865	1930	1,835 (4.7)	1,204 (5.0)
University of California-Berkeley	1868	1920[a]	1,806 (4.6)	812 (3.4)
Ohio State University	1870	1921	1,760 (4.5)	907 (3.8)
University of California-Davis	1908	1949	1,458 (3.7)	1,112 (4.6)
Texas A&M University	1876	1940[a]	1,157 (3.0)	876 (3.6)
Rutgers University	1766	1920	1,042 (2.7)	497 (2.1)
University of Missouri	1839	1920[a]	1,022 (2.6)	660 (2.7)
Oregon State University	1868	1935	1,010 (2.6)	695 (2.9)
North Carolina State University	1887	1947	986 (2.5)	743 (3.1)
Total All Land Grant Universities			39,095 (100.0)	24,137 (100.0)

[a]The first year for which data are available is 1920.
[b]The numbers in parentheses are the percentage of all degrees awarded
by land grant universities in fields associated with agriculture and
home economics.
Source: National Science Foundation--National Research Council, Survey
of Earned Doctorates, various years.

The Institutional Distribution

A large share of the Ph.D. degrees awarded in fields associated with
agriculture and home economics is concentrated in the top 20 percent of
the doctorate-granting land grant universities. For the sixty-year period,
1920–1979, 58 percent of all Ph.D.s awarded in the nineteen fields associated
with agriculture and home economics by land grant universities were awarded
by the top ten Ph.D.-producing universities. For the last fifteen years (1965–
1979), the share of Ph.D.s awarded by the top ten universities is only
slightly lower (49 percent) (see Table 16.2). For the sixty-year period, 1920–
1979, and the most recent fifteen-year period, the University of Wisconsin
is the leading producer of Ph.D. degrees in the nineteen fields associated

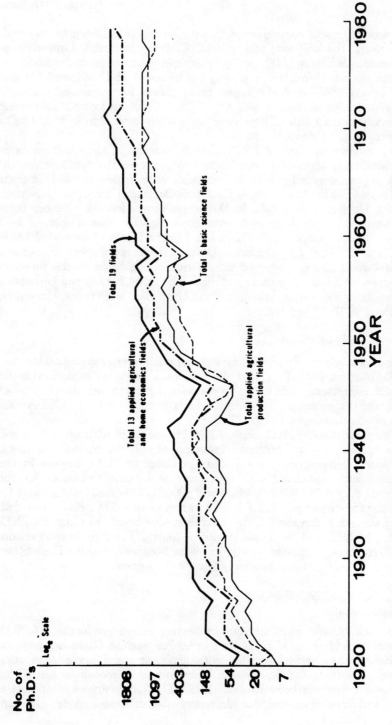

Figure 16.1 Total number of Ph.D. degrees awarded by U.S. land-grant universities in fields associated with agriculture and home economics, 1920-1979.

with agriculture and home economics, with 3,624 and 1,622 degrees awarded, respectively. For the sixty-year period, Cornell University, University of Minnesota, University of Illinois, and Michigan State University, respectively, are the second- through-fifth leading producers of Ph.D. degrees. For the later period 1965–1979, Michigan State moves up to second, Cornell University drops to third, University of Illinois remains fourth, and Purdue University rises to fifth.[5] These same universities rank high in total Ph.D.s awarded in all academic fields.

The relative number of Ph.D. degrees awarded in the nineteen fields associated with agriculture and home economics to the total number of Ph.D. degrees awarded in all academic fields varies widely across land grant universities. For the University of California–Berkeley, Ohio State University, and the University of Illinois, Ph.D. degrees awarded in the nineteen fields associated with agriculture and home economics are a small share (6.5–13 percent) of total academic Ph.D.s awarded in the fifty-five-year period 1920–1974. The University of California–Davis is an exception, with 50 percent of total Ph.D. degrees awarded during this period being in the nineteen fields associated with agriculture and home economics. For Cornell University, University of Minnesota, Michigan State University, and Purdue University, the share is 17–24 percent.

The Geographical Distribution

Because much of agricultural research, especially crops research, is location specific (Ruttan, 1982:Ch. 7) and Ph.D. research frequently focuses on issues of local importance, it is useful to consider the geographic distribution of Ph.D. degrees awarded. This study groups states by the ten USDA-ERS farm production regions (Table 16.3).

The production of Ph.D. degrees in fields associated with agriculture and home economics is concentrated geographically in the midwestern states. The Corn Belt region is the leading producer of Ph.D. degrees in the nineteen fields associated with agriculture and home economics for the sixty-year period 1920–1979 with over 9,000 Ph.D. degrees awarded and for the latest fifteen-year period 1965–1979 with more than 5,000 Ph.D.s awarded. The Lake States are second, the Northeast (due largely to Cornell's Ph.D. output) is third, and the Pacific region is fourth. The Appalachian region, Southern Plains, Mountain, Northern Plains, Southeast, and the Delta States are regions that produce relatively few Ph.D. degrees.

The Institutional Distribution
by Field Groups

The list of land grant universities leading in the production of Ph.D. degrees by field group changes over time. For *total Ph.D. degrees* awarded in the nineteen fields associated with agriculture and home economics, Cornell University is first, and the University of Wisconsin is second for all five-year intervals between 1920–1949.[6] The University of Minnesota is third, and Iowa State and the University of California–Berkeley alternate as the fourth and fifth place universities for each of the intervals, 1925–1949. For each five-year interval, 1950–1979, the University of Wisconsin is the leading producer of total Ph.D. degrees in the nineteen fields associated with agriculture and home economics. In second place are Cornell University for the period 1950–1964, University of Illinois during 1956–1969, and Michigan State University for the 1970–1979 period. The University of California–Berkeley and Iowa State drop from the list of top five Ph.D.-producing universities in the 1960–1979 period and are replaced by Michigan State University and Purdue University.

In applied agricultural production sciences (field group I), Cornell University is the leader, and the University of Wisconsin is second for each five-year interval, 1920–1954; then, the leadership alternates. The University of Wisconsin is first, 1955–1959 and 1965–1969; Michigan State University is first, 1960–1964; the University of Illinois is first, 1970–1974; and Cornell University is first, 1975–1979. Iowa State ranks consistently in the top five except for 1930–1934 and 1975–1979, and Michigan State reaches the top during the last thirty years. Texas A&M University and Purdue University are ranked in the top five for field group I for the first time in 1975–1979.

The set of land grant universities leading in the production of Ph.D. degrees in basic sciences for agriculture (field group II) has been quite stable over the period 1920–1979. During 1920–1954, the top six universities are the University of Wisconsin, University of Minnesota, University of California–Berkeley, Cornell University, University of Illinois, and Iowa State University. Cornell University and Iowa State are replaced in the later periods by the University of California–Davis and Purdue University. The leaders are Cornell, 1920–1924; University of Minnesota, 1925–1934; University of Wisconsin, 1935–1974; and University of California–Davis, 1975–1979.

Some Characteristics of Ph.D. Recipients

Three characteristics of Ph.D. recipients are focused upon in this section. They are the sex and citizenship composition of individuals receiving Ph.D. degrees. The third characteristic is the post-Ph.D. plans of Ph.D. recipients.

Sex

The total number of women receiving Ph.D. degrees in nineteen fields associated with agriculture and home economics for which data are available has been increasing since 1960. In the 1960–1964 period, 413 women and 5,159 men received Ph.D. degrees in these fields, or 7.4 percent of the recipients were female (see Table 16.4). In contrast, in the 1975–1979 period, 1,913 women received Ph.D. degrees in these fields, a 4.6-fold increase over the 1960–1964 period. In 1975–1979, women received 16.0 percent of the 11,981 Ph.D. degrees awarded in these fields, and in 1980–1982, women received 22.3 percent of the Ph.D. degrees awarded in these nineteen fields. Thus, there is strong evidence that the share of Ph.D. degrees in these

TABLE 16.3. Number of Ph.D. Degrees Awarded in Nineteen
Fields Associated with Agriculture and Home
Economics by USDA Farm Production Regions,
1920-1979 and 1965-1979.

Regions	Number of Ph.D. degrees awarded	
	1920-1979	1965-1979
Corn Belt	9,060	5,068
University of Illinois	2,339	1,314
Iowa State University	2,104	983
Purdue University	1,835	1,204
Ohio State University	1,760	907
University of Missouri	1,022	660
Lake States	8,164	4,139
University of Wisconsin	3,624	1,622
University of Minnesota	2,392	1,052
Michigan State University	2,148	1,465
Northeast	6,930	3,602
Cornell University	3,154	1,350
Rutgers University	1,042	497
Penn. State University	971	579
University of Maryland	745	404
University of Massachusetts	493	309
University of Connecticut	178	149
University of Vermont	80	74
University of New Hampshire	72	60
University of Rhode Island	69	64
University of Delaware	68	58
University of Maine	58	58
Pacific	4,894	3,034
University of Calif.-Berk.	1,806	812
University of Calif.-Davis	1,458	1,112
Oregon State University	1,010	695
Washington State University	620	415
Appalachian	2,402	1,996
North Carolina State Univ.	986	743
Virginia Polytechnic Institute	446	403
University of Tennessee	435	384
University of Kentucky	315	291
West Virginia University	220	175
Southern Plains	1,769	1,358
Texas A&M University	1,157	876
Oklahoma State University	612	482

TABLE 16.3 (continued)

Regions	Number of Ph.D. degrees awarded	
	1920-1979	1965-1979
Mountain	1,679	1,493
Colorado State University	488	468
University of Arizona	420	372
Utah State University	325	248
University of Wyoming	163	139
University of Idaho	135	133
Montana State University	114	99
New Mexico State University	28	28
University of Nevada	6	6
Northern Plains	1,534	1,184
Kansas State University	707	512
University of Nebraska	540	410
North Dakota State University	182	176
South Dakota State University	105	86
Southeast	1,449	1,263
University of Florida	631	505
University of Georgia	415	391
Auburn University	267	238
Clemson University	136	129
Delta States	907	716
Louisiana State University	557	396
Mississippi State University	274	251
University of Arkansas	76	69
Others	307	284
University of Alaska	18	18
University of Hawaii	289	266
Overall Total	39,095	24,137

Source: National Science Foundation--National Research Council, Survey of Earned Doctorates, various years.

fields going to women has been increasing quite dramatically over the past twenty-two years.

The share of Ph.D. degrees awarded to women differs across fields over time. In the five-year interval 1960-1964, only eighteen Ph.D. degrees were awarded to women in the applied agricultural production field group (I) or less than 1 percent of all degrees in this group, and twenty-four Ph.D. degrees were awarded in the agricultural production maintenance field group or 2.1 percent of the total. The largest number (364) and largest share (13.7 percent) of total degrees awarded to women in a field group were awarded in the basic science for agriculture group (II) during this early period.

TABLE 16.4 Number of Ph.D. Recipients in Fields Associated with Agriculture and Home Economics by Sex: Five-Year Intervals, 1960-1982

Field	1960-1964			1965-1969			1970-1974			1975-1979			1980-1982		
	M	F	T	M	F	T	M	F	T	M	F	T	M	F	T
Agronomy, inc. soils	709	3	712	891	3	894	1167	24	1191	1048	31	1079	670	69	739
Horticulture	244	5	249	332	8	340	311	12	323	302	20	322	202	44	246
Forestry	164	0	164	301	1	302	386	0	386	393	13	406	237	16	253
Entomology	471	12	483	694	46	740	892	58	950	719	56	775	412	62	474
Phytopathology	377	12	389	465	17	482	475	26	501	396	46	442	269	62	331
Plant physiology	144	14	158	357	39	396	373	57	430	218	54	272	143	33	176
Animal husbandry, sci. and nutrition	565	9	574	639	11	650	645	10	655	633	43	673	415	52	467
Vet. medicine b Animal physiology	345	54	399	1041	188	1229	1445	273	1718	1264	303	1567	752	224	976
Agric. engin.	101	0	101	182	0	182	310	1	311	234	1	235	175	5	180
Agric. economics	-a	-a	-a	92	0	92	790	16	806	751	29	780	462	45	507
Food sci & tech	-a	-a	-a	38	1	39	336	52	388	423	110	533	234	82	316
Agric. and food chem.	178	10	188	226	14	240	136	28	164	40	7	47	-	-	-

Fish & wildlife	98	0	98	127	1	128	252	7	259	302	9	311	181	23	204
General and other agric.	116	1	117	321	8	329	520	13	533	392	20	412	255	34	289
Nutrition and Dietetics	—[a]	—[a]	—[a]	—[a]	—[a]	—[a]	20	7	27	151	213	364	117	191	308
Other Home Ec.[b]	—[a]	—[a]	—[a]	—[a]	—[a]	—[a]	—[a]	—[a]	—[a]	—[a]	—[a]	—[a]	—[a]	—[a]	—[a]
Biochemistry	1261	230	1491	2001	484	2485	2459	601	3060	2329	727	3056	1425	543	1968
Genetics	366	56	422	534	104	638	561	156	717	473	234	707	308	182	490
Total	5159	413	5572	8241	925	9166	11,058	1334	12,392	10,068	1913	11,981	6257	1767	7924

[a] Not a separate degree category during this period.
[b] Data are not available by sex for veterinary medicine and other home economics.

Source: "Science and Engineering Doctorates: 1960-1982," Special Report NSF 83-328, National Science Foundation.

During 1975–1979, women received 4.2 percent of the degrees awarded in the applied agricultural production field group, but they received 8.4 percent and 23.5 percent, respectively, of the Ph.D. degrees awarded in the agricultural-production-maintenance field group and the basic science for agriculture group, respectively. In more recent data for 1980–1982, women received less than 10 percent of the degrees awarded in agricultural engineering, agronomy and soils, agricultural economics, and forestry. In contrast, women received 62 percent of the Ph.D. degrees awarded in the field of human nutrition and/or dietetics, which is the major home economics field.

Citizenship

The proportion of all academic Ph.D. degrees awarded by U.S. Ph.D.-granting institutions to individuals who are not U.S. citizens has increased steadily over time. The National Research Council started collecting data on citizenship of doctoral degree recipients in 1960. Earlier data on foreign origins of Ph.D. recipients can be derived from an analysis of baccalaureate origins of Ph.D. recipients. These data show a long-term upward trend in the number of Ph.D. recipients who earned their bachelor's degrees abroad, being 7–9 percent of the doctorate total until the 1960s, and then the trend is sharply upward (Harmon, 1978:47). For 1970–1974, 20.5 percent of all U.S. Ph.D. recipients in the sciences were not U.S. citizens. The proportion of foreign-origin Ph.D. recipients varies by field, being highest in agricultural sciences and engineering.

In the nineteen fields associated with agriculture and home economics, the proportion of Ph.D.s awarded to non-U.S. citizens has increased from 21.8 percent in 1960–1964 to 25.2 percent in 1975–1979, and the number of Ph.D. degrees awarded to non-U.S. citizens increased from 961 to 2,017 over the same period (see Table 16.5).[7] For 1960–1964, agricultural and food chemistry and genetics had the largest share of Ph.D. recipients being non-U.S. citizens, 39 percent and 31 percent, respectively. In 1975–1979, agricultural engineering, agronomy (including soils and soil sciences), and agricultural economics were leading with more than 38 percent of the Ph.D.s awarded in these fields being to non-U.S. citizens.

Although the number of Ph.D. degrees awarded in most fields associated with agriculture and home economics peaked in the 1970–1974 period, the decline that occurred during 1975–1979 would have been much larger if the foreign share had not been rising. Attracting foreign graduate students has helped maintain the size of many U.S. graduate programs in the face of a declining demand for Ph.D. training by U.S. citizens.[8] Non-U.S. citizens generally bring their own financial aid when they enroll in the U.S. Ph.D. programs but given that university tuition rates do not cover the marginal cost of training large numbers of students, the states seem to be providing a sizable amount of aid to foreign countries in the form of Ph.D. training for non-U.S. citizens. Furthermore, in some fields, immigrant Ph.D. recipients may become an important source of U.S. science manpower.

TABLE 16.5 Total Number of Ph.D. Degrees Awarded in Nineteen Fields Associated with Agriculture and Home Economics and the Proportion of Degrees Awarded to Non-U.S. Citizens with a Temporary Visa [a]

Field	1960-1964			1975-1979		
	Total giving citizenship[a]	Total for-eign[b]	Per-cent for-eign	Total giving citizenship[a]	Total for-eign	Per-cent foreign
Agronomy, inc. soils and soil sciences	698	186	26.6	997	409	41.0
Horticulture	231	61	26.4	298	92	30.9
Forestry	65	5	7.6	289	66	22.8
Entomology	432	97	22.4	635	127	20.0
Phytopathology	379	111	29.3	398	112	28.0
Physiology--plant[c]	96	26	27.1	176	45	25.6
Physiology--plant and animal	157	18	11.5	-	-	-
Animal husbandry[d] Animal sci. and nutrition	562	79	14.0	629	166	26.4
Veterinary medicine	96	25	26.0	136	51	37.5
Physiology--animal	160	12	7.5	561	47	8.4
Agricultural engineering	95	19	20.0	226	98	43.4
Agricultural economics[e]	-	-	-	691	267	38.6
Food science and technology	-	-	-	487	156	32.0
Agriculture and food chemistry	158	62	39.2	36	8	22.2
Fish and wildlife	63	7	11.1	246	20	8.1
General and other agriculture	112	28	25.0	354	125	35.3
Nutrition and/or dietetics[f]	23	6	26.1	265	52	19.6
(Other) home economics	93	18	19.4	254	17	6.7
Subtotal	(3,420)	(760)	(22.2)	(6,669)	(1,858)	(27.9)
Biochemistry	689	111	16.1	977	90	9.2
Genetics	291	90	31.0	346	69	19.9
Total	4,400	961	21.8	7,992	2,017	25.2

[a] For these fields, data were missing on the citizenship of 89 and 486 recipients in 1960-1964 and 1975-1979, respectively.
[b] Foreign is defined as a Ph.D. recipient of a U.S. university who has a temporary visa.
[c] In FY 1962, "physiology" was broken up into "animal physiology" and "plant physiology."
[d] "Animal science" added as a field in FY 1973. Field changed to "animal science and nutrition" in fiscal year 1977.
[e] Added as a field in FY 1969.
[f] "Nutrition" dropped as a field in FY 1960. "Nutrition and/or dietetics" added as a field in FY 1976.
Source: National Science Foundation--National Research Council, Survey of Earned Doctorates, various years.

Post-Ph.D. Activity

Historically, more than 50 percent of U.S.-citizen, new-Ph.D. recipients have taken immediate post-Ph.D. employment in colleges and universities where they can combine research and teaching.[9] However, during the late 1960s and 1970s, an increasing share of new Ph.D. recipients continued their research training beyond the Ph.D. degree through postdoctoral study. For Ph.D. recipients in the sciences, the percentage choosing postdoctoral study increased from 14 percent in 1960–1964 (Harmon, 1978:78) to 42 percent in 1978–1982 (NSF, 1983:100–02). Postdoctoral study historically was restricted to a few outstanding scholars or scientists. As a rule, the objective was to obtain research experience under the guidance of a professor recognized for his/her research achievements and ability to communicate knowledge, technique, or approach to scholars and scientists. However, when the academic labor market became depressed during the late 1960s, Ph.D. recipients in some fields were in excess supply for available assistant professor positions. This reduced the opportunity cost of additional training. An increasing number of Ph.D. recipients chose the next best available university position, postdoctoral study, as a way to raise their probability of obtaining an assistant professorship in the future.

For fields associated with agriculture and home economics, data on four different post-Ph.D. activities of U.S. citizens are reported: postdoctoral study and employment in an educational institution, government, or other (business, nonprofit organization, and other). During 1960–1964, 47 percent of the new Ph.D. recipients in the fields associated with agriculture and home economics (52 percent excluding recipients in biochemistry and genetics) chose employment in educational institutions. Fields with the highest rates of educational sector employment were: home economics, 81 percent; agricultural engineering, 79 percent; veterinary medicine, 65 percent; and horticulture, 64 percent. Fields with low educational sector employment of new Ph.D.s were biochemistry, 28 percent, and agricultural and food chemistry, 32 percent. In 1960–1964, an average of only 14 percent of all Ph.D. recipients in fields associated with agriculture and home economics (9 percent, excluding biochemistry and genetics) chose postdoctoral study as an immediate post-Ph.D. activity. Fields in which postdoctoral study was relatively frequent were: biochemistry, 38 percent; animal physiology, 27 percent; and genetics, 21 percent.

During 1960–1964, government sector employment was the choice of 14 percent of all Ph.D. recipients, and other employment was the choice of 12 percent. Two Ph.D. fields, forestry and fish and wildlife, had 36 percent of their Ph.D. recipients accepting employment in the government sector. Fields that had a relatively high frequency of other employment were agricultural and food chemistry (39 percent), agriculture (general and other, 25 percent), and biochemistry (23 percent).

In the fields associated with agriculture and home economics, new Ph.D. recipients during 1975–1979 had significantly lower employment rates in the educational sector and higher rates of postdoctoral study than new doctorates of 1960–1964. For all fields combined, the proportion of recipients taking employment in educational institutions decreased to 40 percent (47 percent excluding biochemistry and genetics). The share taking postdoctoral study increased to 32 percent (21 percent excluding biochemistry and genetics). For Ph.D. recipients in 1975–1979, postdoctoral study was the immediate post-Ph.D. activity for more than half of the recipients in biochemistry (81 percent), animal physiology (67 percent), genetics (62 percent), and plant physiology (52 percent). Educational institutions continued to employ at least a majority of new Ph.D. recipients in home economics (87 percent); horticulture (67 percent); agricultural engineering (65 percent); forestry (54 percent); animal husbandry, animal science, and nutrition (53 percent); agricultural economics (54 percent); fish and wildlife (52 percent); and nutrition or dietetics (50 percent).

In almost all fields, the share of Ph.D. recipients employed by the government declined from 1960–1965 to 1975–1979. Agricultural economics, which had 29 percent of Ph.D. recipients during 1975–1979 employed by the government, seems to be an exception. Although data are not available for 1960–1965, the share of new doctorates in agricultural economics during 1970–1974 taking employment in the government sector was 23 percent. Among Ph.D. recipients receiving degrees during 1975–1979, the proportion taking "other" employment from the fields of agronomy (including soils and soil sciences), horticulture, plant physiology, and agricultural engineering more than doubled over the 1960–1965 level, but the proportion from biochemistry and genetics choosing the other category dropped by more than 50 percent.

The data on post-Ph.D. plans of non-U.S. citizens start in 1970, so less information is available on their activities. Initial employment in an educational institution was considerably lower and employment in the government sector was considerably higher for non-U.S. citizens than it was for U.S. citizens. For doctorates during 1975–1979, about 39 percent obtained employment in educational institutions in the United States or abroad, 25 percent chose postdoctoral study, and 22 percent chose government sector employment. Postdoctoral study, which is one method for non-U.S. citizens to prolong their stay in the United States, does not seem to be at an unusually high rate.

Summary and Conclusions

The Doctor of Philosophy degree is the highest recognized level of training for scientists. It signifies excellence in mastery of an appropriate body of scientific knowledge and skills to perform research. Well-trained and motivated scientists are the source of most new ideas leading to advances in science and technology.

This study has focused on the production of scientists in nineteen fields of science associated with agriculture and home economics. These fields cover applied agricultural sciences; basic agricultural sciences; production maintenance sciences; and food, nutrition, and economic sciences. The main findings are:

1. The fifty-one land grant universities produced 39,000 Ph.D. degrees in these nineteen fields over the sixty-year period 1920 to 1979. Sixty-two percent of these degrees were awarded during the last fifteen years of this period. However, the number of Ph.D. degrees awarded per year peaked in 1971, and the trend has been downward since then.
2. A large share of the Ph.D. degrees awarded in fields associated with agriculture and home economics is concentrated in the top 20 percent of the granting institutions. Over time, this concentration has, however, declined in all fields. The University of Wisconsin–Madison awarded the largest number of degrees in the nineteen fields of science for the sixty-year period 1920–1979 and for the latest fifteen years. Cornell University ranks second for both these time periods.
3. The production of Ph.D. degrees in these nineteen fields and in most of the individual fields is concentrated geographically in the midwestern states. In the ten USDA agricultural production regions, the Corn Belt states are the leading grantors of Ph.D. degrees in these fields for the sixty-year period and for the last fifteen years. The Lake states are second, the Northeast is third, and the Pacific Region is fourth.

Three characteristics of Ph.D. recipients were focused upon in this study: sex, citizenship, and postdoctoral activity. Additional findings are:

1. The total number of women receiving Ph.D. degrees in fields associated with agriculture and home economics has been increasing since 1960 and perhaps longer. Only 413 Ph.D. degrees were awarded to women in these fields during 1960–1964, or 8.0 percent of the total Ph.D. degrees awarded. In the 1975–1979 period, women received 16.0 percent of the 11,981 degrees awarded.
2. The share of total Ph.D. degrees awarded to women is significantly lower in the applied agricultural science fields than in the basic agricultural science fields.
3. The proportion of Ph.D. degrees awarded to non-U.S. citizen recipients has increased steadily since 1960. In several fields, noncitizens receive 40 percent or more of the Ph.D. degrees awarded.
4. The share of American citizen recipients in the nineteen fields obtaining immediate post-Ph.D. employment in educational institutions has been declining since 1960, and the share pursuing postdoctoral study has been increasing. In the period 1975–1979, postdoctoral study was the primary post-Ph.D. activity of recipients in biochemistry (81 percent), animal physiology (67 percent), genetics (62 percent), and plant physiology (52 percent). For seventeen fields (excludes biochemistry and genetics), the proportion of doctorate recipients obtaining a job in an

educational institution declined from 52 percent in 1960-1964 to 40 percent in 1975-1979.

5. In almost all fields, the share of Ph.D. recipients employed by government (federal, state, or local) declined between 1960-1964 and 1975-1979. Agricultural economics is the only field in which new Ph.D. recipients are reversing this trend.

Notes

Professor of Economics, Iowa State University. Helpful comments were obtained on an earlier draft of this paper from T. Paul Schultz, Robert Evenson, Vernon Ruttan, Roland Robinson, and Lawrence Busch. Stephanie Mercier provided research assistance. Funding was obtained from the USDA, Cooperative State Research Service, and the Iowa Agriculture and Home Economics Experiment Station. This is journal paper no. J-12071 of the Iowa Agriculture and Home Economics Experiment Stations, Ames, Iowa, Project No. 2516.

1. The number of Ph.D. specialties in fields related to agriculture and home economics for the NRC-NSF surveys changes over time. I, however, use the number of nineteen fields throughout the paper to refer to the "complete" set of specialties. Although colleges of home economics receive a small share of the research funds allocated by agricultural and home economics experiment stations, Ph.D. degrees in home economics are included in this study for completeness.

2. The 1890 land grant colleges and universities are not included in this study. They did not award any Ph.D. degrees.

3. A total of 14.4 percent of World War II veterans obtained some college level training that was paid for by the G.I. Bill, and 706,821 graduate degrees have been awarded to G.I. Bill beneficiaries (1945-1982).

4. Exactly where Ph.D. degrees awarded in agricultural economics are recorded before 1969 is unclear. Some were undoubtedly reported as being in economics. Others may have been counted in the field called "other agriculture." It is known that they are included under some category of National Research Council's field classification scheme. Also, Ph.D. recipients at Iowa State University and North Carolina State University can obtain their degree in either economics or agricultural economics.

5. Note that the University of California-Davis awarded its first Ph.D. degree in 1949. This is much later than for any of the other major Ph.D.-granting universities.

6. As one means of condensing the annual data on earned degrees, five-year aggregates were formed. Much of the discussion uses these five-year aggregates rather than annual data.

7. The increase in the share of Ph.D. degrees awarded to non-U.S. citizens may have been larger than these numbers suggest. Citizenship data were missing for only 2.0 percent of these doctorates in 1960-1964, but it increased to 5.5 percent during 1975-1979.

8. Several studies have shown that the expected rate of return on a college degree, including advanced degrees, has declined dramatically in the 1970s compared with the 1960s (Freeman, 1976:Ch. 4).

9. Data collection on employment plans of Ph.D. recipients started in 1960.

References

Freeman, Richard B. *The Overeducated American.* New York: Academic Press, Inc., 1976.

Harmon, L. R. *A Century of Doctorates.* Washington, D.C.: National Academy of Sciences, 1978.

Kuznets, S. *Economic Growth of Nations.* Cambridge: Harvard University Press, 1972.

——. "Two Centuries of Economic Growth: Reflections on U.S. Experiences." *American Economics Review* 67 (February):1–14, 1977.

National Science Foundation. *Science and Engineering Doctorates: 1960–1982.* Special Report NSF 83-328. Washington, D.C.: NSF, 1983.

Ruttan, Vernon. *Agricultural Research Policy.* Minneapolis: University of Minnesota Press, 1982.

Syverson, Peter D. *Summary Report: 1979–1982, Doctorate Recipients from United States Universities.* Washington, D.C.: National Research Council, National Academy Press, 1980–1983.

17

The Contribution
of U.S. Universities to Training
Foreign Agricultural Scientists

Burton E. Swanson

Introduction

The primary objective of this chapter is to summarize the contribution of U.S. land grant universities to the education and training of agricultural scientists, particularly from developing countries. In particular, this analysis differentiates the output of doctoral graduates by geographical area, gender, and field of study. A second objective is to describe some factors that have limited the educational contribution of U.S. universities to strengthening the agricultural research capacity of developing nations.

Number of Foreign
Students Trained at U.S. Universities

There are no precise estimates about the number of agricultural students from developing countries that have received education and training at U.S. universities. Most data are highly aggregated, and only selected years are available. The Institute of International Education (1981) reports that the number of foreign agricultural students studying at U.S. universities increased from only about 1,200 students in 1954–1955 to about 8,880 students in 1981–1982, or about a 24 percent annual increase. However, these data include all foreign agricultural students, including degree, nondegree, and technical level students from both developing and industrially developed countries. In recent years, many participants have been sent to U.S. universities for short courses and other nondegree training. So, while the total number of students enrolled has increased substantially over this period, the number of degree recipients has probably increased more slowly.

The geographic spread of foreign students studying agriculture at U.S. universities is of particular interest in determining where the relative contribution of U.S. universities might be greatest. Table 17.1 provides

TABLE 17.1 Total Foreign Student Enrollment in Agricultural
Sciences at U.S. Universities by Geographic Regions
for Selected Years (1955-1974)[a]

	Africa	Far East	Latin America	Near & Middle East	Total	Percent of Graduate Students
1955-1956	73	317	468	242	1,100	
1960-1961	153	508	522	324	1,507	
1963-1964	314	562	531	323	1,730	(60.3)
1965-1966	542	846	556	382	2,326	(62.4)
1970-1971	401	1,304	919	309	2,933	(71.7)
1973-1974	482	1,366	814	314	2,976	(71.9)
Overall Percent	14.8	37.5	31.5	16.2	100	

[a]1955-1956 through 1962-1963 includes both degree and nondegree
students; proportion of students pursuing graduate degrees
indicated in parentheses from 1965-1974.
Source: International Institute of Education, Open Doors,
1956-1974.

enrollment data for foreign students from developing countries in undergraduate and graduate degree programs by geographic area for selected years.
Unfortunately, published data for these enrollment categories are not available
after 1974. However, during the reporting period, the proportion of foreign
students studying agriculture from each geographical region can be summarized as follows: Africa, 15 percent; Far East, 37.5 percent; Latin America,
31.5 percent; and Near and Middle East, 16 percent. During the decade of
1963-1964 through 1973-1974, there was a 7 percent annual increase in
the number of students from developing countries pursuing degrees in all
fields of agriculture; however, the number of graduate students increased
at 10.5 percent per year.

Relatively good data are available from the National Research Council
on the number of foreign students receiving doctoral degrees from U.S.
universities. Table 17.2 presents the total and average number of nonresident
aliens receiving doctoral degrees, by field of study, for selected years. Over
the past decade, about 350 foreign students have received doctoral degrees
annually in the agricultural sciences from U.S. universities. This output
represents about 30 percent of the total output of doctoral recipients in
the agricultural sciences.

The extent of U.S. educational capacity devoted to training foreign
doctoral students in the agricultural sciences ranges from approximately 11
percent in fish and wildlife to 47 percent in agricultural engineering. The

TABLE 17.2 Total and Average Number of Doctoral Degrees Conferred to Nonresident Aliens at U.S. Universities in Agricultural and Related Science for Selected Years (1974-1980, 1982)

	Total Degrees Conferred to Nonresident Aliens, 1974-1980, 1982			Average Number of Degrees Conferred Per Year		
	Males	Females	Total	All Students[c]	Nonres. Aliens	Percent[d]
Agronomy	427	24	451	140	56	40.0
Soils & Soil Sci.	275	9	284	82	36	43.9
Plant Physiology	77	10	87	57	11	19.3
Phytopathology	207	8	215	96	27	28.1
Horticulture	156	9	165	66	21	31.8
Forestry	147	6	153	80	19	23.8
Animal Husbandry	32	-	32	22	4	18.2
Ani. Sci. & Nutrition	239	14	253	119	32	26.9
Veterinary Science[a]	89	8	97	34	12	35.3
Fish & Wildlife	49	6	55	63	7	11.1
Food Sci. & Tech.	238	50	288	106	36	34.0
Agr. Engin.	186	3	189	51	24	47.1
Agr. Economics	471	18	489	163	61	37.4
Agr. Education	53	2	55	30	7	23.3
Agr. General/ Other	218	13	231	85	29	34.1
Home Economics	1	33	34	73	4	5.5
Nutrition/ Diet[b]	54[b]	42[b]	96[b]	95[b]	16[b]	16.8
Totals	2,919	255	3,174	1,362	402	29.5

[a]Veterinary Science does not include Doctor of Veterinary Medicine degrees.
[b]Includes 1976-1980 and 1982 or six years only.
[c]This column includes the average number of U.S. citizens and resident and nonresident aliens receiving doctoral degrees from U.S. universities for the period indicated.
[d]This column is the average percentage of degrees received by nonresident aliens as a proportion of all degrees conferred.
Source: National Research Council, Office of Scientific and Engineering Personnel, Doctorate Records File.

disciplines having the largest numbers of foreign students include agricultural economics and agronomy. Home economics training is the least popular field of study included in the analysis with an average output of only four foreign doctoral recipients per year or about 5.5 percent of total output.

These data are also differentiated by gender to determine the specific proportion of women being trained by field of study. In the agricultural sciences, food science and technology have the highest proportion of women (17.4 percent), while animal husbandry does not have a single female (foreign) doctoral recipient during the reporting period. Overall, in the agricultural sciences alone, only about 6 percent of foreign doctoral recipients are women.

Another important dimension of the analysis is the geographic distribution of those foreign students receiving doctoral degrees in the agricultural sciences. These data are presented in Table 17.3. Over the past decade, approximately 19 percent of the students are from Latin America and the Caribbean, 51 percent from Asia and Oceania, 15 percent from Africa, and 15 percent from industrialized nations.

The problem of "brain drain" has been a persistent concern of scholars and development planners. Seldom have empirical data been available to infer the magnitude of this problem. The National Research Council asks all doctoral recipients their plans following graduation. These data are also presented in Table 17.3. The proportion of students intending to return to their home country or region ranges from only 43 percent for students from Asia and Oceania to 81 percent for students from Latin America and the Caribbean. This table includes both *resident* and *nonresident* aliens, so the actual number and proportion of foreign students (i.e., nonresident aliens) planning to return home is understated somewhat.

In addition, it should be noted that some regions have sizeable numbers of students reporting "uncertain" plans. These have been coded as not planning to return home, since there is no clear intention to do so. Some of these third world students have a preference to find employment in North America or Europe or with an international organization. If unsuccessful in finding employment abroad, these graduates may eventually return home. However, these data suggest that for some regions and subregions, external "brain drain" may be a real and sizeable problem (internal "brain drain" is discussed in the next section).

Given the growing food crisis in Africa, Table 17.3 contains important findings that merit discussion. The output of African students with doctoral degrees in the agricultural sciences represent only about 15 percent of the total foreign student output. Furthermore, the subregions of Eastern and Southern Africa are only averaging about five and six doctoral graduates per year, respectively. The fact that fewer than two-thirds of African students intend to return to their home country makes these data even more important.

Furthermore, as reported elsewhere (Swanson, 1984), with the exceptions of Egypt, Nigeria, and South Africa, the remaining countries of Africa are sorely lacking in higher agricultural education capacity, particularly at the

TABLE 17.3 Doctoral Degrees Conferred to Non-U.S. Citizens[a] from 1973-1982 Who Were Studying Selected Agricultural Sciences;[b] and the Number and Percent Planning to Return to Their Home Country or Region

Region of Citizenship	Total Degrees Conferred	Average Number of Deg. Conf. Per Year	Percent of Students Planning to Return Home[c]
Central America	116	12	80.2
Caribbean	23	2	43.5
South America	522	52	83.3
Subtotal	661	66	81.4
East Asia	762	76	41.7
West Asia	793	79	41.1
Oceania	215	22	56.7
Subtotal	1,770	177	43.3
Northern Africa	206	20.5	63.6
Western Africa	196	19.5	66.3
Eastern Africa	53	5	52.8
Southern Africa	57	6	71.9
Subtotal	512	51	64.5
Canada	131	13	84.0
Austr. & New Zealand	109	11	75.2
Northern Europe	125	13	33.6
Eastern Europe	60	6	46.7
Western Europe	90	9	35.6
Subtotal	515	52	57.1
TOTAL	3,458	346	55.8

[a]Students could only be directly categorized by country of citizenship from 1979-1982. Data from 1973-1978 are based on country where the student's bachelor's degree was received. This table includes both resident and nonresident aliens.
[b]Agricultural sciences includes agronomy, agricultural economics, animal husbandry, food science and technology, fish and wildlife, forestry, horticulture, soils and soil science, animal science and nutrition, phytopathology, and agriculture general/other. It does not include other agricultural fields, such as agricultural engineering, agricultural education, and home economics.
[c]This table reflects the "intention" of the student to return to his/her home country or region following graduation. It does not indicate what actually happened to the student.
Source: National Research Council, Office of Scientific and Engineering Personnel, Doctorate Records file.

graduate level. Access to graduate-level education capacity, either in national or foreign universities, is essential to strengthening national agricultural research capacity. In addition to cost, the lack of sufficient agricultural universities within most African countries may be an important factor limiting the number of African students attending doctoral degree programs in the agricultural sciences at U.S. universities. Regardless of the reasons, the number of Africans receiving doctoral degrees in the agricultural sciences from U.S. universities is small. The implications of this finding for strengthening agricultural research capacity in Africa and increasing agricultural production through technological change seem apparent.

Factors Limiting the Contribution of U.S. Universities to Training Foreign Agricultural Scientists

Without question, U.S. universities have made a major contribution to strengthening scientific capacity in developing countries by training substantial numbers of agricultural scientists at the masters and doctoral degree levels. At the same time, this experience has not been without its problems and limitations. These problems and deficiencies relate to (1) those characteristics associated with foreign agricultural students as a group, and (2) those institutional characteristics associated with advanced degree programs in the U.S. that make such programs less than appropriate for foreign students from developing countries.

There is a general consensus that the majority of foreign agricultural students studying at U.S. universities come from urban rather than rural backgrounds. Mellor indicates that the basic cause of this situation:

> lies with a history of inadequate rural school systems, with the result that acquiring a secondary school education and the college education for which it is requisite, requires urban living. Historically, even the village boy who has become educated has managed it only by moving to live with relatives in town. As a result he has become urban oriented and experienced (Mellor, 1963:227).

This lack of a rural background tends to result in a number of related consequences. One problem is that many foreign students have a general lack of understanding about the agriculture of their own country and/or about production agriculture in particular. Mellor summarizes the problem succinctly: "The problem of the foreign student is less one of not knowing American agriculture than one of not knowing any operating agriculture at all" (Mellor, 1963:228).

The lack of a rural background and knowledge of production agriculture must have considerable influence on the attitudes and motivations of agricultural research workers. The obvious question to ask is why do these types of individuals enter the agricultural sciences in the first place? Both Mellor (1963) and Wharton (1959) point out that it is common for students to prefer careers in the professions such as law, medicine, or engineering than to one in agriculture but find that the competition excludes them from their first or second choice.

A related issue is whether they are motivated to provide service to rural people once they have returned home. Lewis, in discussing this problem among foreign graduate students in agricultural economics, states that these students "do not hold their own peasant farmers in respect. . . . Many of them cannot communicate with farmers. They will not listen to farmers and have no common ground of understanding with them" (Lewis, 1959:5). Wharton finds in a survey of professors in the U.S. that they:

> feel strongly that there is a need to send students for training (in the United States) who have a greater desire to serve their own agriculture. These persons say that the present levels of development in underdeveloped areas make it necessary to concentrate greatest attention on those individuals with service-oriented motivations (Wharton, 1959:37).

Inasmuch as the background and attitude of many foreign agricultural students may be a serious limiting factor to their future effectiveness as agricultural research workers, what consequences might result regarding the type of research they prefer to undertake? McMeekan thinks that foreign-trained agriculturalists:

> return home with outlooks and techniques much too advanced for their countries' needs. . . . They absorb a philosophy of modern science that attaches more merit to publication in a scientific journal to enhance their specialist reputation than to the dignity of immediate useful but unpublishable work. It is difficult to induce these young specialists to take on such mundane jobs as the testing of different cultivation practices (McMeekan, 1965:72).

Mellor also thinks that many students prefer theoretical rather than applied research. He finds many students working under the dubious assumption that "work with basic theory is thought to be possible without an operating knowledge of agriculture" (Mellor, 1963:228). While these are some of the potential problems that agricultural students from developing countries may bring with them to U.S. universities, the problems are not all one-sided.

One of the more serious institutional constraints that directly influences the type of training foreign students receive in U.S. universities is the continuing movement toward increasing specialization within disciplines. Advanced graduate education programs require original research studies as part of the degree requirement. As the frontiers of knowledge continue to expand, this results in many U.S.-trained foreign students focusing on more and more specialized research problems. Graduate education of this type tends to produce agricultural scientists who know "more and more of less and less." Yet, when these students return home, they find themselves in positions where they are expected to know a great deal more than what they have studied.

According to Borlaug, an originator of the Green Revolution and recipient of the Nobel Peace Prize in 1970, a U.S. graduate degree may be more of a problem than a solution in strengthening national agricultural research capacity. "The most discouraging thing in the world is to see a well-qualified Ph.D. in a developing country who has isolated himself in his own private laboratory to do research on minutiae, extending his doctoral thesis" (quoted in Wolff, 1983:14). According to Borlaug, the roots of the problem are in the American agricultural colleges and universities, where many developing country scientists are trained. "Most of our land-grant colleges and universities want to forget their agricultural heritage," he says. "The research they do is very sophisticated and generally has less and less to do with agriculture. . . ." Foreign students "get imbued with the idea that you can't do research without having very expensive gadgets. Then when they get their degrees they go back home with these ideas" (quoted in Wolff, 1983:14).

Another aspect of the specialization problem is the appropriateness of research problems studied by foreign students while in the United States. Most obvious in agriculture is the difference between doing research in temperate versus tropical climatic environments. Less obvious, yet perhaps more important, are differences in conditions such as: small-scale subsistence versus large-scale commercial types of agricultural production and "growing the same crops under conditions of affluence and sophistication versus that of producing under conditions of crude facilities and scarce resources" (Castillo, 1968:239).

Another problem is the research method and techniques taught to graduate students in U.S. universities. McMeekan points out that foreign agricultural students and research workers see agricultural research in the U.S. as it exists today, not as it operated yesterday.

> They see thousands of scientists in the United States engaged in highly specialized studies geared to a future already within the grasp of such a sophisticated agricultural nation. . . . Their work of today is no longer dominated by immediate usefulness. It lies in fields that are often only remotely connected with agricultural production, as it now exists (McMeekan, 1965:72).

When foreign students return home, they continue to be interested in specialized research problems that challenge the international scientific community in their discipline. The net effect, in cases where U.S.-trained third world scientists continue to work on these specialized, basic research problems, is to contribute to what Singer (1971) characterizes as the "internal brain drain." In this case, these agricultural scientists use the scarce scientific resources of their (developing) country to pursue scientific problems that are largely determined by their North American and European colleagues.

One alternative that may help overcome some current limitations of graduate education at U.S. universities is to allow and even encourage more foreign students to conduct their dissertation research at home country research institutions or at an international agricultural research center. Allowing foreign students to initiate their research careers by focusing on a research problem of significance to their home country could have an important, positive impact on the long-term agricultural research capacity of developing countries.

Another alternative would be the increased use of cooperative degree programs between third world and U.S. universities. In these joint programs, U.S. universities provide foreign students with needed advanced level graduate courses, while other courses and the dissertation research are conducted at the home university. Depending on the formality of relationship between the cooperating universities, the graduate degree may be offered jointly by both institutions or solely by the national university.

The overall objective of both approaches is to strengthen national agricultural research capacity by increasing the educational relevance of these degree programs for foreign students. It should also help reduce both internal and external "brain drain."

Conclusions

To summarize, each year about 350 foreign agricultural scientists receive doctoral degrees at U.S. universities. This represents about 30 percent of the doctoral student output of U.S. universities in the agricultural sciences. This output of new scientists has considerable potential to strengthen the agricultural research and educational capacity of developing nations.

There are several factors that appear to limit this impact. Most important is the problem of "brain drain," with over 40 percent of these foreign students expressing no clear intention to return to their home country or region. There are, however, major regional differences; Latin American doctoral recipients are most likely to return home, while Asian graduates are least likely to return home. Overall, there appear to be too few agricultural doctoral recipients from Africa, especially from Eastern and Southern Africa.

Finally, there appear to be problems related to the types of foreign students being sent for graduate study as well as the type of education received. More attention to nonacademic selection criteria by sponsoring agencies as well as encouraging more home-country thesis research and/or cooperative degree programs with national universities may help improve the quality and long-term impact of graduate education for foreign students at U.S. universities.

References

Castillo, Leopoldo S. "Graduate Training in the United States as Seen by a National from a Developing Country." *Journal of Dairy Science* 51(2):239, 1968.

Institute of International Education. *Open Doors, 1956–1974.* New York: Institute of International Education, 1981.

Lewis, Arthur B. *Thoughts of the American Training of Graduate Students of Agricultural Economics from Less Developed Countries.* New York: The Council on Economic and Cultural Affairs, 1959.

McMeekan, C. P. "What Kind of Agricultural Research?" *Finance and Development* II(2):72, 1965.

Mellor, John W. "Professional Training in Agriculture for Foreign Students." In Irwin T. Sanders (ed.), *The Professional Education of Students from Other Lands.* New York: Council on Social Work, 1963.

National Research Council. Office of Scientific and Engineering Personnel, Doctorate Records File. Washington, D.C.: National Academy of Sciences, various years.

Singer, Hans W. "A New Approach to the Problems of the Dual Society in Developing Countries." *United Nations International Social Development Review,* 3:23-31, 1971.

Swanson, B. E. "Agricultural Education in African Agricultural Development." *African Agricultural Education Conference.* Yaounde, Cameroon, July 1984.

Wharton, Cliffton R., Jr. *The U.S. Graduate Training of Asian Agricultural Economists.* New York: The Council on Economic and Cultural Affairs, 1959.

Wolff, Anthony. "Borlaug Remembers." Pp. 13-14 in *RF Illustrated,* December 1983.

PART SIX

Dissemination and Impact of Experiment Station Science

18

U.S. Agricultural Research and International Agricultural Research Centers: An Institutional Comparison

Hemchandra Gajbhiye and Don F. Hadwiger

Introduction

Agricultural research policy studies seldom have reflected the issues of international concern despite awareness that problems of international poverty, malnutrition, and low productivity are tied to national economic and security interests (Koppel, 1981). Most national and international systems have been studied in isolation without due consideration of international relations and the framework within which the agricultural research systems operate. Most of the studies have reflected local, state, or national perspectives.

The reasons for this are logical and stem from several factors. Historically, science and technology have been seen by governments as a means of serving national interests. They developed from within particular social and political settings, and there are inherently greater opportunities for productive research within a national setting. Unfortunately, this basically national research orientation has some undesirable effects: lack of anticipation and understanding of the international changes brought by science and technology, and poor ability to cope with issues as they impinge on international affairs (Skolnikoff, 1977:508).

The international agriculture research system, which was established and is still supported to a great extent by American resources, has served as a very important link between U.S. agricultural research and small farmers of the third world. However, not much attention has been paid to the relationship between the U.S agricultural research system and the international agricultural research system (Koppel, 1981). Are they competing or complementary? What are the issues that can bring both the systems onto one platform? And most important, how can this relationship be functional for U.S. agriculture as a whole?

What follows is a kind of overview comparing the U.S. agricultural research system and the international agricultural research system, which is represented by the network of International Agricultural Research Centers (IARCs) under the umbrella of the Consultative Group on International Agricultural Research (CGIAR). The purpose of this comparison is to assess the institutional consequences of the wholesale transfer of the U.S. agricultural research system to an international setting where the fundamental features of rural life and work, of society and politics, are wholly different. A viewpoint that may emerge in this chapter is that if U.S. agricultural research is on a decline as reflected in the reduced funding, the IARCs may serve as alternative forms of organizing agricultural research in the U.S. for the next century.

To understand some of these issues, a study was conducted involving senior- and middle-level scientists in two major international institutes: the International Rice Research Institute (IRRI), Manila, Philippines, and the International Crops Research Institute for Semi-Arid Tropics (ICRISAT), Hyderabad, India. The data were obtained by personal interviews and self-administered questionnaires in June–August 1984. Of the 145 potential respondents, 108 scientists participated in this study.

A number of questions, responses from which are used in this chapter, are identical to those used by Busch and Lacy in interviews of U.S. scientists (Busch and Lacy, 1983). It should be recognized that the Busch and Lacy (1983) sample of U.S. public agricultural scientists, used for comparison with our sample of IARC scientists, includes scientists from the federal research agencies as well as from state agricultural experiment stations and the land grant colleges of agriculture.

Appropriateness of the Model

To some extent the international agricultural research institutes are modeled after the land grant system in the United States (Busch and Sachs, 1981:146). The replication of this model involved the transfer of specific cultural practices and biomedical and mechanical innovations as well as entire institutions and the value system associated with them. Both the IARCs and the land grant systems have tended to utilize scientific knowledge to transform agriculture into a more productive system. The package of goods that has been introduced by the international institutes is essentially the same as that which has been developed in the United States except the international institutes are more crop specific than the land grant system (Busch and Sachs, 1981:146).

However, the systems differed on some philosophical issues. The American agricultural research system has transformed American agriculture into a business and science with the emphasis on efficiency. For most of the beneficiaries of international systems, agriculture remains a way of life and of subsistence and not a capitalistic enterprise. Second, the American system has encouraged mechanization, whereas the international system has to work for social systems where agriculture continues to be based upon manual and bullock power.

Some thinkers have expressed the fear that the U.S. research system, characterized by a highly developed institutional infrastructure linking the university to other private and public institutions involved in technical, social, and economic change, rarely performs as an effective instrument of technical, social, and cultural change when transported into societies where the presumed institutional infrastructure does not exist (Ruttan, 1982:123). But the excellent results achieved by the international institutes in the transformation of agriculture in many areas of the world may have demonstrated the soundness, efficacy, and relevance of the pattern of the American agricultural research system for agricultural research systems that operate in a different resource base and level of development.

Comparing Funding Systems

The land grant system is supported by two research funding mechanisms. First, the institutional research support system provides funds to support the research program of a particular research institution. Second, a competitive grants system provides support through project grants to individual scientists or research teams.

The international agricultural research system is supported mainly through the institutional research mechanism. The funds from donor countries and organizations are channeled through the Consultative Group on International Agricultural Research (CGIAR), a multilateral group of donors. In addition to the original cosponsors—Ford and Rockefeller Foundations—the CGIAR system is supported by thirty donors including twenty national governments from both developed and developing countries plus a number of additional private foundations. CGIAR provides a forum in which international institutes set forth their program and funding needs, and the donors make known their funding commitments.

Interacting Roles of U.S. and International
Agricultural Research Systems

Activity by agricultural institutions can be conceptualized in terms of several roles that they play. The contributions of the American system and the international system are compared here, and notice is taken of their apparent interdependence or conflict. The first of these roles is that of creating and maintaining the research system. This role includes founding institutions, developing the necessary facilities such as germplasm banks in the case of plant biology, and rationalization or integration of the knowledge process. A second role is that of recruitment and training of personnel. A third role, which is in a strict sense the output of the research system, is the production and distribution of knowledge; and within this role, further distinctions are made among the kinds of knowledge produced. A fourth role is that of developing support for the research endeavor. Support may be defined broadly as the means to existence and sustenance within the environment. Support involves legitimacy, which means acceptance and approval from those who share and control the environment. Beyond accepting public research as a proper activity of government, support includes the provision of material resources or funding required to maintain and advance the research institutions.

In an ideal situation, perhaps, the roles of the various research institutions would reinforce and strengthen the support for all others. The international centers and the American experiment stations are two of many actors in agricultural research. Another set of actors particularly to be kept in mind is the national research institutions within less industrialized countries, which have essential linkages with both the IARCs and with the land grant institutions and experiment stations.

Founding and Development of Institutions

Although the colleges of agriculture or experiment stations did not play a direct role in the founding of the international research centers, their structure and experience provided important models that the IARCs could emulate or avoid. The U.S. agricultural colleges have made a large effort in the development of national research institutions in less industrialized countries, and the IARCs have reinforced this effort through their personnel training, cooperative research, leadership, and sharing of resources with national institutions.

Both sets of institutions have been important in performing preliminary and underlying tasks such as collection and storage of germplasm. Support for disciplinary associations and journals is provided by scientists at both institutions, as indicated later in the report on publications.

Both institutions play a part in integrating the knowledge process but in different ways. The colleges provide a common location for major and minor academic disciplines, enabling students to become exposed to various fields of knowledge. These institutions produce leaders who serve in all sectors of the agricultural industry. Through conferences and short courses, the experiment stations and extension find the opportunity to refresh the knowledge of agricultural scientists and others who work in the industry. The agricultural colleges are centers for communication as well as for research. The international research centers pursue an integrative function by bringing together various disciplines to do research on a particular sector. The IARCs, as well as the U.S. Agricultural Research Service, can assemble research teams across disciplines, which occurs less routinely at the land grant institutions because of disciplinary demands and competition for resources.

Recruitment and Training of Personnel

Given these interactions between IARCs and land grant colleges in personnel selection and training, it is not surprising that the human resources of these two sets of institutions are remarkably similar on many dimensions.

Education. The level of educational attainment among scientists at international agricultural research institutes appears high. In our survey, more than 94 percent of scientists have received the doctoral degree. About 20 percent of the scientists reported that they have some post-doctoral training. These percentages are slightly higher than public sector agricultural researchers in the U.S. Busch and Lacy (1983:58) reported that 92 percent of agricultural scientists in the U.S. have received the doctoral degree and 16 percent have post-doctoral training.

Next, we examined how many scientists in international institutes have received their educational training in the United States. Over 48 percent of our respondent scientists reported that their last educational degree was obtained in the United States, over 90 percent of these in the land grant colleges. In addition, many scientists received multiple degrees from the land grant colleges.

The appropriateness of this graduate education has been continually disputed. A prominent criticism is that it is too narrow for use in less developed countries, both as to discipline specialization and as to physical environment. If about one-half of the international agricultural scientists are trained in this piecemeal approach, which certainly is not sufficient for the multiplicity of environments and scarce resources of the third world, then scientists at the international centers must pay a professional penalty when they go beyond the narrow lines of their disciplines. If the land grant colleges will not allow their students to go beyond the piecemeal approach, where in the developed countries can a future scientist of the international institutes or the third world national institutes gain training in holistic agriculture? Where can he/she receive training in testing combinations of components? How does he/she develop a design capability for the crop sequences or for the animal-crop relations that are crucial to the development of agriculture all over the third world?

Family Origins. When the occupation of a scientist's father is used as an indicator of family origin, a strong influence of farm background can be observed in the IARCs, as it is in the U.S. research system. About 26 percent of the IARC scientists reported that their father's occupation was farming. In the U.S. system about 30 percent of agricultural scientists came from farm backgrounds (Busch and Lacy, 1983).

To the extent that agricultural science has a large attraction for rural youth, it can be presumed that a considerable proportion of interested students will be found in the developing countries where agriculture still predominates. This will be particularly evident as schooling spreads into the rural areas of these countries. In the future, therefore, the number of agricultural scientists from such areas may grow.

Besides farming background, the other important professions that were reported as father's occupation in international centers are small business owners (12 percent), minor executives (11 percent), and teachers (11 percent). The data indicate that the scientists in IARCs are drawn from a broader social base and they bring a more varied background to these institutes.

Sex. Given the growing awareness that women play a major role in food production and consumption throughout the world, not enough attention has been paid to analyzing the scientific activities of female agricultural scientists. Our study reveals that only 3.7 percent of scientists in the international agricultural research centers are female. This observation is not very different from the American agricultural research system where only 4 percent of scientists are reported to be female (Busch and Lacy, 1983:51). In the U.S., women are concentrated in such disciplines as nutrition, social science, and food science. In the international centers studied, they work in economics, journalism, and soil science.

Such a low percentage of women in research may be attributed to the cultures, where intellectual competence and achievement, independence, and readiness for competition are judged as masculine (Shapley, 1975). Unfortunately, even if these cultural values are overcome, there seems to be a certain reluctance on the part of the institutions to accept women as agricultural scientists. The dual career conflict may provide some explanation. Mobility for a married and family-oriented female scientist is likely to be dependent upon that of her husband (Fisch, 1977:292).

The institutions may have different problems resulting from the dearth of women: In developing countries, since women are important actors in agriculture, a male science establishment will lack sensitivity to the problems faced by farmers. In U.S. agricultural colleges, faced with a diminished pool of farm youth from which to recruit, women might have become, as in some nonagricultural major fields, an alternative new pool from which to recruit able scientists.

Age. Concern over the age distribution of scientists in the U.S. agricultural research system has been recently expressed by Busch and Lacy (1983:52). In the U.S., 35.2 percent of agricultural scientists are over 50 years of age compared with only 20.4 percent in the IARCs. The comparative youth of IARC scientists is something of an enigma, for the founders of the centers were said to have sought scientists with the breadth and management skills that come from experience. Perhaps, the lower age of IARC scientists is due to the youth of the Centers themselves, their scientists having been recently recruited.

In our survey of IARCs, age is related to various criteria of problem choice. Scientists younger than 50 years of age are more likely to select a research problem based on the priorities of the research organization. Scientists older than 50 years are more likely to choose a research problem with potential creation of new methods. These results are in contrast with the U.S. system, where younger scientists are more likely to choose a research problem if it is a hot topic or because of publication probability in professional journals.

Our findings for the IARCs challenge the assumption that older scientists are less flexible in accepting new views. Among possible explanations, perhaps those scientists who are well settled in the disciplines can take the risk of doing new things, or perhaps a well-established scientific hierarchy may not allow the younger scientists to try new approaches or new methods. It has also been argued that a change in outlook always involves bitter dispute and generates strong opposition (Mulkay, 1977:121), which younger people cannot afford.

Creation of Knowledge

Agricultural scientists often divide their research time among basic research, applied research, and development (Busch and Lacy, 1983:64). The particular orientation they perceive may have major consequences for the results and products of the work. The international centers, which are being called "an adventure in applied science," are basically created for applied research. Although IARC scientists may tend to chafe a bit under an agenda of applied research, the centers apparently dictate such an agenda not as a means of complementarity with other research institutions but because major improvements in yields result from adaptations rather than from new theory (Evenson and Kislev, 1973:1309–29). However, basic research is also carried out to some extent. As pointed out by Chandler (1982:102), "None of this was pure research or research for its own sake but rather a search for the answers to questions that arose as they attempt to breed superior varieties."

When scientists in international centers were asked how they perceive their own work in the context of orientation, they classified 10 percent of their research as basic, 62 percent as applied, and 20 percent as development. The comparable study of U.S. scientists (Busch and Lacy, 1983) revealed that U.S. scientists on an average classified 30 percent of their research as basic, 55 percent as applied, and 13 percent as development. However, a majority within both sets of scientists felt that more time should be spent on basic research than what they were actually spending, and, correspondingly, less time should be spent on applied research. Farming system scientists and agronomists felt that more time should be spent on development; whereas agricultural engineers felt that less time should be spent on development, and research efforts in both basic and applied research should be increased.

It seems that scientists in international centers identify with their organization and concentrate on meeting its requirements. However, their perceived need for more basic research needs to be explained. It is argued that the high commitment to organization tends to separate researchers from their professional reference groups and to reduce their access to certified scientific knowledge, which lowers their productivity (Shepard, 1956). This may often lead to frustration and disillusionment because a researcher's professional aspirations almost inevitably conflict with his/her organizational responsibilities (Kornhauser, 1962).

In their choice of research problems, IARC scientists were more influenced by factors associated with an applied research agenda. As noted, the priorities of their research organization were most important to them in contrast with U.S. scientists who ranked a number of criteria higher, including following their own preferences as to research they enjoyed doing or questions that piqued their curiosity. Also, in choosing research, IARC scientists were more likely than U.S. scientists to consider potential marketability and the potential creation of new methods, useful materials, and devices. Demands raised by clientele and clientele needs as assessed by the scientists as well as feedback from extension personnel were more important criteria for IARC scientists. These scientists were more sensitive to the length of time required, possibly in the interest of producing a timely product, and less inclined to choose research because of publication possibilities in a professional journal (they preferred research service bulletins and reports).

There were other indicators of emphasis upon applied research. In the designation of persons who were influential in their research choice, IARC scientists were more responsive to "clients and users" and also to immediate supervisors and research review committees. Further, IARC scientists were more likely than U.S. scientists to communicate with an administrator, client, and funding agency regarding their research. Finally, IARC scientists were more likely to publicize their findings in a research bulletin or report in contrast to a journal or book.

Communication of scientific and technical information is clearly one of the most important aspects of scientific research, for it is the process that leads to its widespread use and ultimate benefits (King et al., 1976:3). Among scientists, the principal means of this communication is the publication process, which allows scientists to verify the reliability of information, to acquire a sense of the relative importance of a contribution, and to obtain critical response to work. Correspondingly, it is through publication that scientists receive professional recognition and esteem as well as promotion, advancement, and funding for future research (Fox, 1983). In our survey of international institutes, it was found that in a five-year period (1979–1983) agricultural scientists at IARCs have produced more scientific publications than the U.S. scientists. The mean numbers of journal articles, books, book chapters, abstracts, bulletins, and reports produced by international scientists and U.S. scientists over five years are summarized in Table 18.1.

For a possible explanation for comparatively lower publication rate among U.S. agricultural scientists, it might be argued that they spent less time in research than did international agricultural scientists. However, our study reveals that there is a marginal difference in time spent in research in both the systems. The scientists at international institutes reported that they spent about 68 percent of their time in research, whereas U.S. scientists spent 65 percent of their time in research (Busch and Lacy, 1983:120). Busch and Lacy argue that "after approximately 65 percent of a scientist's time is spent in research, it appears that additional increments of time do not result in an increase and may even result in a decrease in the production of journal articles and abstracts." So, the causal factor for higher publication productivity in international institutes is not the mere research time but something else. Researchers in this area have looked for individual level

TABLE 18.1 Five-Year Scientific Publication Rates Per Scientist by Type

Scientific Literature	Authored		Co-Authored	
	U.S. Scientists (1974-1979)	International Institutes (1979-1983)	U.S. Scientists (1974-1979)	International Institutes (1979-1983)
Journal Articles	4.54	6.05	6.64	7.34
Books	.09	.78	.11	.64
Book Chapters	.62	2.00	.44	2.38
Abstracts	2.71	3.83	3.57	4.00
Bulletins	.96	3.57	.99	2.62
Reports	4.05	10.49	2.59	8.56
Other	1.59	5.85	.86	3.20

Source: Data on U.S. agricultural scientists are based on Busch and Lacy (1983:80).

variables such as psychological traits, work habits, and demographic characteristics. Some studies examined the organizational factors such as organizational freedom, leadership, and group cohesion. However, there have not been enough data reported to justify strong conclusions. One of the possible explanations for higher publication productivity of IARC scientists compared to U.S. scientists may be stated as a response to the environmental threat to IARCs in the form of budgetary constraints. When many IARCs are finding it difficult to continue some of their existing programs or to establish new programs because of shrinking funding resources, producing more publications may be one strategy of organizations to cope with the threatening external environment. By producing more publications, legitimacy of the research organizations can be maintained. The fact that IARCs have higher publication rates in all categories of scientific literature perhaps reflects their struggle for survival.

Development of Political Support

As indicated earlier, political support may be manifested both in the form of legitimacy or acceptability and in the form of specific material resources. U.S. public agricultural research has been regarded for more than a century as a legitimate function of state and national governments. There have been only occasional challenges to the belief, which underlies public support, that agricultural progress is obtained through improved technology.

Concerns about resource depletion and hazards to the environment resulting from technology change prompted effective opposition to public agricultural research institutions, which were alleviated when the research and regulatory agencies seriously addressed these concerns. Concerns about impacts upon farming structure have been more enduring because U.S. agricultural research did facilitate, though it did not dictate, increased size and decreased number of farming units.

It can be argued on behalf of the IARCs that, because their emphasis is upon improving genetic materials, new technology that they produce is scale neutral and has aided small farm agriculture. Scientists surveyed at the international centers believed that small farmers are the principal beneficiaries of their research and publications. If the work of international centers has increased productivity and also distributed benefits widely, it will have enhanced the worldwide legitimacy of public agricultural research.

Legitimacy is but one level of support for agricultural research. With legitimacy it becomes possible to move to the second level of providing the material resources needed to maintain a research establishment. Several motives may be identified for providing such resources, whether they be from public or private sources common to governments, nonprofit foundations, or private entities. First, legitimacy itself may lead to support "in the public interest." Agricultural research has always had "public interest" advocates who would not personally benefit from research outcomes. Supporters during the nineteenth century were likely to be utopians who envisioned a future of abundance and leisure brought about by technological development (Hadwiger, 1984:194–95). No longer do such payoffs exist only in an imagined distant future, so it is not surprising that private foundations that seek the public interest should have provided leadership and generous support in the development of the international research centers. It should be noted that even in seeking the public interest, success has its rewards: the satisfaction and public acclaim from helping in a good cause. In the U.S. Congress, influential legislators seeking a fitting memorial to their own years of service have sometimes dictated new budget lines for agricultural research. Such assistance can produce a large increment in a relatively small budget such as that for agricultural research.

A second kind of material support is that based upon client interest. Among the beneficiaries and potential clients of agricultural research are the producers and/or consumers of food and fiber—a rather large constituency. Consumers, unfortunately, are rarely mobilized as clienteles, though they are considered to be the largest research beneficiaries (Hildreth, 1982:241). Among the explanations offered for this anomaly are the following: (1) consumer benefits are diffuse rather than exclusive, so it pays no consumer to advocate for himself/herself; (2) research institutions cater to producers as clients, so when consumer groups perceive that consumer benefits are unintended, they become defensive rather than supportive.

Producer interests, too, are difficult to mobilize. In the U.S., much producer support is decentralized: groups attach themselves to a particular research institution in the expectation that it will be responsive to their unique geographic or commodity needs. Producers accept the likelihood that any new knowledge of which they are first users may later be adapted to the needs of competitors, and they have been disinclined to support activities such as those at an international research center that would speed the process of dissemination. Sometimes they have directly opposed such aid, as in the use of U.S. agricultural attachés to promote agricultural reform in foreign countries.

It seems the task of maintaining public and clientele support for agricultural research does in the end fall to the research institutions themselves. For many years now, the U.S. research institutions have cultivated a network of industry groups including the general farm organizations—particularly the American Farm Bureau Federation—and also commodity organizations. They have also maintained close ties with the farm legislators and with agricultural bureaucracies who form a subgovernment that makes agricultural policy decisions in the state and national governments.

The international research centers, too, have clienteles, judging from the survey finding that IARC scientists communicate with their clients twice as often as do U.S. public agricultural scientists. It is likely that IARC scientists were not referring to the governments and organizations that sponsor the international centers. Rather, they may have been referring to the beneficiaries who, according to another of the scientist responses, are small farmers. Small farmers as clients, though they enhance legitimacy, may provide little effective political support.

While it seems that international centers themselves appear to have little grass roots support, they do on the other hand provide a persuasive argument for public interest assistance. Although anxiety as well as hope attends the progress of technology, the international centers have had an enormous impact upon developing country agriculture. Most observers see the changes wrought by technology as being necessary to meet increasing food needs.

Realistically, there are likely to be periods of recession in which prices are below cost of production for many farmers. Even now, increased production for export from developed countries may be induced by export subsidies rather than by world export prices.

However, there are particularly strong reasons for the development of commodity interests on a world basis that have a complementarity of interest with respect to some aspects of agricultural research: for example, basic or fundamental research that would make a product more resilient, more attractive to consumers, or more competitive with potential substitutes. Rice producers, as one case, have a large potential Asian market if rice continues to be competitive in price with wheat or other grains. Rice may also have an enlarging world market, including countries such as the United States where domestic producers promote its use.

Public interest support for research institutions may be forthcoming based on their achievements. These institutions have demonstrated their potential for meeting increasing world food needs. Efforts of the international research centers have shown the potentiality for technology to serve the small producers and poor consumers. The research institutions may have good access to the decision makers within governments and private funding agencies who are able to increase budgets for reasons of public interest. In effect, there may be a worldwide institutional lobby with an attitude of mutuality and a fairly large vision of the international research system.

Given that the research output will continue to be impressive and the cost will be small relative to other public budgets, it would seem that the prospects are good for a healthy and expanding international research system. The future of international research centers may be more promising than that of other international systems such as the United Nations and its agencies.

Concluding Comments

While the formal structure of agricultural research institutions is highly decentralized, there is a global research system in which the experiment stations, land grant colleges, the developed country research agencies, the national institutes of developing countries, and the international research centers are interdependent parts.

1. There is complementarity in the development of research institutions. Aspects of the U.S. system have served as models for the international research centers. Both the U.S. system and the international centers played important roles in the development of the national research institutions within the developing countries, and these in turn will play a crucial role in meeting world food needs. In addition, the research institutions respectively rely on the infrastructures of the others, including the germplasm banks. Both IARCs and national research systems play coordinating and integrating roles.

2. There is interdependence in training and recruitment and in career development of public agricultural scientists. U.S. institutions may have trained half or more of those at the IARCs. They also trained a large number of scientists in developing country institutes on whose function both the national and the international centers depend. The agricultural science career becomes more rewarding with the opportunities for interchanging positions among the various institutions.

3. All institutions contribute in the development of the various types of knowledge. The IARC scientists, whose major mission is to provide applied knowledge, nevertheless contribute much to mainstream academic literature. In the U.S. agricultural system, scientists are somewhat more likely to engage in "basic" research; however, support from U.S. agricultural research results more from its capacity to provide technologies for specific sets of users.

4. The U.S. agricultural system and the international research centers are complementary, on balance, in their efforts to develop support for their own missions. In particular, the IARCs, in exhibiting an ability to help small unit farming, help to reassure those who fear that new technology may not be beneficial to the world's smaller farmers. The

combined achievements of the agricultural institutions provide a strong rationale for continuing support from public interest groups, eleemosynary foundations, and benevolent governments.

Research institutions have a great potential constituency among those who want adequate and low cost food for themselves and others. Agricultural institutions have been remarkable in their progress to this goal. They should recognize and explain to others that current success as well as the prospect for ultimate world food abundance derives from working together.

Notes

Funding for this project was provided by the World Food Institute, Iowa State University, Ames, Iowa.

References

Busch, Lawrence, and Lacy, William B. *Science, Agriculture, and the Politics of Research.* Boulder, Colorado: Westview Press, 1983.

Busch, Lawrence, and Sachs, Carolyn. "The Agricultural Sciences and the Modern World System." Pp. 131–56 in Lawrence Busch (ed.), *Science and Agricultural Development.* Totowa, New Jersey: Allanheld, Osmun, 1981.

Chandler, R. E., Jr. *An Adventure in Applied Science.* Manila: International Rice Research Institute, 1982.

Evenson, Robert E., and Kislev, Y. "Research and Productivity in Wheat and Maize." *Journal of Political Economy* 81:1309–29, 1973.

Fisch, R. "Psychology of Science." Pp. 277–318 in I. Spiegel-Rosing and D. de Solla Price (eds.), *Science, Technology and Society: A Cross-Disciplinary Perspective.* Beverly Hills, California: Sage Publications, 1977.

Fox, M. F. "Publication Productivity Among Scientists: A Critical Review." *Social Studies of Science* 13:285–305, 1983.

Hadwiger, Don. "U.S. Agricultural Research Politics: Utopians, Utilitarians, Copians." *Food Policy* 9:193–205, 1984.

Hildreth, R. J. "The Agricultural Research Establishment in Transition." Pp. 235–48 in Don F. Hadwiger (ed.), *Food Policy and Farm Programs.* New York: The Academy of Political Science, 1982.

King, D. W.; McDonald, D. D.; Roderes, N. K.; and Wood, B. L. "Statistical Indicators of Scientific and Technical Communication 1960–1980." Vol. 1. A Summary Report for the National Science Foundation. Rockville, Maryland: Center for Quantitative Sciences, 1976.

Koppel, Bruce. *Report of a Workshop on Linkages Between the International and Domestic Functions of the Land-Grant System.* Honolulu: East-West Center, 1981.

Kornhauser, W. *Scientists in Industry.* Berkeley: University of California Press, 1962.

Mulkay, M. J. "Sociology of the Scientific Research Community." Pp. 93–147 in I. Spiegel-Rosing and D. de Solla Price (eds.), *Science, Technology and Society.* Beverly Hills, California: Sage Publications, 1977.

Ruttan, Vernon W. *Agricultural Research Policy.* Minneapolis: University of Minnesota Press, 1982.

Shapley, Deborah. "Obstacles to Women in Science." *Impact of Science on Society* 25:115-23, 1975.
Shepard, H. A. "Basic Research and the Social System of Pure Science." *Philosophy of Science* 23:48-57, 1956.
Skolnikoff, E. B. "Science, Technology and the International System." Pp. 507-33 in I. Spiegal-Rosing and D. de Solla Price (eds.), *Science, Technology and Society.* Beverly Hills, California: Sage Publications, 1977.

19

The Interrelationships of Agricultural Research and Farm Structure

Fred C. White

Introduction

The agricultural research system was established to make farms more efficient and profitable at a time when U.S. agriculture was characterized by a large number of small farms. The number and size of farms have changed dramatically since the agricultural research system was developed and are projected to continue to change in the future. If current trends continue, U.S. agriculture in the future may be characterized by a bimodal distribution of many small part-time farms used to supplement operators' incomes and a few large farms producing the vast majority of U.S. farm products.

Agricultural research obviously impacts on farm structure. Adoption of new technologies by particular types or sizes of farms may improve the competitive positions of these farms relative to other farms and hence may lead to changes in farm structure. Farm structure, on the other hand, impacts on agricultural research in a direct but not well-understood manner. The demand for agricultural research, both the aggregate level and type of research demanded, is related to farm structure. These interrelationships are explored in this chapter.

The overall objective of this chapter is to examine the agricultural research system's impact on and response to the changing farm structure. In particular, the chapter examines the agricultural research system's (1) contribution to past structural changes; (2) response, in terms of goals and operations, to past structural changes; (3) alternative options to influence future structural changes; and (4) alternative options for serving agriculture in the future that account for potential structural changes.

Farm Structure

An Operational Definition

Structure as related to agriculture is a multifaceted concept. Penn (1979:5) identified the following components of structure:

1. Organization of resources into farming units;
2. Size, management, and operation of those units;
3. Effects of different types of organizations and techniques on natural resources;
4. Ease of entry into the food and agricultural industry;
5. Manner in which the firm procures its inputs and markets its output;
6. Performance of the food and agricultural industry in providing the quality and quantity of food sought by the consumer;
7. Degree of freedom to make business decisions, and the degree of risks borne by the operator;
8. Restrictions on land use;
9. Manner of asset transfer to succeeding generations.

In the broadest sense, agricultural research could affect farm structure by affecting any of these components. Operationally, structure is often focused on the number of farms and the size distribution of farms. The major public concern over research and extension and structure was explicitly brought to public attention by Hightower in 1973. He alleged the research and extension system gave a preference to large farms and geared research toward large-scale operations.

In order to examine the effect of agricultural research on the number and size of farms, an operational definition of structure that accounts for the number and size of farms is utilized. Penn (1979) used the term "family farm structure," referring to a relatively large number of modest-sized farms operated by a family unit. Within the context of this operational definition of structure, agricultural research would be characterized as structurally neutral if it does not favor farms of a particular size. Alternatively, agricultural research would be considered structurally nonneutral if it favors farms of a particular size, contributing to a changing farm structure.

Historical Trends in Farm Structure

The changes in farm structure characteristics over the last 100 years are reviewed in this section. Farm numbers, the distribution of farms by size category, and average farm size over the 100-year period are shown in Table 19.1. Expansion in output during the first half of the period can be attributed largely to expanded use of conventional inputs of land, labor, and capital. Hence, farm numbers continued to increase throughout the first half of the period, reaching a peak during the depression. The last fifty-year period has been a unique period in the history of American agriculture. For the

TABLE 19.1   Number of Farms--by Size of Farm and Average Size
             of Farm: 1880-1982

Year	Under 50 Acres	50-99 Acres	100-499 Acres	500-999 Acres	1,000 Acres and Over	Total	Average Size
	------------------thousands-------------------						acres
1880	1,175	1,033	1,696	76	29	4,009	133.70[a]
1900	1,933	1,366	2,291	103	47	5,740	146.55
1920	2,306	1,475	2,457	150	67	6,454	148.54
1940	2,291	1,291	2,255	164	101	6,102	174.55
1959	1,057	658	1,660	200	136	3,711	302.75
1982[b]	637	1,238		204	162	2,241	439.40

[a]U.S. Dept. of Agriculture, ERS. Farm Real Estate Historical Series
Data: 1850-1970, ERS-520, Washington, D.C., June 1973.
[b]U.S. Dept. of Commerce, Bureau of the Census. 1982 Census of
Agriculture, Preliminary Report, United States, AC82-A-00-000(P),
U.S., G.P.O., Washington, D.C., May 1984.
Source: U.S. Dept. of Commerce, Bureau of the Census. Historical
Statistics of the United States, Colonial Times to 1970. U.S.,
G.P.O., Washington, D.C., 1976.

first time, increases in agricultural output can be explained largely by
expansion of nonconventional inputs such as research, extension, and
education (Tweeten, 1979). As a consequence, farm numbers have been
reduced to one-third of the peak 1935 level. Average farm size has doubled
in the last fifty years. The number of farms in the large farm categories
in Table 19.1 has continued to increase, while the number of farms in other
categories has been decreasing dramatically.

Recent trends in farm structure also are examined by considering the
distribution of farms by value of sales class. In analyzing the changing farm
structure issue, it is important to maintain a consistent classification scheme
through time. Classification of farms by value of sales, which is one of the
most frequently used classification systems, can be used if adjustments are
made for inflation. A correction for inflation can be made between 1972
and 1983, because, first, the index of prices received by farmers doubled
between 1972 and 1983 and, second, each sales class is double the lower
adjacent sales class. Farms that had over $100,000 in sales in 1972 would
have over $200,000 in 1983 dollars. The distributions of farms by sales class
for 1972 and 1983 are presented in Table 19.2. Approximately one-half of
the reduction in farm numbers in the lowest sales category can be directly
attributed to a change in definition of a farm. After adjusting for the change
in definition, it is evident that the rate of decline in farm numbers is much
lower between 1972 and 1983 and earlier periods. All categories with less
than $40,000 in sales experienced a decline in farm numbers between 1972

TABLE 19.2   Number of U.S. Farms by Sales Class
with Adjustments for Inflation Using
Constant 1983 Dollars

| | Number of Farms | |
Farms with Sales of:	1972	1983
	(thousands)	
Less than $5,000	1,222	829
$5,000-$9,999	347	325
$10,000-$19,999	353	279
$20,000-$39,999	347	272
$40,000-$199,999	512	558
$200,000 and over	79	107
All Farms	2,860	2,370

Source: U.S. Department of Agriculture, ERS. Economic
Indicators of the Farm Sector, Income and Balance Sheet
Statistics, 1983, Washington, D.C., September 1984.

and 1983. The two categories with the largest level of sales experienced
an increase in farm numbers.

Current Farm Structure

Agriculture is characterized by a heterogeneous structure of various sizes
of farms as indicated by the data in Table 19.3. Large farms dominate sales:
4.5 percent of the largest farms (sales over $200,000 per year) accounted
for 44.4 percent of total sales in 1983. Small farms are more numerous;
71.9 percent of total farms in 1983 had annual sales of less than $40,000.
These small farms accounted for only 17.2 percent of total farm sales.
Medium-sized farms (sales of $40,000–$200,000 per year) accounted for 23.6
percent of total farm numbers and 38.4 percent of gross farm income in
1984.

The small farm category is particularly heterogeneous, being made up
of both part-time farmers and low resource farmers. Low resource farmers
are often characterized by little if any off-farm income and low levels of
farm sales. Many part-time farmers have full-time nonfarm jobs. The average
off-farm income for the small farm group is $19,194 per year (Table 19.3).
The level of farm prices and government payments has little impact on
total family income for many small farms, because income from farm sources
is only a small part of their total income (Tweeten et al., 1983).

The uneven distribution of net income creates problems in debt servicing.
The largest farms received two-thirds of the net income but held only a
little over one-third of the debt (USDA, ERS, 1984). The medium-sized
farms received 31.6 percent of the net farm income but held 42.4 percent
of total debt (USDA, ERS, 1984). Small farms, in aggregate, had little net

TABLE 19.3   Selected Characteristics of Farms by Volume of Sales
in 1983

	Large Farms (Sales $200,000 and Over)	Medium Farms (Sales $40,000 to $199,999)	Small Farms (Sales Under $40,000)	All Farms
NUMBERS				
Number of Farms	107,000	558,000	1,705,000	2,370,000
(Percent of all farms)	(4.5)	(23.6)	(71.9)	(100.00)
(Percent of all sales)	(44.4)	(38.4)	(17.2)	(100.00)
		(Dollars per Farm)		
INCOME				
Net income from farming	175,583	15,738	243	15,518
Off-farm income	17,299	11,424	19,194	17,299
Total income from farm and off-farm sources	192,882	27,162	19,437	32,817
BALANCE SHEET				
Assets, Dec. 31	2,294,523	804,905	197,241	435,120
Debt, Dec. 31	733,972	163,440	26,335	90,591
Equity, Dec. 31	1,560,551	641,465	170,906	344,529

Source: U.S. Department of Agriculture, ERS, Economic Indicators of the Farm Sector, Income and Balance Sheet Statistics, 1983, Washington, D.C., September 1984.

farm income to service debt. However, much of the debt on small farms was serviced by income from nonfarm sources.

Impact of Agricultural Research on Farm Structure

Economists theorize that the adoption of new technology is dependent on the profitability of the new technology and on the asset positions of firms (Mansfield, 1963). From a profitability standpoint, large farms generally have more to gain from adoption of a new technology than small farms, because large farms have more output to which the cost savings can be applied. In other words, a given cost savings per unit of output multiplied by more units of output on large farms than on small farms results in larger total savings on the large farms.

Farmers who make the most use of research results are often characterized as more innovative, more aggressive, and better managers of larger farms (Paarlberg, 1981). Even when farmers in general do not benefit from technological change, the larger, progressive ones can benefit from a new technology through early adoption. Adoption lags, which systematically favor the larger farmers, occur because it is more profitable for large farms than for small farms to invest in acquiring information. Some technologies such as specialized mechanical equipment are economically feasible only for large farms that can spread the high investment costs over a large volume of output. Technologies that could efficiently be applied to farms of any size tend to be adopted more quickly on large farms. In a study of adoption of new crop varieties, Perrin and Winkelman (1976) noted that new seed varieties and fertilizer, which should help both large and small farms, favored larger farms because the small farms lagged behind in the early stage of adoption.

Response of Agricultural Research to Changing Farm Structure

This section explores how agricultural research institutions have responded to changes in farm structure. Goals and operations are discussed.

Paarlberg (1981) stated that agricultural research was initially intended to make the family farm more efficient and thus more profitable. Articulation of the justification and motivation for public support of agricultural research appears to have changed over time with less direct reference to farm structure concepts such as the family farm. Arndt and Ruttan (1977:3-25) indicate that agricultural research constitutes an investment aimed at improving society's well-being by raising returns to factors of production through lowering costs or increasing output, by improving product quality or introducing new products, and by reducing farmers' vulnerability to forces beyond their control. Changing the emphasis of the stated goals from farmers' well-being to society's well-being can be attributed to the realization that the ultimate beneficiaries of agricultural research are society as a whole rather than agricultural producers. Although new technologies may offer economic incentives for adoption by innovative producers, initial profits from innovation are eroded over time as a technology becomes widely used.

A task force appointed by the Experiment Station Committee on Organization and Policy (1981) recently assessed the role of agricultural research in bringing about changes in structure, particularly dealing with the concentration of production on larger farms. Results from that study indicated that production research of agricultural experiment stations was not slanted toward large farms. Of all production research, 78 percent was judged to be applicable to all farms, 10 percent primarily useful to small farms, 7 percent primarily useful to moderate-sized farms, and 5 percent primarily useful to large farms. However, the task force concluded that even though the research effort may be characterized as producing knowledge applicable to all sizes of farms, the interaction of that knowledge with the economic environment results in a significant contribution by the experiment stations to a growing concentration of production in the larger-sized firms.

Even though the research activities conceptually are structurally neutral, this assumption often breaks down in reality in the technology adoption process. Research and extension personnel may make information available to all farmers, but the large farmers tend to make the most use of the research results and extension information. These farmers utilize information they consider to be useful to them, while discarding other information deemed to be inappropriate. The more innovative, more aggressive, and better managers of large farms are also generally vocal, which provides a feedback to research and extension personnel, indicating what information has been useful and what information has not been useful. The natural response on the part of research and extension pesonnel has been to provide more of the useful information and less of the information that was not useful. Consequently, research and extension activities tend to respond to users of this information, who generally are larger farmers. Even though there may be no overt effort made to exclude particular groups such as small farmers, the net result is that many research and extension programs become oriented toward select groups that avail themselves of the information (Paarlberg, 1981).

Farm Structure's Influence on Public Support for Agricultural Research

Farm structure is postulated as influencing the level of public support for agricultural research. This section explores the impact of farm structure characteristics on public funding decisions for agricultural research, particularly in state agricultural experiment stations.

Agricultural research expenditures by state agricultural experiment stations amounted to $939 million in 1982 (USDA, SEA, 1983). State appropriations accounted for 61.8 percent of this total, with federal and private funding accounting for 32.1 percent and 6.1 percent, respectively. The largest component from federal sources was formula funds, which include Hatch funds. Over the period 1966–1982, state appropriations (in constant dollars) grew at an annual rate of 2.8 percent compared to 1.2 percent for federal funds (in constant dollars). With this background on the levels and sources of funding, attention is next focused on how farm structure affects funding decisions.

Federal funds allocated under the Hatch Act are allocated by a formula, which is based largely on a state's rural and farm population. At least 52 percent of these funds have been allocated on the basis of the size of each state's rural population and farm population relative to total U.S. rural and farm population (Peterson, 1969:46). Hence, the distribution of federal funds among states is affected by farm structure, but the overall level of Hatch funding is not explicitly linked to farm structure.

Schultz (1956) and Heady (1961) argue that the level of total income within a state is a major determinant of state appropriations for state agricultural experiment stations. Heady (1961) further indicated a negative relationship exists between the proportion of a state's income generated by agriculture and its appropriations to experiment stations.

Peterson (1969) concludes that state income, both farm and nonfarm, was the most important variable influencing the size of experiment stations. Farm population of the state appeared to be a relatively minor factor affecting level of funds available to a state. The number of dollars of income generated in the state, not the number of farmers, seemed to be the most important variable determining the support of experiment stations.

Huffman and Miranowski (1981) examined the effects of size distributions of farms and the tenure status of farmers on research expenditures in state agricultural experiment stations. Variables reflecting the proportion of large farms and the proportion of medium-sized farms had positive impacts on the level of expenditures. An interaction term between the proportion of large farms and the size of the subregional applied research stock had a negative coefficient. This result implies that large farmers have a greater ability than other farmers to borrow applied research from the available stock in similar subregions outside their state. Hence, large farmers are less likely to support indigenous applied agricultural research within their own state if similar research is being conducted elsewhere.

Rose-Ackerman and Evenson (1985) find that state appropriations for agricultural research and extension were influenced by the level of farm income and farm population and by the political effectiveness of farmers. Farm population had a greater influence on extension expenditures than on research expenditures. The ability of farmers to elect other farmers to the legislature increased state support for research and extension.

Implications for the Future

Prospects for future changes in farm numbers differ markedly by farm size category. The large farm category (sales of over $200,000 per year), which experienced the greatest relative increase in numbers in recent years, is projected to continue to grow in the future because of economies of size. Costs per unit of output are lower for the large farm category than for any other category. Agricultural products from these farms move into international markets, and, hence, the economic well-being of these farms is heavily dependent on developments in international markets. Many of these farms were expanded in response to favorable export markets in the mid-1970s, and future expansions in this category will be dependent on future developments in the export markets.

Full-time medium-sized family farms (sales of $40,000 to $200,000 per year) appear to be vulnerable in the long run. The cost of production is higher, on the average, on these farms than on the larger farms, because the medium-sized farms have not achieved the economies of size that many larger farms have achieved. The medium-sized farms have more debt to service relative to net income than large farms.

Many small farms are heavily dependent on off-farm income. A strong nonfarm economy providing abundant job opportunities is more important to this group of farmers than farm profits, because more of their income is derived from nonfarm sources than from farming. Low resource farmers generally benefit more from general social programs for the poor, aged, and disabled than from traditional government efforts to increase farm profits, including traditional research and extension programs.

Agricultural research has markedly influenced farm structure and will continue to influence farm structure. However, Ruttan (1982:344) argued that agricultural research should not be the tool used by policy-makers to achieve some desired future farm structure. His induced innovation model indicates that the agricultural research system responds to the economic incentives signaled from the marketplace. Asking the research system to respond to some other objective would result in technologies that would not be adopted without facilitating government actions. Diverting research activities away from market incentives would eventually erode the scientific capacity of the research system to meet society's needs. Ruttan (1982:346) further argued that research is too blunt an instrument to use in achieving a particular farm structure. Other government programs including income transfers, tax policies, and land reform measures may be more efficient techniques for achieving a desired farm structure.

An increasing number of large farms in the future will place additional demands on the agricultural research system. The empirical results by Huffman and Miranowski (1981) indicated that large farmers effectively demand more research than others. Some states have already experienced large farmers bypassing extension agents and coming directly to research scientists to solve production and marketing problems. This type of action would be expected to increase in the future with a rising proportion of large farms if the extension service is not upgraded to deal with the problems of large farmers. If the extension service does not respond to these demands, there will be a greater demand placed on research scientists to be involved in problem solving and consulting large farmers.

Broad public support for agricultural research was initially based on the fact that a large portion of the population was involved in farming. Agricultural research has contributed to a marked decline in the number of farms through time. Busch and Lacy (1983:237) pointed out that these changes have contributed to "sweeping away the foundations of legitimacy that made possible broad public support for agricultural research in the first place." They have suggested that the support base for agricultural research will need to be broadened through the cultivation of other support groups. However, expanding the base of support may carry with it the possibility for changing directions for future agricultural research. Changes in direction will depend on which additional support groups might become involved in the political process.

References

Arndt, Thomas M., and Ruttan, Vernon. "Valuing the Productivity of Agricultural Research: Problems and Issues." *Resource Allocation and Productivity in National* and *International Agricultural Research*. Minneapolis: University of Minnesota Press, 1977.

Busch, Lawrence, and Lacy, William B. *Science, Agriculture, and the Politics of Research*. Boulder, Colorado: Westview Press, 1983.

Experiment Station Committee on Organization and Policy. *Research and the Family Farm*. Ithaca, New York: Media Services, College of Agriculture and Life Sciences, Cornell University, 1981.

Heady, Earl O. "Public Purpose in Agricultural Research and Education." *Journal of Farm Economics* 43:566–81, 1961.

Hightower, Jim. *Hard Tomatoes, Hard Times*. Cambridge, Massachusetts: Schenkman Publishing Company, 1973.

Huffman, Wallace E., and Miranowski, John A. "An Economic Analysis of Expenditures on Agricultural Experiment Station Research." *American Journal of Agricultural Economics* 63:104–18, 1981.

Mansfield, E. "Intrafirm Rates of Diffusion of an Innovation." *Review of Economics and Statistics* 45:348–59, 1963.

Paarlberg, Don. "The Land Grant Colleges and the Structure Issues." *American Journal of Agricultural Economics* 63:129–34, 1981.

Penn, J. B. "The Structure of Agriculture: An Overview of the Issue." *Structure Issues of American Agriculture*. U.S. Department of Agriculture, Ag. Econ. Report 438, 1979.

Perrin, Richard, and Winkelman, Don. "Impediments to Technical Progress on Small Vs. Large Farms." *American Journal of Agricultural Economics* 58:888–94, 1976.

Peterson, Willis L. "The Allocation of Research, Teaching, and Extension Personnel in U.S. Colleges of Agriculture." *American Journal of Agricultural Economics* 51:41–56, 1969.

Rose-Ackerman, Susan, and Evenson, Robert. "The Political Economy of Agricultural Research and Extension: Grants, Votes, and Reapportionment." *American Journal of Agricultural Economics* 67:1–14, 1985.

Ruttan, Vernon W. *Agricultural Research Policy*. Minneapolis: University of Minnesota Press, 1982.

Schultz, T. W. "Agriculture and the Appreciation of Knowledge." *A Look to the Future*. W. K. Kellogg Foundation Conference Proceedings, Battle Creek, Michigan, 1956.

Tweeten, Luther G. *Foundations of Farm Policy*. Second edition, revised. Lincoln: University of Nebraska Press, 1979.

———. "The Economics of Small Farms." *Science* 219:1037–41, 1983.

Tweeten, Luther G., et al. *The Emerging Economics of Agriculture: Review and Policy Options*. Council for Agricultural Science and Technology Report No. 98, Ames, Iowa, 1983.

U.S. Department of Agriculture, ERS. *Farm Real Estate Historical Series Data: 1850–1970*, ERS-520. Washington, D.C., June 1973.

———. *Economic Indicators of the Farm Sector, Income and Balance Sheet Statistics, 1983*. Washington, D.C., 1984.

U.S. Department of Agriculture, SEA. *Inventory of Agricultural Research*. Washington, D.C., 1983.

U.S. Department of Commerce, Bureau of the Census. *Historical Statistics of the United States, Colonial Times to 1970*. Washington, D.C.: Government Printing Office, 1976.

———. *1982 Census of Agriculture, Preliminary Report, United States*, AC82-A-00-000(P). Washington, D.C.: U.S. Government Printing Office, May 1984.

PART SEVEN

Future Directions

20

Toward a New Covenant
for Agricultural Academe

J. Patrick Madden

Introduction

In his book, *The Next Economy,* Paul Hawken (1983) has envisioned the U.S. economy as it is likely to emerge from the current financial crisis. Agriculturalists ought to do a similar kind of thinking. We should ask ourselves what kind of agriculture is going to emerge from the current financial crisis in which farm bankruptcies are becoming endemic, land prices and equipment values are plummeting, and the structure of agriculture is a blur. The past decade has seen unprecedented changes in U.S. agriculture. And the rate of change seems to be accelerating. How will the land grant institutions and other realms of academia adapt to "The Next Agriculture"? And more to the point, what will be our role in shaping the future of agriculture?

Success as a Mixed Blessing

American agriculture is heralded as a great success. Nurtured by scientific and educational systems, farmers not only make two or three blades of grass grow where none grew before, but they produce an abundance of food perhaps unprecedented in history. However, agricultural abundance has been both a blessing and a curse; food is plentiful for those who can afford it; prices are relatively low; and Americans spend a lower share of their income on food than any other industrial nation. Because some commodities have been supported above market clearing prices, massive surpluses have been produced, causing a ruinous drain on the federal treasury. Farm mechanization has reduced the drudgery and risk of most farming operations (Splinter, 1980), but it has contributed to a loss of agricultural employment and depopulation of some farming areas while enriching other locations (Martin and Olmstead, 1985). Yield-enhancing fertilizers, pesticides, and herbicides are heralded as an example of man's conquest over nature, while an increasing number of experts and consumer advocates have become alarmed about potential health hazards due to chemical residues appearing in ground water, streams, and foods. Meanwhile, the increasingly prevalent exercises in setting national priorities for agricultural research and extension are frustrated by the absence of a clearly articulated set of national goals and an increasing number of vocal participants.

Interviews conducted during the Penn State study (Feller et al., 1984, Vol. 2) illustrate the dedication of extension personnel to help farmers solve their various production problems. One of the interviewees, a prosperous Utah farmer, said he didn't know how he would have survived had it not been for the help of the county extension agent and his staff. Then, upon further reflection, the farmer mused, "On the other hand, if extension didn't do its job quite so well, maybe we wouldn't have all these burdensome surpluses."

The Voices of Dissent

One interviewee likened the demise of millions of small family farms to the holocaust. He contended that small farms are being exterminated through the overt actions of some extension personnel and the indifference of others. He said extension personnel are analogous to the "good tame Jews who led the other Jews into the gas chambers. They are saying 'just file your clothes over here, put your eyeglasses and shoes over there, and follow me. I will take you to a place where you can get a nice warm shower.'"

I personally reject the charge that extension pretends to be the friend of the farmer while deviously jerking the rug out from under him, as inferred by some of the critics. The intentions are honorable. But sometimes the aggregate impact is the opposite of what was intended, as in the case of excess production suppressing prices in national and international markets. Critics argue that the land grant university system is not highly responsive to the needs of small- to moderate-scale family farms and that adequate safeguards and guidelines do not exist for insuring that judgments regarding negotiation of grants from private industry would remain within the institution's public interest. Researchers, according to some critics, tend to focus on increasing efficiency and production rather than on attaining any structural ideal with regard to survival and prosperity of family farms. These critics view the primary clientele of the land grant agricultural research and extension system as wealthy farmers, agribusiness, chemical and machinery corporations, and other nonfarm interests. These "fat cats," according to this group of critics, are able to exert strong leverage on the mission and priorities of the system. By contributing a small amount of money to support research, they are able to persuade researchers and research administrators to alter the nature and scope of their research projects in a way that provides substantial in-kind contributions from the institutions to the firms in the form of nonreimbursed input of faculty time, laboratory or field research resources, and general overhead. Simultaneously, as a result of this kind of shift in emphasis, often little faculty time or research money remains to address the specific concerns of small- to moderate-scale family farms. Consequently, the wealthy interests are able to gain an even greater advantage over the already beleaguered small- to moderate-scale family farm (Strange, 1984; Strange et al., 1982). University officials and scientists respond that private grants are accepted only if they are compatible with established publicly supported research and with the overall mission of the institution, which includes service to industries and to large as well as small farm operators. From this perspective, private grants are viewed as augmenting and quickening the research process.

Furthermore, critics allege that researchers develop a vested interest in ignoring the ecological impacts of toxic chemicals and that no incentive exists within the system for researchers to find economically and environmentally sound methods of conserving and enhancing the productivity of the nation's natural and human resources. It is further contended that the motivation of private funding sources (principally the agribusiness corporations) is the hope that the research will enhance their after-tax net income. Little if any concern is focused on the ecological, community, or humanitarian impacts of the manufacture or use of the technology resulting from such grants and contracts.

For example, a chemical company may give researchers a grant of a few thousand dollars plus a supply of their chemical pesticide or herbicide to be tested under the field conditions found in that state. The researcher then would allocate certain experimental plots to the testing of this chemical for comparison with other competing chemicals and a control plot. Critics contend that the real beneficiaries of this research are the chemical companies who can use the results of the university tests to advertise their products. Meanwhile, according to the critics, the chemical companies reap all the benefits while paying only a small fraction of the total cost of the research.

The View from Within

The researchers interviewed had quite a different perspective. They agree that the chemical companies are not paying the full cost of evaluating their chemicals. But the researchers contend that it costs proportionately little to add one more set of test plots to an experimental design. Furthermore, they say that it is essential for researchers to arrive at their own independent assessment of the effectiveness of the chemicals in different locations as the basis for recommendations to farmers in their state. Critics claim that it is inappropriate for publicly supported universities to perform contract testing of chemicals for private industry. Researchers respond by asking a rhetorical question, "Would it be better to have the fox guarding the chicken house?" That is, would it be in the long-run interest of farmers and of society to have all the testing of chemicals done by private industry rather than by scientists who subscribe to standards of objectivity and repeatability and to peer review of methodology? The dialogue is at times shrill, and agreements are few (Hadwiger, 1982).

Public debate regarding the optimum mix of scientific autonomy and social responsibility in publicly funded research organizations has intensified in recent years. For example, a public interest organization, California Rural Legal Assistance (CRLA), has brought suit against the University of California (UC) and that state's Cooperative Extension program with charges that funds are being misappropriated and the fundamental mission of the land grant system is betrayed in the choice of research objectives and extension methods. CRLA is demanding as relief that UC be required to delay initiation of publicly supported agricultural research until the potential social impacts have been studied and a committee of noninvolved persons has approved the proposed research. Kendrick (1984:1) has responded as follows:

> This allegation fails to recognize the nature of the benefit [of agricultural research] and its distribution among producer, supplier, and consumer.
> The social impact analysis of contemplated research called for by the plaintiffs would have a destructive impact on creativity and innovation in research. All *research*, whether in agriculture, engineering, physical science, medicine, the arts, humanities, or social sciences, *has potential positive and negative impacts* on societal values and structural configurations.
> The challenge to us as a people is not to stifle inquiry into the unknown, but to be wise enough to incorporate new knowledge into the fabric of living a better life within an organized society. Programs conducted by the Land Grant Agricultural Experiment Stations and Cooperative Extensions are under-taken on the assumption that an *enlightened society will accept or reject* findings and practices based on what it sees as being in its best interests.
> The broadest participation in the benefits from a technologically based agriculture in the United States accrues to the *consuming public*. The national interests of the United States are served by supporting, through research, extension, and other actions, the efficient production, processing, and marketing of the products of agriculture. (Emphasis added.)

In this statement, Kendrick is clearly emphasizing the impact of agricultural research on increasing consumer purchasing power through lower prices for food. The contention that society will serve its own best interest by abundantly supporting agricultural research, with no "social accounting" strings attached seems to be based on three implicit value assumptions:

1. The "greatest good for the greatest number of people" is assumed to be promoted by an ever-increasing abundance of agricultural commodities. Agricultural research that enables producers to increase production, productivity, and efficiency is assumed inevitably to enhance the welfare of consumers through greater availability at lower prices.
2. It is assumed that if emerging technologies carry detrimental side effects (pollution, social dislocation, unemployment, carcinogenic residues, etc.), then society will omnisciently anticipate these side effects.
3. It is further assumed that, in view of the anticipated impacts, an "enlightened society," presumably including entrepreneurs and other

decision makers, will automatically reach a rational decision whether these disadvantages outweigh the advantages; that is, if the social disadvantages are expected to outweigh the anticipated advantages of adopting a technology, that technology will be rejected. If and only if the social advantages are expected to prevail will the technology be adopted.

These assumptions have been subject to extensive criticism both from within and outside the agricultural academic establishment. For example, the axiom that "more is better than less" can be questioned in view of agricultural surpluses costing billions in federal funds. It is reasonable also to question whether the human condition is improved indefinitely with successively higher levels of consumption at a time when obesity is a major threat to health (Strumpel, 1976; Madden, 1986). This incongruity does not imply, however, that further efforts to increase agricultural productivity should necessarily be terminated but that a more holistic constellation of goals should be incorporated into the debate over the future of agriculture.

The second and third assumptions have also been severely questioned. Predictions of the harmlessness of chemicals and other technology have frequently been found to be incorrect years or even decades after widespread adoption. And the adoption of technology by private decision makers is known to be affected more strongly by the promise of profit than by anticipated social and environmental impacts whose costs are not borne by the firm adopting the technology. Thus, the apparent assumptions underlying the argument for a laissez-faire approach to agricultural research are doubtful.

Among the most eloquent critics of the agricultural research system are some enlightened economists within the land grant university system. For example, Bonnen (1983:964) has written:

Organizations, foundations, legal advocacy groups, and others . . . now constitute a Greek chorus of criticism of the performance of U.S. agricultural institutions. Most cluster around the growing externalities of agricultural technology and public policy. These issues include environmental degradation; concerns for animal welfare; impacts on health and safety of farmers, agricultural workers, and consumers; adverse nutritional effects of production and processing technologies; the extrusion of smaller family farmers from agriculture; erosion of rural communities; the concentration of agricultural production and economic wealth; inadequate conservation; and commercial exploitation of fragile lands that should not be in cultivation. . . .

Focusing R&D investment on productivity and ever increasing growth is not enough today. Equity, but also safety, quality of life, stability, and preservation of the environment for future generations, to name a few, must become major goals of agricultural R&D, as well as productivity and growth. In an urban society, soured on paying for malfunctioning farm programs to support farmers who are far wealthier than the typical taxpayer, these concerns must be dealt with or agricultural scientists can expect to lose public support of agricultural R&D. . . . Greed is not a sufficient condition upon which to base public policy. . . .

Changes in society's values and social agenda, in part the consequence of externalities to agricultural policy and production, will remain an important source of disequilibria. This will require not only social science and physical and biological science, but also humanities research on the ethical and value conflicts in the choices that must be made. (Emphasis added.)

Various public interest organizations, highlighting possible links between agricultural research and the well being of society, have called for conscious social planning. For example, Strange (1984:20) of the Nebraska-based Center for Rural Affairs has taken issue with the laissez-faire approach to agricultural research:

There is a sort of feeling throughout the land that the unwanted is necessary. I simply can't accept that. I don't believe American agriculture has to unfold in any pre-determined way—we can have the kind of agriculture we want. That is, we can have the kind of agriculture we want within the limitations of nature, within the constraints established by the laws of nature—which [sic] constraints we've pretty well ignored in the last 100 years.

Castle (1981:51) has noted, "There seems to be an inability [of the land grant–USDA system] to identify and then work with the major trends which are shaping our social environment." During a conversation with the director of one of the major foundations associated with agriculture, I asked him what it would take to get the land grant universities to change, to provide articulated cooperation between research and extension among various disciplines and between basic research specialists and other academics and extension personnel as described by Irwin Feller in Chapter 21 of this book. The director's response, after several pulls on his pipe, was that it may already be too late to save the land grant system. That was in 1978.

Johnson (1984) has revealed a counterproductive feature of agricultural academia that blocks attainment of what he considers the preeminent goals of the system. He contends that while the attainment of these goals requires an effective integration of problem solving, subject matter, and disciplinary types of research, the various "chauvinisms" found on academic campuses inhibit the growth and development of the optimum balance of these three kinds of research.

For example, the philosophic chauvinism, which posits the superiority of logical positivism, is seen as the most damaging where it elevates the pursuit of hard science "positive" knowledge while denigrating as "unscientific" the kinds of knowledge about human values that are crucial to problem definition. Somewhat less damaging, in Johnson's view, is the converse or "normative chauvinism," which downplays the importance of hard science positive knowledge while focusing on values and prescriptions of action to attain highly valued goals. Both forms of chauvinism are seen as "anti-intellectual," running the risk of opening the door to "mysticism and flights from knowledge" (Johnson, 1984:6).

Other forms of chauvinism that thwart the attainment of ultimate goals of agriculture are various disciplinary chauvinisms: the self-perceived superiority of one particular discipline inhibits interdisciplinary respect and, therefore, cooperation in addressing agricultural problems and opportunities.

Allied with the various disciplinary chauvinisms is what Johnson (1984) terms "academic excellence as a chauvinism." Increasingly, academic institutions are establishing elitist criteria of academic excellence, which elevate intradisciplinary research featuring innovative methodological and theoretical devices, while denigrating the more applied problem-solving and subject matter types of research.

In a recent paper, Schuh (1984) observed that the land grant system has lost its way. Initially created as a response to the elitism and limited relevance of private universities in this country, the land grant college system was intended to provide practical (what Johnson and Wittwer [1984] call "problem-solving") research and education, especially in agriculture and the mechanical arts. Gradually, the commitment to problem solving began to erode. Practicality began to be replaced with a disciplinary orientation. At many of the more prestigious institutions, applied work is now frowned upon, or at best tolerated, by those who bestow prestige and monetary rewards upon academics. Schuh observes:

> There is almost a perverse turning away from institutional responsibility. Professionals are self and professional-peer oriented. They are concerned with advancing the state of knowledge and hence publishing for their professional peers, not generating and applying knowledge for the solution of society's problems. . . .
>
> . . . As a modern research university we want to be in on and contributing to knowledge on that frontier. And in my judgment we should be. The challenge is how to bridge that ever widening gap between the frontier of knowledge and the problems the new knowledge we generate can ultimately solve. . . . Basic research needs to be effectively articulated with the applied research (1984:4, 9).

Schuh contends there is an abundance of research and educational work to do in dealing with the problems of society. Increasingly, private industry, community colleges, and other institutions are usurping the roles formerly considered the exclusive domain of the land grant institutions. Ominously, he reasons, "if we in the Land Grant Universities really want to specialize in basic research and graduate training . . . if those are the things we want to limit ourselves to, then we need to be much smaller institutions" (1984:23). Schuh goes on to predict that if we specialize ourselves into irrelevance, we can expect further reductions in political and financial support for our programs. He continues: "But that is not my main concern. My main concern is what we will have sacrificed for society as a consequence of our growing irrelevance and the loss of effectiveness and payoff to a society from its investment in the sciences and the arts" (1984:23).

Commenting on the almost exclusive dedication to disciplinary interest, with professors catering to elites within their own professions, Schuh observes, "The net effect of these developments is effectively to neuter university administrators. They would have a very difficult time developing a strong mission orientation even if they wanted to" (1984:27). One of the research administrators interviewed for the Penn State study was bemoaning the lack of effective control or persuasive influence on professors. He said trying to influence the research agenda of a tenured full professor was a little like pushing on a string. And trying to influence a department is like pushing on a plate of spaghetti. Their reward system is oriented more toward their own discipline rather than toward the mission of the university as perceived by administrators.

The point of Schuh's paper is not to argue that academics should cease the quest for scientific excellence and quality. Rather, he challenges the notion that publishing for one's disciplinary colleagues is the only, or even the most, important criterion for determining that quality and excellence. He challenges the institutions to figure out a way to revitalize the land grant sense of institutional mission and to reward and encourage excellence in service to society as well as disciplinary excellence—and to accomplish all this without making dictators out of university administrators. He closes his essay by writing: "It won't be easy to extricate ourselves from the box into which we have forced ourselves. But we owe it to both ourselves and the society of which we are a part to at least make the effort" (1984:23).

Concurring with Schuh's central argument, Johnson (1984) contends that academia needs a "new covenant," a dedication to attainment of superordinate societal goals, while setting aside our various chauvinisms and seeking the most effective combination of disciplinary, problem-solving, and subject matter research. He calls for an increase in funding for all three types of research.

While a case could be made for an increase in funding for agricultural research of all three general types, in a time of budget austerity such as we seem to be entering, significant budget increases are highly unlikely. Past experience has demonstrated clearly that some organization and institutional strategies are much more effective than others in attaining agricultural goals. Rather than relying on larger budgets to finance more of all kinds of research, we may have to rely on better ways of organizing our research so as to achieve an institutional "hybrid vigor."

Perils of Success

In contemplating possible ways that academia might formulate a new covenant, one must be aware that there are dangers inherent in succeeding. Castle (1970:839) has observed a recurrent theme circa 1970:

This is a notion that if the university could but (1) reorder their priorities and (2) organize properly to tackle "real" social problems, rather than "just increasing agricultural production," we would be off and running in our attempt to give rebirth to the land grant philosophy. As commendable as such an objective is, a word of caution must be raised. It is now clear that the success of the first land grant effort was largely in terms of first-round and direct effects, with other effects largely being ignored. *The social problems we are now addressing are, in large part, a manifestation of these indirect effects coming to the surface.* (Emphasis added.)

We have succeeded so well, for example, in increasing yields of various crops and dairy enterprises that the nation's warehouses are stuffed with surplus corn, wheat, cotton, dairy products, and other price-supported commodities. The strong dollar, caused in large part by the massive federal budget deficit, has further supressed domestic prices by undermining historically strong export markets. Meanwhile, back on the farm, some of the other indirect effects of our successes include environmental pollution by agricultural chemicals, clogging of municipal water facilities and waterways with eroded soil, and hundreds of thousands of farmers on the verge of bankruptcy.

The classic example of a success going sour is the biologist who succeeded in transplanting the Gypsy Moth to these shores in the hope of creating a local silk industry; instead, he created a monster that has denuded and killed millions of acres of forest. Chemists and entomologists who have succeeded in creating a powerful arsenal of pesticides have inadvertently visited upon mankind a veritable Pandora's box of lethal surprises just now beginning to be detected in our soils, water, and foods. Federal policymakers who succeeded in removing the great price fluctuations in major crops have inadvertently provided the income guarantees needed by farmers as collateral to finance the purchase of huge machines and vast blocks of land. *Ipso facto*, they have sealed the fate of the moderate-scale family farm. Castle goes on to challenge the social sciences to figure out how to treat successfully these indirect effects. I would add that it is not enough simply to treat the detrimental indirect effects of our "successes." Rather, we must develop our sciences to the point where we can anticipate and prevent detrimental impacts and thereby achieve a much greater benefit for society.

Spurred on by the Winrock report (Rockefeller Foundation and Office of Science and Technology Policy, 1982), universities are clamoring to create biotechnology programs. Buttel (1984:137) observes that the products of biotechnology research can be extremely beneficial in substituting renewable for nonrenewable resources by coming up with high-yielding plant and animal species, genetic disease resistance, nitrogen fixation capabilities in nonleguminous crops, and other innovations not yet imagined. He warns, however, of the potential ecological and social impacts that could emerge, and he makes a plea for monitoring the development and diffusion of biotechnology.

Cycles of Policymaking

Creation of these biotechnology institutes and a plethora of other such entities is an example of a policymaking philosophy that favors creation of new organizational structures rather than modifying or improving traditional ones. This kind of policymaking process is illustrated in Figure 20.1. First, a "Great Problem" is identified; the policymaker decides this problem can and must be solved. The knee-jerk tendency of many policymakers (especially those of a liberal persuasion) is immediately to create a "New Program" to solve the Great Problem. Familiar examples include the creation of a new nutrition education program, a rural development program, or a new regional research laboratory.

After a period of program operation, congressional oversight hearings are held to review the New Program. Findings of the assessment are influenced by political pressure exerted through various interested organizations and individuals, by the administration's attitude toward a program, and sometimes by the results of scientific studies, including possibly an evaluation of the program. Depending on the outcome of the assessment, the program may receive accolades followed by more funds to continue or expand the program.

Or, in the case of disenchantment with the program, it will be either modified or terminated. In this case, if the Great Problem has been "solved" or is no longer important to powerful interests, the policymaker's attention is directed toward the identification of a new Great Problem, and so on.

This continuous cycle is also operative in academic institutions. In response to clientele group or legislative mandates, university administrators may attempt to promote research to solve a particular problem or to enhance the institution's ability to cope with some specific type of problem. In this case, however, the ability of the institution to contribute to the solution of the problem may not be limited by a lack of knowledge, but by the focusing of faculty attention toward research and educational resources away from practical problem solving toward activities that are professionally rewarding in a disciplinary context. As Leontief (1971:3) has observed, "Methods known to be valid and useful for solving practical problems are often laid aside by academics and replaced by more esoteric (not to say more valid or more useful) methods . . . because they are new and different."

Beyond Success

During the Penn State study we interviewed over 300 persons in various land grant and other institutions, in government agencies and private firms, and many others. We were amazed at the complexity of the agricultural technology delivery system and the speed with which parts of the system are changing. We have seen exemplary organizational and institutional arrangements in some states, where cooperation and respect between research and extension personnel seem to occur spontaneously. We have seen basic research specialists housed among applied researchers to the immense benefit of both the disciplinary and problem-solving capabilities of the institution. We have been impressed by the quality of cooperation between and among private and public actors in the system. We have also found institutional and organizational arrangements that seem inherently perverse as though

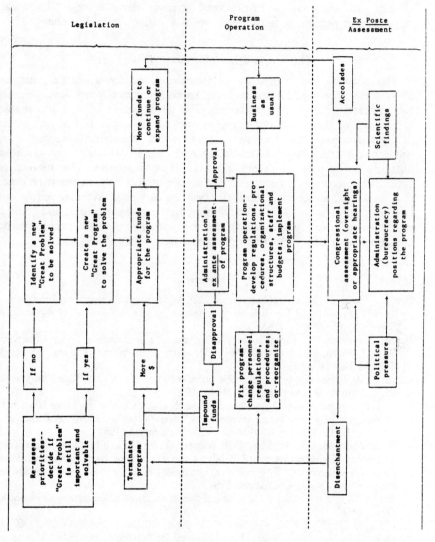

FIGURE 20.1 CYCLES OF POLICYMAKING--Legislation, Operation, Assessment, Recyling

designed to block cooperation between research and extension, to discourage problem solving, and to perpetuate separateness throughout the system.

When one observes a truly outstanding institution, one is tempted to advocate a transplant of its organizational and institutional features to the less fortunate. We have become convinced it is not that easy. The success of any organizational or institutional strategy depends upon historical, cultural, and personnel factors that are not easily or quickly changed.

The Imperative of a New Covenant

The survival and prosperity of agricultural academia require that we adopt a new covenant, a commitment to be scientifically excellent, socially relevant, and ecologically responsible. The development of such a covenant is complicated by the rapidly changing roles of the public and private actors in the technology delivery system, as well as the constantly changing array of problems and opportunities facing agriculture and society as a whole. Difficult as the task may seem, however, it is imperative. The survival of agricultural academia demands it. Even more importantly, in the hard times that lie ahead, society will need the best we can offer. We can deliver our best only as we lay aside our chauvinisms, heal our separateness, and commit ourselves and our institutions to the solution of important problems and the attainment of worthwhile opportunities.

References

Bonnen, James T. "Historical Sources of U.S. Agricultural Productivity: Implications for R&D Policy and Social Science Research." *American Journal of Agricultural Economics* 65:958-66, 1983.

Buttel, Frederick H. "Biotechnology and Agricultural Research Policy: Emergent Issues." Ithaca, New York: Cornell University, Department of Rural Sociology, Bulletin No. 140, 1984.

Castle, E. N. "Priorities in Agricultural Economics for the 1970s." *American Journal of Agricultural Economics* 52(5):831-40, 1970.

———. "How to Change Agricultural Research and Extension to Make It a Better Investment." Pp. 49-53 in *Increasing Understanding of Public Problems and Policies—1981*. Oak Brook, Illinois: Farm Foundation, 1981.

Feller, I.; Kaltreider, L; Madden, J. P.; Moore, D.; and Sims, L. "The Agricultural Technology Delivery System: A Study of the Transfer of Agricultural and Food-Related Technologies." Five volumes. University Park, Pennsylvania: Institute for Policy Research and Evaluation, 1984.

Hadwiger, D. F. *The Politics of Agricultural Research*. Lincoln: University of Nebraska Press, 1982.

Hawken, P. *The Next Economy*. New York: Holt, Rinehart, and Winston, 1983.

Johnson, G. L. "Academia Needs a New Covenant for Serving Agriculture." Mississippi State: Mississippi Agricultural and Forestry Experiment Station, Special Publication, 1984.

Johnson, G. L., and Wittwer, S. H. "Agricultural Technology until 2030: Prospects, Priorities, and Policies." East Lansing: Michigan State University, Agricultural Experiment Station, Special Report 12, 1984.

Kendrick, J. B. "Agricultural Research Is on Trial." *California Agriculture* 38(5 and 6):1, 1984.

Leontief, W. "Theoretical Assumptions and Nonobserved Facts." *American Economic Review* 61(1):1–7, 1971.

Madden, J. P. "Beyond Conventional Economics—An Examination of the Values Implicit in the Neoclassical Economic Paradigm as Applied to the Evaluation of Agricultural Research and Productivity." In K. Dahlberg (ed.), *New Directions for Agriculture and Agricultural Research: Neglected Dimensions and Emerging Alternatives.* Totawa, New Jersey: Rowman and Littlefield, 1986.

Martin, P. L., and Olmstead, A. L. "The Agricultural Mechanization Controversy." *Science* 227(February 8):601–06, 1985.

Rockefeller Foundation and Office of Science and Technology Policy. *Science for Agriculture.* Report of a Workshop on Issues in American Agriculture. New York: The Rockefeller Foundation, 1982.

Schuh, G. E. "Revitalizing the Land Grant University." St. Paul: University of Minnesota, Strategic Management Research Center. Paper presented at a colloquium on September 28, 1984.

Splinter, W. E. "Agricultural Mechanization: Who Wins? Who Loses?" *Agricultural Engineering* 61(5):14–17, 1980.

Strange, M. "Down on the Farm." NOVA television program, interview. First broadcast on March 20, 1984.

Strange, M. et al. *The Path Not Taken.* Walthill, Nebraska: The Center for Rural Affairs, 1982.

Strumpel, B., ed. *Economic Means for Human Needs: Social Indicators of Well-Being and Discontent.* Ann Arbor: The University of Michigan Survey Research Center, 1976.

21

Research and Technology Transfer Linkages in American Agriculture

Irwin Feller

Introduction

This is a buoyant time for the agricultural research community. Recent congressional action for the FY 1985 budget triples the amount available for a competitive grant program to $46 million and includes funds for biotechnology research as well. The Division of Agriculture of the National Association of State Universities and Land Grant Colleges (NASULGC) and the Experiment Station Committee on Organization and Policy–The Cooperative State Research Service (ESCOP-CSRS) have each issued reports, *Emerging Biotechnologies in Agriculture: Issues and Policies* and *Research 1984*, respectively, that, in response to almost fifteen years of criticism, assert the willingness of agricultural scientists to demonstrate their scientific mettle in the arenas of basic research and competitive award processes. USDA, Science and Education–Agricultural Research Service (ARS), long the target of repeated criticisms for its pork-barrel proclivities and the failure of its political leadership to defend the integrity of its research functions and to provide any coherent research policy (Bonnen, 1983), has received praise for its new leadership and its initiatives under its six-year research plan (Fox, 1984). ARS must now also find some solace in the growing criticism of political logrolling increasingly evident in the location of major research facilities by the Departments of Energy, Health and Human Services and elsewhere (Shapley *et al.*, 1985).

The nature of the changes in the agricultural research system is the principal subject of this volume and thus is only alluded to in this presentation. Instead, the focus of this chapter is how these changes relate to the combined capability of public-sector organizations to generate, convert, adopt, and disseminate research findings in a manner that permits profit-oriented producers to incorporate them into firm-specific production functions. The importance of linkages between research and technology transfer in agriculture is so widely demonstrated in empirical and historical studies that it is taken as the hallmark of the American agricultural system. Indeed, agriculture is widely cited as the model for public-sector technology delivery systems (NSF, 1983:162; Nelson, 1984).

This concept of a technology delivery system, although couched and partitioned in different phrases by different authors, is integral to any treatment of the impacts of agricultural research. The technology delivery system includes activities (or stages) for (1) the delineation of research priorities; (2) the performance of various types—basic/applied—of research; (3) the conversion of research findings into economically useful production practices and technologies; (4) the development of ancillary information on the use of newly developed practices and technologies to accord with site-specific production settings; (5) the demonstration of new research findings and new technologies to an initial set of users; (6) the subsequent spread of the new practices to a larger set of users; and (7) the iterative feedback of changes in research activities, adaptive modifications, and consequent changes in use patterns that follow from use of the technology (Ezra, 1975:707-713).

The concept of a technology delivery system underpins findings of the high social rates of return to agricultural R&D. Numerous case histories also illustrate the way in which this system operates. Cooperative efforts among agricultural researchers, extension specialists, and county agents have often been required in order first to develop new scientifically based approaches to agricultural production and then to educate producers as to how to incorporate them into a larger cultivation system. One recent technological innovation—the mechanical tomato harvester—provides a useful illustration of this linkage. Most attention in the development of the technology has focused on the work of G. C. "Jack" Hanna, a plant geneticist at the Department of Vegetable Crops at the University of California-Davis, who developed a tomato appropriate for mechanical harvesting, and Coby Lorenzen, an agricultural engineer, Department of Agricultural Engineering, who is credited with the creation of the first successful prototype. Successful operation of the mechanical tomato harvester, however, also required very specific conditions in the field. The soil could not be too wet; irrigation just prior to harvesting was forbidden. Growers were required to shape their seedbeds in specific ways to conform with the shape of the machine. Weeds had to be strictly controlled. Initially, flat areas at least thirty feet wide were required at each end of the field. Only the approved variety of tomato (in the early days, only VF-145) could be planted. Agricultural extension in California became involved in an educational program on how to use the harvester. William Sims, extension specialist at the University of California, has observed that the university contributed to tomato harvesting technology in four areas: variety of tomatoes, harvesting machinery, cultural practices, and postharvest technology. The university contributed to each of these four components, but more significantly, according to Sims, "The four components had to be put together and it had to be extended" (Feller et al., 1984:101).

The thesis of the chapter is that strains are emerging between research and technology transfer activities within the public-sector agricultural technology delivery system. These strains are the product of three overlapping issues: (1) the portfolio of basic/applied research to be performed by agricultural scientists; (2) the responsibilities of extension specialists, including both the mix of applied research/in-service training and "program" activities that they perform and their organizational placement within colleges of agriculture; and (3) the functional relevance of the county-based cooperative extension system.

Central to this thesis is the view that recent changes moving agricultural scientists toward a more basic orientation are not themselves the first or indeed the primary cause of these strains, although they clearly intensify them. Agricultural researchers, extension administrators and personnel, private industry representatives, and observers of the organizational evolution of agricultural research and extension have identified many factors that have served to blur traditional lines of responsibility within a linked set of research-adoption-dissemination-education activities. Prominent among them are changes in the technical complexity and interdependency of agricultural production practices, the increased educational level of producers, the increased concentration of production into fewer units, the increased activity of the private sector in both research and technology transfer activities, and the reduction in the cost of transmitting information.

These centrifugal changes raise the question of whether the two principal holding companies for publicly conducted agricultural research and technology transfer activities—USDA-Science and Education and colleges of agriculture at land grant universities—can conceptually and programmatically maintain and improve the functional integration of research and technology transfer activities.

The thesis applies to both the federal and state sectors. It includes, for example, the efforts by the ARS to move simultaneously to a more basic research orientation, as highlighted in its six-year plan, to take on a more active technology transfer role and to forge closer functional linkages among ARS, Federal Extension Service (FES), and the state extension services. This chapter, though, focuses principally on land grant universities. It raises several concerns about the long-term meshing of functional activities and organizational roles of agricultural researchers, extension specialists, and county extension agents. It also describes changes underway in the land grant university system that seek to maintain effective links between research and technology delivery.

Its documentation is a national study, funded by USDA-Science and Education, of organizational relationships in agricultural research and technology transfer. The study was conducted between 1981 and 1984 by my colleagues and myself at The Pennsylvania State University. The study is unique among several contemporaneous inquiries in that it focuses on linkages among the component organizations. Thus, it served to bring more sharply into analytical focus issues that are raised but generally treated as tangential to most of these studies (Feller et al., 1984).

The study included field interviews with administrators, researchers, and extension personnel in land grant universities in nine states (Alabama,

California, Michigan, Nebraska, New York, South Carolina, Texas, Utah, and Vermont); with senior officials and program leaders in ARS, CSRS, Extension Service (ES), Food and Nutrition Service, and other units within USDA; other federal agencies, including the National Science Foundation, National Institutes of Health, and Department of Energy; non-land grant universities; chemical, seed, and equipment manufacturers; equipment distributors; the agricultural press; and foundations. The study also entailed the development of case histories that focused on the (changing) roles of public- and private-sector organizations and of relationships among them in the development and diffusion of selected agricultural technologies.

The term thesis is used to frame this presentation in order to emphasize its problematic and future-oriented tone. Indeed, the thrust of this presentation is that the future effectiveness of the agricultural technology delivery system may rest on (or require) a fundamental redefinition of roles and relationships among its current constituent parts as much as it rests on the array of modifications now being taken or likely to be taken to strengthen the integration of research and technology transfer activities.

Interorganizational Linkages as a Policy Issue

Although widely referred to in studies on the rate of return to publicly supported agricultural R&D and extension, little current descriptive information exists on the character of the functional linkages between research and technology transfer or of the organizational linkages between and among agricultural scientists, extension specialists, and county extension agents. The subject, for example, falls between the major studies by Busch and Lacy (1983) on the research priorities of agricultural scientists and the assessment of cooperative extension by Warner and Christenson (1984) and is not directly treated in several other recent careful examinations of agricultural research (Hadwiger, 1982; Paarlberg, 1981). It is covered in the recent study by Marshall and Summers (1985), but the main force of their findings relates to comparisons of the research base for extension programming among extension's four principal program areas and not to technical or structural changes in agricultural production.

The "policy" literature that has so affected discussions of agricultural research also pays little attention to the subject of linkages between research and technology transfer. The principal documents in the decade-long critique of agricultural research—the 1972 National Academy of Sciences (Pound) report, Report of the Committee on Research Advisory to the U.S. Department of Agriculture, the 1981 Office of Technology Assessment report, An Assessment of the United States Food and Agricultural Research System, and the 1982 Winrock report, Science for Agriculture (Rockefeller Foundation and Office of Science and Technology Policy), are primarily concerned with the "quality" and "direction" (basic/applied) of agricultural research—the issue of "science in agriculture." The reports are largely silent about functional or organizational linkages between (a more) science-based agriculture and technology transfer. Similarly, the 1984 oversight hearings on agricultural research extension by the House Committee on Agriculture's Subcommittee on Department Operations, Research and Foreign Agriculture focused on many issues. Only in a passing inquiry into ties between ARS and the Federal Extension Service, however, did the questions of linkage between research and technology transfer surface (Carr, 1984).

NASULGC, ESCOP, The Extension Committee on Organization and Policy (ECOP), and USDA documents and reports are similarly not informative about current relationships between research and technology transfer activities within the land grant system. They assert the existence of the linkage but in fact give little attention to the strength of existing linkages or the possible effects that the paths each is preparing to follow have on these linkages. NASULGC's report, *Emerging Biotechnologies*, for example, sets forth major initiatives to strengthen the basic research capabilities of ARS and the state agricultural experiment stations. The report, again, is largely silent on the question of the land grant university's activities in transferring this technology. It notes that Cooperative Extension would have to move forward, but basically it asserts:

> Cooperative Extension, the education and technology transfer component of the land grant system, is the delivery system which ensures that new knowledge and technology will be placed in the hands of users as quickly as possible and also provides the feedback mechanisms which bring new problems back to the researcher (NASULGC, 1983:5).

The ESCOP-CSRS report, *Research 1984*, similarly makes only passing reference to extension and then only in the context of using new communication technologies to facilitate/improve communications (ESCOP, 1984:15).

In like manner, reports emanating from Cooperative Extension, such as *Extension in the 80s*, tend to assert the historic contribution of cooperative extension, to identify several factors prompting a reevaluation of extension's operations, and to emphasize the research base of extension programming. The reports do not address how effective ties between research and technology transfer activities are to be maintained, tending at most to focus mainly on program initiatives for new clientele or on the users of computer and other information technologies for disseminating research results (GAO, 1981:21).

The unquestioned acceptance of the existence of an integrated system, of a smooth hand-off of responsibilities and functions, would be appropriate if in fact the system continued to work that way. But it does not appear, at least in a sufficient number of settings, to be cause for concern. There is, for example, evidence that the ties between research activities and extension activities are far looser than expected. Busch and Lacy's findings (1983) suggest that extension personnel are relatively unimportant as a source of research priorities for agricultural scientists. Wolek's (1984) study of technology transfer in ARS suggests that extension personnel are seldom involved in the transfer of ARS research. Along similar lines, Lipman-Blumen and Schram, in their study, *Paradox of Success*, write:

> Many interviewees report that while the theoretical relationship between research and extension is clear (i.e., Extension translates and demonstrates new research findings for users and simultaneously reports users' research needs to scientists), in reality, the relationship is not well articulated. Some Extension personnel worry about a growing separation of researchers and Extension workers (1984:3).

More broadly, Ruttan has observed:

> Although the evidence is not yet conclusive, it is hard for me to escape the conclusion that the institutional changes introduced to implement national science policy after World War II have contributed to the disarticulation rather than to the strengthening of the linkages between advances in knowledge and technology development. There is a critical need for the architects of national science policy to give attention to the problem of how to institutionalize more effective articulation between advances in knowledge and advances in technology. And we must be particularly careful, in those areas where articulation is effectively institutionalized, that the reforms that are introduced do not lead to further disarticulation (1983:811–812).

Overall, many recent statements from both the research and extension communities involve declamation as much as documentation. This shared declamation provides a common front to the external world. One interpretation of these statements is that the linkages are so strong as to be self-evident. Another is that each sector, although aware of the difficulties of maintaining effective linkages to the other, is preoccupied with responding to the set of pressures unique to it, with issues of linkages being relegated to lesser importance.

A Historical Perspective

The context and point of this thesis should be noted. First, on the occasion of an examination of the one hundred year history of the Hatch Act, it is appropriate to move beyond a focus on annual budgets or multi-year reauthorizations of Title XIV to consider the evolutionary character of the correspondence between functions and organizations, both within the public sector and between the public and private sectors. What is fundamentally at issue here is the recurrent need to integrate two different frameworks, one, a functionally derived framework relating to the stages of technological change, the other, an organizational framework that links the individuals who perform these functions. For as Lambright and Teich have argued, "technology transfer is best understood as fundamentally a problem in interorganizational relationships" (1976:30).

Second, the issues raised here are not new ones; they are part of the early history of the state experiment station and of the inherent contradictory pulls on publicly supported agricultural research in America. Debates over the mix between "basic" and "applied" research and conflicts between the stations and the USDA Office of Experiment Stations are found in the early history of many experiment stations. So, too, are found conflicts between the role of the experiment station scientists as "researchers" and as sources of expertise and information to state farmers (Rosenberg, 1971).

Third, this focus on induced changes in relationships among the component organizations is itself not a judgment on the capabilities of the organizations to change. If anything, the ability of the traditional system to adapt effectively to changing conditions has been identified as one of the reasons why research and extension activities have been found to have contributed to agricultural productivity over long periods of time and to have yielded high rates of social return. As Evenson has noted:

> . . . these research and extension institutions were productive over the whole of the past century. This sustained productivity was attributed to a capacity for institutional change which in turn was associated with a capacity to respond to clientele interests (1984:268).

Adaptability is one desired characteristic. But another is that the organizations move in an articulated manner. If, or as, each of the principal organizations involved in the public-sector system responds to the criticisms raised about its respective performance and does so in a manner that is responsive to that set of criticisms alone (e.g., "better science" in agricultural research; a more diversified clientele in cooperative extension), the risk increases that the integrated linkages between research and technology transfer may be attenuated.

Fourth, there is a fundamental difficulty in developing a "tight" analytical framework involving linkages between functions and organizational roles in a technology delivery process and the "looseness" of the functions performed in part by agricultural researchers but especially extension personnel. The span of activities of Cooperative Extension, the conflicting pressures on it concerning its program priorities, and the inherently formidable task it confronts as it seeks to introduce directed changes into a "grass roots" system are subjects beyond the scope of this presentation. Still, it is necessary to recognize that Cooperative Extension is more than a component of the technology delivery system. Even if one omits its other program areas (e.g., home economics, 4-H) and focuses only on agricultural production and natural resources, the range of services offered by Cooperative Extension to its traditional agricultural clientele extends beyond the activities that are contained within the technology delivery model. For example, a recent description printed in the *Centre Daily Times* of the services offered by the Cooperative Extension agricultural agent in Centre County, Pennsylvania (the home of The Pennsylvania State University), reads as follows:

> Agricultural services provided for most of the farmers in Centre County include meetings such as: forage, small grain and soybean production, corn

production and soil fertility, sprayer callibration, pesticide recertification, no-till sod seeding, farm income tax, farm business analysis, farm safety, dairy day, Dairy Herd Improvement Association records workshops, mastitis prevention and maintenance of milk equipment. . . .

. . . Demonstrations were done last year on alfalfa variety plots, manure management plots and NIR mobile van forage analysis. . . .

. . . Data collection programs provided are the five-acre alfalfa growing program and the five-acre corn club. . . .

. . . The county agent also provides support to the Centre County Crop Improvement Association and the two crop technicians. . . . This is an agronomic crop consulting service owned and directed by farmers who use the service to collect data that can be used to make more precise crop production decisions (Russell, 1984:D-7).

Fifth, the complexity and diversity of American agriculture produces a wide range of functional activities and organizational arrangements. Interactions among the changing characteristics of producers, the technical orientation of research and extension personnel, the nature of the technologies being developed, the R&D intensity of agriculture in a particular region, and the changing role that organizations play over the life cycle of a technology are numerous. So, too, are the services being performed by agents, specialists, or researchers across the country. For example, extension specialists in those university systems that pride themselves on basic research were found to emphasize roles as applied researchers, responsive in varying degrees to county agents and growers. These specialists were heavily influenced by academic standards including publication of research results in refereed journals. The specialists and their administrators viewed such publications as important for promotion and tenure decisions. In other states, extension specialists were essentially technical consultants to both agents and producers, taking on heavily service roles, e.g., drafting drawings of irrigation systems. They transmitted already known state-of-the-art knowledge; they are only marginally involved in either their own research problems or in disseminating emerging findings.

Sixth, there are many organizational changes currently being implemented at land grant universities that seek to improve the integration of research and extension activities. These changes include formal modifications such as greater use of joint research-extension appointments for extension specialists, establishment of regional centers staffed by both researchers and extension specialists, increased attention in recruiting both researchers and specialists for individuals who can "crosswalk" between the two functions, establishment of institutes of agriculture that organizationally place experiment station and extension activities under a more coordinated administrative structure, and the move towards functionally integrated budget submissions for state support. Informal modifications include a greater recognition of the interdependence of the activities of the experiment station and Cooperative Extension, including improved lines of internal communication, and the *de facto* repositioning of the activities of researchers, specialists, and agents such that as researchers move towards a more basic research orientation, specialists increase their commitment to applied research, and agents take on enlarged "problem-solving" research activities.

It is thus not possible to generalize as to the strengths of linkages between research and technology transfer activities across all the states or even necessarily across commodity or scientific areas within a state. Even less so is it possible to prescribe remedies, particularly of an organizational form, that are uniformly or, indeed, even widely applicable across the variegated settings of land grant universities.

Research-Extension Linkages
in Land Grant Universities

In the prototypical public-sector agricultural technology delivery system, the various functions of basic research, applied research, demonstrations, etc., are performed by individuals located in different organizations: researchers at federal laboratories and land grant universities, extension specialists located at the land grant university, and extension agents located in counties.

The decentralized, flexible, and iterative character of roles and relationships has been the hallmark of the combined contribution of public- and private-sector organizations to sustained increases in agricultural productivity (Johnson, 1981). The functioning of the system has involved both the "mixing of functions" by individuals, i.e., performing research and transfer activities, and the linkage of activities among these individuals, both formally in project teams or informally through working networks.

The degree of separation or its opposite, integration—functional as well as organizational—between research and extension is difficult to measure. Still, in the Penn State study the emphasis accorded by numerous respondents from both research and extension communities to improved relationships in recent years suggests that if the organizational relationships were not rigidly comparative, they were at least difficult to penetrate (Porter, 1979:85).

The strains in relationships occur at all levels of the land grant university, affecting at the "macro-level," its commitment to a mission orientation and at its "micro-level," the activities and functional relevance of county extension agents.

One of the historic themes that permeates colleges of agriculture in land grant universities is that of a mission orientation. This theme is voiced in the statements of both academic and research administrators who see their institutions as "world class" research universities and by those who see the principal identification of their universities with the citizens (and producers) of their states. Such an orientation legitimizes not only applied research but the activities and roles that link research and technology transfer activities. It rewards and nurtures linkage activities and serves as an organizational thermostat, calling forth corrective measures when the links become attenuated.

Concern, however, has been expressed about the vitality of the land grant university's sense of a mission orientation, particularly in the resources and prestige accorded to applied research or to "problem-solving" activities as it increases its commitment to basic research. Schuh (1984), for example, has expressed concern over the commitment of the land grant university to applied research. This concern is the one most expected in the context of the shift to basic research. It might, if not interconnected with other developments, call for little more than attention to the ever present "balancing act" that goes on within experiment stations to the multiple influences on its research priorities (Feller *et al.*, 1983; Huston, 1980; Ruttan, 1980; Schuh, 1984) and to reminders that basic research and mission orientation are not necessarily antithetical concepts. (The University of California–Davis's research plan, for example, emphasizes the concept of "targeted basic research," which is designed to provide for the concurrent pursuit of scientific discoveries at the frontiers of knowledge and of the generation of useful and technical findings to producers.)

Added to the basic/applied mix, however, is the concern, as expressed for example by Glenn Johnson (1984), that to a great extent the former also tends to diminish the value placed in colleges of agriculture on what Johnson terms "problem-solving" activities, particularly as they relate to the standing of extension personnel. Combined, these two concerns point to the principal thesis, namely, that a potential risk exists of losing sight of the need to maintain a mission orientation in the shift towards a basic research commitment.

Three other university-wide influences reinforce this trend towards loosened ties between research and technology transfer activities. First is the infusion of new scientists. The combination of the aging of the existing corps of agricultural scientists and research administrators coupled with the new scientific areas that are to be cultivated requires an infusion of new scientific talent. Given the long-term contraction of agricultural and rural sectors, it is likely that newly appointed faculty in colleges of agriculture will have less direct experience with agricultural production than has the current generation. The inculcation of a mission orientation into new members in a mission-oriented organization is not automatic. It requires an ability to demonstrate the complementarity of quality research efforts with a mission orientation. It requires the melding of research skills and personalities into project-oriented teams, so that the relative scientific competencies of newer and older generations of scientists do not invidiously become associated with basic/applied orientations.

Second, there is also the question of how institutional mores affect the orientation of experiment stations (and to a lesser extent, Cooperative Extension). Colleges of agriculture and experiment stations are part of larger organizations. Their standing, in terms of funding, influence, and prestige, may vary from great to small, from "academic crown jewel" to "country cousin," in Emery Castle's (1980) words, but they are not autonomous organizations, if only for the protection of tenure-track researchers and extension specialists from the criteria of university-wide promotion and tenure committees. Internal performance standards must be adopted that are compatible (although not necessarily identical) with those of other parts of the university. The influence of the American Council of Education rankings on intra-university priorities and rewards may be subtle, but it is nevertheless real.

Third, the current fascination with improved collaborative relationships between university researchers and private industry may serve to improve the transfer of university-based research but in a way that reduces the importance of the extension component of the land grant system. Strengthened university-industry ties may produce a situation in which industry is able to have academic research bring a product closer to the market. The firm, buttressed by the tacit university endorsement of the technical qualities of its product, then relies on its already developed and apparently newly strengthened technology delivery mechanisms to provide information to producers. Sales representatives, supported by a firm's technical staff, also may be able to reach into research-based supporting material generated by the SAES system directly to reach and benefit farmers. Over time, the more access that firms have to the land grant system's research findings, the less necessary are the services of a "neutral" third party. If this pattern does, in fact, emerge, the university may find itself subject to competing internal pressures, as the efforts of the experiment stations to transmit effectively their new findings may lead to more close linkages with a competitor for the county extension system.

Moving from the macro- to the micro-level, several issues emerge concerning relationships among researchers, specialists, and county agents. The organizational changes noted earlier concerning greater use of joint appointments, regional research centers, placement of specialists in academic departments, and, in general, improved communications between research and extension personnel serve mainly to strengthen ties between researchers and extension specialists; they leave unanswered the question of the function of the county extension agent, or of how closer linkages between research and specialists affect the accessibility or utility of the specialist to the agent.

The Penn State study confirms many traditional verities about the various ways county agents transfer and interpret the most recent findings from their experiment stations to growers and also pass on to researchers questions arising from producers. The study also identifies several important roles county agents perform that are seldom identified, such as serving as a link between commodity marketing order boards and university researchers in defining projects that combine scientific interest and commodity-specific relevance. The study, however, also suggests a debate, muted at most times but occasionally breaking through, concerning the functional importance of the county agent in the transfer of agricultural technologies.

Interviews with persons both within and outside the land grant universities suggest that farmers and other clients are turning increasingly to extension specialists and researchers at the land grant university for answers to agricultural technology problems because of the increasing complexity of agriculture. In some states the ratio of specialists to agents has increased as a consequence. In these instances, county agents see the specialists as intruding on the agent's job, even though the agents concede they originally pushed for more specialized assistance. Strains between specialists and agents are identified in almost every state visited, except where agents perceive themselves to have independent expertise based upon their own research and study.

Extension administrators and personnel widely recognize that advances in agricultural technology have been substantial and increasingly complex. Producers are seen as wanting information not only on recommended "best practices" but also on answers to the more difficult "what if" sort of questions concerning the interdependency of decisions involved in agricultural production. Extension officials believe that the state extension systems have responded to these demands for technical expertise by staff development and professional improvement programs. Extension is seen as the leading source of information on selected practices. Its contribution to improved production practices, however, in the view of extension personnel does not always require it to be the first or only source of information on these practices. Extension's ability to provide information that reinforces information provided from other sources, public or private, and its standing as a "neutral" source to which to turn when producers are in doubt about the validity of the information they have otherwise received are seen as contributing to the acceptance of the most economically useful items from the overall streams of new products or practices that research makes possible. As noted by Palm (1966:9), "It is not a question of whether industry or the county agent should do the job. Both can and indeed do perform excellent service, hopefully, each telling the same story."

On the other hand, respondents from all sectors interviewed expressed concerns that county agents are falling behind in their ability to comprehend and communicate new practices. To some extent, this observation relates mainly to the rate at which in-service staff development programs are able to keep pace with the changing technical complexity of production techniques for specific commodities and with changes in the mix of commodities produced within a state. It relates also to the training and qualifications of agents relative to those of producers in the state, itself a trend that is related to higher levels of education for producers and the advent of professionally managed farms. It also relates to the multiple responsibilities often assigned to county agents, including agricultural agents, which limit the time they have to develop the competencies required to provide the services requested by their more technically sophisticated clients.

Attenuation of ties between research and extension programs paradoxically may involve greater pressure on university researchers to make themselves more accessible to producers. The need to maintain the continued support of the public through continuing demonstrations of the application of its research endeavors will perhaps serve as the major prod for the "research" segment of the public agricultural research sector—the state experiment stations system as well as ARS—to integrate forward into a more active technology transfer role. However begrudgingly done, as a matter of self-interest, academic scientists may take on more "extension-like" work, not as part of their "formal" budgeted assignments, but as a pragmatic accommodation to the demands of those who support them. However much obeisance is paid to traditional organizational boundaries, the research system will not by the default of its "marketing" arm permit its new products to remain in the laboratory. It will seek its own outlets.

This pressure may reflect itself in an increase in the number of extension specialists and/or in the relative elevation (in terms of compensation, status, and promotability) of the specialist role within colleges of agriculture. In practice, the combined influence of a shift to a more basic research orientation by agricultural scientists, the concentration of agricultural productivity, and the increasingly competitive character of private-sector suppliers of agronomic information and its equivalent may lead to technology delivery systems involving scientists, specialists, and producers. County extension agents may, as outlined above, continue to deliver many services to producers and may in the aggregate continue to enhance the economic well-being of producers, but their importance in those activities that constitute technology transfer may diminish, as indeed it already has (Cochrane, 1970:251).

It is at this point that the contradictions in what is occurring between the research and extension communities most clearly need to surface. If the research community is content to leave "transfer" activities to Cooperative Extension either because it accepts extension's claims to this function or because it prefers to concentrate on more "intellectually" gratifying tasks and if extension claims this role even if it is not able to perform it effectively, a societal loss will occur in terms of the foregone gains in productivity achievable if the new knowledge had been incorporated into production. Furthermore, over time, this lack of transferable benefits from research will find its voice in the growing disenchantment of producers within the research and extension communities.

There are other potentially adverse elements in this emphasis on the research content. It is commonplace to speak of feedback that extension personnel provide to researchers concerning "grassroots" research needs. Busch and Lacy's study suggests that this factor is quite insignificant, ranking fifteenth of sixteen possible criteria (although there may be more indirect channels). It would be ironic if at the same time contemporary treatments of corporate excellence place increasing weight on contact with customers, the public system most associated with this desirable trait suffers a loss in this capability.

Conclusion

The futures of public-sector research and extension organizations are interconnected. Unless changes are made to maintain strong linkages between research and technology transfer components, it is likely that both segments will suffer and that the attainment of important societal goals will fall short of optimum. Public-sector research organizations will suffer if basic research activities are emphasized to the detriment of the more client-oriented applied research needed to justify continuing levels of public and political support. The debates of the 1960s and early 1970s concerning the public return from its investment in R&D clearly demonstrate that mission-oriented research must be linked to research utilization/technology transfer programs to maintain continuing public support.

Recent congressional approval of competitive grant funds can readily be withdrawn in subsequent budgets, especially if in the context of strong pressures to reduce federal deficits these funds are seen as being subtracted from even nominal increases in formula funding. Already a backlash against the excessively basic research orientation of ARS and the experiment stations can be detected in the statements of agricultural representatives (Berg, 1985:34).

The "honeymoon" period within which the research community has to demonstrate its claim that the path to significant advances in agricultural productivity and agricultural profitability may be quite short. While public funding to support basic research in agricultural biotechnology can at present be justified in terms of "science" alone, past experience suggests that potential "pay-off" is never absent from the executive or congressional bottom-line. For its part, without linkages to new research, the technology transfer component will suffer because of accelerated obsolescence, which erodes the productivity of the information and technical assistance it offers.

References

Berg, G. "Bridge Over Troubled Waters." Editorial. *Ag Consultant and Fieldman* 41 (January):34, 1985.

Bonnen, James. "Historical Sources of U.S. Agricultural Productivity: Implications for R&D Policy and Social Science Research." *American Journal of Agricultural Economics* 65(5) (December):958–66, 1983.

Busch, Lawrence, and Lacy, William. *Science, Agriculture, and the Politics of Research.* Boulder, Colorado: Westview Press, 1983.

Carr, A. B. *Critical Issues in Agricultural Research, Extension and Teaching Problems.* Washington, D.C.: Library of Congress, Congressional Research Service, October 1984.

Castle, E. "Agricultural Education and Research: Academic Crown Jewels or Country Cousin." Kellogg Foundation Lecture, National Association of State Universities and Land Grant Colleges, Washington, D.C., 1980.

Cochrane, W. *The Transformation of American Agriculture.* Minneapolis: University of Minnesota Press, 1970.

Evenson, R. "Agriculture." Pp. 233–82 in Richard Nelson (ed.), *Government and Technical Progress.* New York: Pergamon Press, 1984.

Experiment Station Committee on Organization and Policy–The Cooperative State Research Service. *Research 1984.* Washington, D.C.: The Cooperative State Research Service, 1984.

Ezra, A. A. "Technology Utilization: Incentives and Solar Energy." *Science* 187 (February 28):707–13, 1975.

Feller, I.; Kaltreider, L.; Madden, P.; Moore, D.; and Sims, L. "The Structure of Agricultural Research in the United States: An Overview." Report prepared for Science and Education, USDA. University Park: Institute for Policy Research and Evaluation, March 1983.

————. *The Agricultural Technology Delivery System: A Study of the Transfer of Agricultural and Food-Related Technologies.* Volume 5. Report to USDA–Science and Education, Contract No. 53-32R6-1-55. University Park: Institute for Policy Research and Evaluation, 1984.

Fox, J. "USDA Struggles to Reform Its Research." *Science* 22 (September 21):1376–78, 1984.

General Accounting Office. *Cooperative Extension Service's Mission and Federal Role Need Congressional Clarification.* CED-81-119. Washington, D.C.: General Accounting Office, 1981.

Hadwiger, D. *The Politics of Agricultural Research.* Lincoln: University of Nebraska Press, 1982.

Huston, K. "Priority Setting Processes in the State Agricultural Experiment Stations." Pp. 21–32 in OTA, *An Assessment of the United States Food and Agricultural Research System.* Volume II, Commissioned Papers, Part B. Washington, D.C.: U.S. Congress, 1980.

Johnson, D. G. "Agricultural Productivity in the United States: Some Sources of Remarkable Achievement." Seaman-Knapp Lecture. Annual meeting of the National Association of State Universities and Land Grant Colleges, Washington, D.C., 1981.

Johnson, G. "Academia Needs a New Covenant for Serving Agriculture." Paper presented at Mississippi State University as a university-wide lecture, April 16, 1984.

Lambright, H., and Teich, A. "Technology Transfer as a Problem in Interorganizational Relationships." *Administration and Society* 8:29–54, 1976.

Lipman-Blumen, J., and Schram, S. *The Paradox of Success.* Washington, D.C.: USDA, Science and Education, 1984.

Marshall, P. H., and Summers, J. *Strengthening the Research Base for Extension.* Final Report, USDA–Extension Service cooperating with the West Virginia and Missouri Cooperative Extension Service. Morgantown: West Virginia University, 1985.

National Academy of Sciences, National Research Council. *Report of the Committee on Research Advisory to the U.S. Department of Agriculture.* Springfield, Virginia: National Technical Information Service, 1972.

National Association of State Universities and Land Grant Colleges, Division of Agriculture, Committee on Technology. *Emerging Biotechnologies in Agriculture: Issues and Policies,* Progress Report II. Washington, D.C.: NASULGC, November 1983.

National Science Foundation, Division of Industrial Science and Technological Innovation. *The Process of Technological Innovation: Reviewing the Literature.* Washington, D.C.: National Science Foundation, May 1983.

Nelson, R. (ed.). *Government and Technical Progress.* New York: Pergamon Press, 1984.

Office of Technology Assessment. *An Assessment of the United States Food and Agricultural Research System.* Washington, D.C.: U.S. Congress, OTA, 1981.

Paarlberg, D. "The Land-Grant Colleges and the Structure Issue." *American Journal of Agricultural Economics* 63 (February):124–34, 1981.

Palm, C. "How County Agents Can Work Closer with Industry." *Farm Technology* 22(8) (September-October):9–10, 1966.

Porter, J. "Experiment Stations in the South, 1877–1940." *Agricultural History* 53 (January):84–101, 1979.

Rockefeller Foundation and Office of Science and Technology Policy. *Science for Agriculture*. Report of a Workshop on Critical Issues in American Agriculture. New York: The Rockefeller Foundation, 1982.

Rosenberg, C. E. "Science, Technology, and Economic Growth: The Case of the Agricultural Experiment Stations Scientist, 1875–1914." *Agricultural History* 45:1–20, 1971.

Russell, Joni. "Extension Service Farms Out Know-how." *Centre Daily Times.* November 25:D-7, 1984.

Ruttan, Vernon. "Bureaucratic Productivity: The Case of Agricultural Research." *Public Choice* 35:529–47, 1980.

———. "Agricultural Research Policy Issues." The B. Y. Morrison Memorial Lecture. *HortScience* 18(6):809–18, 1983.

Schuh, G. E. "Revitalizing the Land Grant University." Paper presented at Colloquium, Strategic Management Research Center, Minneapolis, University of Minnesota, 1984.

Shapley, W.; Teich, A.; and Pace, J. *Congressional Action on R&D in the FY 1985 Budget.* Washington, D.C.: American Association for the Advancement of Science, 1985.

USDA/NASULGC. *Extension in the 80s.* Washington, D.C.: USDA, 1983.

Warner, Paul, and Christenson, James. *The Cooperative Extension Service: A National Assessment.* Boulder, Colorado: Westview Press, 1984.

Wolek, F. *Technology Transfer and ARS.* Villanova, Pennsylvania: Villanova University, 1984.

22

Industry/Land Grant University Relationships in Transition

Frederick H. Buttel, Martin Kenney, Jack Kloppenburg, Jr., J. Tadlock Cowan, and Douglas Smith

Introduction

The changing tenor of the 1980s was perhaps no better captured when *Science*, no critic of Big Science, published an article in 1982 with the intriguing title, "The Academic-Industrial Complex" (Culliton, 1982). The new forces discussed in Culliton's *Science* article—stagnation and insufficiency of public research funding, huge transnational corporation investments in basic or fundamental research departments in elite universities, the growing interest in academic-industrial-government cooperation to promote U.S. technological leadership in a changing world economy—were later in the pages of this same periodical referred to by Stanford University President Donald Kennedy (1985:483) as among the major elements of a "sea change in science policy." In this chapter, we will examine some of the implications of this "sea change" for agricultural research in general and the land grant university (LGU)/state agricultural experiment station (SAES) system in particular.

While we would not disagree with Culliton that there has emerged an "academic-industrial complex," with Kennedy that this complex is at the heart of a "sea change in science policy," or with those more critical of the complex and the "sea change" (e.g., Dickson, 1984; Heirich, 1979) who argue that fundamental changes in the relationship between science and society are taking place, the hopes and fears of these diverse observers cannot necessarily be directly applied to the LGU/SAES system. Indeed, from their very beginnings the LGUs have assumed a distinctively public role as well as a close relationship with clientele groups in the private sector. The Morrill Act of 1862, which created the LGU system, was enacted in order to broaden the access of rural youth to education in the agricultural and "mechanic" arts—creating, in effect, a public alternative to elitist private colleges and universities. Twenty-five years later Congress passed the Hatch Act of 1887, which provided federal support of SAESs. The Hatch Act dictated that SAES research was to benefit the mass of the rural population—especially farmers as private sector producers.

Subsequent legislation further deepened the dual roles—the public-private "mission orientation"—of the LGU/SAES system. Of particular importance were the Adams Act of 1906, the Smith-Lever Act of 1914, the Bankhead-Jones Act of 1935, the Agricultural Marketing Act of 1946, and the Food and Agriculture Act of 1977. In each case, legislation was predicated on public institutions providing "public goods" (activities that are not privately profitable for individuals or firms in the private sector to undertake) in service to a constituency external to the LGU/SAES complex. Thus, the research and education roles of the LGU/SAES system have never been predicated solely on the intellectual interests and curiosities of instructors and researchers. Service to client groups has been integral to the system from its very inception.

To the degree to which there has been a "sea change" in the LGU/SAES system, it has no doubt been induced by dramatic transformations in the structure of its clientele groups. One such transformation has been the rise of agribusiness firms, especially large transnational companies with science-based product lines (Martinson and Campbell, 1980), an entity essentially absent at the time that the LGU system was founded save for a handful of small machinery companies. The second has been the breathtaking decline in the number of farmers and in the farm population. From the writing of the Morrill Act to the present, the U.S. has been radically transformed from a largely agrarian society to one in which there are only about 800,000 commercial farmers and an additional 1.4 million "small" or subcommercial—largely part-time—farm operators (Office of Technology Assessment, 1985). Concomitant with these structural changes has been the fact that the lion's share of value added in the U.S. agricultural system is now accounted for by agricultural input-provider and output-processor firms rather than by farmers and ranchers.

The impacts of these more-than-century-long changes in the structure of clientele groups on the LGU/SAES system have, nonetheless, been manifested relatively recently. As recently as three decades ago, the LGU/SAES technology transfer system could be characterized as follows: LGU relationships with *farmers* were strong and direct through cooperative extension. The bulk of technology transfer occurred through noncommodity agronomic advice (albeit with variations by commodity). That is, the bulk of new technology was transferred to farmers in the form of production advice from extension agents rather than in the form of purchased inputs. Relationships with *private industry* were quite decentralized and occurred largely in two ways. The first was through small, largely development-oriented grants from an industry to a particular LGU researcher. The second way was through LGUs delivering public-domain commodity products—prototypically, finished crop varieties—to private firms and quasi-private organizations such as seed improvement associations.

By the mid-1980s the nature of LGU technology transfer had changed considerably. In terms of LGU relationships with *farmers*, there has been a trend for the largest, most dynamic farmers to get information directly from university-based personnel rather than through extension agents (Feller *et al.*, 1984). There has also been a much more important role played by private management consultants and industry sales representatives in providing information to farmers (Sonka, 1983). In terms of LGU relationships with *private industry*, these relationships have become closer, more formalized, and more substantial in terms of the industry share of SAES research budgets. As we will demonstrate later, industry grants are for larger amounts, are more likely to involve proprietary considerations, and are more likely to involve fundamental or "basic" rather than highly applied or developmental research than was the case three decades ago. Further, LGUs have largely moved away from releasing public-domain products such as finished crop varieties.

The transition in LGU relationships with farmers and private industry that we have depicted has longstanding historical roots (Kloppenburg, 1985). But there is wide agreement that both the pace of the transition and debate over its long-term socioeconomic impacts were dramatically quickened during the era of "synthetic biology" that began in the late 1970s, a phenomenon that we will discuss at some length below. Nevertheless, nearly twenty-five years have passed since Carson (1962) fired the opening salvo in what has now become an enduring skirmish over how the LGU system should balance its public mission and its commitment to service to external clientele groups. The publication of Hightower's *Hard Tomatoes, Hard Times* in 1973 upped the ante; Hightower went beyond Carson's argument that SAES researchers had used questionable scientific judgment in helping to develop pesticide-dependent production systems, alleging instead that the LGU/ SAES system had become a tax-supported subsidy to an elite of agribusiness interests. The most recent popularized critique of the public research system, Doyle's (1985) *Altered Harvest*, has changed the plane of debate yet again; instead of depicting, as Hightower did, the LGU system as an autonomous behemoth that had cast its lot with agribusiness instead of the mass of rural people, Doyle's writing conjures up an image of the LGU system as a junior partner in an agricultural research system dominated by a handful of large transnational corporations.

Critiques of the structure and functioning of the public agricultural research system—especially of the character of LGU-industry relationships— have by no means been confined to persons outside of the system, to nonacademics, or to left-leaning positions. Stimulated in large part by Hightower's provocative, but severely flawed analysis, there has been generated a substantial academic social science literature on LGU-industry relationships (see, for example, Busch and Lacy, 1983; Friedland and Kappel, 1979; Hadwiger, 1982; Lewontin, 1982; McCalla, 1978; Vogeler, 1981), much of which has been written by LGU academicians and has taken positions that resembled Hightower's critical views. To this social justice and environmental criticism has been added criticism of a very different sort. Beginning with the Pound Report (National Academy of Sciences, 1972), the LGU system has been attacked for over a decade for emphasizing routine, low-quality research that is too highly applied, too commodity focused, and insufficiently oriented toward basic biology. Echoing the basic science-oriented criticism of the Pound Report, the Rockefeller Foundation/Office of Science and Technology Policy (1982) bombshell, *Science for Agriculture*, took this argument one step further—arguing that the LGUs were lagging behind in doing basic biological research and in transferring this research expeditiously to private firms to aid them in enhancing the U.S. position in a new high-technology world economy (Kenney and Kloppenburg, 1983).

The LGU system thus has found itself cornered in the midst of contradictory social forces. And at the heart of each of these social forces lie rival judgments about the appropriate configuration of industry-university relationships. On one hand, LGU administrators must confront social justice and environmental critics who believe that the public research system puts efficiency, productivity, and corporate interests before the needs of the public and basic science and industry critics who allege that the system has eschewed opportunities for productivity advance and for U.S. corporate supremacy in the global high-technology sweepstakes in favor of a complacent, moribund bureaucracy. On the other hand, the LGU system is being asked to do more and more. It is being asked to continue its traditional research programs while responding to the new concerns of groups as diverse as organic farmers and biotechnology companies and addressing the needs of its rural community constituencies that are becoming increasingly nonagricultural every year. And it must do so at the same time that public funding levels have stagnated, and it faces dire threats in the future due to the Gramm-Rudman deficit reduction legislation of 1985.

In this chapter we make some observations on contemporary criticisms that have been made concerning the LGU system and its emerging patterns of relationships with industry. In doing so we comment briefly on historical patterns of private funding of university research and on similarities and differences in private funding patterns of land grant and non–land grant research universities. We then summarize two case studies of the role of private funding of LGU research, giving particular emphasis to biotechnology research. Our concluding comments summarize the implications of these data and seek to reconceptualize current controversies over the relationships between LGUs and private industry.

A Historical Perspective on Private Funding of University Research

There has been a strong tendency in analyses of industry-LGU relationships to treat the LGU/SAES system as unique and (along with the USDA Agricultural Research Service [ARS]) a largely self-contained system. Accordingly, the major benchmark for analyzing change is seen to be evolution of the public agricultural research system and of the structure of the client industries (principally the farm and agribusiness sectors) that are served by this public system. Most observers—both defenders and critics—of public agricultural research stress the growing role of and dilemmas surrounding private funding of research in the SAES. Often appeal is made to the "good old days" when private influences on public agricultural research presumably were minor or to some imagined state of purity of the nonagricultural sciences, which are assumed to be unafflicted by dilemmas about the mixing of public and private funds in the context of public academic research institutions.

In a certain sense these perspectives have some justification, as we indicate at the outset of this chapter. The LGU/SAES system is unique in many respects. It was an early federally supported research program and the largest and most comprehensive federally funded applied research program until World War II. This system of federal intervention was established in the late nineteenth century, which is otherwise considered to be an era of laissez-faire government. The principal assumed beneficiary of the system is an economic sector—food and fiber production—that, by comparison with other industrial sectors, is conspicuously decentralized; accordingly, the rationale for publicly funded research has long been that of conducting research and development (R&D) that is not privately profitable for such small enterprises to perform themselves. The depth of the federal-state partnership in agricultural research is matched by no other area of basic or applied research. One may also argue, with some justification, that the system has aspects of self-containment. After all, many observers of public agricultural research have seen fit to refer to it as an "island empire" (Mayer and Mayer, 1974) that historically has been insular in terms of the backgrounds and training of scientists (Busch and Lacy, 1983) and in terms of the patterns of communication with scientists outside of the system (Lipman-Blumen and Schram, 1984; National Academy of Sciences, 1972; Rockefeller Foundation and Office of Science and Technology Policy, 1982).

Despite some important elements of uniqueness and self-containment in the public agricultural research system, we feel that it is somewhat misleading to confine an assessment of industry-university relationships to this system alone. There is a long history of university-industry relationships in non-land grant universities and in the nonagricultural colleges and departments of LGUs in which many of the concerns that have been recently raised about private sector penetration of publicly funded research have been struggled over and dealt with before (see, for example, Weiner, 1982). And, as some of our data to be presented later will show, the LGU system has recently experienced major shifts in the content and organization of research. These shifts have led the LGUs to approximate more closely the nonagricultural science fields such as chemistry, biomedicine, geology, and engineering in terms of the social organization and role of private funding in university research. One can thus exaggerate the purity of nonagricultural science from the "contamination" of industry relationships (or the degree to which the free flow of information prevails and to which research problem choices are dictated by investigator curiosity and peer review by disinterested scientists). One can also exaggerate the extent to which industry-university relationship issues were absent from the LGU system prior to World War II; for example, the SAESs (and USDA) have been under almost continual pressure for about seventy years by private plant breeding firms and industry groups to withdraw from releasing finished crop varieties in species that are considered privately profitable by industry (Kloppenburg, 1985).

Let us begin by examining broad patterns of R&D spending in the U.S. The National Science Foundation (1984) has reported data on sources of funding of research and development (R&D) for the federal government, industry, universities and colleges, and other performers of R&D for 1953, 1960, and individual years for 1965 and after. With regard to long-term changes in the sources of funding for university and college R&D, we see that the trend in industry funding of R&D has been upward but at a significantly slower pace than for the other sources of funding, especially the federal government. In fact, the massive increase in university and college R&D since the 1950s has been accounted for by the explosion of federal—not industrial—funding. In the early 1960s, industry funding accounted for about 13 percent of university and college R&D, but this proportion has *declined*, to about 8 percent, as of 1984. The NSF data do indicate, however, that the industry share of funding of university and college R&D has begun to increase relative to that of the federal government during the early 1980s. Nonetheless, U.S. universities and colleges have had a long history of significant industrial support of R&D.

One of the implications of the NSF data for understanding the dynamics of university research is that principal emphasis must be given to the rapid expansion of federal (as opposed to private) funding. It is, of course, important to stress that the LGU/SAES system is somewhat unusual with regard to federal funding in that the bulk of federal funding of the SAESs is in the form of Hatch and other "formula" (or "block grant") funds. The fifty-four SAESs received from USDA a yearly average from FY 1978 to FY 1982 of about $116 million in Hatch funds but only $15.1 and $15.6 million, respectively, in competitive and special research grant funds. Total USDA funds to the states (less ARS funds) during this period averaged about $168.3 million (General Accounting Office, 1983). By contrast, most federal funding for nonagricultural R&D is in the form of *competitive grants* that fund *individual investigators*.

It is also important to stress that the rapid expansion of federal research funding during the 1960s contributed to a major shift in the social organization of science. The most dynamic and aggressive scientists became research entrepreneurs and managers and began to relinquish the pattern of solitary bench science that had been typical prior to the late 1950s. The successful scientist became one who was able to obtain large federal grants in order to equip and staff a large laboratory with several postdocs, graduate students, and technicians. More of the scientist's time came to be devoted to grant writing and other managerial duties. Successful scientists—whether they were physicists, geologists, chemists, sociologists, or biologists—came to be increasingly oriented toward the external funding environment (Heirich, 1979). Universities came to expect far more productivity from their research scientists, with the number and size of grants assuming a prominent place along with number of publications in the measurement of productivity.

But slowly over the past fifteen years the federal funding sources that have fueled the rise of entrepreneurial-managerial science and the growth of research programs in nonelite universities began to stagnate.[1] Even major research universities, despite their having long been the major beneficiaries of federal grant and contract programs, began to feel the pinch of stagnation or contraction in federal grant programs, especially in government support for the purchase of capital equipment for research (Kennedy, 1985). Thus, an increasingly prominent component of the orientation of research universities and scientists to the external funding environment came to be that of private sector funding. As noted earlier, private sector funding of university research began to increase at a rapid rate in the late 1970s and early 1980s as scientists sought to compensate for the declining availability of public funding.[2] The strategy of seeking private funding of research became increasingly feasible as industry came to embrace new "high technologies" (semiconductors, biotechnology, fiber optics, and so on) in which the proprietary goals of private firms involved the need to conduct relatively basic or fundamental research of the sort that would be of interest to intellectually ambitious scientists.

We can thus agree with Weiner (1982) that the controversies over industry-university relationships that emerged in the 1970s were, in a sense, an updated version of controversies that occurred prior to World War II before federal funding came to predominate in university research. But we think that Weiner would agree with us that the magnitude of the problems of industry-university relationships has become significantly greater over the past decade. The sheer size of private grants appears to have become larger, private firms' interests in university-based research are shaped by a far more competitive international environment, and issues of proprietary control over university-based research are more intense (Dickson, 1984).

The Role of Private Funding
in Land Grant University/SAES Research

It was noted earlier that private funding of U.S. university and college research has, in general, declined as a proportion of total research funding since the 1950s but that since the late 1970s the trend has been toward a greater role in corporate funding of university and college research. Further, the expansion of university and college research in the 1960s was largely accounted for by federal funding, which, however, began to stagnate in the 1970s. To what degree have these funding trends characterized the LGU system?

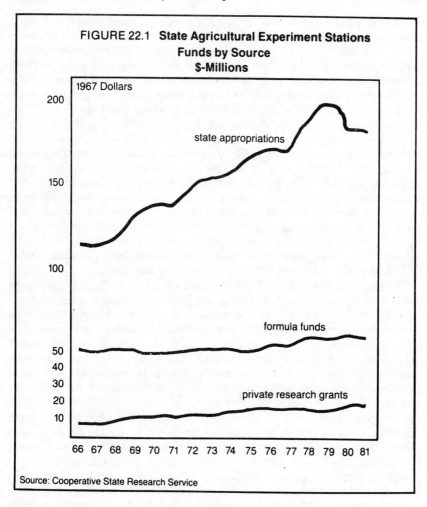

FIGURE 22.1 **State Agricultural Experiment Stations Funds by Source $-Millions**

1967 Dollars

state appropriations

formula funds

private research grants

66 67 68 69 70 71 72 73 74 75 76 77 78 79 80 81

Source: Cooperative State Research Service

Figure 22.1 reports ESCOP (1984) data on trends in the sources of funding for SAES research from 1966 to 1981. The data indicate, first, that like U.S. university and college research in general, there was rapid expansion in SAES research expenditures during the 1960s. This surge in research activity, however, was accounted for almost entirely by increases in *state* government appropriations, not by either federal or private sources. (Note, however, that the data in Figure 22.1 exclude federal funds other than formula funding.) Second, the amount of federal formula funding of SAES research has remained virtually constant in real terms up to the present following some minor declines during the late 1960s. Third, Figure 22.1 indicates that the SAESs suffered major declines in the real value of their state appropriations during the late 1970s, much of which presumably was accounted for by the effects of state government fiscal crises and rapid inflation during this period. Fourth, Figure 22.1 shows that there has been a slow but steady increase in the amount of private research grants and in the proportion of the total SAES research budget accounded for by these private funds. Finally, however, it can be seen that even by the early 1980s private research funds were still far less important than either federal formula funds or state appropriations in the SAES research portfolio.

The modest role of private industry grants in the funding of SAES research has long been recognized. Even critics such as Hightower (1973) have acknowledged that industrially supported projects were generally small, typically on the order of several hundred to a few thousand dollars per year. Interestingly, defenders of the SAES system have argued that this modest role of private funding testifies to the autonomy of the SAESs from undue industry influence. But many critics have looked at these data in a quite different way—suggesting that agribusiness firms with small sums of discretionary grant funds can leverage the efforts of researchers backed by large sums of public resources in the direction of developing products useful to industry (see especially Center for Rural Affairs, 1982).

Because national data such as those in Figure 22.1 do not include all sources of SAES research funding, we have conducted a case study of trends from 1973 to 1983 in the sources of agricultural research funding at Cornell University (including the Cornell University Agricultural Experiment Station in Ithaca and the New York Agricultural Experiment Station in Geneva). The data collection methodology, a more extensive discussion of the results and caveats about their generalizability and interpretation are reported in Buttel et al. (1986). A summary of the results of the case study is reported in Table 22.1.

The data in Table 22.1 corroborate several of the observations made regarding national trends in funding sources found in Figure 22.1. Two other observations are in order. First, at a major LGU such as Cornell University, federal and state competitive funding is very important—representing about 24 percent of Cornell University's agricultural research effort in 1983. Second, the role of private industry funding of Cornell research has increased rapidly, from 4 percent in 1973 to 9 percent in 1983. The Cornell case study also reveals that the upward trend in industrial sponsorship of research was accounted for by a substantial increase in the average size of industrial grants (from $4,049 in 1973 to $27,792 in 1983 in current dollars) along with a slight decrease in the number of industrial sponsors (69 and 67, respectively).

Implications of Changing Patterns
of Industrial Funding
for the Land Grant System

The data we have summarized clarify some of the numbers at issue in recent debates over industry/LGU relationships, but they have little to say

TABLE 22.1 Research Expenditures, College of Agriculture and Life
Sciences, Cornell University, by Source of Funding,
1973, 1978, and 1983

Source of Funds	1973	Percent of Total	1978	Percent of Total	1983	Percent of Total
Budgeted						
College	$ 646,716	4	$ 1,368,006	6	$ 3,014,046	9
State	9,651,332	59	10,382,793	48	15,099,404	46
Federal	1,839,625	11	2,980,685	14	3,568,343	11
Subtotal	(12,137,673)	(74)	(14,731,484)	(68)	(21,681,793)	(65)
Competitive						
Federal	2,366,663	14	3,923,302	18	5,963,759	18
State	594,113	4	888,225	4	1,929,686	6
Foundations	659,045	4	284,285	1	388,443	1
Industry	619,934	4	1,817,729	8	3,182,348	9
Subtotal	(4,239,755)	(26)	(6,913,541)	(32)	(11,464,236)	(35)
Total	16,377,428	100	21,645,025	100	33,146,029	100

Source: Buttel et al., (1986).

about the "numbers game"—whether the still-small proportion of SAES
funding coming from industry indicates SAES autonomy on one hand or
the ability of industry to influence the allocation of large sums of public
money by providing small grants to SAES researchers on the other. (We
do, nonetheless, feel that the Center for Rural Affairs' [1982] case study
of the animal science department at the University of Nebraska provides
significant empirical support for the latter argument.) It is also unclear from
these aggregate data whether the growing importance of industrial funding
of SAES research has led to increased and/or undue industry influence on
the SAES system. And to these uncertainties should be added the fact that
industry-university relationships are not limited to research funding but
also include faculty consulting with industry, university programs for continuing education and training of industry personnel, use of university
facilities for routine product testing, industry representation on university
boards and advisory committees, and the existence of university faculty who
are part-time employees of or who have equity interests in private companies.
Indeed, many of these relationships that do not involve industry funding
of university research—especially faculty consulting with, part-time employment by, and equity interests in private firms—have been at the heart
of contemporary conflicts over industry-university relationships (especially
with regard to conflict of interest problems and debates over the control
and dissemination of scientific information) (see Dickson, 1984; Kenney et
al., 1982). It is becoming increasingly apparent that industry-LGU relationships are complex and, as noted by Feller et al. (1984:26) in the executive

summary of their comprehensive study of agricultural technology transfer, there have yet been "few studies that describe the institutional character of the relationships between the public/private sectors."

Several further observations can be made with regard to the data on the changing role of private research funding at Cornell University. The ten-year trend toward slightly fewer corporate sponsors investing in substantially larger research projects can be seen as a reflection of structural change in the agribusiness sector. This sector has over the past several decades been transformed from a set of small, regional and national, independent, single-product firms into a concentrated industry characterized by fewer multinational, multi-product firms (Martinson and Campbell, 1980), the majority of which on the agricultural inputs side have chemical, petroleum, or pharmaceutical companies as their parent firms (Buttel et al., 1984; Ruivenkamp, 1985). In a market economy, agricultural technology transfer inherently involves relationships between public sector research and private firms. But the contemporary technology transfer process now involves firms vastly different in structure than those of three decades ago. This new breed of firm not only emphasizes "R&D-intensive" products but also the "'coupling' or 'bundling' [of] a product package in which they sell both the core technologies, e.g., the seed or herbicide, and information concerning the best uses of the product"—information that "resemble(s) that traditionally supplied through the SAES-CES system" (Feller et al., 1984:30).

The data on 1979–1983 changes in the average size of industry grants to the Cornell University SAES are also consistent with the widely discussed trend toward high-technology companies investing substantial sums in fundamental or basic research in universities. We noted earlier the cumulation of political forces during the 1970s and early 1980s that led the LGUs to increase their emphasis on fundamental biotechnology research. Chief among these political forces were the changing interests of agricultural input firms and the budgetary retrenchment in the SAESs revealed in Figure 22.1. Beginning with venture capitalists and faculty entrepreneurs in the late 1970s and continuing with large multinational agrochemical/seed companies in the early 1980s, a broad spectrum of private firms recognized the utility of advances in molecular and cell biology for agricultural product lines. At this point, however, the SAES system had only limited expertise and few research programs in these areas, a circumstance that many industry personnel were not hesitant to criticize. Adding their voices to those of longstanding basic-science critics and influential foundations (see especially Rockefeller Foundation and Office of Science and Technology Policy, 1982), agribusiness firms crystallized a formidable coalition seeking to redirect SAES research away from highly applied or developmental activities and toward more fundamental, basic biological research. This rising crescendo of criticism of the traditional SAES research portfolio occurred at precisely the time when the SAESs faced declining public support for research. LGU/SAES administrators, who had largely sidestepped criticism of the lack of basic biological research in the decade following the Pound Report, began to see this research in a new light. Not only would heightened industry interest in SAES biotechnology research promise to shore up shrinking research budgets, but many LGUs perceived the time as ripe to open up new opportunities for expanded state government funding premised on attracting high-technology industry to the states (Cowan and Buttel, 1983).

Three aspects of the LGU/SAES response to the biotechnology revolution, based on case studies of twenty-five SAESs that are discussed more extensively in Buttel *et al.* (1986), stand out most dramatically. First, of the twenty-five SAESs that we contacted, each purported to have made some significant response—ranging from reclassifying professional openings to require biotechnology expertise (e.g., Nebraska) to establishing an interdepartmental or intercollege biotechnology center (e.g., Cornell). Second, 60 percent of the SAESs had either established a biotechnology center or had plans to do so. Third, however, most centers have been or apparently will be established largely with state government funds, and relatively few have been able to attract significant industry funding; and the prospects for ever being able to do so appear to be getting slimmer as the leading agricultural biotechnology companies such as Monsanto appear to be withdrawing from sponsorship of university research.

While attracting industry and state government support and the benefits that might be derived therefrom (e.g., retaining faculty who might otherwise be tempted to move to industry) have been the principal motivations for SAESs to establish biotechnology centers, two other factors have typically been important. One is that extradepartmental biotechnology centers help to foster the interdisciplinary research that has been of acknowledged importance in agricultural biotechnology (e.g., National Academy of Sciences, 1984). Second, and most germane to the purposes of this chapter, the emergence of closer industry-university linkages, especially relating to high-technologies such as biotechnology, has been controversial on many campuses. Many of the most visible early controversies relating to conflicts of interest and control over the dissemination of research findings occurred in colleges of agriculture (e.g., Wisconsin and UC-Davis; Buttel *et al.*, 1984). Thus, many SAES administrators were apparently attracted to the biotechnology center concept as a means of rationalizing potentially problematic relationships with industry and avoiding damaging scandals such as those that occurred in the early 1980s. Biotechnology centers have typically been established with clear guidelines relating to patent and licensing rights, consulting opportunities, access to prepublication information, and the like. SAES administrators have thus sought to replace anarchic *industry-researcher* relationships, which at times have led to abuses and public relations scandals, with more formal *industry-university* relationships focused on a biotechnology center.

Conclusion: Industry-University Relationships and the Changing Division of Labor Between Public and Private Agricultural Research

Many of the conclusions of our analysis correspond fairly well to conventional wisdom. Industrial sponsorship of SAES research has increased significantly over the past decade, although public support—especially state appropriations—remains the funding backbone. The character of industrially sponsored research has changed significantly from a predominance of small, applied projects to a greater prevalence of large grants for more fundamental research. The LGUs have responded very rapidly to a combination of factors—external political pressure, a plateauing of public support, and opportunities for new sources of external funding—in establishing biotechnology programs. The surge of biotechnology activity in the LGU system has occurred with far fewer conflicts over industry-university relationships than might have been expected in the wake of, for example, the controversy over Hoechst, A. G. having essentially purchased the molecular biology program at Massachusetts General Hospital (Harvard University). In part, this has been because NASULGC's Division of Agriculture (1983, 1984) was attentive to the public image of LGU biotechnology efforts and apparently was influential in urging the LGUs to take steps, such as creating formalized biotechnology institutes, to reduce conflict of interest problems and conflicts over the dissemination of research findings.

It should be stressed, however, that another reason why conflicts over LGU relationships with industry have been minimal is that even the majority of LGUs with biotechnology centers have been unable to attract significant industrial funding (i.e., as long-term "industrial associates" or major contributors to constructing facilities or to department or center-based budgets). The key issues in industry-LGU relationships over the next decade are thus unlikely to revolve around managing a gold rush of industrial funding.

Indeed, one might suggest that there is something to be said for the argument that instead of worrying over or discouraging industrial funding of the SAESs, industry should be encouraged to contribute more—to pay for a larger share of the already large benefit that it receives from LGU research. But while this argument has a certain appeal, it does not appear realistic at this point. It is unlikely, in fact, that the industry proportion of total university and college research funding will ever approach the 13 percent figure of the early 1960s. LGU biotechnology efforts may well prove to be typical of what we see as a larger pattern of the first major phase of the industry-university high-technology connection in the early 1980s starting to come to an end. In biotechnology as well as other areas of high-technology research in universities, the initial three- to six-year industry contracts are beginning to run out. We suspect that many are unlikely to be renewed, especially at their initial funding levels—and, ironically so, if state governments have stepped in to provide strong base support to high-technology centers and institutes. Private companies, especially the initial supporters of research centers, from this point forward need to do little more than contribute some nominal sums—probably in traditional areas such as consulting fees paid to faculty and supporting graduate students, libraries, and equipment purchases—to obtain the information they need. This emerging situation in "high-technology" research paradoxically starts sounding very similar to the "industry leverage" arguments that had been advanced with regard to routine, applied, developmental research in the SAESs a decade ago!

We would also argue that popularized and academic treatments of industry-LGU relationships have tended to give too much attention to the micro-level phenomenon of how and to what extent industrial funding directly influences the priorities and activities of researchers. What have largely gone unnoticed have been the full dimensions of shifts in the division of labor between public and private agricultural research (which are discussed more thoroughly in Buttel, 1986; Buttel et al., 1986; Kloppenburg, 1984, 1985; and Kenney and Kloppenburg, 1983). Chief among these shifts has been the growing predominance of private R&D in U.S. agricultural research, the declining role of public research institutions in shaping new trajectories of technological change, the growing dependence of public agricultural research institutions on industry as a political support base, the historic exercise of industry influence on leading the LGUs to refrain from developing public-domain products (prototypically, finished seed varieties) that compete with industry product lines, and the vastly expanded role of intellectual property restrictions in shaping the activities of public and private sector researchers. The absence of analysis and debate at the more macro level of the public/private division of labor has resulted, among other things, in a lack of discussion as to what should be the uniquely public roles of the SAESs and ARS. Clearly, a component of this public role should be what the LGUs have proceeded apace to do: to conduct more fundamental biotechnology research to be transferred to industry. But we would suggest as well that the accomplishment of other public goals—for example, developing reduced-input agricultural systems in the interest of environmental protection—is unlikely to be of interest to industry. Accordingly, accomplishing such goals will require public research along the full range from fundamental to applied—perhaps including the development of public-domain products, such as finished crop varieties, that compete with private sector product lines. Issues of this sort, we would argue, will be far more enduring than those such as the propriety of faculty entrepreneurs enriching themselves through relationships with private industry that have hitherto received the lion's share of attention.

Notes

The authors would like to thank James J. Zuiches and William Pardee of Cornell University for their assistance in collecting data on trends in sources of funding at the Cornell University Agricultural Experiment Station. We also appreciate the cooperation of several college of agriculture and experiment station administrators in providing information on their biotechnology programs. This research was supported, in part, by the Cornell University Agricultural Experiment Station under Hatch #432.

1. It should be noted, however, that stagnation of public research funding has been uneven, both sectorally and over time. Overall, public research funding, which had exhibited a ten-year decline in real dollars during the 1970s, began to increase

to some degree during the end of the Carter Administration. It is also estimated that federal funding of basic research increased from about $5.5 billion to $7.8 billion from 1980 to 1984, even though total nonmilitary research was constant over this period. Basic research was increased at the expense of developmental research, which dropped from 42 percent to 27 percent of nondefense R&D.

2. Mere availability of funding was not the only factor attracting university researchers to industry support. Despite publication delays and complications relating to patents and other modes of proprietary protection, industry funding has tended to come with fewer restrictions and administrative requirements than has government funding.

References

Busch, L., and Lacy, W. B. *Science, Agriculture, and the Politics of Research.* Boulder, Colorado: Westview Press, 1983.

Buttel, F. H. "Biotechnology and Agricultural Research Policy: Emergent Issues." In K. A. Dahlberg, ed., *New Directions in Agriculture and Agricultural Research.* Totowa, New Jersey: Rowman and Allanheld, in press.

Buttel, F. H.; Cowan, J. T.; Kenney, M.; and Kloppenburg, J., Jr. "Biotechnology in Agriculture: The Political Economy of Agribusiness Reorganization and Industry-University Relationships." Pp. 315–43 in H. K. Schwarzweller, ed., *Research in Rural Sociology and Development.* Greenwich, Connecticut: JAI Press, 1984.

Buttel, F. H.; Kenney, M.; Kloppenburg, J., Jr.; and Smith, D. "Industry-University Relationships and the Land-Grant System." *Agricultural Administration*, in press.

Carson, R. *Silent Spring.* Boston: Houghton-Mifflin, 1962.

Center for Rural Affairs. *The Path Not Taken.* Walthill, Nebraska: Center for Rural Affairs, 1982.

Cowan, J. T., and Buttel, F. H. "U.S. State Governments and the Promotion of Biotechnology R&D: A Case Study of the Emergence of Subnational Corporatism." Paper presented at the annual meeting of the British Sociological Association, Cardiff, Wales, April 1983.

Culliton, B. J. "The Academic-Industrial Complex." *Science* 216 (May 28):960–62, 1982.

Dickson, D. *The New Politics of Science.* New York: Pantheon, 1984.

Doyle, J. *Altered Harvest.* New York: Viking, 1985.

Experiment Station Committee on Organization and Policy (ESCOP) and Cooperative State Research Service. *Research 1984.* Washington, D.C.: U.S. Department of Agriculture, 1984.

Feller, I.; Kaltreider, L.; Madden, P.; Moore, D.; and Sims, L. *The Agricultural Technology Delivery System.* University Park: Institute for Policy Research and Evaluation, Pennsylvania State University, 1984.

Friedland, W. H., and Kappel, T. *Production or Perish: Changing the Inequalities of Agricultural Research Priorities.* Santa Cruz: Project on Social Impact Assessment and Values, University of California, 1979.

General Accounting Office. *Federal Agricultural Research Funding: Issues and Concerns.* Washington, D.C.: General Accounting Office, 1983.

Hadwiger, D. F. *The Politics of Agricultural Research.* Lincoln: University of Nebraska Press, 1982.

Heirich, M. "Why We Avoid the Key Question: How Shifts in Funding of Scientific Inquiry Affect Decision Making About Science." Pp. 234–60 in D. A. Jackson and S. P. Stich (eds.), *The Recombinant DNA Debate*. Englewood Cliffs, New Jersey: Prentice-Hall, 1979.

Hightower, J. *Hard Tomatoes, Hard Times*. Cambridge, Massachusetts: Schenkman, 1973.

Kennedy, D. "Government Policies and the Cost of Doing Research." *Science* 227 (February 1):480–84, 1985.

Kenney, M.; Buttel, F. H.; Cowan, J. T.; and Kloppenburg, J., Jr. "Genetic Engineering and Agriculture: Exploring the Impacts of Biotechnology on Industrial Structure, University-Industry Relationships, and the Social Organization of U.S. Agriculture." Ithaca, New York: Department of Rural Sociology, Cornell University, Bulletin No. 125, 1982.

Kenney, M., and Kloppenburg, J., Jr. "The American Agricultural Research System: An Obsolete Structure?" *Agricultural Administration* 14:1–10, 1983.

Kloppenburg, J., Jr. "The Social Impacts of Biogenetic Technology in Agriculture: Past and Future." Pp. 291–321 in G. M. Berardi and C. C. Geisler (eds.), *The Social Consequences and Challenges of New Agricultural Technologies*. Boulder, Colorado: Westview Press, 1984.

————. "First the Seed: A Social History of Plant Breeding in the United States." Unpublished Ph.D. Dissertation. Ithaca, New York: Cornell University, 1985.

Lewontin, R. C. "Agricultural Research and the Penetration of Capital." *Science for the People* (January/February):12–17, 1982.

Lipman-Blumen, J., and Schram, S. *The Paradox of Success: The Impact of Priority Setting in Agricultural Research and Extension*. Washington, D.C.: Science and Education, Office of the Assistant Secretary, U.S. Department of Agriculture, 1984.

Martinson, O. B., and Campbell, G. R. "Betwixt and Between: Farmers and the Marketing of Agricultural Inputs and Outputs." Pp. 215–53 in F. H. Buttel and H. Newby (eds.), *The Rural Sociology of the Advanced Societies*. Montclair, New Jersey: Allanheld, Osmun, 1980.

Mayer, A., and Mayer, J. "Agriculture: The Island Empire." *Daedalus* 103:83–95, 1974.

McCalla, A. "The Politics of the Agricultural Research Establishment." In D. F. Hadwiger and W. P. Browne (eds.), *The New Politics of Foods*. Lexington, Massachusetts: Lexington Books, 1978.

National Academy of Sciences. *Report of the Committee on Research Advisory to the U.S. Department of Agriculture*. Washington, D.C.: National Academy of Sciences, 1972.

————. *Genetic Engineering of Plants*. Washington, D.C.: National Academy Press, 1984.

National Association of State Universities and Land Grant Colleges (NASULGC). *Emerging Biotechnologies in Agriculture, Progress Report II*. Division of Agriculture, NASULGC, November, 1983.

————. *Emerging Biotechnologies in Agriculture, Progress Report III*. Division of Agriculture, NASULGC, November, 1984.

National Science Foundation. *National Patterns of Science and Technology Resources, 1984*. Washington, D.C.: National Science Foundation, 1984.

Office of Technology Assessment. *Technology, Public Policy, and the Changing Structure of American Agriculture: A Special Report for the 1985 Farm Bill*. Washington, D.C.: Office of Technology Assessment, 1985.

Rockefeller Foundation and Office of Science and Technology Policy. *Science for Agriculture*. Report of a Workshop on Issues in American Agriculture. New York: Rockefeller Foundation, 1982.

Ruivenkamp, G. "The Introduction of Biotechnology into the Pesticide Industry and Its Economic and Political Impacts." Paper presented at the Conference on the Production and Use of Agrochemicals. Milan, Italy. January, 1985.

Sonka, S. T. "New Approaches to Farm and Ranch Management." Pp. 202–07 in J. W. Rosenblum (ed.), *Agriculture in the Twenty-First Century*. New York: Wiley-Interscience, 1983.

Vogeler, I. *The Myth of the Family Farm*. Boulder, Colorado: Westview Press, 1981.

Weiner, C. "Science in the Marketplace: Historical Precedents and Problems." Pp. 123–30 in W. J. Whelan and S. Black (eds.), *From Genetic Experimentation to Biotechnology*. New York: Wiley, 1982.

PART EIGHT

Conclusion

23

A Second-Century Agenda for State
Agricultural Experiment Stations:
A View from the Twenty-First Century

Sylvan H. Wittwer

Introduction—The Agricultural Scene

We are a nation in transition, living in a parenthetical time lapse between eras where everything is in a state of flux. In the 1950s and early 1960s, the U.S. led the world in technological innovations and industrial progress. Today, the situation has changed. Japan emerged in the 1970s as did many western European countries with advanced technological products. Until recently, the U.S. had an "effortless" superiority in agriculture. Over 60 percent of the grain of international trade had its origin in the U.S. Export dominance for wheat prevailed beginning in 1973, ushering in an era of an export-oriented agriculture (Flora, this publication). Technically, we were also ahead of the rest of the world. That advantage is no longer true. Many new actors have emerged. Agricultural exports from the U.S. led to the boom of the 1970s and the bust of the 1980s. If American agriculture is to recover, exports will once again have to lead the way (Schuh, 1985).

Particularly the past decade, even the last five years, has seen unprecedented changes in American agriculture (Avery, 1985). A decade ago food was in short supply, and prices were escalating. Experts predicted food shortages would remain commonplace. All-out production would be required with plantings from fence row to fence row, henceforth, to meet diminishing reserves, a rising population, and increased purchasing power. Conservationists were concerned about the tremendous pressure such a food demand would put on soil resources. Farmers of the U.S. responded with increased land purchases at inflated prices and large investments in the latest power equipment.

Contrary to the dire predictions of The Global 2000 Report (1980), the world is neither on the brink of famine nor ecological disaster brought on by unprecedented food needs. Today the world is awash in both grain and oil (Insel, 1985). Oil prices have dropped over 50 percent, and both food and oil prices are expected to drop even lower than they are now. Who, ten years ago, would have predicted the present state of affairs? Today, farm bankruptcies and foreclosures are becoming endemic. Land prices and equipment values are plummeting. These are coupled with mounting surpluses, heavy farm debts, and massive government subsidies (Avery, 1985). The structure of agriculture is a blur (Madden, this publication).

Today, through economic incentives, commodity subsidies, influx of new technologies, a favorable climate, and perhaps scare tactics to stimulate production, we have accumulated the greatest food surpluses the world has ever known. Some are now predicting a continuing age of glut. It has even been suggested that we could feed all our citizens using only half of our farm land. Within less than a decade we have gone the full cycle from shortages, high prices, and low reserves to surpluses, overproduction, low prices, deteriorating farm incomes, and a crisis in farm credit. Expectations of an American public and those that till the land are quite different than a decade ago (Wittwer, 1985a). Much of the current U.S. farm crisis was precipitated by unrealistic advice, scare tactics, and expectations about a world food crisis that never materialized. The penalty is now being extracted from farmers, creditors, and taxpayers (Avery, 1985).

Meanwhile, American agriculture, along with its supporting infrastructures of research support and education, has been heralded as one of the world's great successes. The land grant system is widely cited as the model for a public sector technology delivery system (Feller, this publication).

What has happened to agriculture from the writing of the Hatch Act of 1887 to the present is that the U.S. has been transformed from a largely agrarian society to one in which there are now only about 800,000 commercial farmers that produce over 80 percent of our food supply and an additional 1.4 million small, subcommercial, part-time farm operators that take care of the balance (Buttel et al., this publication). In fact, most American farmers are now part-time and recipients of secondary incomes often exceeding those from agriculture (White, this publication).

What has happened to U.S. agriculture is proving both a blessing and/or a curse depending on the audience (Madden, this publication). Food is plentiful for those who can buy it. Prices are relatively low. Americans spend less for food than any other people in an industrialized nation. But, meanwhile, massive surpluses have accumulated. There is agricultural unemployment from mechanization and automation. An urban society is soured on a malfunctioning support program for farmers far wealthier than typical taxpayers, resulting in the accumulation of even greater surpluses for which there is no foreseeable market or customers. Warehouses are becoming stuffed with wheat, corn, cotton, soybeans, dairy products, tobacco, and other price-supported products nobody wants. The strong dollar has discouraged purchases of American products with an undermining of export markets and a severe imbalance of payments in international trade with 100,000 farmers now on the verge of bankruptcy.

Research and Educational Structure

The U.S. agricultural research and educational system is characterized by a unique network whose genesis occurred 100 years ago (Wittwer, 1985b). Components include local, state, and federal governments, with institutional inputs from land grant and other universities, and from private industries. The system coordinates teaching, research, extension, and international programs in the land grant universities in each of fifty states and at Tuskegee University and sixteen colleges of 1890. The land grant university system has been credited as being eminently successful, with accomplishments as yet unparalleled in other parts of the world. Attempts to emulate the system abroad have met with only partial success.

An integral part of the system is the state agricultural experiment stations. The depth of this federal-state partnership in agricultural research is matched by no other area of applied or basic research (Buttel *et al.*, this publication). Major efforts at altering the system have thus far failed except for minor changes. This system champions public financing of research independent of the private sector. Emphasis has traditionally been on applied research. A unique interaction occurs between research and extension, and educational activities. Finally, it is geographically and administratively a decentralized system, which is now being viewed politically with favor (Schweikhardt and Bonnen, this publication).

Constraints and Challenges

Storm clouds, however, are now on the horizon. How has agricultural research responded to changes in farm structure during the past 100 years or even the past decade? Problem-solving research is eroding, frowned upon, or at best tolerated. How can the gap be bridged between the frontiers of knowledge and the problems that new knowledge generates? How can basic research be best articulated with applied research? Some would say the state agricultural experiment stations and the land grant system have lost their way (Madden, this publication; Rockefeller Foundation and Office of Science and Technology Policy, 1982). Science is no longer seen as a neutral force contributing to societal progress (Schweikhardt and Bonnen, this publication). Confidence in science has declined. Side effects (externalities) of industrialized agriculture, prompted by the introduction of new technologies, are being identified. They include decadence of the family farm; excessive capital requirements and financial instabilities; environmental, financial, and human health impacts from the use and misuse of chemical pesticides, herbicides, fertilizers, and animal medicines (Schell, 1984); the impacts of soil erosion on land and water resources; adverse impacts on quality of life; animal rights; and farm unemployment from mechanization. An issue for the state agricultural experiment stations is one of continuing autonomy and survival within the land grant system. The state stations have lost considerable ground in the hierarchical administration of the land grant system during the past century. If this research institution, now in its 100th year, is to fall into disrepair or become an increasingly insignificant entity, a unique contribution to science and food production will be lost to society (Scheikhardt and Bonnen, this publication).

What should be the research agenda for the second century? The role of scientists in the state agricultural experiment stations has been debated from the beginning and continues today (Marcus, this publication). The call is for new commitments, but what does this mean? Agricultural science is in the midst of a revolution concerning expectations of administrators, funding sources, response to advocacy, special interest groups, and the changing ideologies of researchers (Douglas, 1984; Zuiches, this publication). We are living in a sea of change (OTA, 1985), but this has not yet been translated into changes in research policy (Flora, this publication).

Meanwhile, more than five years have elapsed since U.S. agriculture experienced in 1981 the major shifts in prices received and incomes, which were coupled with increasing costs of inputs. Technical assistance programs for agriculturally developing countries are under fire. The argument is that with our new technologies and their cheap labor, the American farmer is being thrown out of business. Exercises in setting research priorities are increasingly prevalent, but scientists are frustrated by the lack of national goals and ever increasing number of vocal participants with differing views (Madden, this publication).

In summary, many forces, some never before encountered, are affecting agriculture and the research establishment. These include government programs, genetic engineering and other biotechnologies, mechanization and automation, on-farm personal computers (Holt, 1985) and an accompanying communication revolution, changing patterns for agricultural exports and imports, changes in farm size and structure, an increasing number of part-time farmers and those with secondary incomes, and the transition of farming from a way of life to a business (Wittwer, 1985a, 1985b).

Societal trends are also affecting agriculture and impacting the research agenda. There are increases in disposable incomes, a rising interest in physical fitness, and increasing expenditures for "health," "natural," and "organic" foods. A "grazing society" or "grazing craze" has emerged with demands for "fast foods" and "eating on the run." Populations are aging, households are smaller, and there are more single parents. Microwave cookery is taking over. We now have new audiences of consumers with solitary eating habits, and of two-income households. There is an increasing demand for freshness in fruits, vegetables, flowers, and fish. Dietary changes, based on perceived effects on health as well as cost considerations, are having major impacts on some agricultural sectors. An example is the significant reduction in per capita consumption of beef, with parallel increases in marketing of broilers, turkeys, and fish. This transition is having a major effect on U.S. beef cattle producers, with cattle numbers dropping by 6 percent during the past two years (Wittwer, 1985b).

A Research Agenda

While enhancement of agricultural *production* in the U.S. is no longer a problem or a need, increases in agricultural *productivity* hold high priority (Michigan State University and Charles F. Kettering Foundation, 1985). The clarion call should be for resource-sparing technologies and evaluation of alternative systems of production to reduce input costs. Research priorities should now reside in soil, energy, and water conservation and preservation of genetic resources—both seed and clonally propagated as well as natural and genetically engineered micro-organisms (Plucknett et al., 1983). We should seek greater resistance to environmental stresses; crop protection through integrated pest management (McIntyre, this publication) and pesticide resistance management (Brattsten et al., 1986; Dover and Croft, 1986); biological nitrogen fixation and soil microbiological transformation management including the mycorrhizae and root colonizing bacteria (Abelson, 1985); improved nutritional values of crops and livestock products; greater food safety and the protection of human health through genetic development of greater resilience to pests and diseases in both crops and livestock; and better raw product utilization through improved food processing technologies, storage, packaging, and distribution.

What is needed is a research agenda to design institutional arrangements, policies, and programs to prevent overuse of resources in times of surplus agricultural production and also to determine the need for public expenditures to offset the undesirable consequences of resource overuse. When agricultural production resources are overcommitted to product commodities nobody wants, society, as well as the farmer, loses (Michigan State University and Charles F. Kettering Foundation, 1985).

Technology does not automatically expand production in periods of shortages. Appropriate institutions, infrastructures, and entrepreneurial skills must also be in place. If such an untruth is automatically accepted in periods of food shortages and high food prices, it will also be believed in the much more common periods of surpluses and reasonably low prices for farm products and food as now prevail. (In only eight out of the last sixty-five years have we not been plagued with food surpluses.) If such a false premise prevails, the obvious conclusion is that production can be controlled during periods of surpluses, which are chronic in the U.S. and not an aberration, by putting a brake on the generation of new technologies. This is precisely the argument now being faced by the agricultural research establishment (Johnson, 1985; Johnson and Wittwer, 1984). Unfortunately, many scientists through such tactics have used and still use such arguments to garner support from public agencies for their research.

The spinoff is that there are now those who suggest a moratorium on further agricultural research and technology development (Brady, 1985). The argument goes that such a moratorium would slow growth in agricultural production and permit domestic and international markets to absorb the surplus at no real cost to consumers or producers. Such reasoning is flawed (Ruttan, 1986). The competitive capacity of U.S. agriculture to expand foreign markets and to retain its domestic markets will depend upon declines in real costs of production. American agriculture achieved its once preeminence in the world by substituting knowledge for resources. That knowledge, embodied in more productive packages of biological, chemical, and mechanical technologies adapted to the financial resources and managerial skills of farmers, gave the U.S. a world-class agricultural industry at a time when many other sectors of our economy were on the decline. That efficiency must continue to be enhanced by new sources of productivity growth, consistent with changing resource endowments and new scientific opportunities (Ruttan, 1986). The resource base can change with time and technology. Thus, technological superiority is called for in an environment that encourages creativity, innovation, and a vision of the future. Economic and social incentives will foster a search for technological innovation.

There is a complementarity between price incentives on the one hand and investments in science and technology on the other. If there is a flow of productive technology being produced for an agricultural sector, proper price incentives will accelerate the adoption of that technology. The result will be an increase in output. If such a flow is not forthcoming, the best one can expect from policy reform is a one time gain (Schuh, 1985). The agricultural research system also does and should respond to economic incentives signaled from the marketplace. If agriculture responded otherwise, technologies would be developed that would not be adopted except by facilitating actions of governments.

Production Capacity

In face of the dilemmas of uncertainty and instability, the U.S. must seek increased production capacity whether or not that capacity is actually used. All projections indicate that more science and technology must be put into agriculture to double crop production in the next half century. Food reserves and the reserve capacity to produce in times of regional or global conflicts and in the event of natural hazards are strategically important. To design a macroinstitutional system with programs, technologies, and policies to achieve steady long-run production; to meet effective international and domestic market demands; to satisfy current and anticipated nutritional needs and dietary changes; and at the same time to improve and conserve resources and avoid the short term overproduction trap, remains as the supreme challenge for the U.S. agricultural research establishment for its second-century research agenda. Policy is needed for control of short-term overcommitment of resources for both crop and livestock production, realizing that a substantial increase in capacity will be needed in the long term (Johnson and Wittwer, 1984).

Conservation of Natural Resources

There has been much rhetoric with respect to the agricultural exploitation of soil and water resources (Batie et al., 1985; L. Swanson, this publication). While it is important to conserve what we have, it is even more important to recognize that land is a capital good in which we have been investing (improving) for decades. Good examples of soil improvement are along the eastern seaboard of the U.S., in Japan, and in western Europe. For the U.S., the Conservation Reserve Program authorized by the Food Security Act of 1985 can become one of the best and most effective conservation efforts this country has ever known. It has the potential for removing from cultivation—for at least ten years—as many as 40 to 45 million acres of highly erodible and fragile cropland. The constraint will be the recruitment of the national and local leadership required to direct such a program.

Much of the leadership for environmentally oriented agricultural research is now coming from outside the USDA and the land grant system (Batie et al., 1985). The recently established Institute for Dryland Development at the University of Oklahoma is a good example. Nevertheless, agricultural research efforts of state agricultural experiment stations have responded to concerns of conservationists and those promoting more sustainable agricultural production systems. Good examples are research on conservation tillage (Gebhart et al., 1985), integrated pest management (McIntyre, this publication), and greater efficiency of water use through crop irrigation.

What agriculture needs more than anything else is water. The time has come to develop on-farm water conserving practices and computerized systems for crop irrigation. We must seek technologies for greater efficiency in the use of a resource of which 80 to 85 percent in the U.S. is consumed in the irrigation of crops. Policies with respect to water use in agriculture and issues concerning water quality will be high in affecting the agricultural research agenda for the next century. Expansions in irrigation will be sought after to increase both the stability and magnitude of crop production.

Nutritional Values of Food

Equal in opportunity with those of resource conservation, in an age of food abundance, would be to introduce technologies that would improve the nutritional values of food. The fate of American agriculture and the health of the people will rest, in part, in the agricultural sector responsibly meeting the nutritional needs of the public. In times of surplus, agriculture must be responsive to consumer concerns, which from a health perspective are legitimate. Here, the public is ahead of the agricultural community. This public is convinced that health benefits may be derived from reductions in calories, dietary fat, sugar, and salt, and we should not try to convince it otherwise (Wyse et al., 1985). The response to this need by state agricultural experiment station scientists should be clear and direct, whether it be grain to the Soviets, soybeans for Japan, corn for Taiwan, or nutritionally superior fruits and vegetables for a discriminating domestic market (Simon et al., 1985).

The Conference Model

An interesting type of leadership in identifying a research agenda for the second century of state agricultural experiment stations has originated in a unique approach at the state level with donors from foundations, federal agencies, professional societies, and the private sector. It is the conference model (Krogmann and Key, 1981). The recommendations of the international conference on "Crop Productivity—Research Imperatives" held at Boyne Highlands, Michigan, in 1975, joined with those of the National Research Council's "World Food and Nutrition Study" and those of the Office of Technology Assessment of the U.S. Congress for high priority research, set the stage for a competitive grants program in the plant sciences now in its eighth year (Michigan State University and the Charles F. Kettering Foundation, 1975). This constitutes the only real innovation in agricultural research funding strategy in the last forty years. A subsequent national conference, "Animal Agriculture—Research to Meet Human Needs for the Twenty-First Century," served as a catalyst for increased federal support of research for high priorities in the food animal areas (Pond et al., 1980).

More recently (1985), a repeat of the international conference on "Crop Productivity—Research Imperatives Revisited" with the same sponsors, donors, organizers, and editor has not only established a new research agenda in the plant sciences for the decades ahead, but has involved in addition to plant scientists, research administrators and those knowledgeable of policy issues and channels for implementation of research recommendations (Michigan State University and the Charles F. Kettering Foundation, 1985).

A political reality, not anticipated by the participants in the 1985 conference, was the passing of the Gramm-Rudman-Hollings bill during the very course of the conference. This proved both a challenge and an opportunity for developing an agenda of research policy with appropriate biological and social science inputs along with institutional structures and policies for implementation. The model of the international or national conference appropriately structured can be a very effective means for establishing future agricultural research agendas.

The Future

For the past 100 years state agricultural experiment stations have responded to a wide spectrum of research needs. Clearly identified have been problem-solving, subject matter, and disciplinary (basic) research (Johnson and Wittwer, 1984). There has been a heavy bias of research toward the problem-solving or applied areas. Varying degrees of collaboration with the private sector or industrial concerns have occurred, but not without criticism (Buttel et *al.*, this publication). State agricultural experiment stations have also served not only as the knowledge and action base but the financial resource base for up to 90 percent of those acquiring advanced degrees in the agricultural sciences (B. Swanson, this publication). State stations have effectively supplied the human capital for many markets, both domestically and internationally (Huffman, this publication). Many aspects of the functions of the state agricultural experiment station system during the past twenty years have also served as models for the development of international agricultural research centers (Gajbhiye and Hadwiger, this publication). The international agricultural research centers are among the few research institutions where funding for the past decade has exceeded the rising costs of inflation.

New demands have been cast to the responsibility of state agricultural experiment stations, while funding levels have stagnated (Buttel *et al.*, this publication). A continuing of traditional research programs is expected while new constituencies and disciplines are added and human resources are directed to such topics as the conservation sciences; resource conservation; econometrics; automation with its sensors, electronics, and robots; genetic engineering; and, finally, biotechnology (Hansen *et al.*, 1986; National Academy of Sciences, 1984, 1985; Skelsey, 1984; Teich *et al.*, 1985; Wittwer, 1985a). Concurrently, the trend among scientists is toward specialization in these new, highly focused, narrow areas with their attractive competitive federal grants and with goals often far removed from problem-solving research.

The challenge resides with state agricultural experiment station directors. Scientists, as well as administrators, must become more involved in public dialogue (Schweikhardt and Bonnen, this publication). Improved linkages, networking, and collaborative efforts with the private sector need to be forged and a balance struck between what is done for service and for profit (Blumenthal *et al.*, 1986). New state–university–experiment station–industry relationships unlike those of the past, must evolve and pave the way for a second century of growth, progress, and service (Abelson, 1986). To date, most collaborative efforts, nationally and internationally, have been within the public sector, yet the private sector has unique expertise for development of technologies and their delivery. To encourage the private sector to collaborate in agricultural research and development will require both innovation and changes in attitudes of all concerned.

Biotechnology has become both a byword and a slogan. It is ushering in a new technological era for agriculture. It is a green-gene revolution and follows a mechanization era from 1920 to 1950 and a chemical era that began about 1950. Universities, with or without state agricultural experiment stations and with or without federal assistance, are creating biotechnology programs, schools, centers, and institutes. These are playing a role in shaping the new agriculture we will view from the twenty-first century.

Independent crop consultants, with a now well-structured U.S. organization, are beginning to fill a gap formerly occupied by publicly supported agricultural scientists and extension specialists.

Meanwhile, private firms, more for profit than for service, are beginning to function quite differently than they did a decade ago. They are selling product packages, including a core technology (seed or herbicide), and included with the package is information concerning the best use of the product. Chemical companies, many of which have bought seed companies, will sell seed-herbicide packages. Herbicide resistant crops are a goal (Sun, 1986). This is something akin to knowledge and recommendations previously supplied only by the state agricultural experiment station systems. With profit as the ultimate motive, there will be no gold rush of funding to the land grant system by the private sector (Buttel et al., this publication).

The race is on. The parenthetical state of flux we are now in will not continue forever. The integrity of the state agricultural experiment stations, of the land grant system with its federal and state partnerships, the feedback mechanisms from producers to scientists, and the continuing source of trained human capital in the agricultural sciences must continue, but the chart must be clear and the mission redefined.

References

Abelson, P. H. "Plant-Fungal Symbiosis." Science 229:617 (editorial), 1985.

———. "Evolving State-University-Industry Relations." Science 231:317 (editorial), 1986.

Avery, D. "U.S. Farm Dilemma: The Global Bad News is Wrong." Science 230:408–12, 1985.

Batie, S. S.; Shabman, L. A.; and Kramer, R. A. "U.S. Agricultural and Natural Resource Policy." Pp. 127–46 in Dilemmas of Choice. Washington, D.C.: Resources for the Future, Inc., 1985.

Blumenthal, D.; Gluck, M.; Louis, K. S.; and Wise, D. "Industrial Support of University Research in Biotechnology." Science 231:242–46, 1986.

Brady, N. C. "Agricultural Research and U.S. Trade." Science 230:317 (editorial), 1985.

Brattsten, L. B.; Holyoke Jr., C. W.; Leeper, J. R.; and Raffa, K. F. "Insecticide Resistance: Challenge to Pest Management and Basic Research." Science 231:1255–60, 1986.

Douglas, G. A. (ed.). Agricultural Sustainability in a Changing World Order. Boulder, Colorado: Westview Press, 1984.

Dover, M. J., and Croft, B. A. "Pesticide Resistance and Public Policy." BioScience 36(2):78–85, 1986.

Gebhart, M. R.; Daniel, T. C.; Schweizer, E. E.; and Allmaras, R. C. "Conservation Tillage." Science 230:625–30, 1985.

Hansen, M.; Busch, L.; Burkhardt, J.; Lacy, W. B.; and Lacy, L. R. "Plant Breeding and Biotechnology." BioScience 36(1):29–39, 1986.

Holt, D. A. "Computers in Production Agriculture." Science 228:422–27, 1985.

Insel, B. "A World Awash in Grain." Foreign Affairs 63(4):892–911, 1985.

Johnson, G. L. "Agricultural Surpluses—Research on Agricultural Technologies, Institutions, People and Capital Growth." In M. Gibbs and C. Carlson (eds.), Crop Productivity—Research Imperatives Revisited. Proceedings of an International Conference. East Lansing: Michigan Agricultural Experiment; and Yellow Springs, Ohio: Charles F. Kettering Foundation, 1985.

Johnson, G. L., and Wittwer, S. H. "Agricultural Technology Until 2030: Prospects, Priorities, and Policies." Special Report 12. East Lansing: Michigan State University Agricultural Experiment Station, 1984.

Krogmann, D. W., and Key, J. L. "The Agricultural Grants Program." Science 213:178–82, 1981.

Michigan State University and the Charles F. Kettering Foundation. Crop Productivity—Research Imperatives. Proceedings of an International Conference. Boyne Highlands, Michigan, October 20–24, 1975.

————. Crop Productivity—Research Imperatives Revisited. Proceedings of an International Conference, Stage I, Boyne Highlands, Michigan, October 14–18, and Stage II, Airlie House, Virginia, December 11–13, 1985.

National Academy of Sciences. Genetic Engineering of Plants. Agricultural Research Opportunities and Policy Concerns. Board on Agriculture, National Research Council. Washington, D.C.: National Academy Press, 1984.

————. New Directions for Bioscience Research in Agriculture. High Reward Opportunities. Committee on Bioscience Research in Agriculture, Board on Agriculture, National Research Council. Washington, D.C.: National Academy Press, 1985.

Office of Technology Assessment. Technology, Public Policy, and the Changing Structure of American Agriculture: A Special Report for the 1985 Farm Bill. OTA-F-272. Washington, D.C.: U.S. Congress, March 1985.

Plucknett, D. L.; Smith, N. J. H.; Williams, J. T.; and Anishetty, N. Murthi. "Crop Germplasm Conservation and Developing Countries." Science 220:163–69, 1983.

Pond, W. G.; Merkel, R. A.; McGilliard, L. D.; and Rhodes, V. I. (eds). Animal Agriculture, Research to Meet Human Needs in the Twenty-First Century. Boulder, Colorado: Westview Press, 1980.

Rockefeller Foundation and Office of Science and Technology Policy. Science for Agriculture. Report of a Workshop on Issues in American Agriculture. New York: The Rockefeller Foundation, 1982.

Ruttan, V. W. "Increasing Productivity and Efficiency in Agriculture." Science 231:781 (editorial), 1986.

Schell, O. Modern Meat. Antibiotics, Hormones, and the Pharmaceutical Farm. New York: Random House, 1984.

Schuh, G. E. "Improving U.S. Trade." Pp. 59–126 in The Dilemmas of Choice. Washington, D.C.: Resources for the Future, Inc., 1985.

Simon, P. W.; Wolff, X.; and Peterson, C. E. "Selection for High Carotene Content in Carrots." Abstract of a paper presented at the 82nd annual meeting of the American Society for Horticultural Sciences, Virginia Polytechnic Institute and State University, Blacksburg, Virginia, July 28–August 2, 1985.

Skelsey, A. F. Biotechnology in Agriculture—New Tools for the Oldest Science. Joint Council on Food and Agricultural Sciences. Washington, D.C.: USDA, 1984.

Sun, M. "Engineering Crops to Resist Weed Killers." Science 231:1360–61, 1986.

Teich, A. H.; Levin, M. A.; and Pace, J. H. (eds.). Biotechnology and the Environment, Risk and Regulation. Washington, D.C.: American Association for the Advancement of Science, 1985.

The Global 2000 Report to the President. A report prepared by the Council on Environmental Quality and the Department of State. Washington, D.C.: The White House, 1980.

Wittwer, S. H. "Technology Needed to Sustain Increased Food Production." Pp. 1–55 in Food for the Future. Bicentennial Forum Proceedings, 1785–1985. Philadelphia, Pennsylvania: Philadelphia Society for Promoting Agriculture, 1985a.

_____. "Change, Choices and Challenges." Pp. 3–12 in *1985 Accomplishments for Research, Extension and Higher Education*. Washington, D.C.: Joint Council on Food and Agricultural Sciences, USDA, 1985b.

Wyse, B. W.; Hansen, R. G.; and Windham, C. T. "The Status of Human Nutrition and Agricultural Productivity." Paper presented at a symposium-workshop on Diet and Health, University of California, Davis, September 19, 1985.

About the Contributors

ORVILLE G. BENTLEY is the first Assistant Secretary for Science and Education, U.S. Department of Agriculture. He is responsible for USDA research and education programs in the food and agricultural sciences. He has authored scientific and technical publications on animal science and biochemical research activities and on the administration of research and education programs in agriculture.

JAMES T. BONNEN is Professor of Agricultural Economics at Michigan State University. His research interests are in the areas of information systems theory, the design and management of statistically based policy decision systems, and agricultural research policy.

JEFFREY BURKHARDT is Assistant Professor of Philosophy and Coordinator of the Program in Philosophical Studies in Agriculture and Natural Resources in the University of Florida College of Agriculture. He has published papers on political philosophy and ethics, the philosophy of economics, ethical and value issues in agriculture and agricultural science, and biotechnology.

LAWRENCE BUSCH is Professor of Sociology at the University of Kentucky in Lexington with joint appointments in the College of Agriculture, the College of Arts and Sciences, and the College of Medicine. He is also the Co-chair of the Committee for Agricultural Research Policy and has published on agricultural research policy.

FREDERICK H. BUTTEL is Associate Professor of Rural Sociology at Cornell University. His current research focuses on biotechnology and U.S. and international agricultural research. Buttel is co-author of *Environment, Energy, and Society* (1982), *Rural Sociology of the Advanced Societies* (1980), and *Labor and the Environment* (1984).

ROBERT L. CHRISTENSEN is currently Deputy Associate Director of Extension and Professor of Agricultural Economics at the University of Massachusetts, Amherst. He worked at the University of New Hampshire prior to his appointment at the University of Massachusetts in 1968 and has served in short-term assignments with Agriculture Canada, CSRS-USDA, ES-USDA, and the University of Nevada, Reno.

J. TADLOCK COWAN is a Ph.D. candidate in the field of Development Sociology at Cornell University. He is currently completing his Ph.D.

327

dissertation on the role of the state in the U.S. and the U.K. in promoting and regulating biotechnology research and products.

STAN DUNDON is Professor in the Philosophy Department at California Polytechnic State University, San Luis Obispo. He specializes in History and Philosophy of Science and Technology, with a focus on agricultural sciences. He directs the Agriculture and Human Values program at the university. His chapter, "Hidden Obstacles to Creativity in Agricultural Science," appeared in *Agriculture, Change and Human Values* (1982).

ROBERT E. EVENSON is Professor of Economics at Yale University. He has authored or co-authored a number of articles and discussion papers on national and international political and economic development, and agricultural research and technology. He has also served as Visiting Professor and Visiting Lecturer in Economics on several occasions.

IRWIN FELLER is Professor of Economics and Director, Institute for Policy Research and Evaluation, The Pennsylvania State University. His most recent publications are a multi-volume study, *The American Agricultural Technology Delivery System* and *Universities and State Governments: A Study in and about the Use of Policy Analysis* (Praeger). His current research centers on university-industry contracting for research and development.

DEBORAH FITZGERALD is Assistant Professor and Head Tutor in the History and Science Department, Harvard University. She has just completed a dissertation entitled "The Business of Breeding: Public and Private Development of Hybrid Corn in Illinois, 1890–1940."

CORNELIA BUTLER FLORA is Professor of Sociology at Kansas State University and associated with the Agricultural Experiment Station and the International Agriculture Program there. She works with farming systems and their institutional bases in the U.S. and developing countries. Recent publications deal with economic development policy and rural development in the U.S. and Latin America.

JAN L. FLORA is Professor of Sociology at Kansas State University, where he has an appointment with the Kansas Agricultural Experiment Station. Current research deals with the relationship between agricultural structure and community change. Recent publications focus on the interaction between cropping strategy and farm organization in a frontier wheat region in Kansas, and agricultural change and social structures in Central America.

HEMCHANDRA GAJBHIYE is a scientist with the Central Cotton Research Institute (Indian Council of Agricultural Research), Nagpur, India, and presently is completing a study at Iowa State University of the organization of the International Agricultural Research Centers. He is author of several forthcoming articles on the management of agricultural research organizations.

DON F. HADWIGER is Professor of Political Science at Iowa State University. He is author of books and articles on agricultural politics, rural development, and agricultural technology, including *The Politics of Agricultural Research* (University of Nebraska, 1982). He has served as visiting scholar at the USDA on two occasions, as a Congressional Fellow, and as staff for a Washington-based public interest group.

DON HOLT is Associate Dean of the College of Agriculture at the University of Illinois and Director of the Illinois Agricultural Experiment Station. Prior to his present assignment he served on the faculty of Purdue University for fifteen years and as head of the University of Illinois Agronomy Department.

WALLACE E. HUFFMAN is Professor of Economics at Iowa State University. His research has focused on human capital issues in agriculture, allocative efficiency, productivity of research and extension, human time allocation, and illegal immigration.

JOHN PATRICK JORDAN is Administrator of the Cooperative State Research Service, USDA. He is also a Fellow of the American Association for the Advancement of Science and the American Institute of Chemists. He has published widely in agriculture, space medicine, and educational technology and for the last decade has authored the Food and Agriculture article in Encyclopaedia Britannica's *Yearbook of Science in the Future.*

MARTIN KENNEY is Assistant Professor of Rural Sociology at The Ohio State University. He has published widely on issues relating to biotechnology, agriculture, and industrial reorganization. His book on the development of the U.S. biotechnology industry will be published later this year by Yale University Press.

JACK KLOPPENBURG, JR. is Assistant Professor in the Department of Rural Sociology at the University of Wisconsin–Madison. His research focuses on the political economy of science and on the social impacts of new technologies. His book, *First the Seed: Plants, Profits, and the Politics of Agricultural Research*, is forthcoming from Cambridge University Press.

WILLIAM B. LACY is Professor in the Department of Sociology at the University of Kentucky in Lexington with joint appointments in the College of Arts and Sciences and the College of Agriculture. He is also the Co-chair of the Committee for Agricultural Research Policy and Director of the Food, Environment, Agriculture, and Society in Transition program.

JEAN LIPMAN-BLUMEN holds the Thornton F. Bradshaw Professorship in Public Policy and Organizational Behavior at the Claremont Graduate School and the Claremont Executive Management Center. She is the senior author of *The Paradox of Success: The Impact of Priority Setting in Agricultural Research and Extension* (1984). Her research focuses on agricultural research policy, Third World policy, power, and crisis management.

J. PATRICK MADDEN is Professor of Agricultural Economics at The Pennsylvania State University. His research has included a national study of the agricultural technology delivery system, an examination of the ethical foundations of economic analysis, and various program evaluations and policy analyses. He is currently studying the economics of the transition from chemical-intensive to organic or low-input farming.

ALAN I MARCUS is Associate Professor in the Program in the History of Technology and Science, Department of History, and Director of the Center for Historical Studies of Technology and Science, Iowa State University. He is the author of several works on agricultural colleges and experiment stations, including "Constitutents and Constituencies: An Overview of the History of Public Agricultural Research Institutions in America," in Don F. Hadwiger and William P. Browne, eds., *Public Policy and Agricultural Technology: Adversity Despite Achievement* (forthcoming, Macmillan); and "The Ivory Silo: Farmer–Agricultural College Tensions in the 1870s and 1880s," *Agricultural History* (Spring 1986).

GARY A. McINTYRE is head of the Department of Plant Pathology and Weed Science and Professor of Plant Pathology at Colorado State University. He is also coordinator of Western Regional Integrated Pest Management. His research interests are in potato tuber diseases.

ALAN RANDALL is Professor of Resource Economics and Environmental Policy at The Ohio State University. Until recently, he held a similar position at the University of Kentucky. He also maintains an active interest in philosophy of science and, especially, the methodology of economics.

ROLAND R. ROBINSON is an Agricultural Economist with the Cooperative State Research Service, USDA. His responsibilities include planning for, coordinating, and conducting reviews of subject matter programs; reviewing research project proposals; and assisting in program planning and budgeting. He has authored or co-authored publications in dairy science, agricultural economics, and research administration.

DAVID B. SCHWEIKHARDT is a graduate research assistant in the Department of Agricultural Economics at Michigan State University. His research has examined the history and organization of the state agricultural experiment stations.

DOUGLAS SMITH is an undergraduate in the Department of Rural Sociology at Cornell University. He has recently completed a thesis concerning organic farmers in New York State and will graduate with honors in June of 1986.

BURTON E. SWANSON is Professor of International Agricultural Education and Associate Director of the International Program for Agricultural Knowledge Systems (INTERPAKS) at the University of Illinois at Urbana–Champaign.

LOUIS SWANSON is Assistant Professor of Sociology at the University of Kentucky. His current research areas include the sociology of agriculture, rural development, and social history.

FRED C. WHITE is Professor of Agricultural Economics, University of Georgia, Athens. He is a member of the technical committee on National and Regional Analysis, Evaluation, Planning, and Financing of Agricultural Research.

SYLVAN H. WITTWER is Director Emeritus of the Agricultural Experiment Station and Professor of Horticulture at Michigan State University, East Lansing. He has traveled extensively as a consultant' for international agricultural research centers and for assisting in agricultural development research programs for several countries. Interests include protected cultivation for crops, plant growth regulation, limits of biological productivity for crops and food animals, research and technologies for global food production, and agricultural communications.

JAMES J. ZUICHES is Associate Director for Research in the New York State College of Agriculture and Life Sciences at Cornell University, Associate Director of the Cornell University Agricultural Experiment Station, and Professor of Rural Sociology. He works with faculty on project development in technology transfer; regional, socio-economic, and demographic studies; and rural and community development. His research interests are demography, particularly migration models and population redistribution between urban and rural areas, and the processes of funding and research administration.

Index